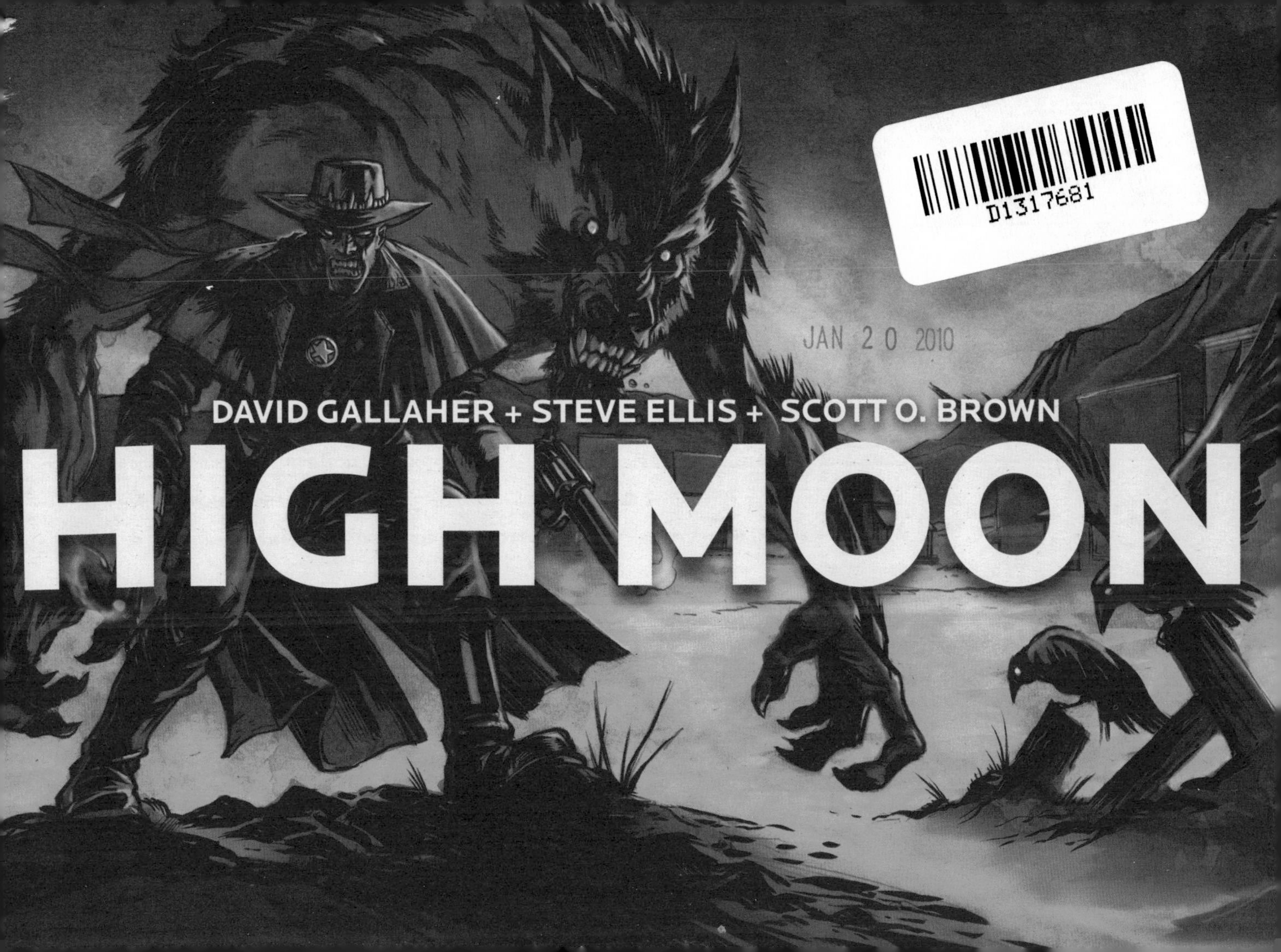
DAVID GALLAHER + STEVE ELLIS + SCOTT O. BROWN
HIGH MOON

HIGH MOON VOLUME 1   Published by DC Comics. Copyright © 2009 David Gallaher and Steve Ellis. All rights reserved. Originally published online at ZUDACOMICS.COM. All characters, their distinctive likenesses and related elements featured in this publication are trademarks of David Gallaher and Steve Ellis. Zuda Comics and the Zuda logo are trademarks of DC Comics. The stories, characters and incidents featured in this publication are entirely fictional. Visit ZUDACOMICS.COM for Zuda Comics submission information. DC Comics, 1700 Broadway, New York, NY 10019. A Warner Bros. Entertainment Company. Printed in Canada. First Printing. ISBN: 978-1-4012-2462-2

CHAPTER *1*

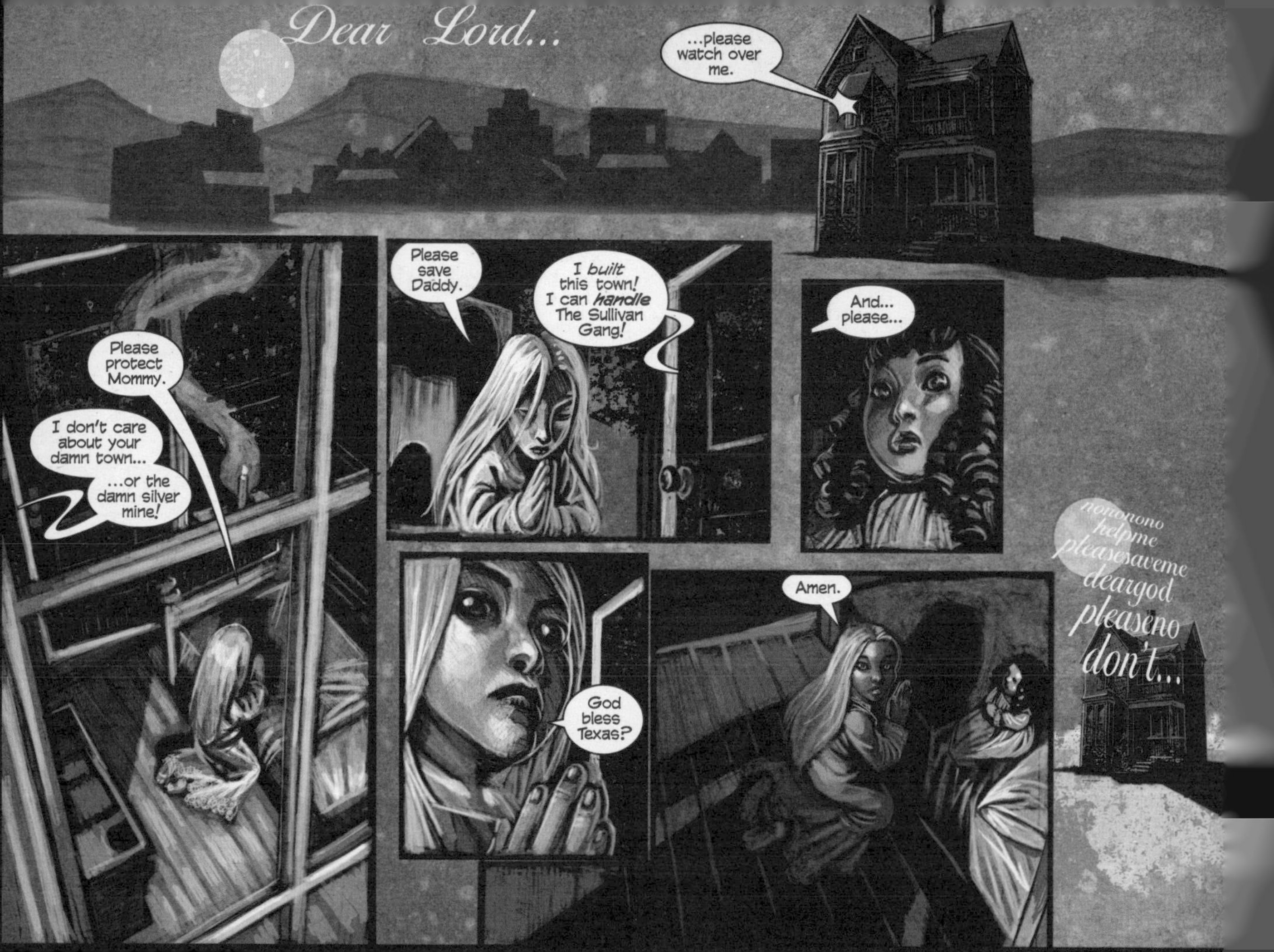
Dear Lord...
...please watch over me.
Please protect Mommy.
I don't care about your damn town...
...or the damn silver mine!
Please save Daddy.
I built this town! I can handle The Sullivan Gang!
And... please...
God bless Texas?
Amen.
nononono
helpme
pleasesaveme
deargod
pleaseno
don't...

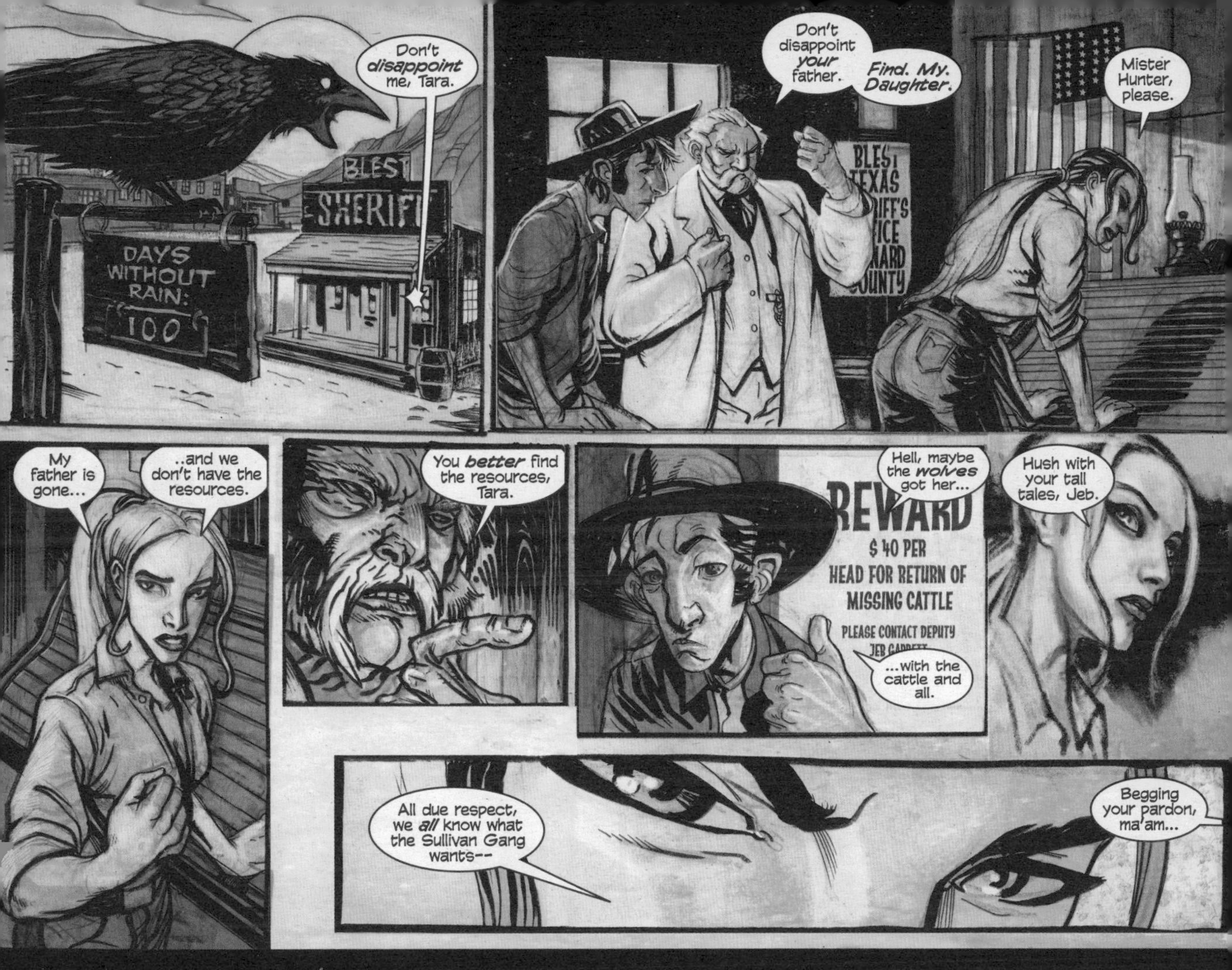

BLEST
SHERIF
DAYS WITHOUT RAIN: 100
Don't *disappoint* me, Tara.
Don't disappoint *your* father.
Find. My. Daughter.
BLEST TEXAS
Mister Hunter, please.
My father is gone...
..and we don't have the resources.
You *better* find the resources, Tara.
REWARD
$ 40 PER HEAD FOR RETURN OF MISSING CATTLE
PLEASE CONTACT DEPUTY
Hell, maybe the *wolves* got her...
...with the cattle and all.
Hush with your tall tales, Jeb.
All due respect, we *all* know what the Sullivan Gang wants--
Begging your pardon, ma'am...

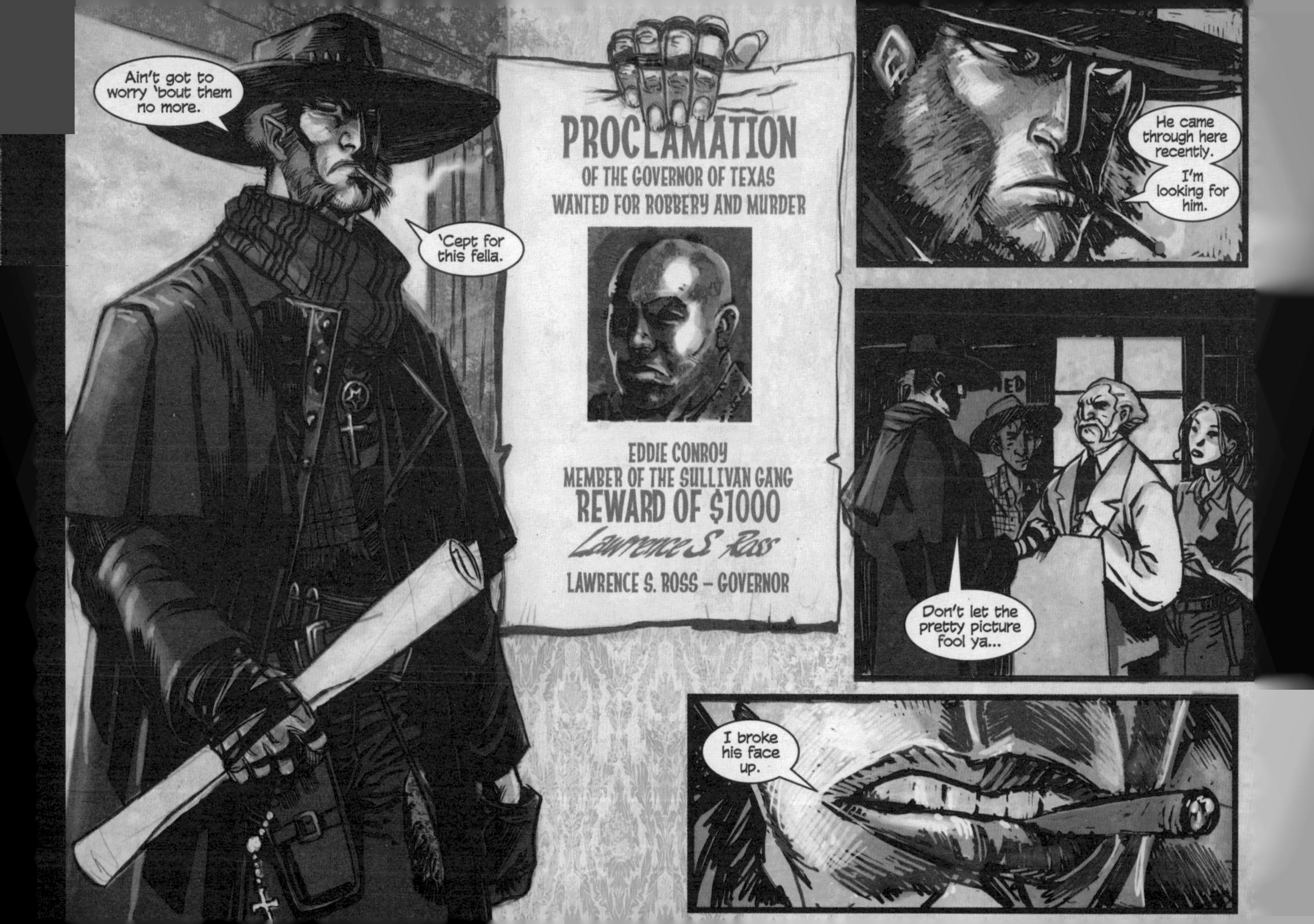
Ain't got to worry 'bout them no more.
'Cept for this fella.
PROCLAMATION
OF THE GOVERNOR OF TEXAS
WANTED FOR ROBBERY AND MURDER
EDDIE CONROY
MEMBER OF THE SULLIVAN GANG
REWARD OF $1000
Lawrence S. Ross
LAWRENCE S. ROSS – GOVERNOR
He came through here recently.
I'm looking for him.
Don't let the pretty picture fool ya...
I broke his face up.

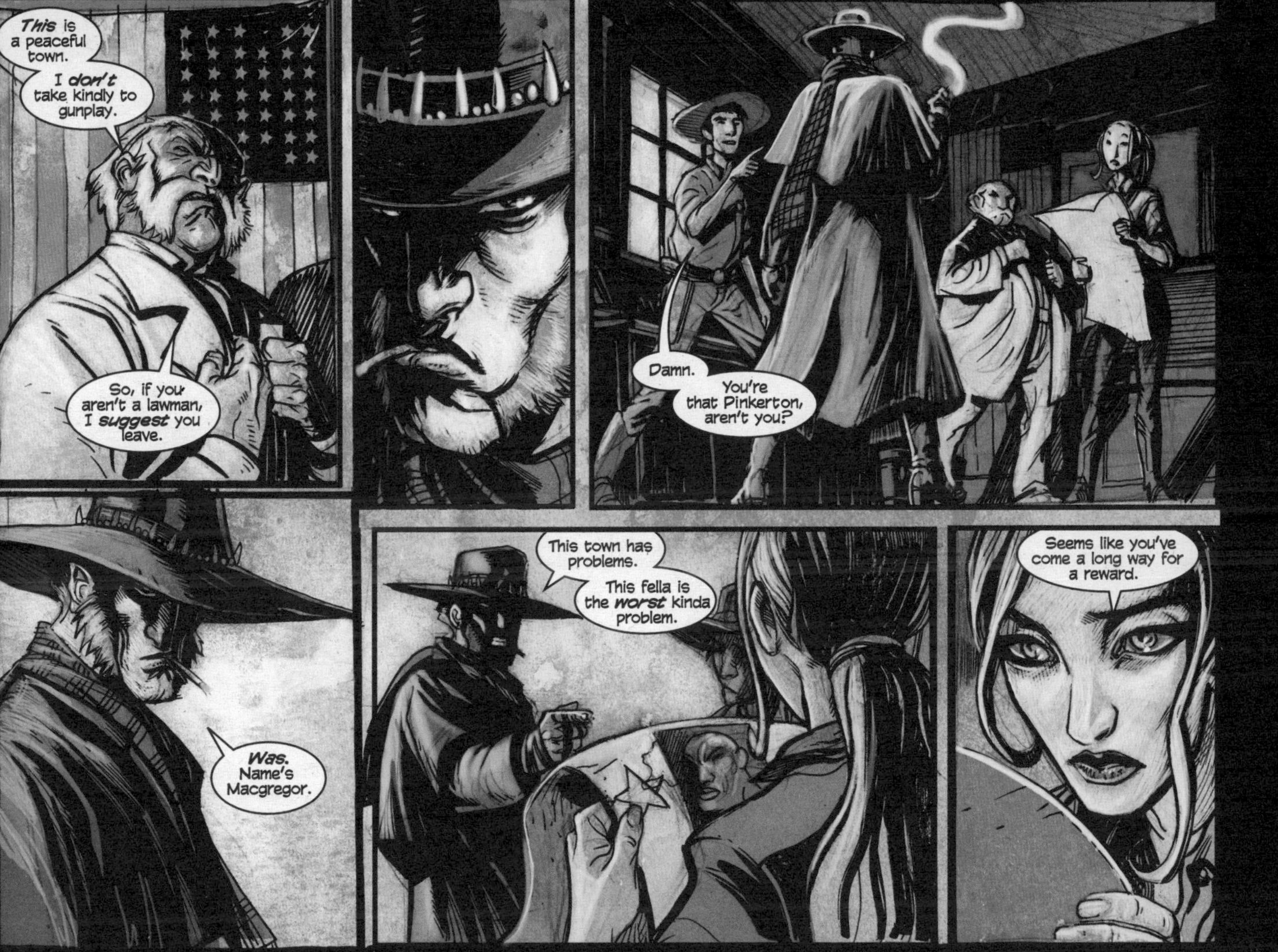
This is a peaceful town.
I don't take kindly to gunplay.
So, if you aren't a lawman, I suggest you leave.
Damn.
You're that Pinkerton, aren't you?
Was. Name's Macgregor.
This town has problems.
This fella is the worst kinda problem.
Seems like you've come a long way for a reward.

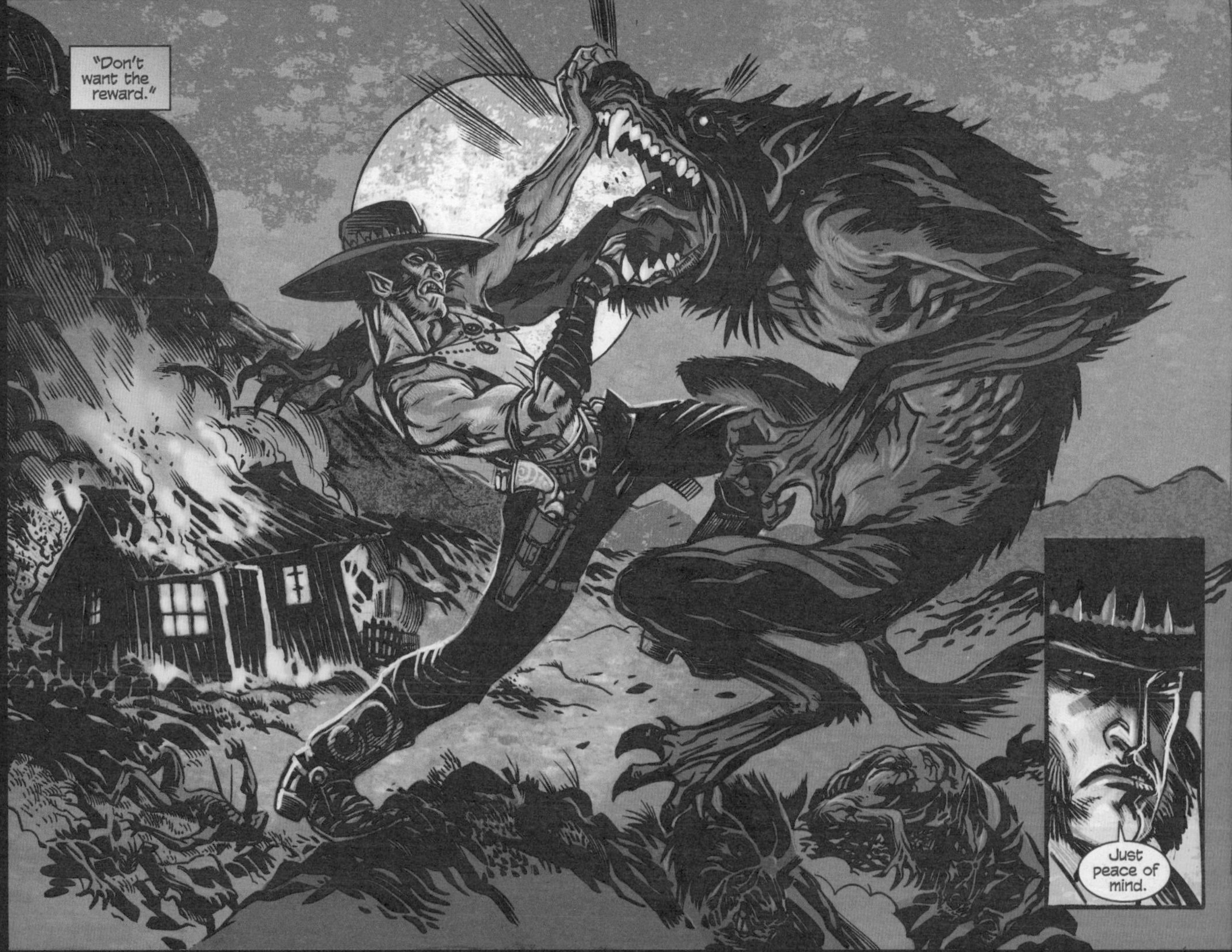
"Don't want the reward."
Just peace of mind.

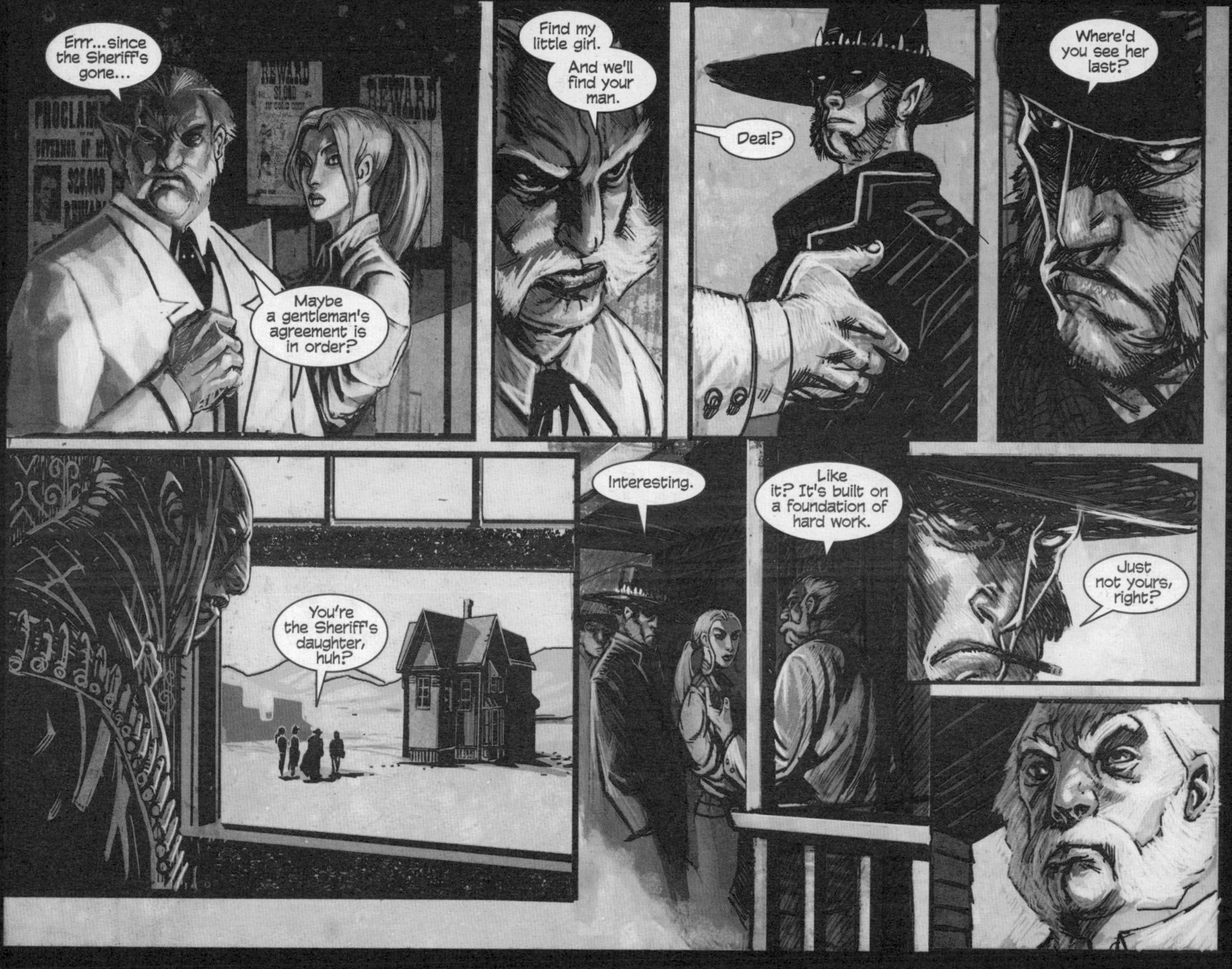

Errr...since the Sheriff's gone...
Maybe a gentleman's agreement is in order?
Find my little girl.
And we'll find your man.
Deal?
Where'd you see her last?
You're the Sheriff's daughter, huh?
Interesting.
Like it? It's built on a foundation of hard work.
Just not yours, right?

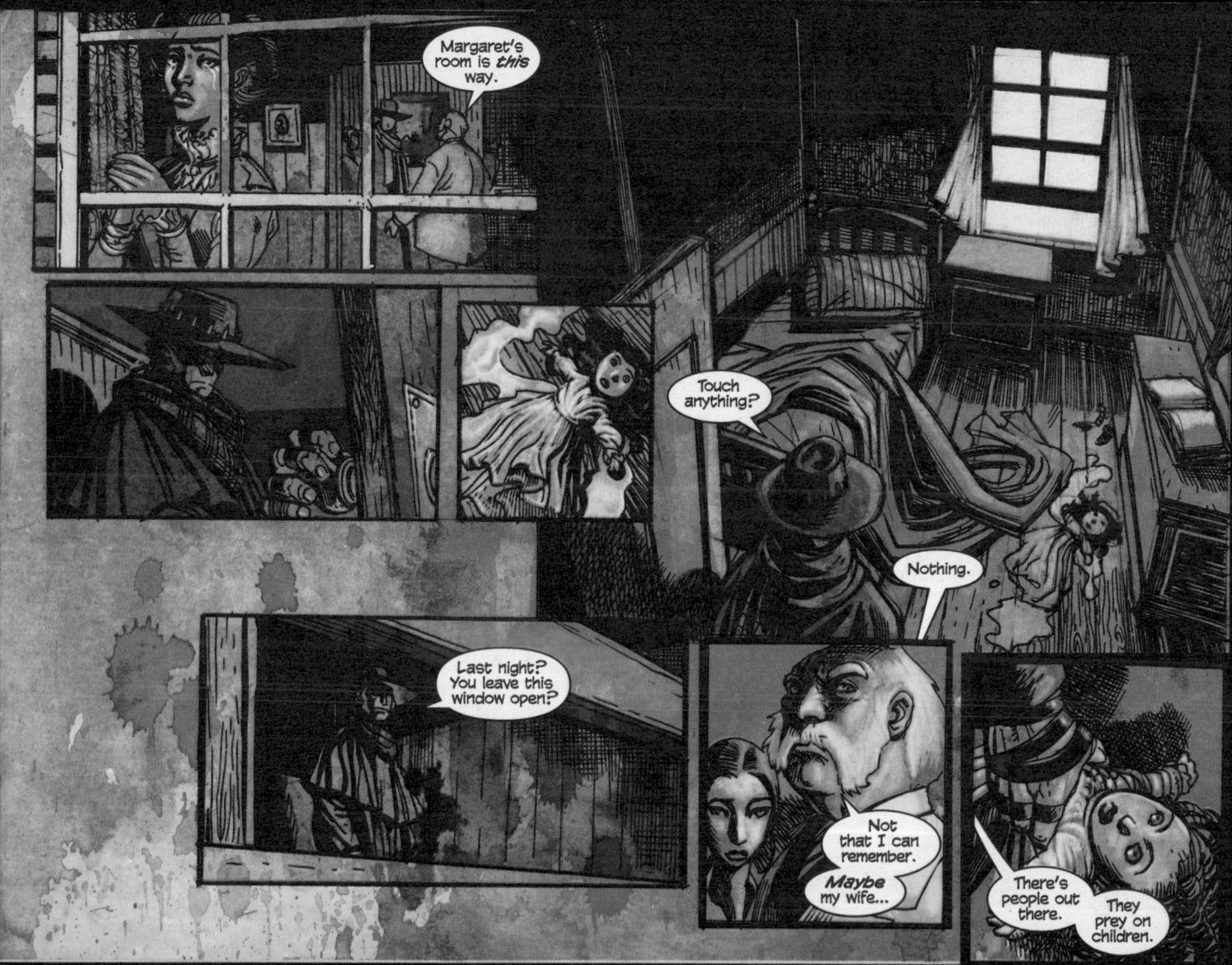
Margaret's room is *this* way.
Touch anything?
Nothing.
Last night? You leave this window open?
Not that I can remember.
Maybe my wife...
There's people out there.
They prey on children.

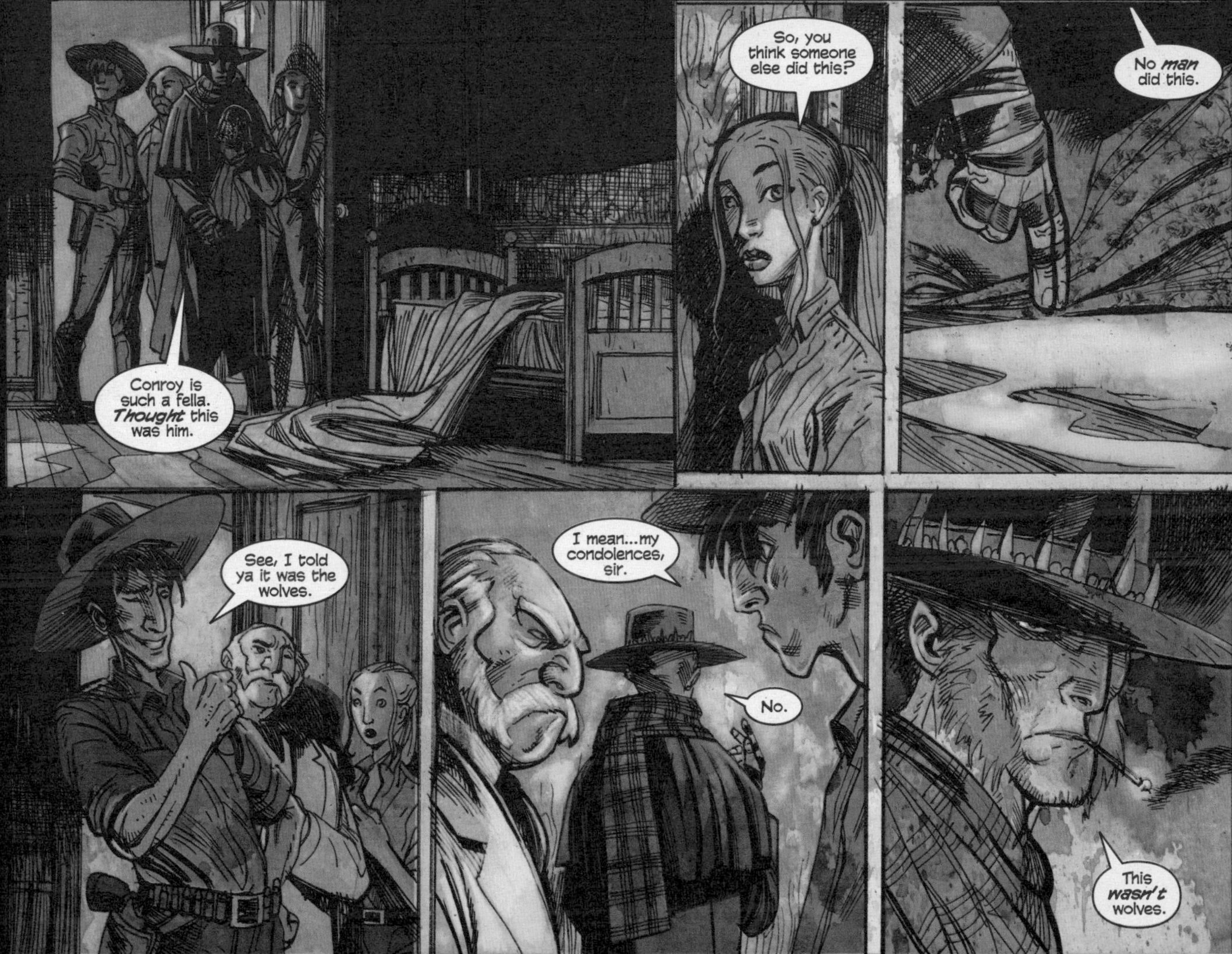
Conroy is such a fella. *Thought* this was him.
So, you think someone else did this?
No *man* did this.
See, I told ya it was the wolves.
I mean...my condolences, sir.
No.
This *wasn't* wolves.

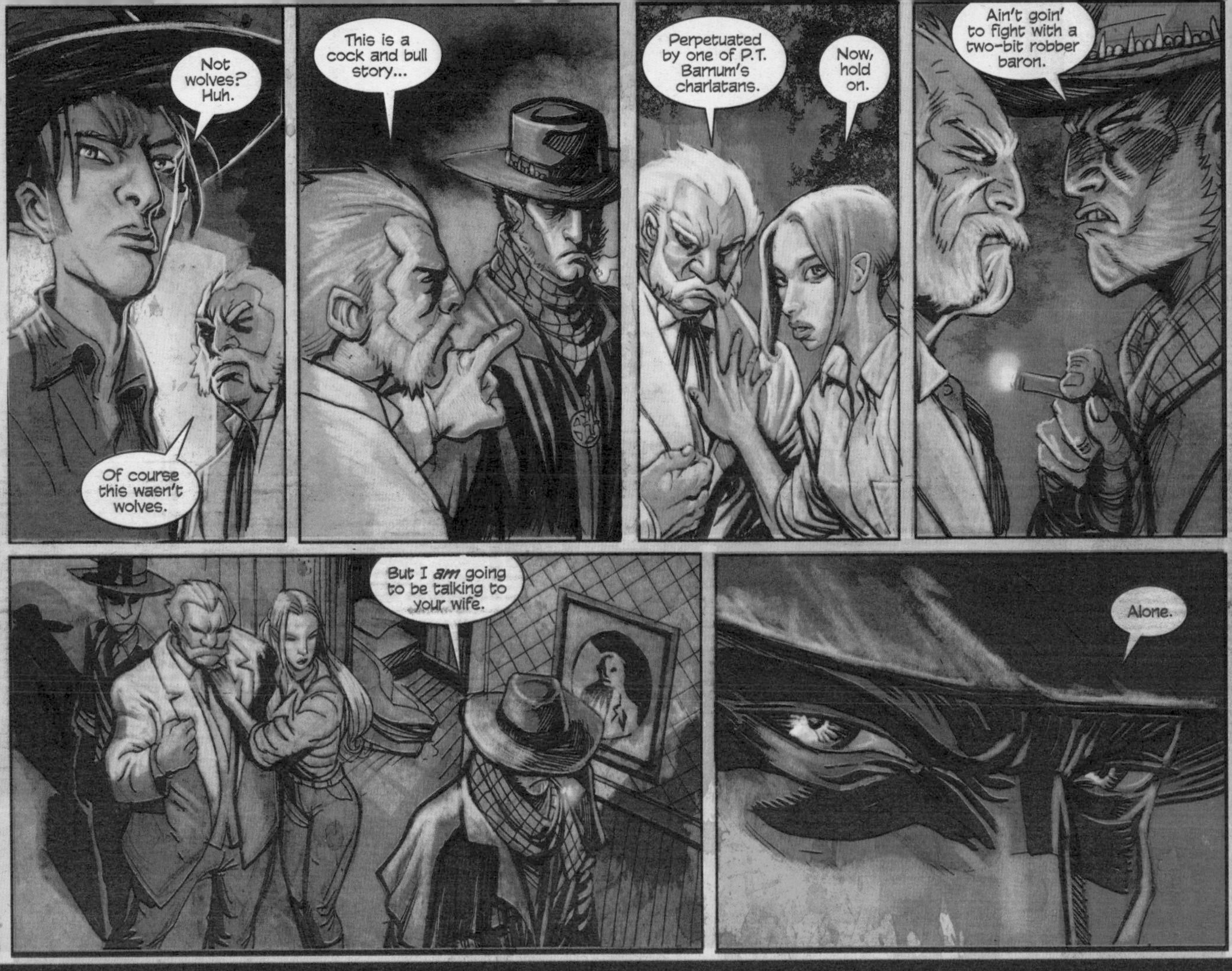
Not wolves? Huh.
Of course this wasn't wolves.
This is a cock and bull story...
Perpetuated by one of P.T. Barnum's charlatans.
Now, hold on.
Ain't goin' to fight with a two-bit robber baron.
But I *am* going to be talking to your wife.
Alone.

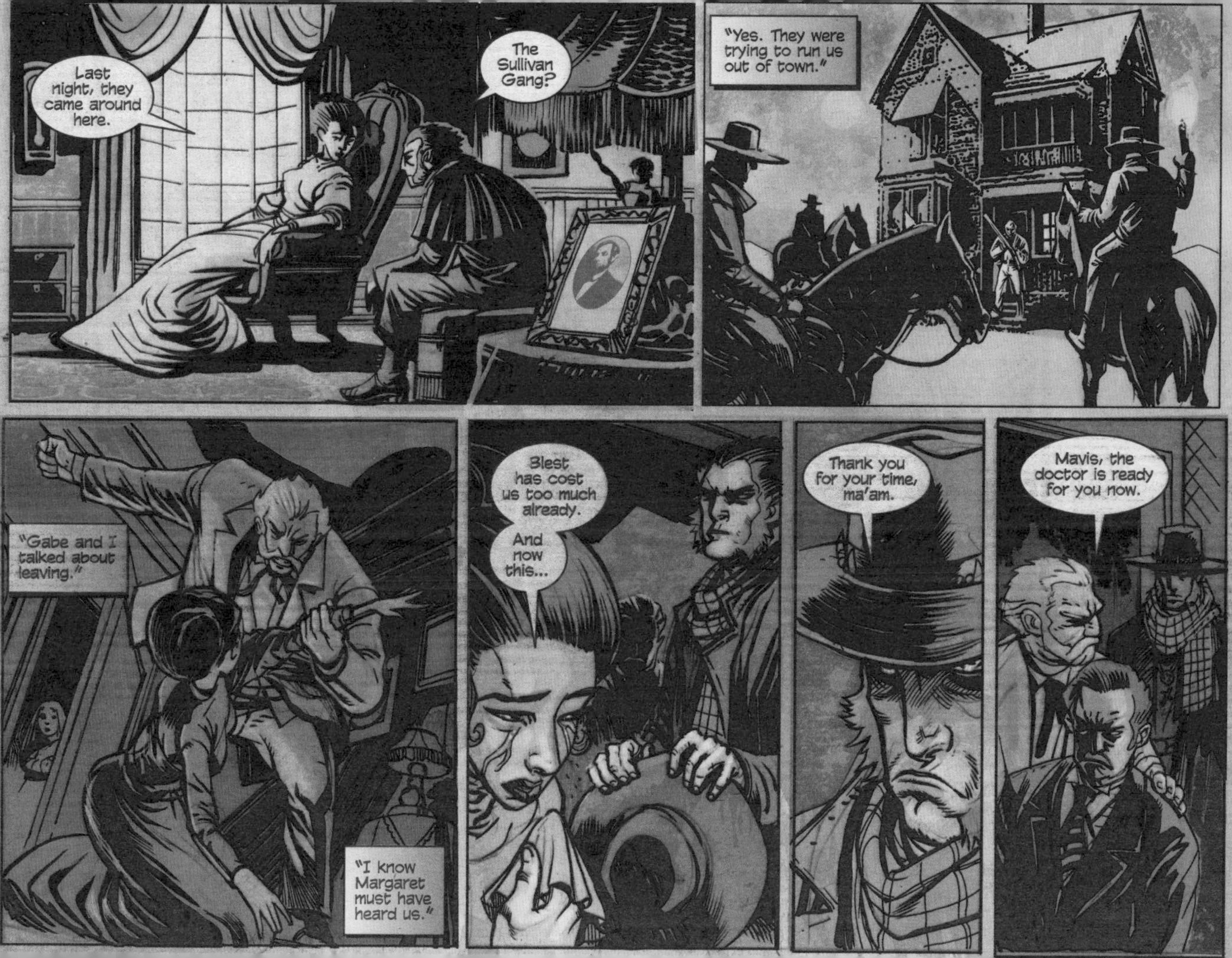
Last night, they came around here.
The Sullivan Gang?
"Yes. They were trying to run us out of town."
"Gabe and I talked about leaving."
"I know Margaret must have heard us."
Blest has cost us too much already.
And now this...
Thank you for your time, ma'am.
Mavis, the doctor is ready for you now.

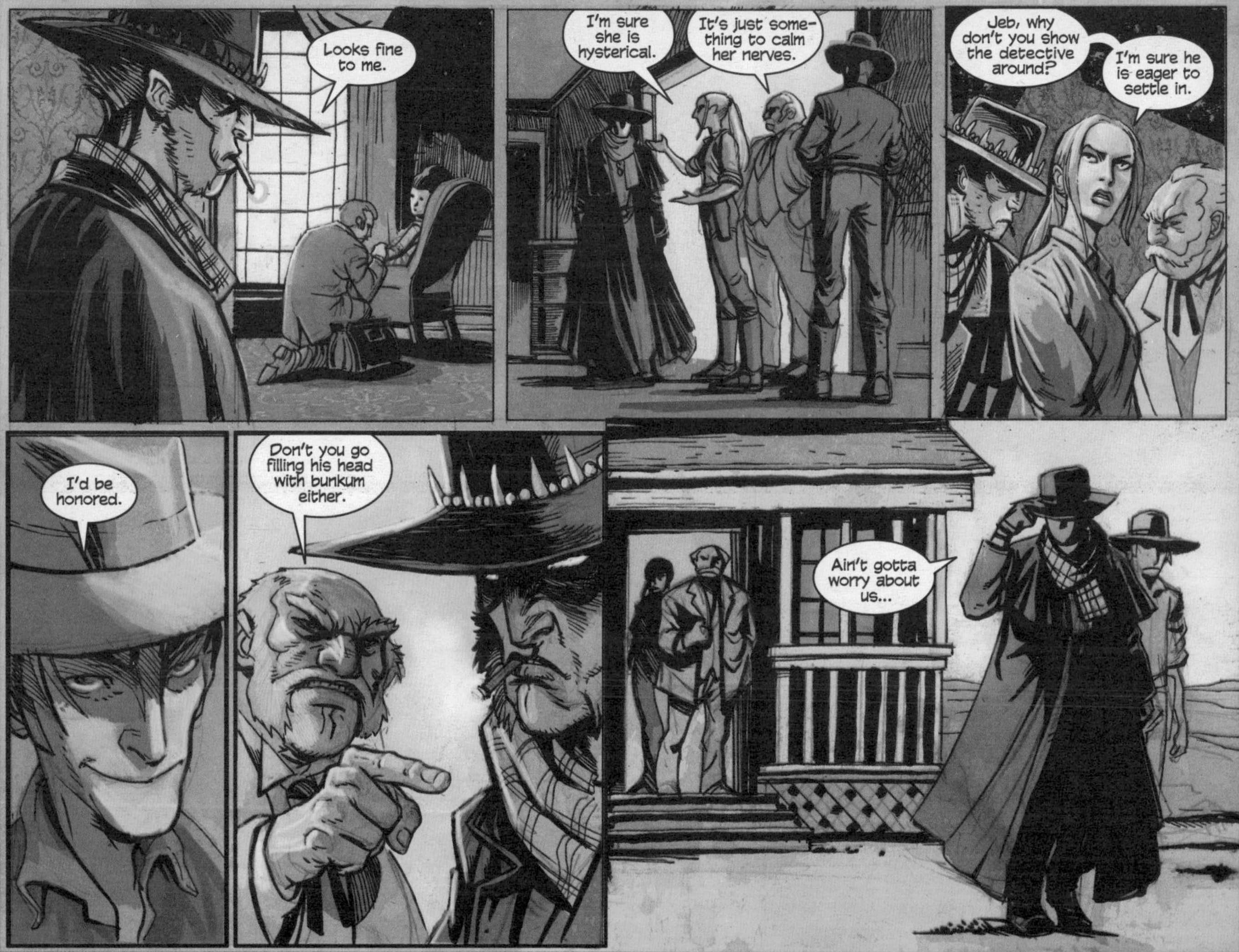
Looks fine to me.
I'm sure she is hysterical.
It's just something to calm her nerves.
Jeb, why don't you show the detective around?
I'm sure he is eager to settle in.
I'd be honored.
Don't you go filling his head with bunkum either.
Ain't gotta worry about us...

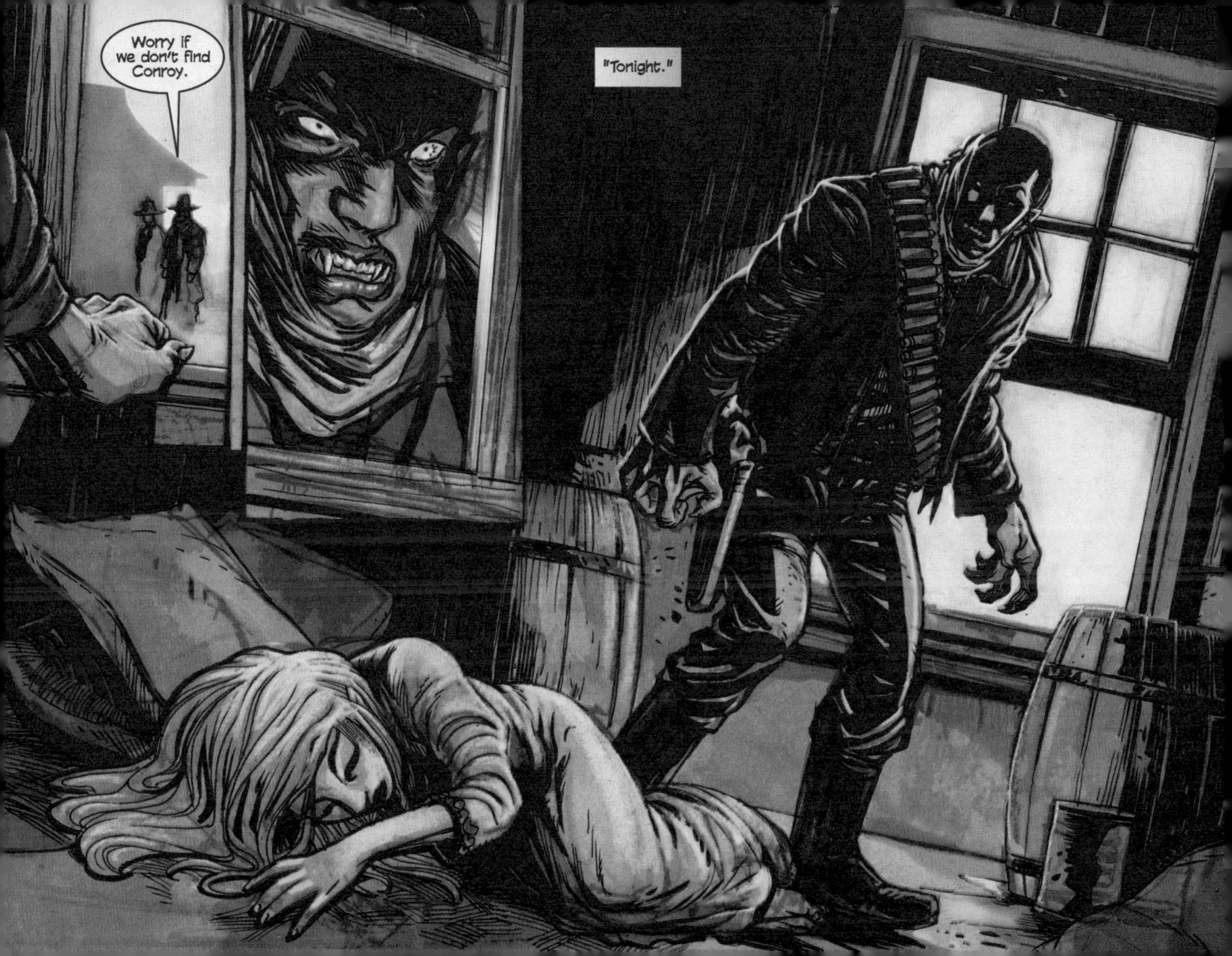
Worry if we don't find Conroy.
"Tonight."

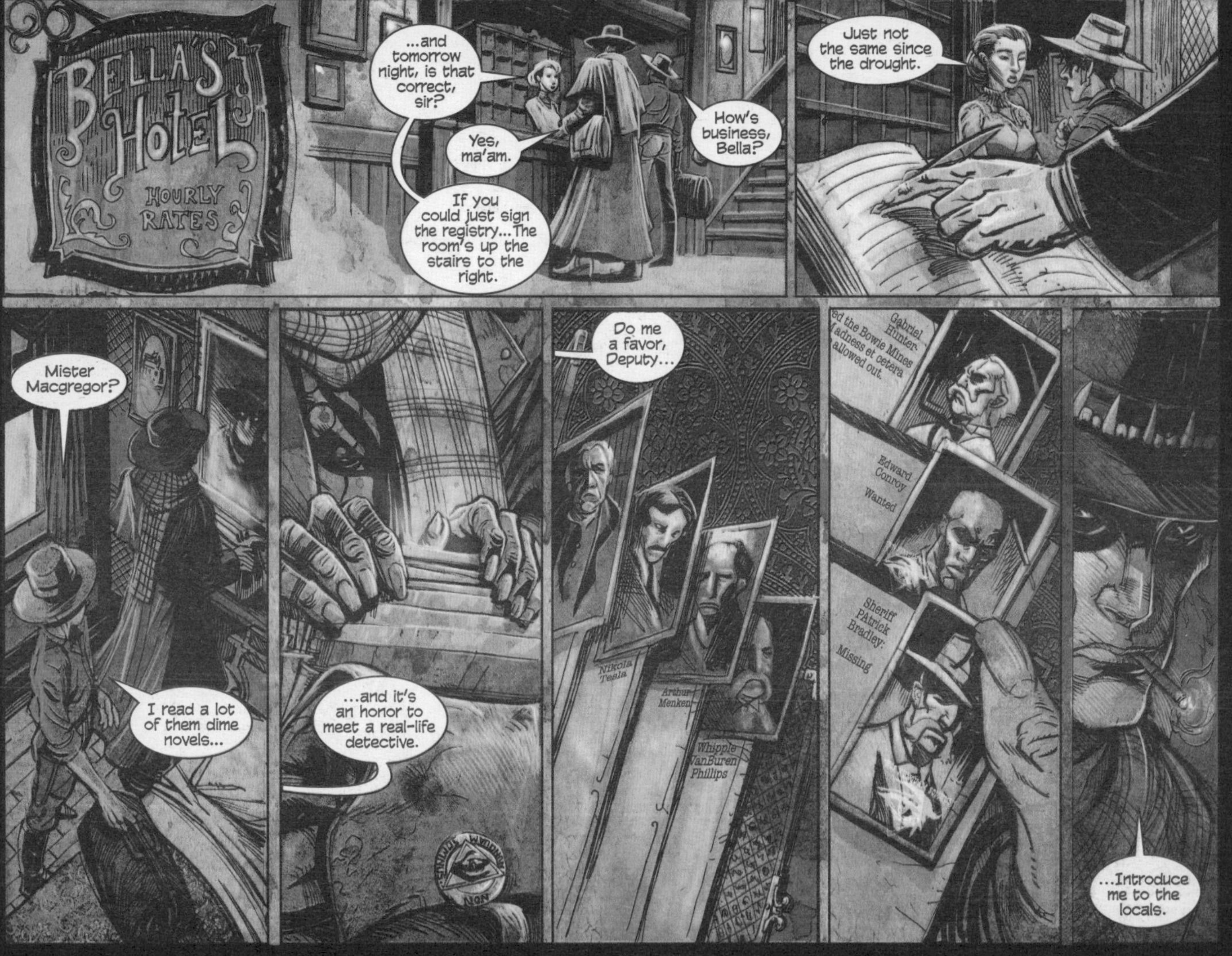

BELLA'S HOTEL
HOURLY RATES
...and tomorrow night, is that correct, sir?
Yes, ma'am.
If you could just sign the registry... The room's up the stairs to the right.
How's business, Bella?
Just not the same since the drought.
Mister Macgregor?
I read a lot of them dime novels...
...and it's an honor to meet a real-life detective.
Do me a favor, Deputy...
Nikola Tesla
Arthur Menken
Whipple VanBuren Phillips
Gabriel Hunter
Edward Conroy
Wanted
Sheriff PAtrick Bradley:
Missing
...Introduce me to the locals.

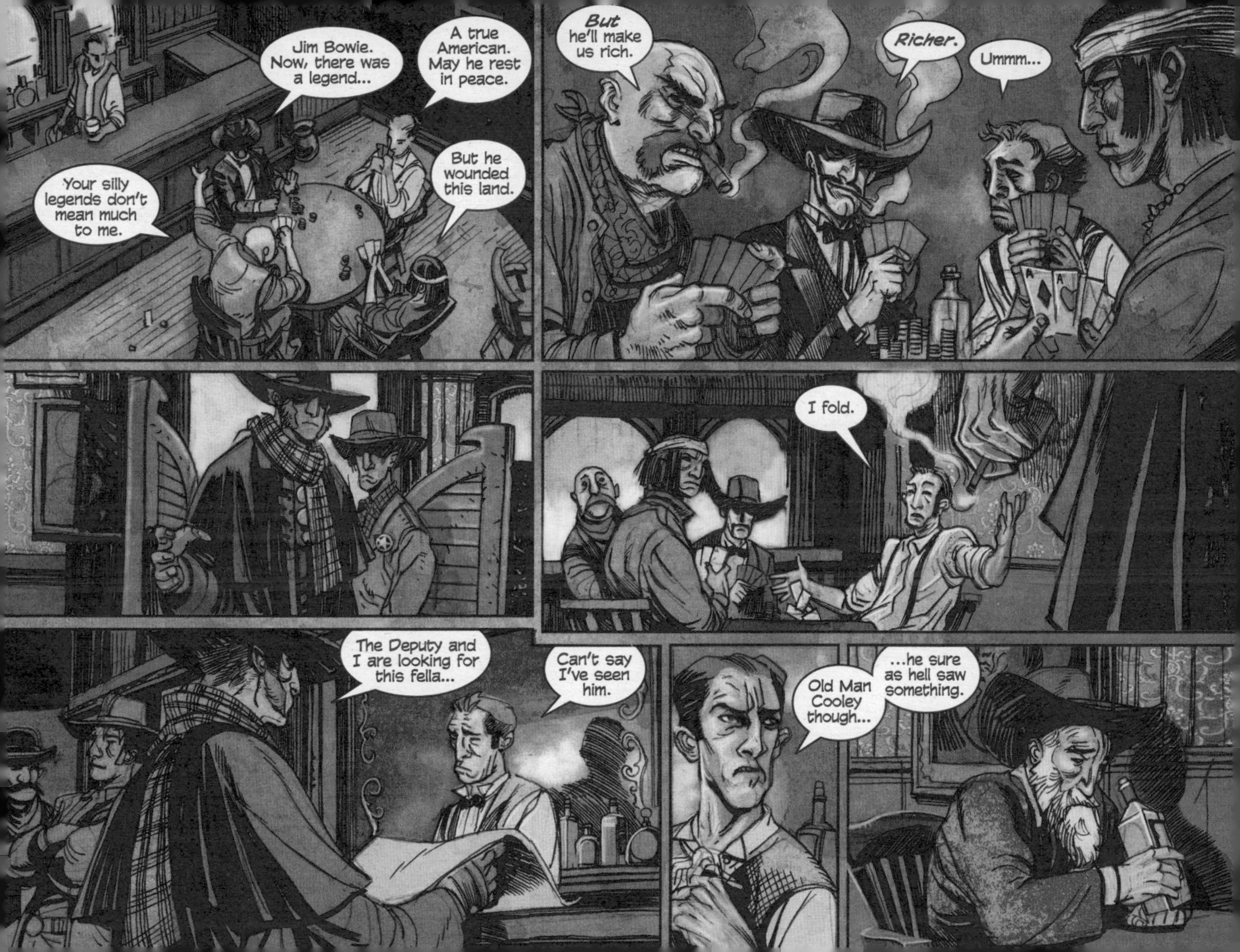
Jim Bowie. Now, there was a legend...
A true American. May he rest in peace.
Your silly legends don't mean much to me.
But he wounded this land.
But he'll make us rich.
Richer.
Ummm...
I fold.
The Deputy and I are looking for this fella...
Can't say I've seen him.
Old Man Cooley though...
...he sure as hell saw something.

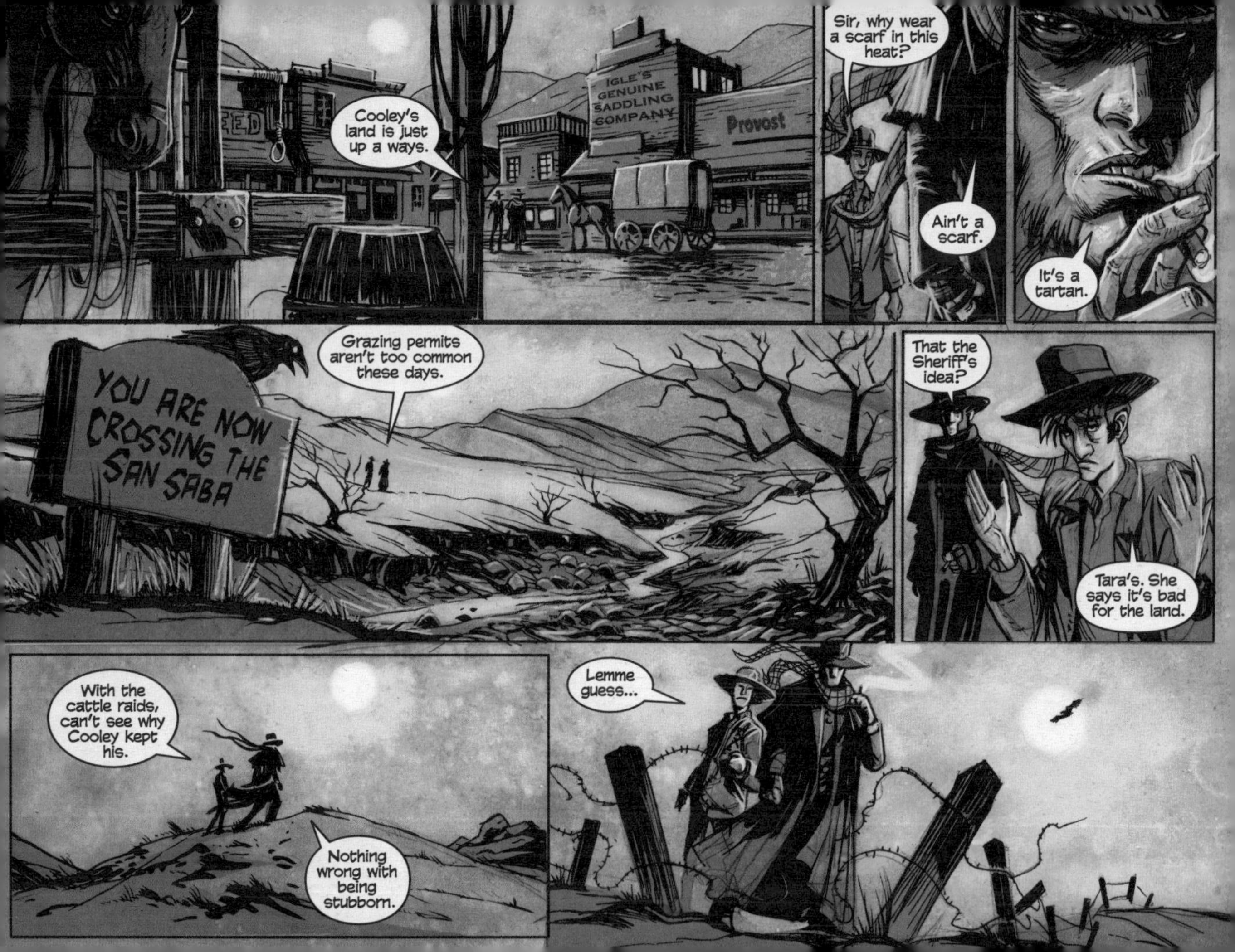
Cooley's land is just up a ways.
FEED
IGLE'S GENUINE SADDLING COMPANY
Provost
Sir, why wear a scarf in this heat?
Ain't a scarf.
It's a tartan.
YOU ARE NOW CROSSING THE SAN SABA
Grazing permits aren't too common these days.
That the Sheriff's idea?
Tara's. She says it's bad for the land.
With the cattle raids, can't see why Cooley kept his.
Nothing wrong with being stubborn.
Lemme guess...

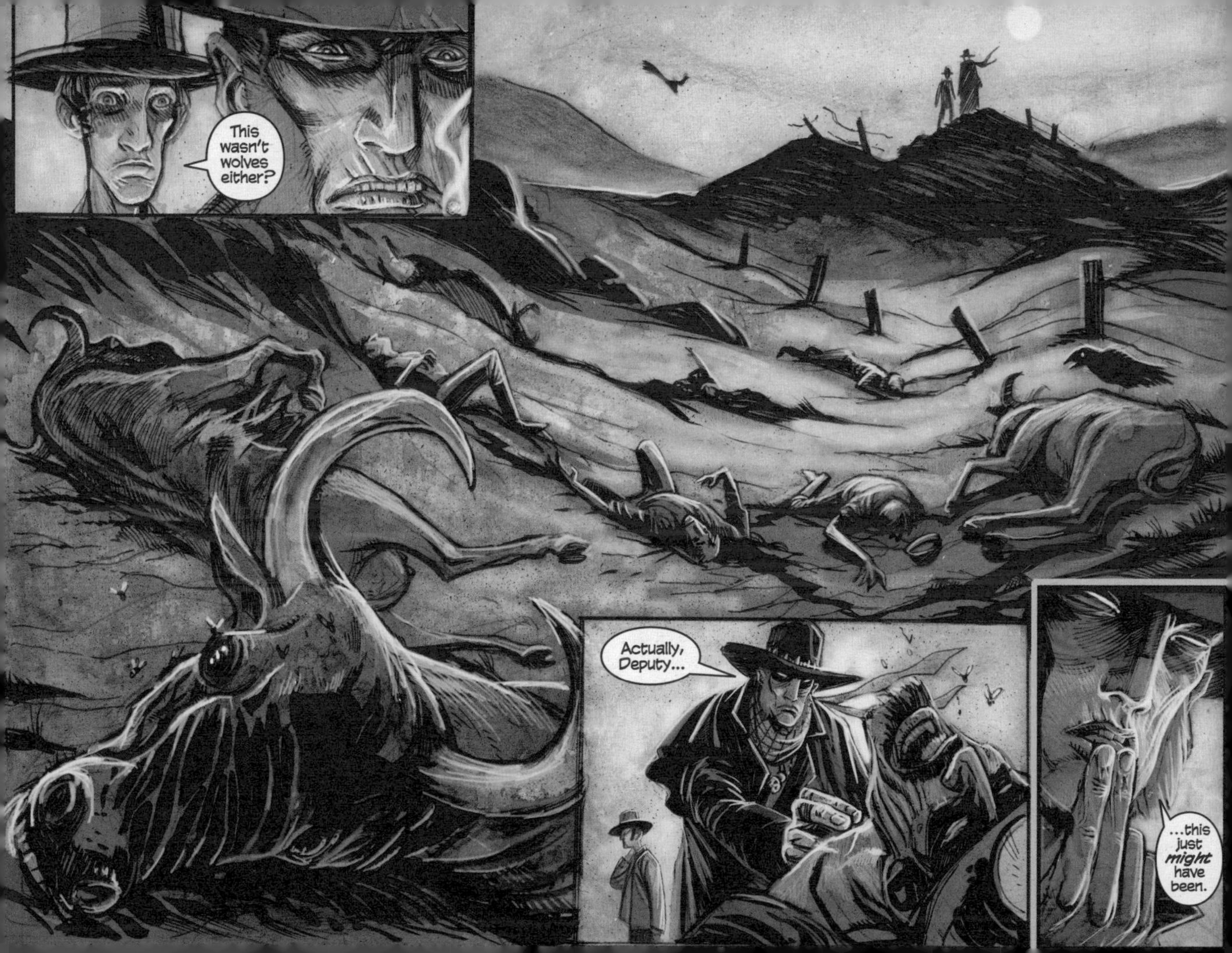
This wasn't wolves either?
Actually, Deputy...
...this just *might* have been.

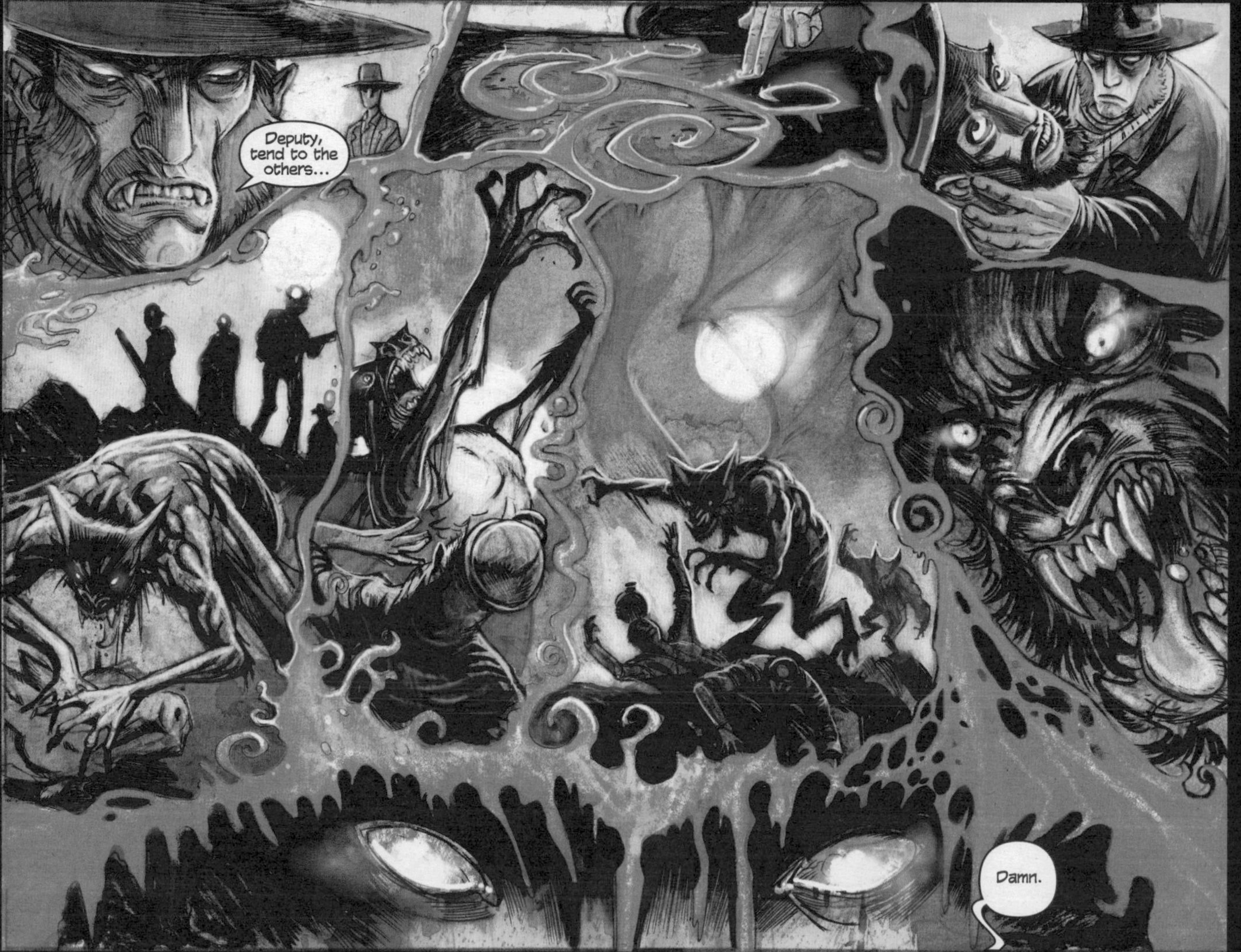
Deputy, tend to the others...
Damn.

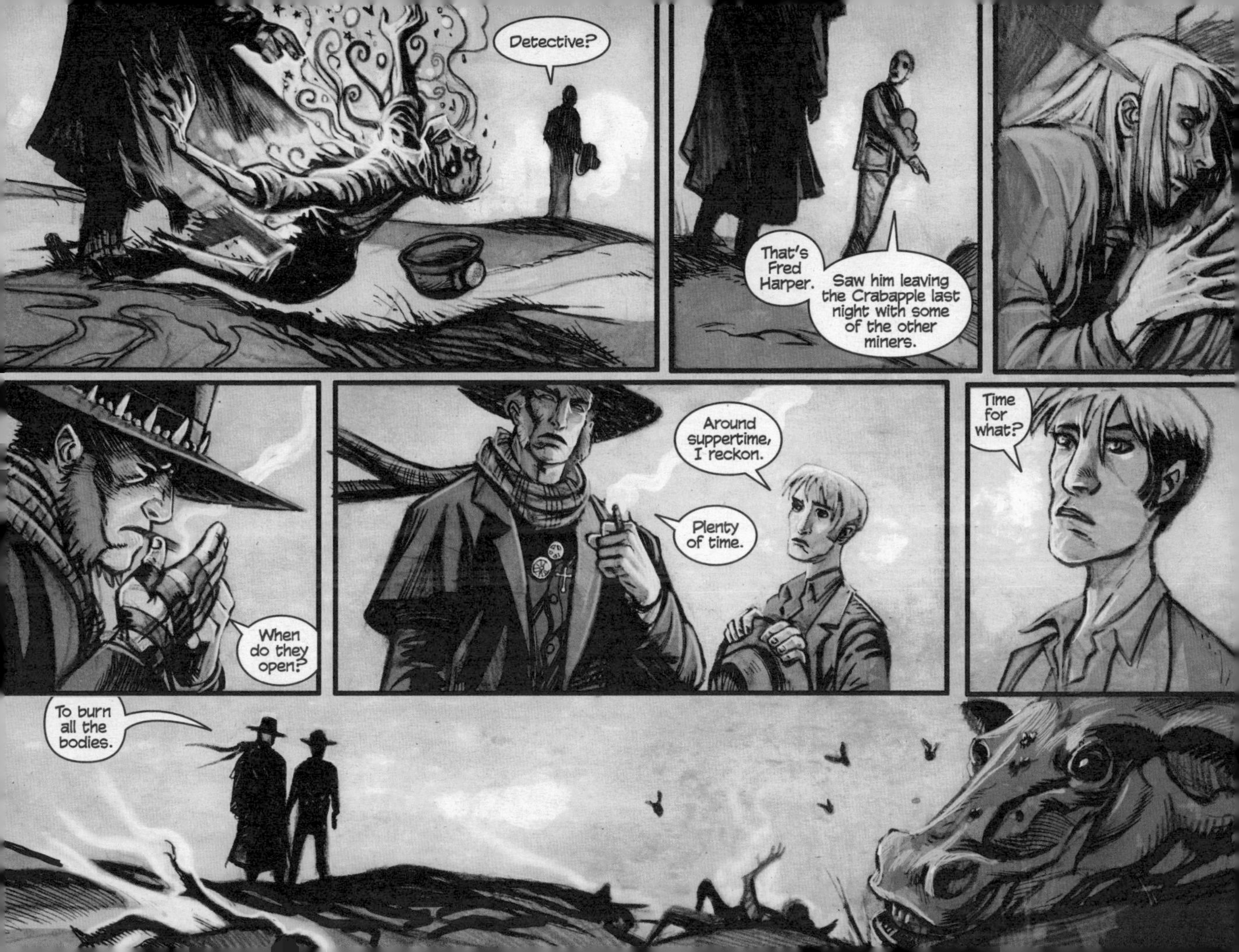
Detective?
That's Fred Harper.
Saw him leaving the Crabapple last night with some of the other miners.
When do they open?
Around suppertime, I reckon.
Plenty of time.
Time for what?
To burn all the bodies.

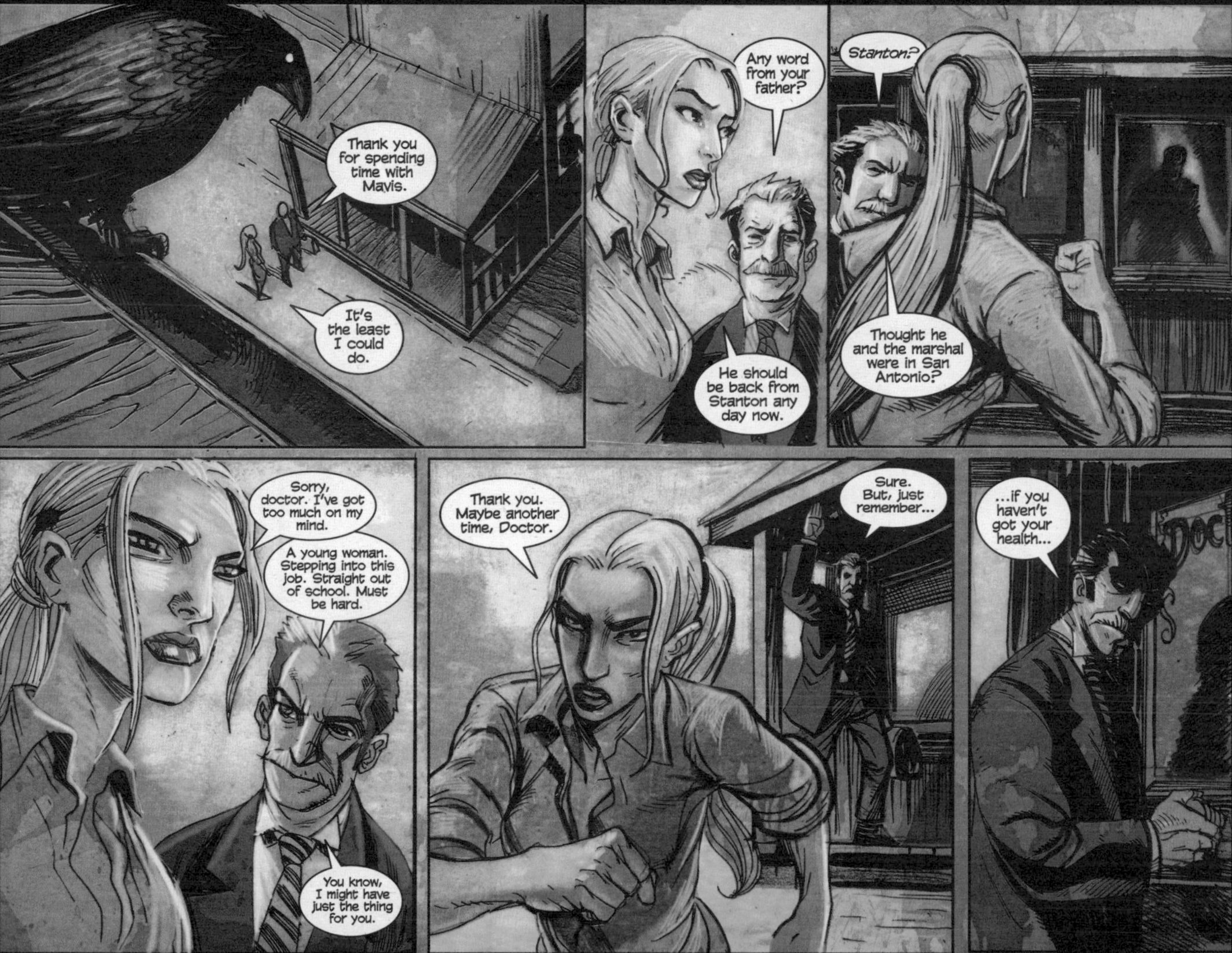
Thank you for spending time with Mavis.
It's the least I could do.
Any word from your father?
He should be back from Stanton any day now.
Stanton?
Thought he and the marshal were in San Antonio?
Sorry, doctor. I've got too much on my mind.
A young woman. Stepping into this job. Straight out of school. Must be hard.
You know, I might have just the thing for you.
Thank you. Maybe another time, Doctor.
Sure. But, just remember...
...if you haven't got your health...

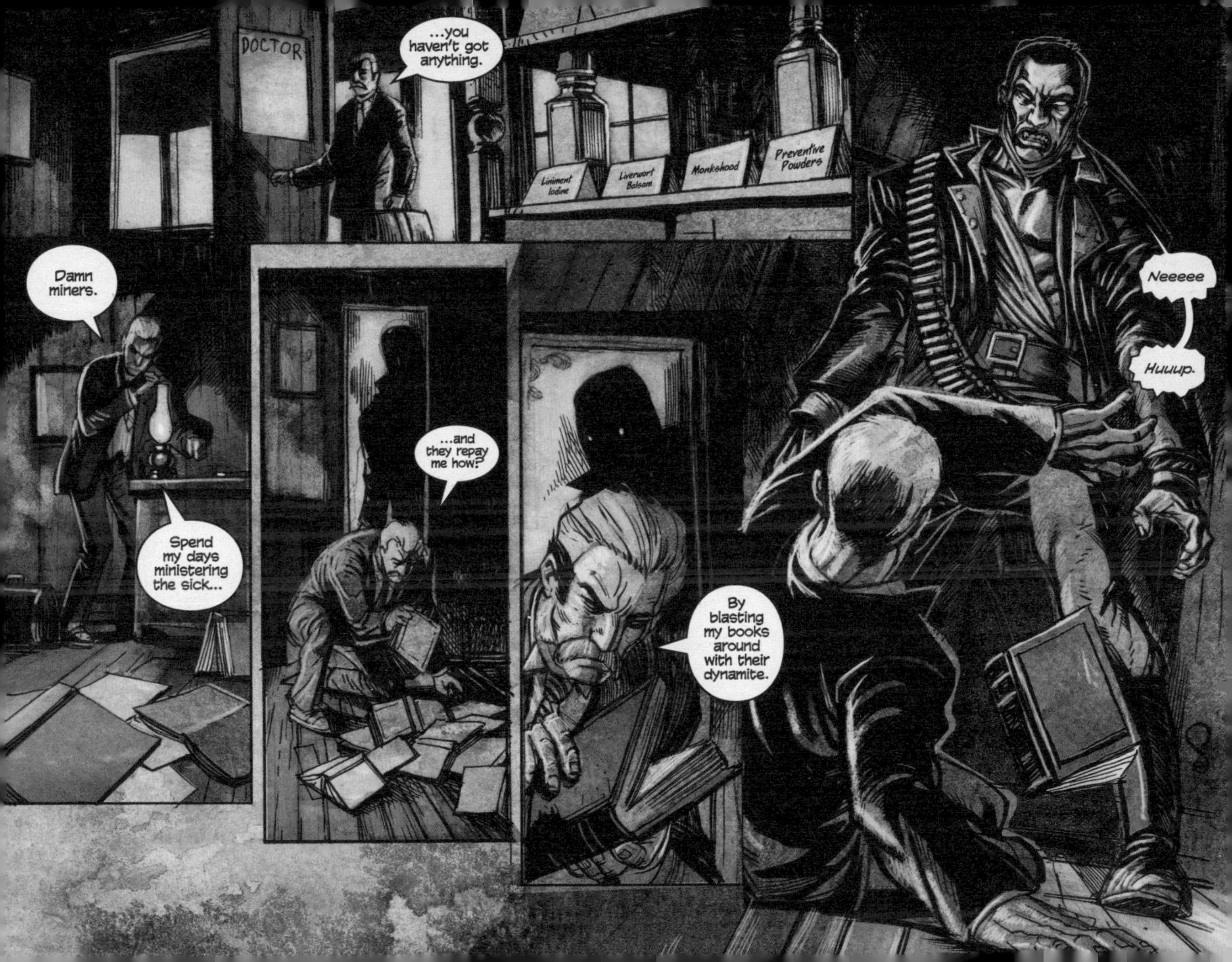
DOCTOR
...you haven't got anything.
Liniment Iodine
Liverwort Balsam
Monkshood
Preventive Powders
Damn miners.
Spend my days ministering the sick...
...and they repay me how?
By blasting my books around with their dynamite.
Neeeee
Huuup.

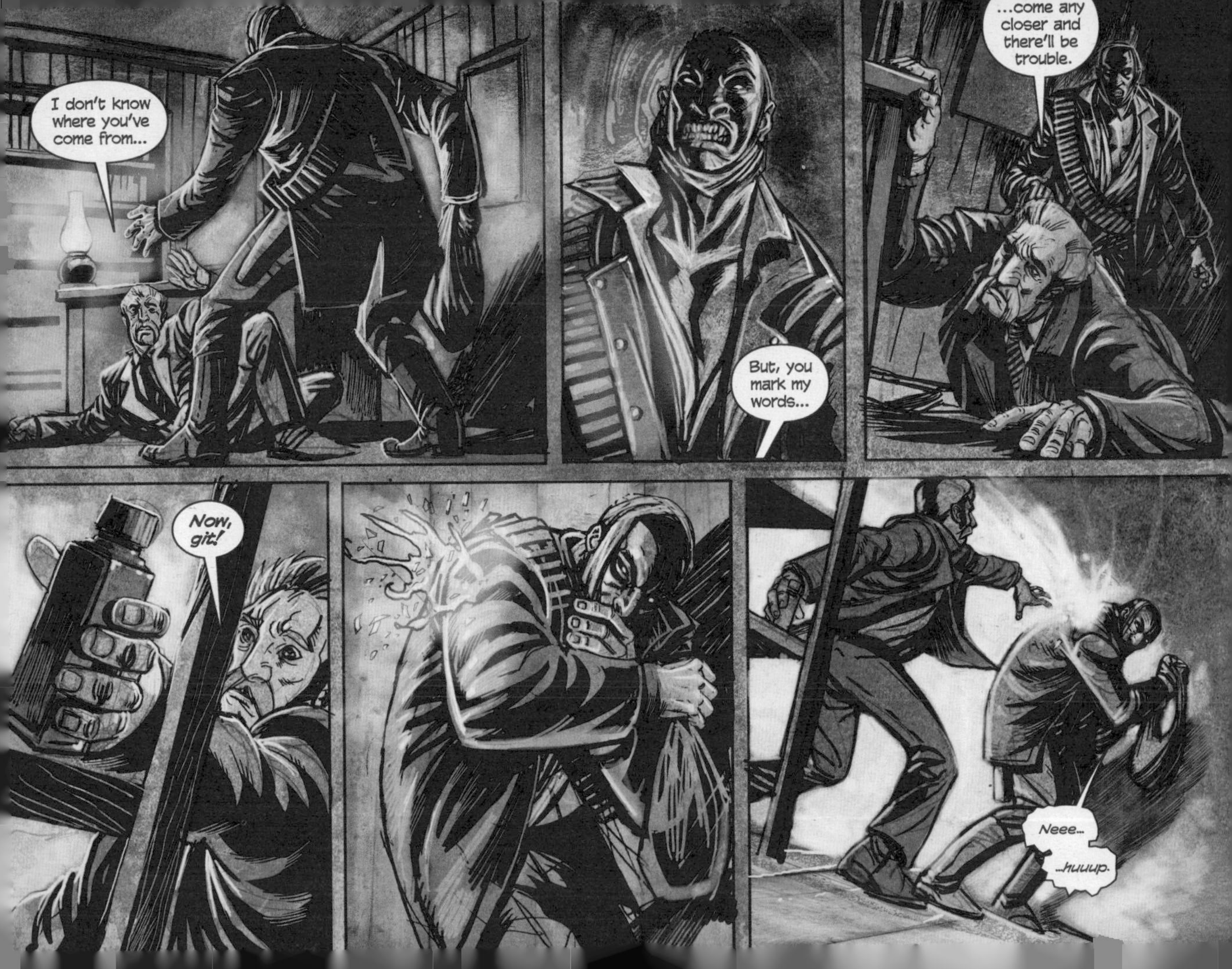
I don't know where you've come from...
But, you mark my words...
...come any closer and there'll be trouble.
Now, git!
Neee...
...huuup.

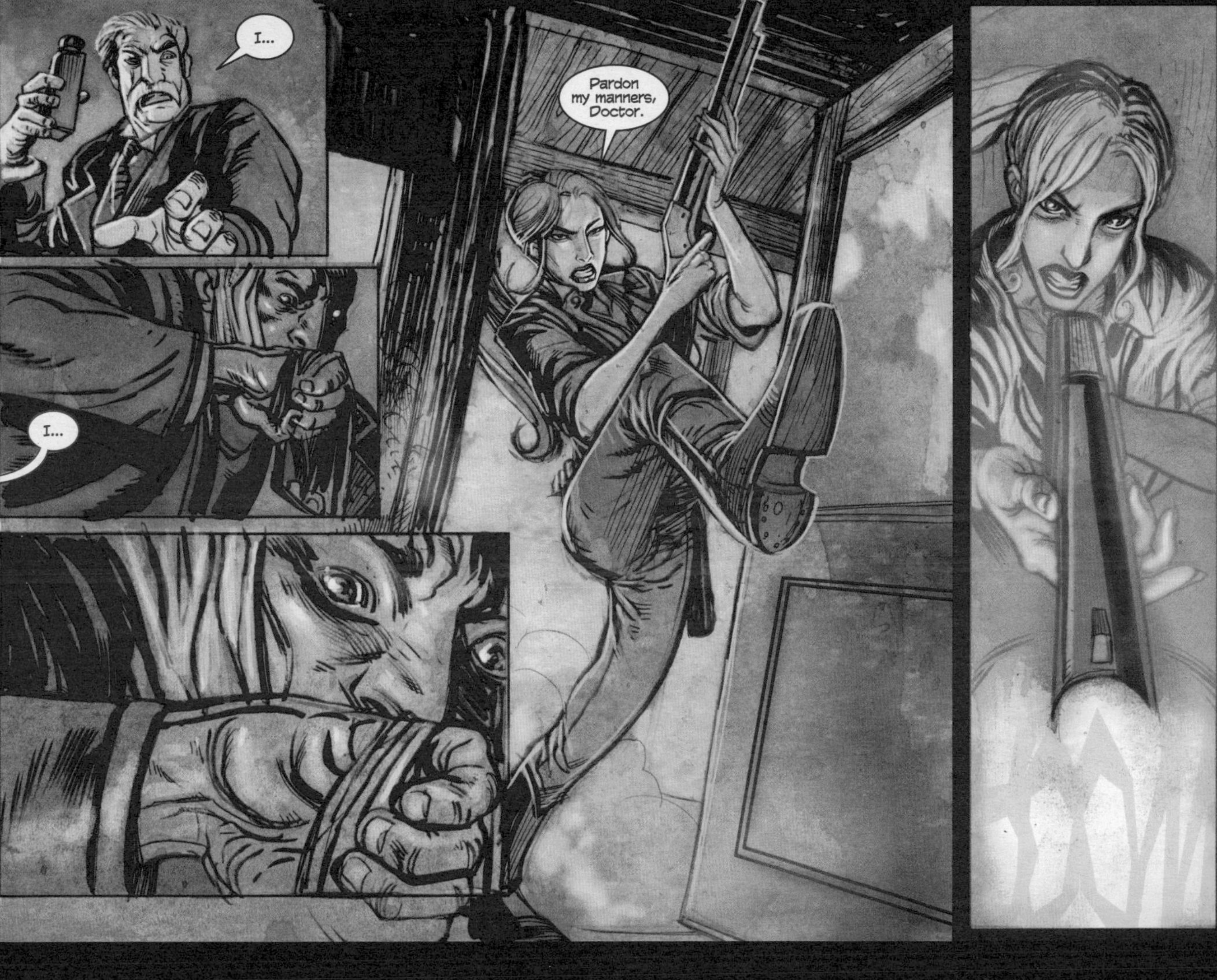
I...
I...
Pardon my manners, Doctor.

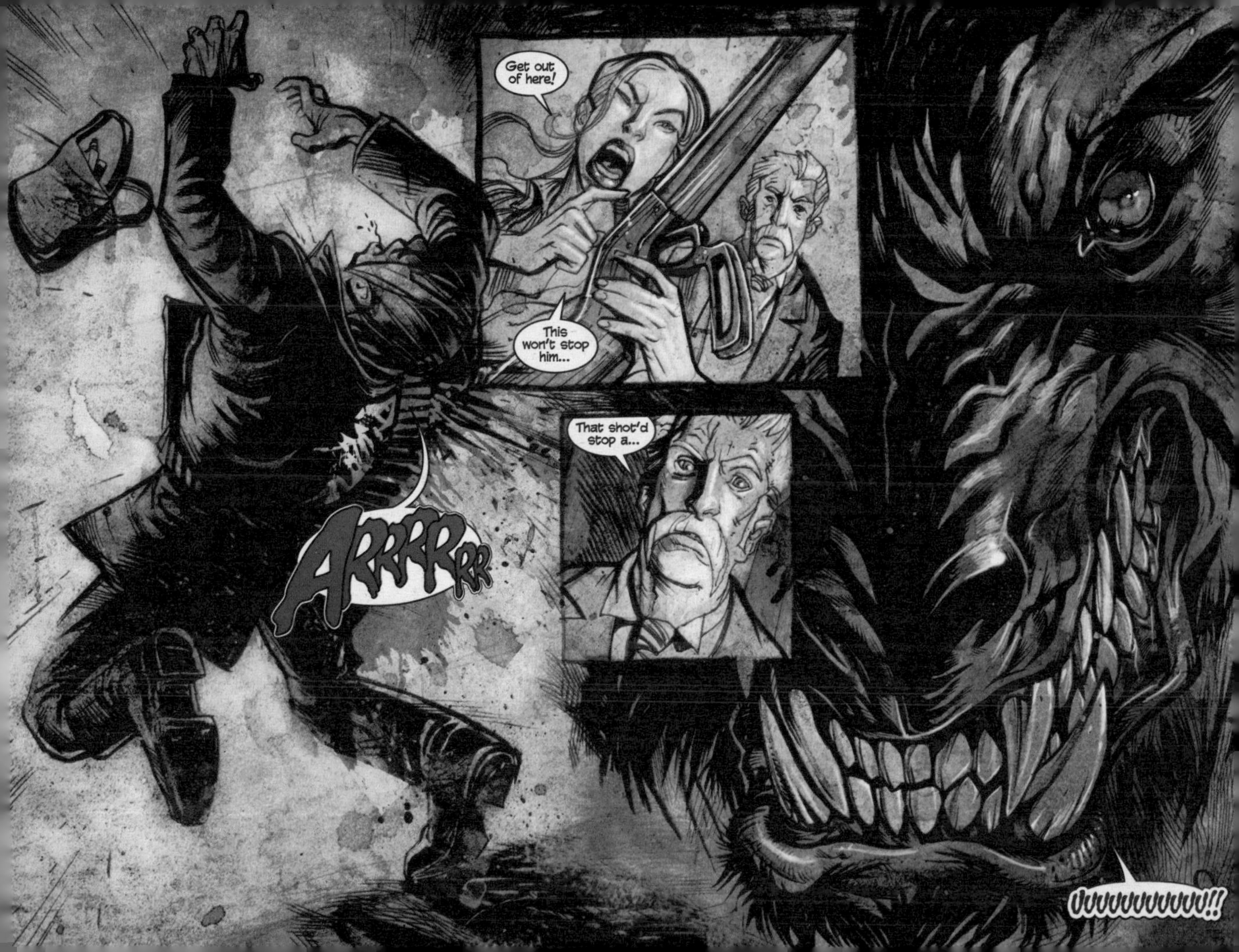
Get out of here!
This won't stop him...
ARRRRRRR
That shot'd stop a...
UUUUUUUUUUU!!

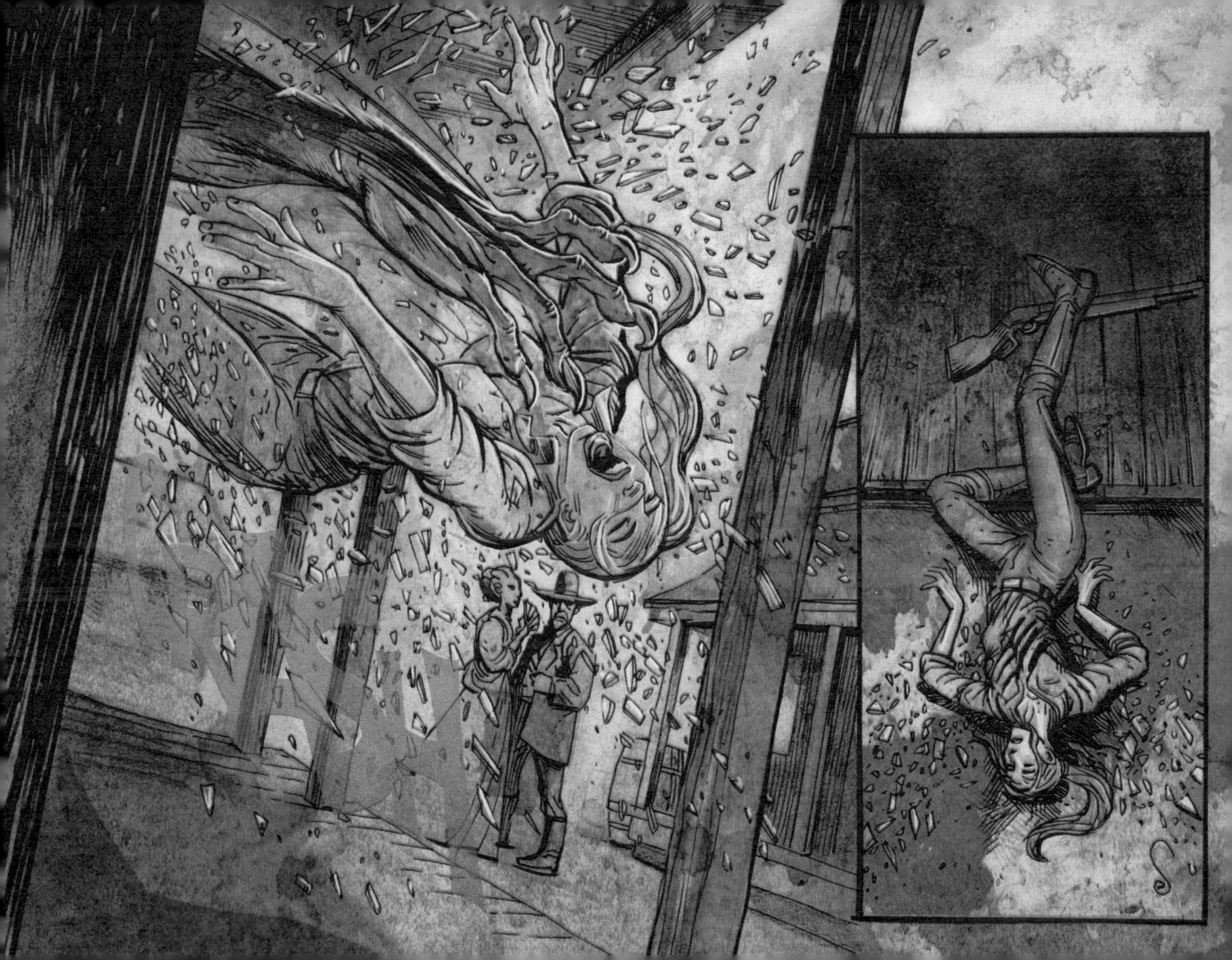

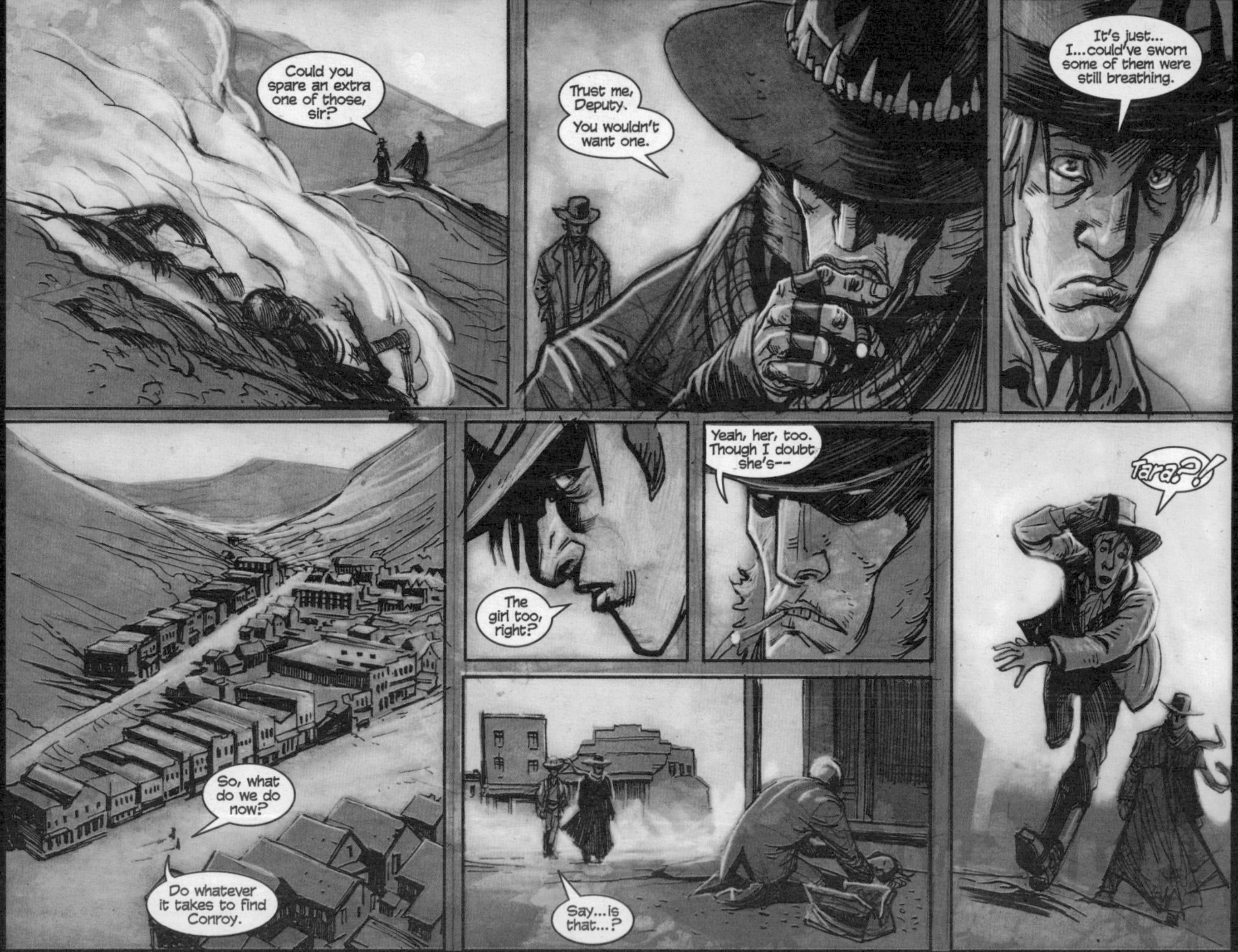
Could you spare an extra one of those, sir?
Trust me, Deputy.
You wouldn't want one.
It's just... I...could've sworn some of them were still breathing.
So, what do we do now?
Do whatever it takes to find Conroy.
The girl too, right?
Yeah, her, too. Though I doubt she's--
Say...is that...?
Tara?!

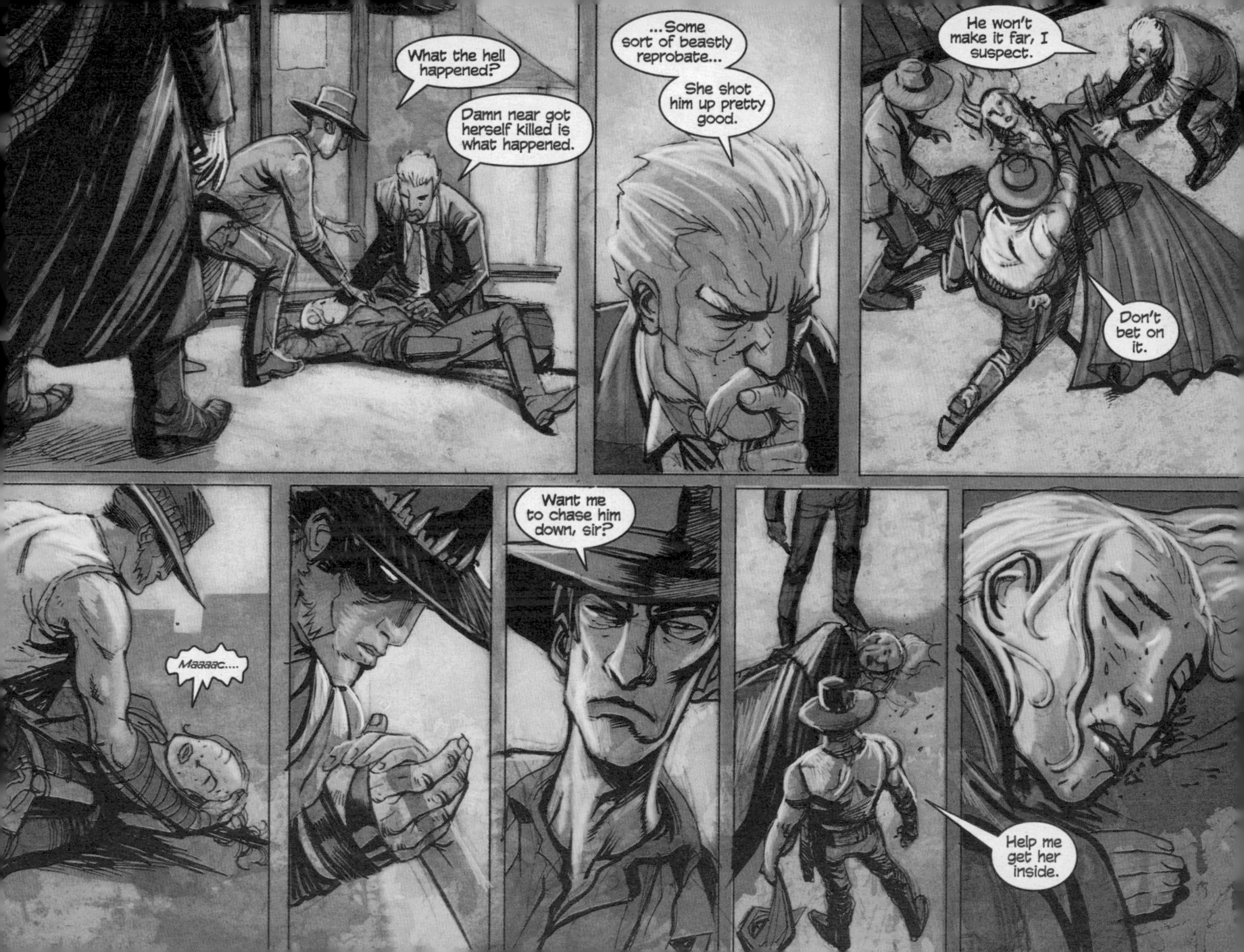
What the hell happened?
Damn near got herself killed is what happened.
...Some sort of beastly reprobate...
She shot him up pretty good.
He won't make it far, I suspect.
Don't bet on it.
Maaaac....
Want me to chase him down, sir?
Help me get her inside.

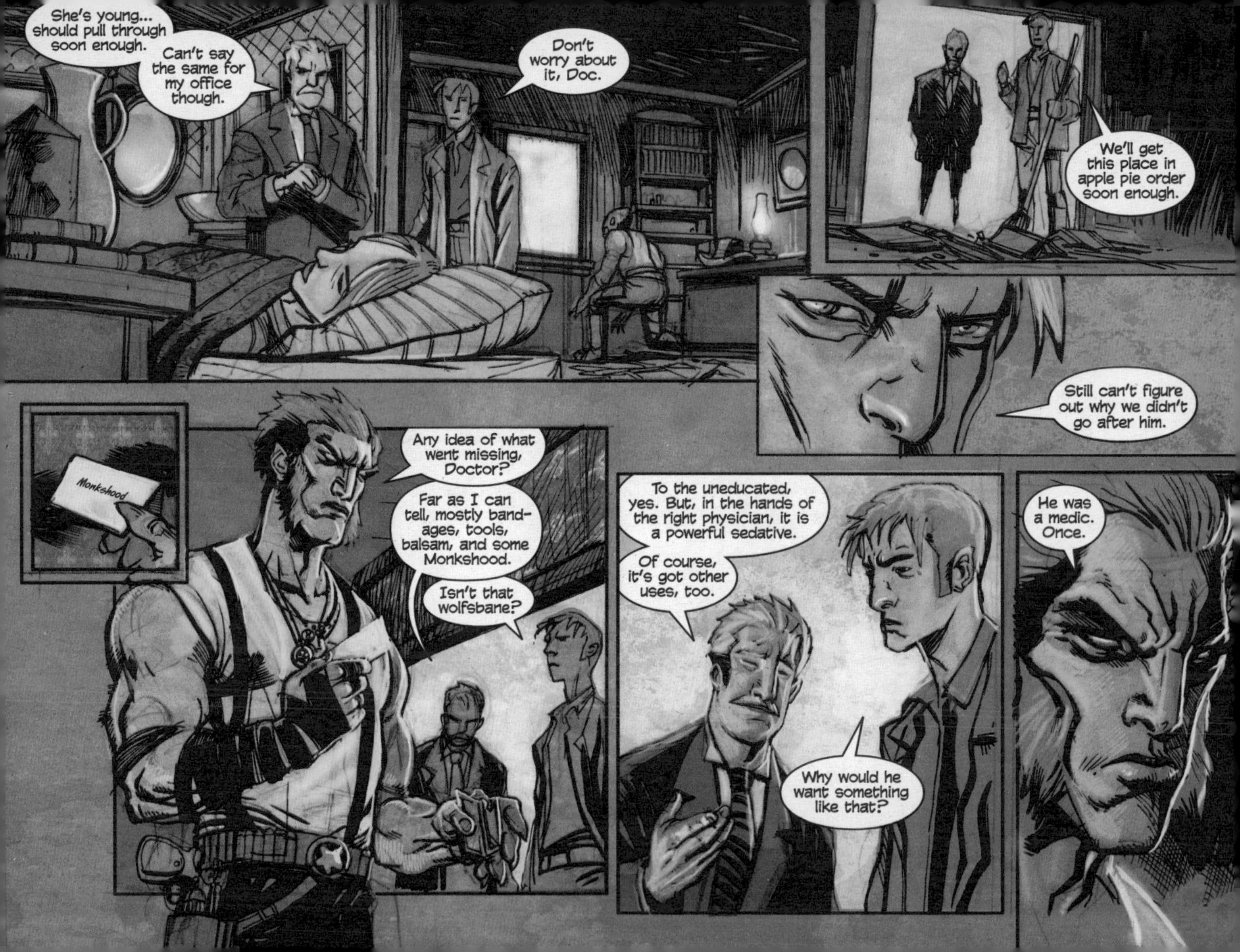

She's young... should pull through soon enough.
Can't say the same for my office though.
Don't worry about it, Doc.
We'll get this place in apple pie order soon enough.
Still can't figure out why we didn't go after him.
Monkshood
Any idea of what went missing, Doctor?
Far as I can tell, mostly bandages, tools, balsam, and some Monkshood.
Isn't that wolfsbane?
To the uneducated, yes. But, in the hands of the right physician, it is a powerful sedative.
Of course, it's got other uses, too.
Why would he want something like that?
He was a medic. Once.

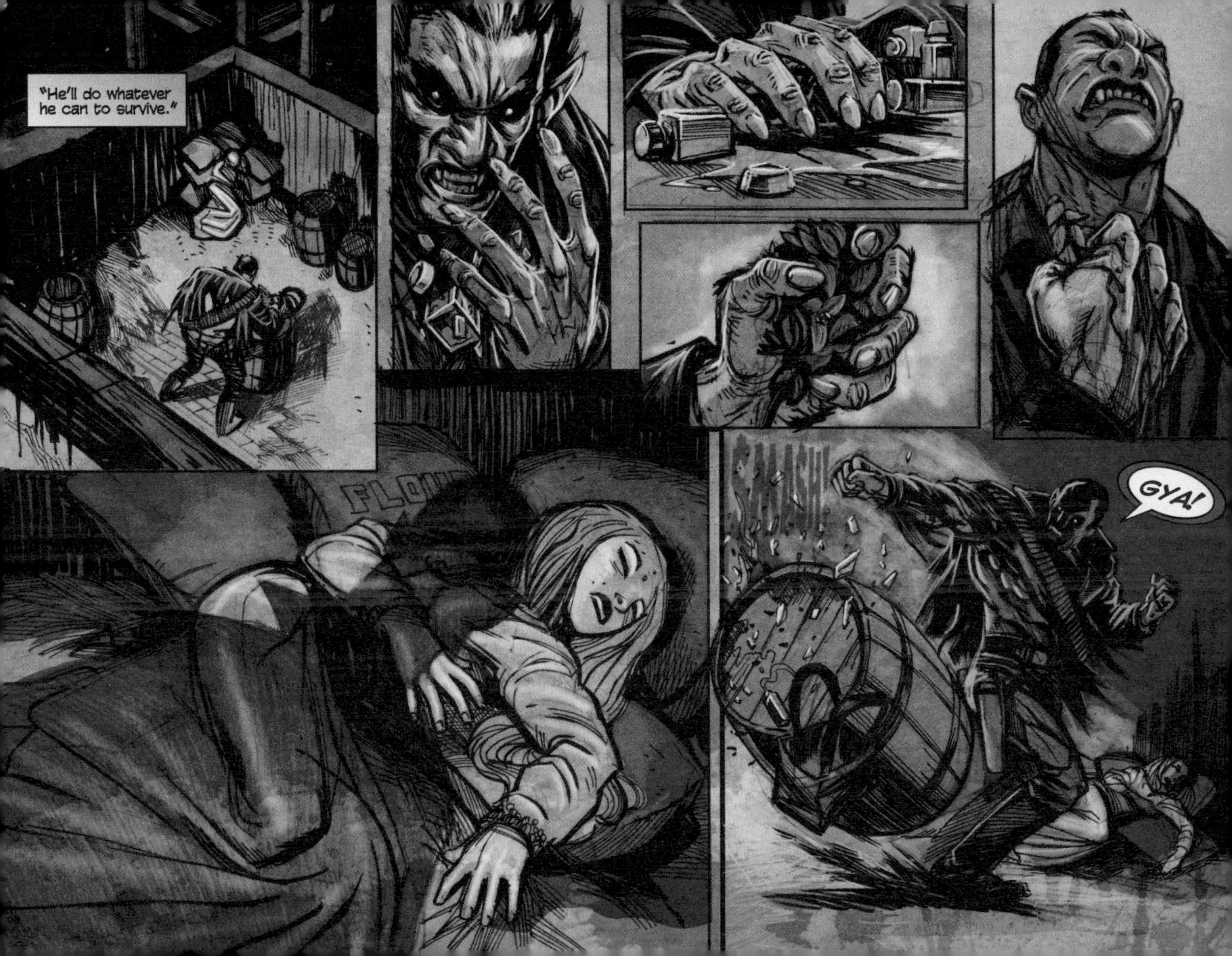
"He'll do whatever he can to survive."
FLOUR
SMASH!
GYA!

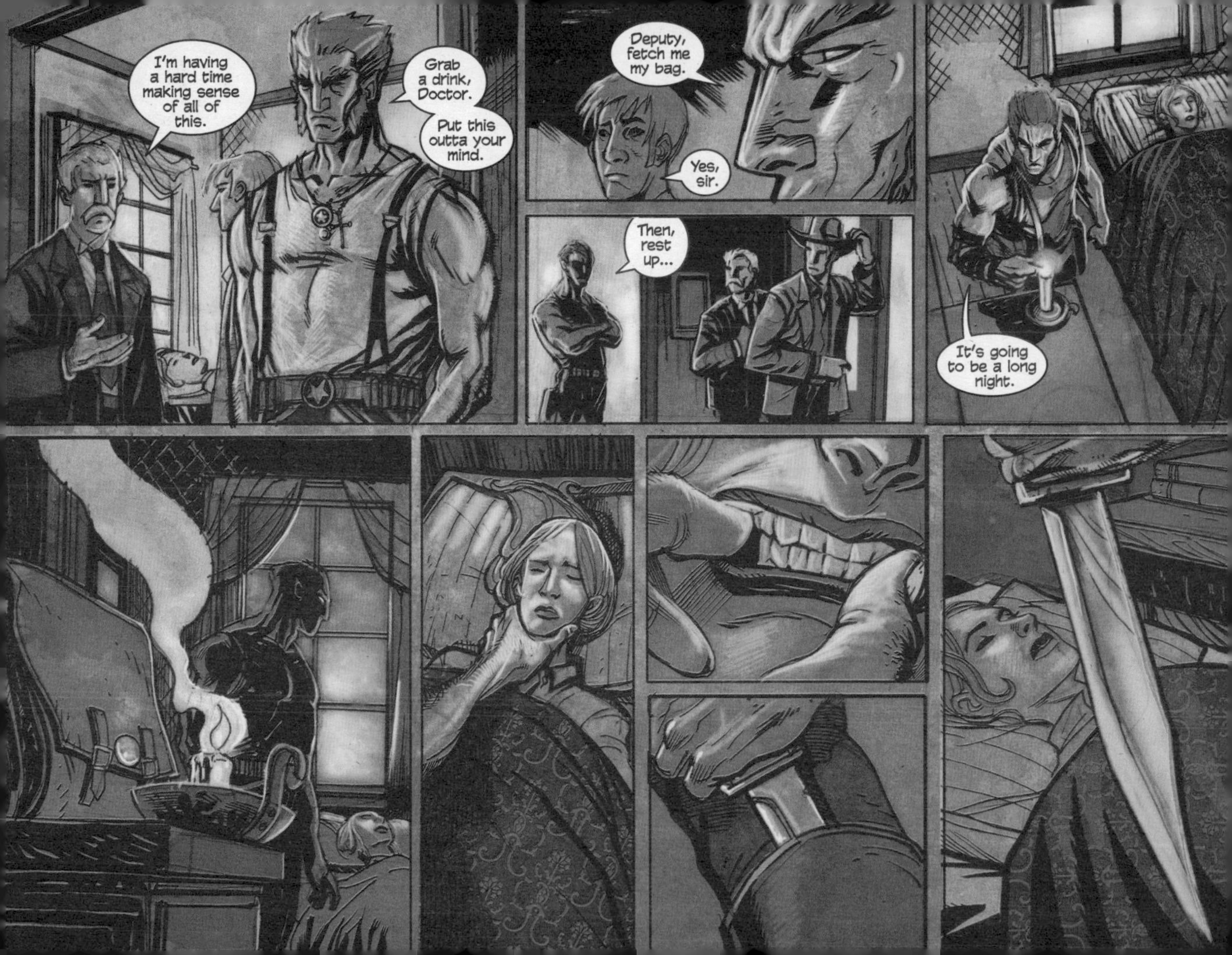
I'm having a hard time making sense of all of this.
Grab a drink, Doctor.
Put this outta your mind.
Deputy, fetch me my bag.
Yes, sir.
Then, rest up...
It's going to be a long night.

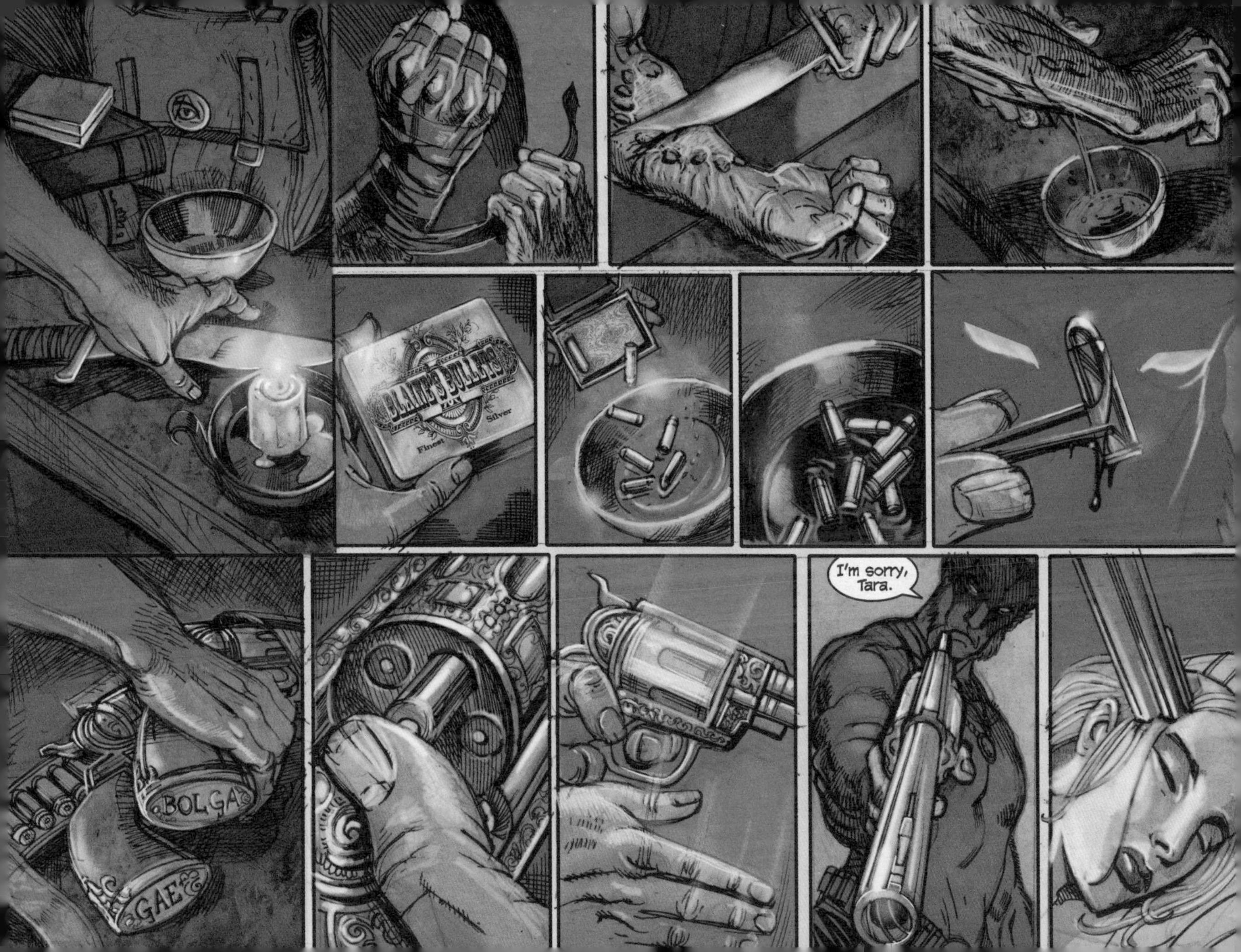
BLAINE'S BULLETS
Finest
Silver
BOLGA
GAE
I'm sorry, Tara.

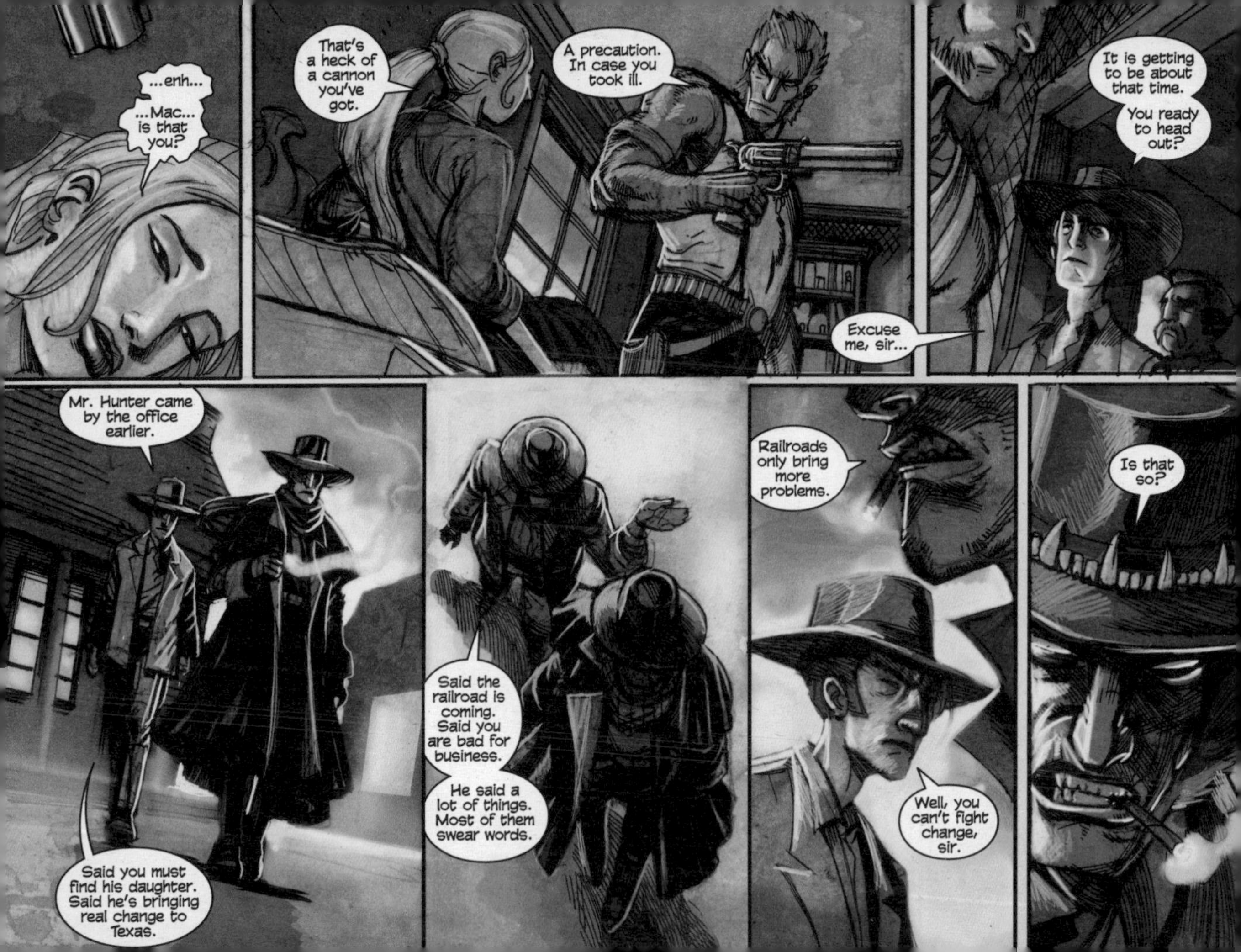
...enh...
...Mac... is that you?
That's a heck of a cannon you've got.
A precaution. In case you took ill.
Excuse me, sir...
It is getting to be about that time.
You ready to head out?
Mr. Hunter came by the office earlier.
Said you must find his daughter. Said he's bringing real change to Texas.
Said the railroad is coming. Said you are bad for business.
He said a lot of things. Most of them swear words.
Railroads only bring more problems.
Well, you can't fight change, sir.
Is that so?

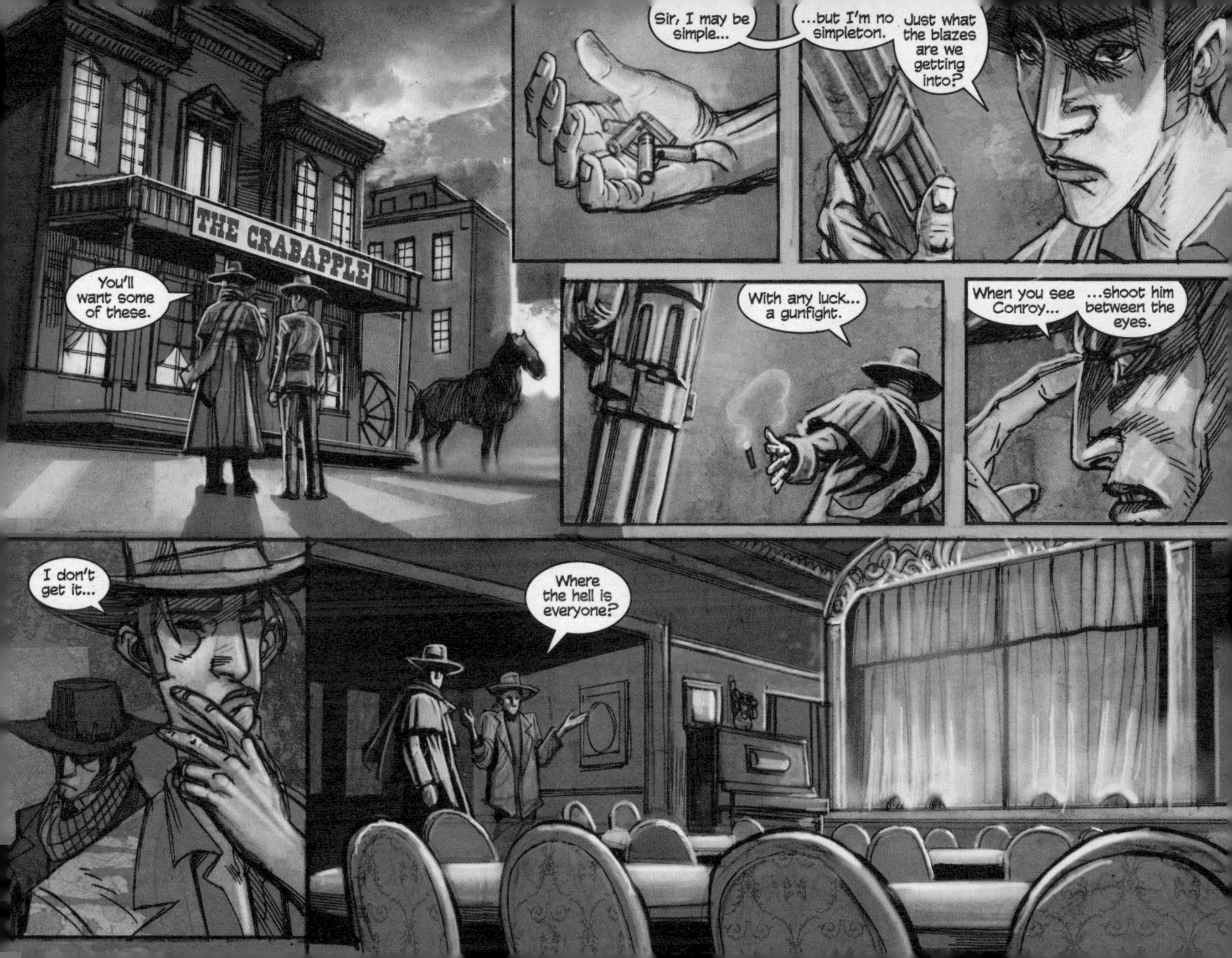
THE CRABAPPLE
You'll want some of these.
Sir, I may be simple...
...but I'm no simpleton.
Just what the blazes are we getting into?
With any luck... a gunfight.
When you see Conroy...
...shoot him between the eyes.
I don't get it...
Where the hell is everyone?

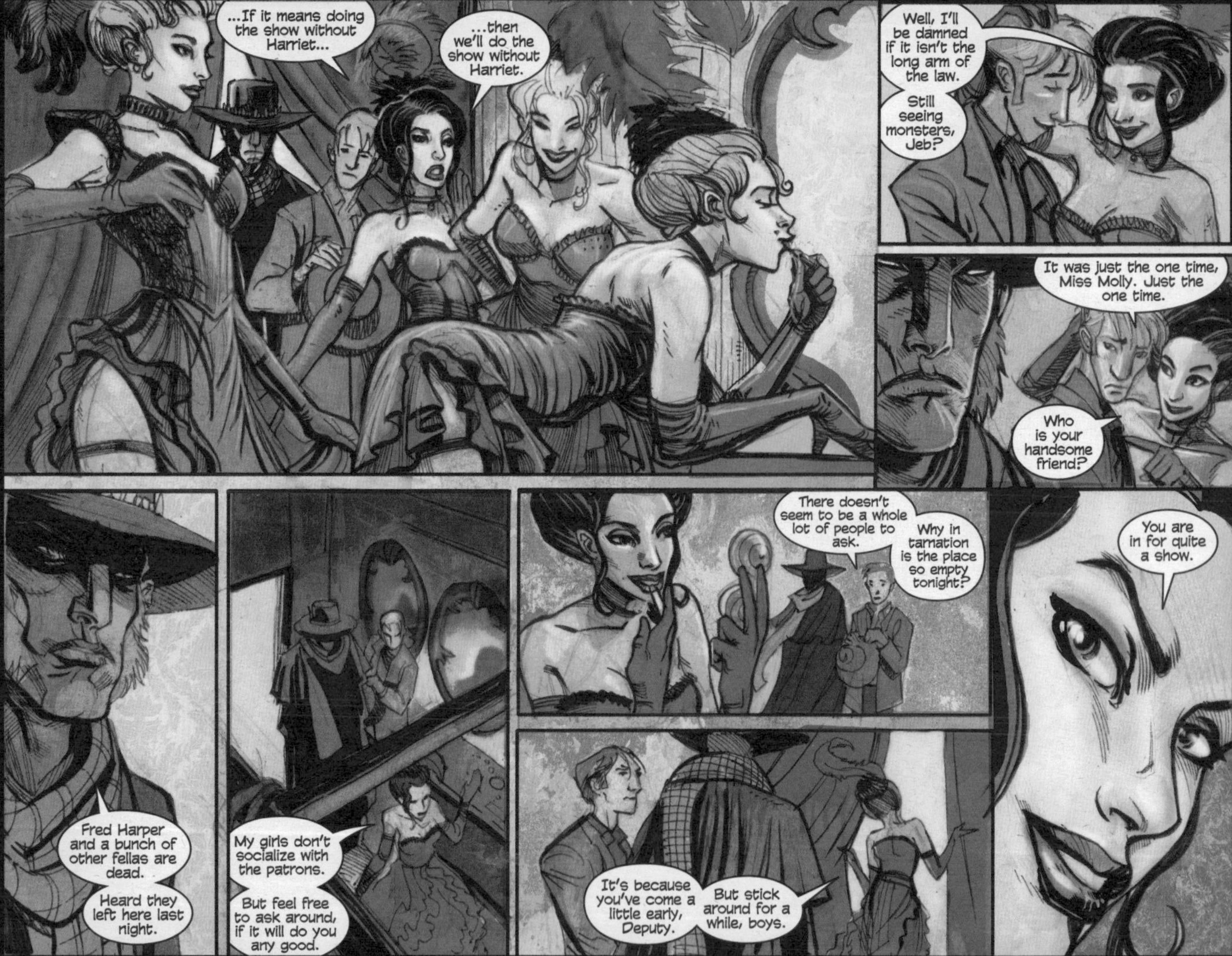
...If it means doing the show without Harriet...
...then we'll do the show without Harriet.
Well, I'll be damned if it isn't the long arm of the law.
Still seeing monsters, Jeb?
It was just the one time, Miss Molly. Just the one time.
Who is your handsome friend?
Fred Harper and a bunch of other fellas are dead.
Heard they left here last night.
My girls don't socialize with the patrons.
But feel free to ask around, if it will do you any good.
There doesn't seem to be a whole lot of people to ask.
Why in tarnation is the place so empty tonight?
It's because you've come a little early, Deputy.
But stick around for a while, boys.
You are in for quite a show.

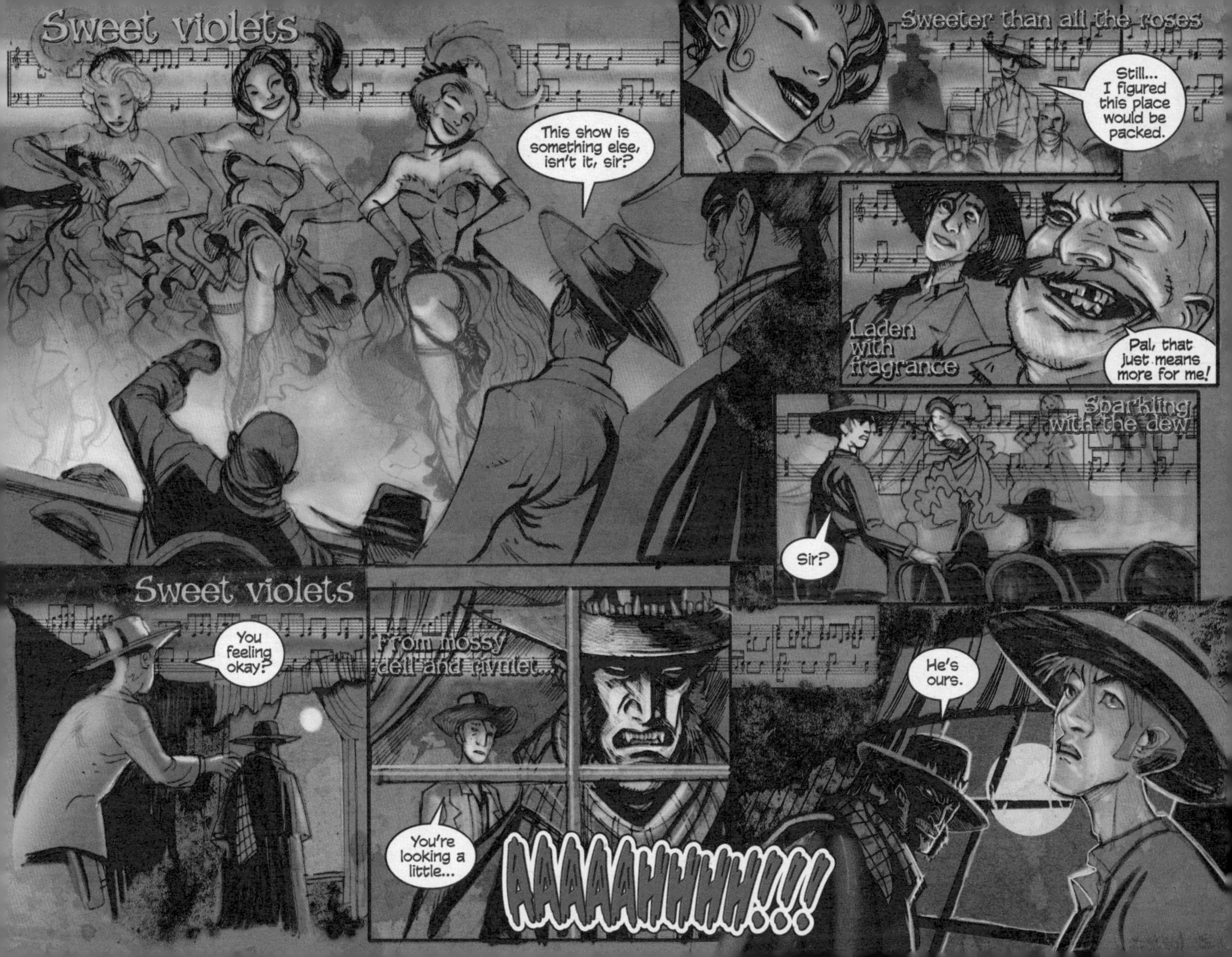
Sweet violets
This show is something else, isn't it, sir?
Sweeter than all the roses
Still... I figured this place would be packed.
Laden with fragrance
Pal, that just means more for me!
Sparkling with the dew
Sir?
Sweet violets
You feeling okay?
From mossy dell and rivulet...
You're looking a little...
AAAAAHHHH!!!
He's ours.

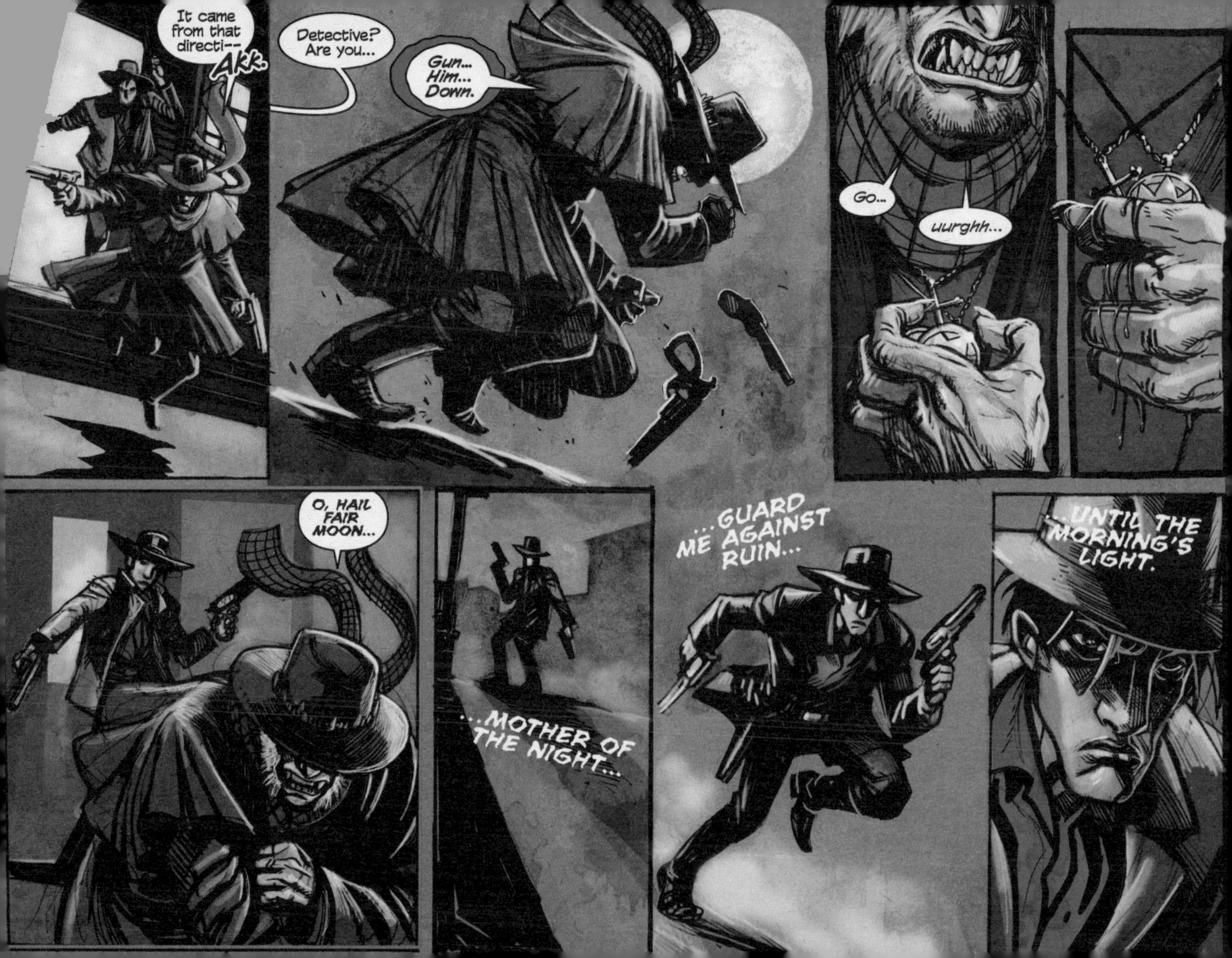
It came from that directi--
AKK.
Detective? Are you...
Gun... Him... Down.
Go...
uurghh...
O, HAIL FAIR MOON...
...MOTHER OF THE NIGHT...
...GUARD ME AGAINST RUIN...
...UNTIL THE MORNING'S LIGHT.

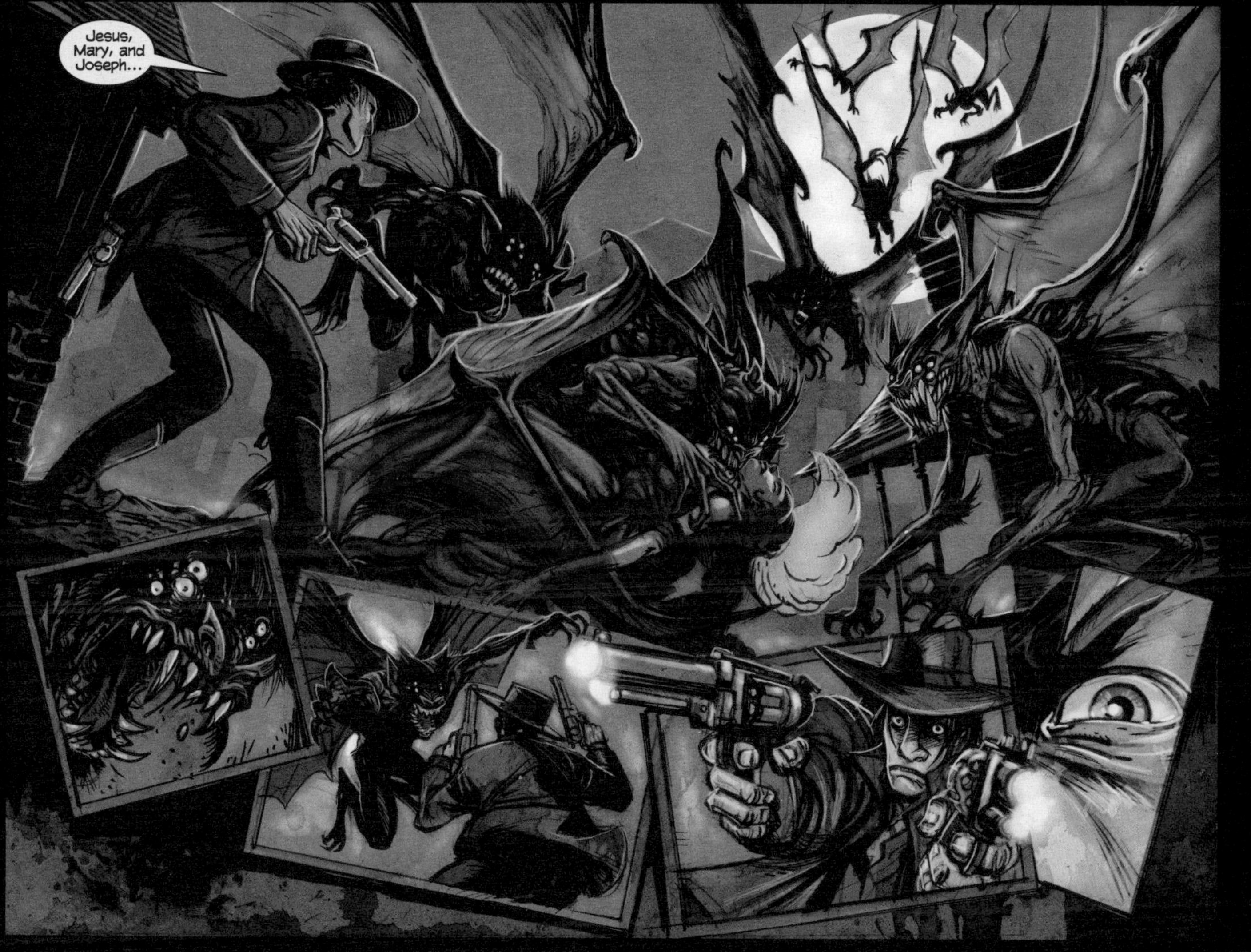
Jesus, Mary, and Joseph...

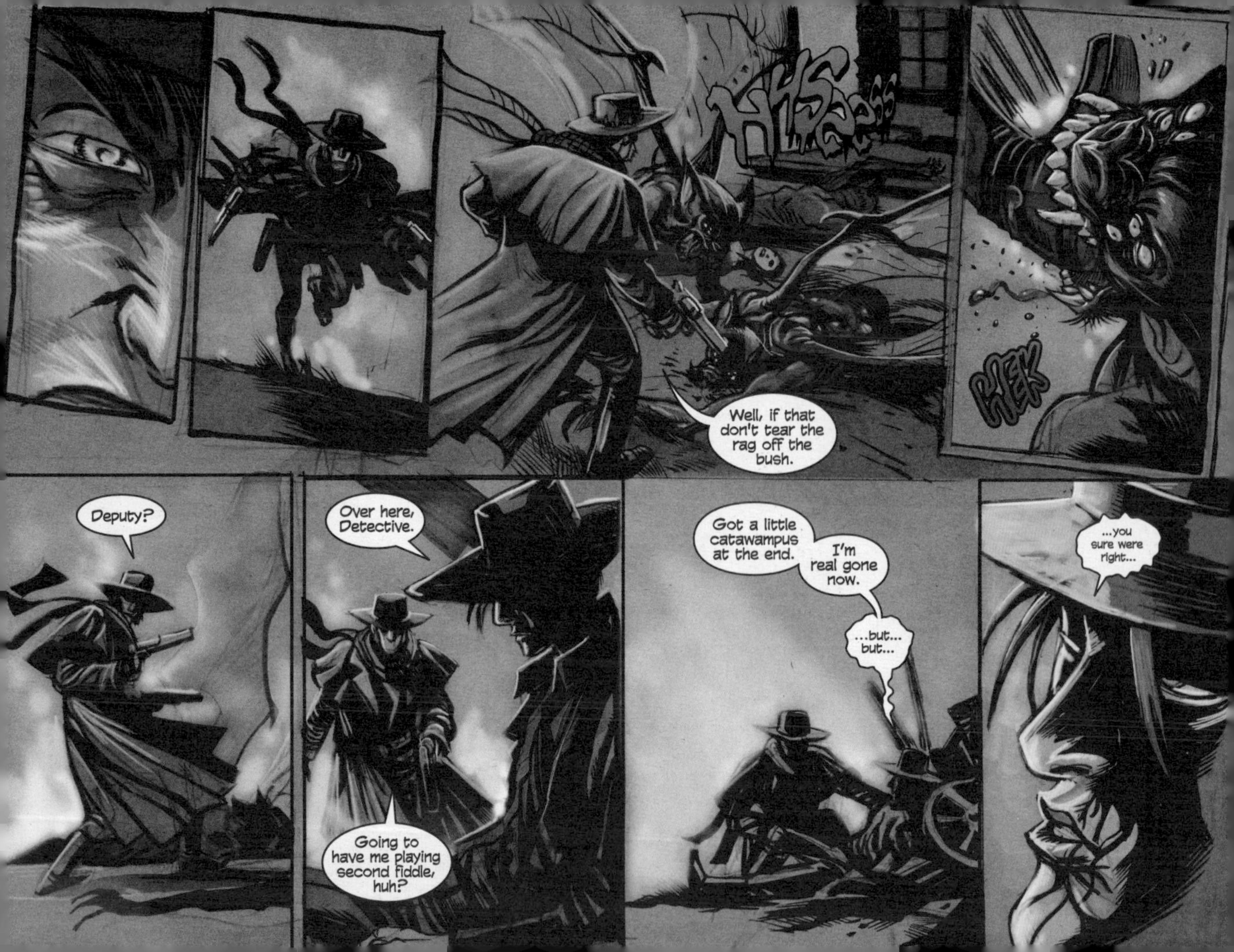
Well, if that don't tear the rag off the bush.
Deputy?
Over here, Detective.
Going to have me playing second fiddle, huh?
Got a little catawampus at the end.
I'm real gone now.
...but... but...
...you sure were right...

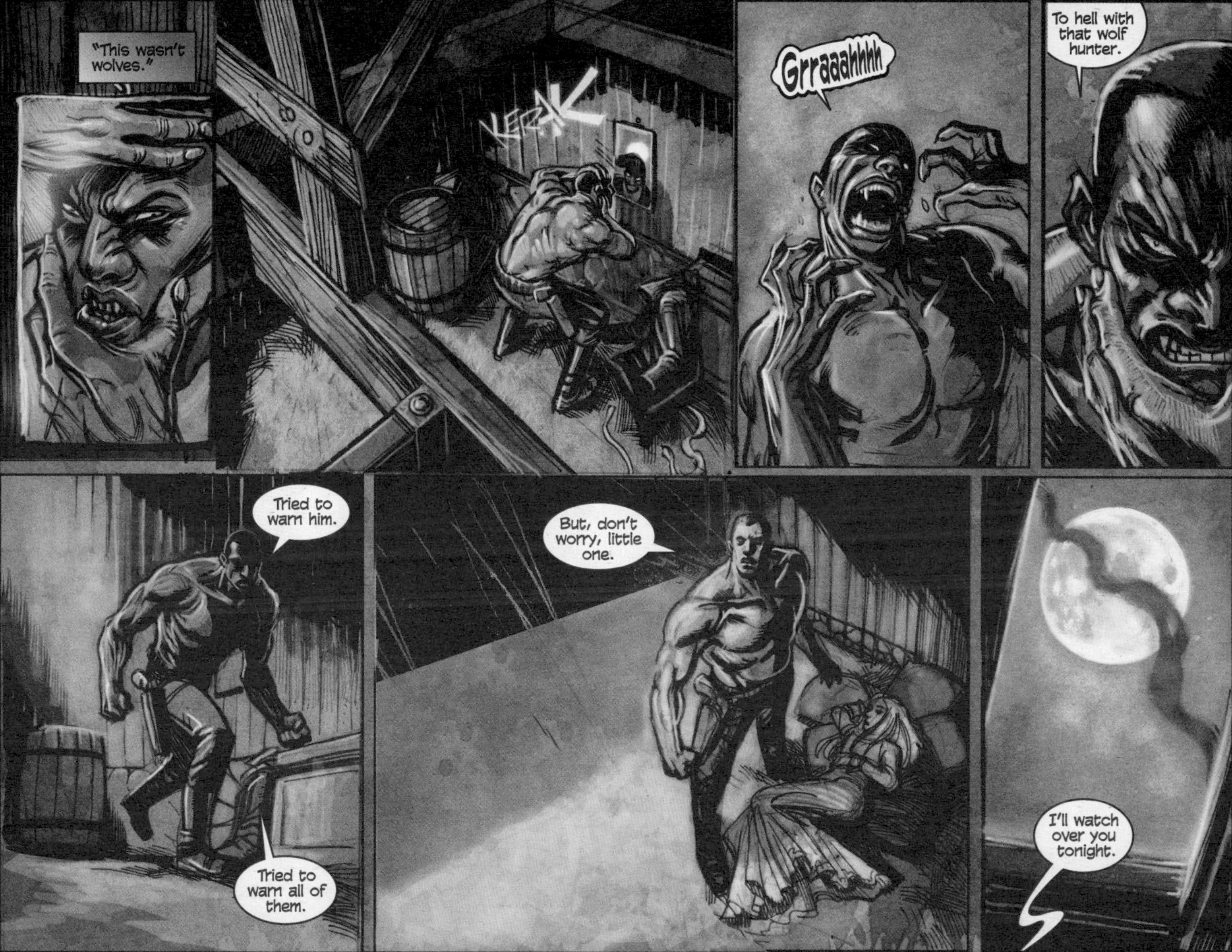
"This wasn't wolves."
KERAK
Grraaahhhh
To hell with that wolf hunter.
Tried to warn him.
Tried to warn all of them.
But, don't worry, little one.
I'll watch over you tonight.

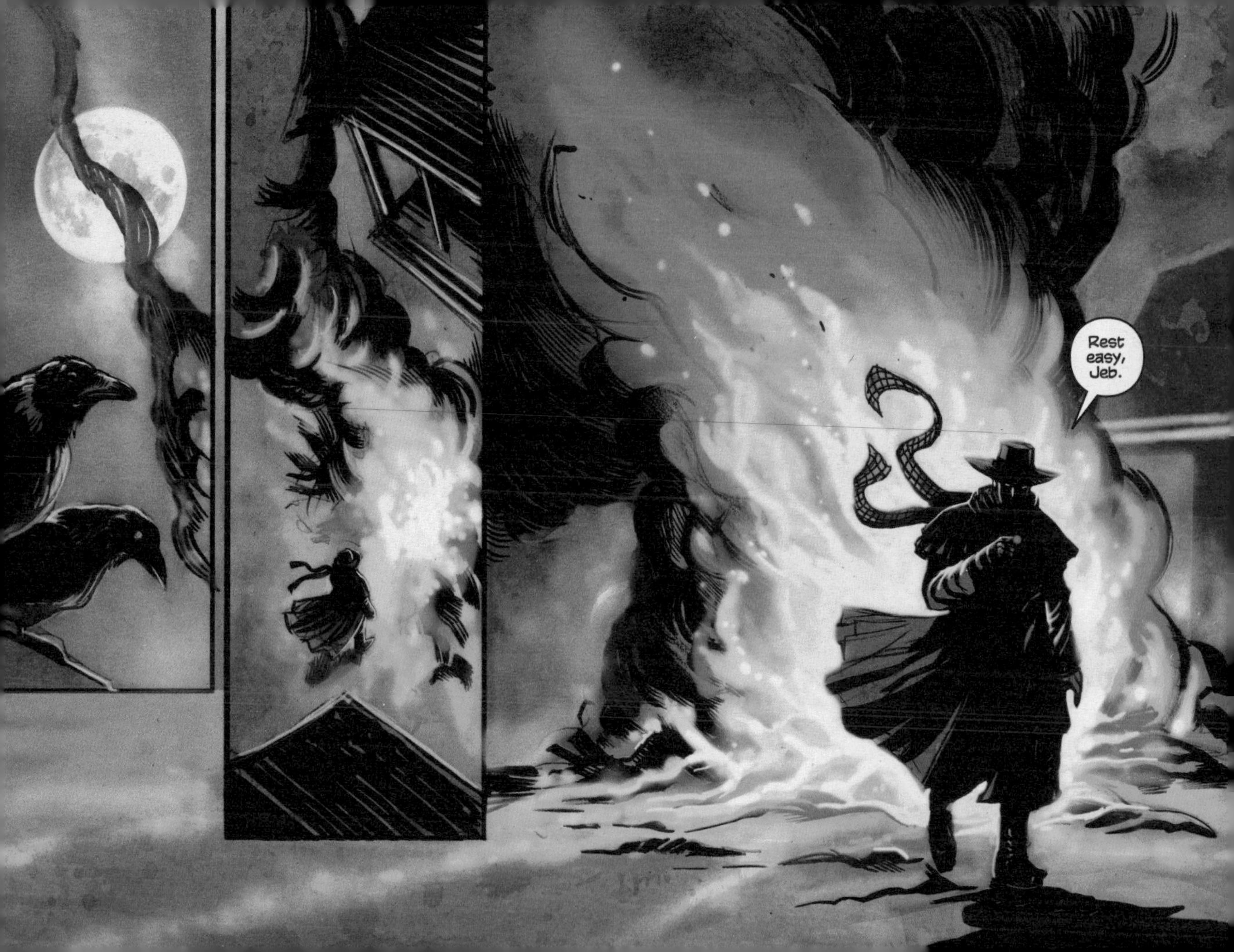
Rest easy, Jeb.

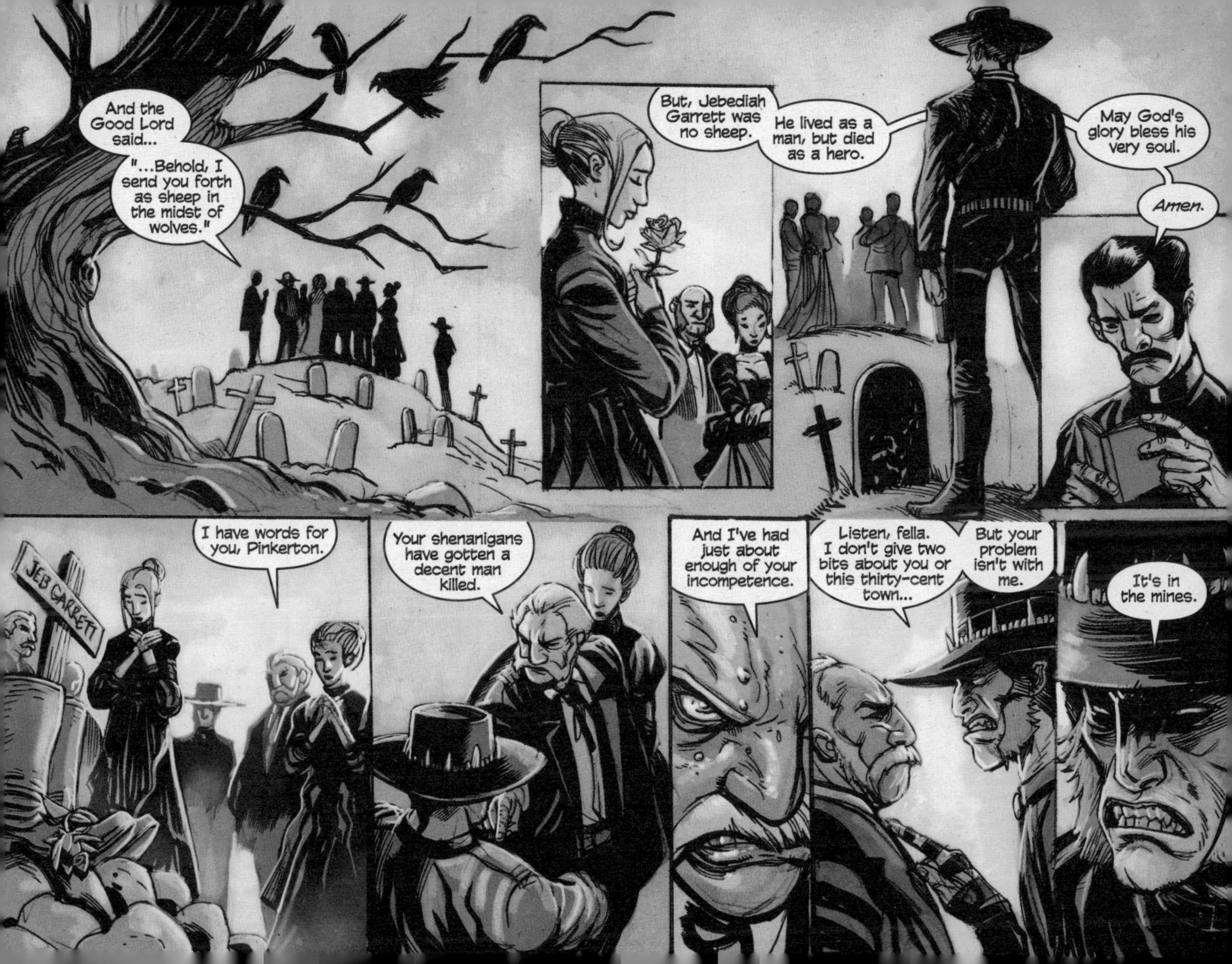
And the Good Lord said...
"...Behold, I send you forth as sheep in the midst of wolves."
But, Jebediah Garrett was no sheep.
He lived as a man, but died as a hero.
May God's glory bless his very soul.
Amen.
JEB GARRETT
I have words for you, Pinkerton.
Your shenanigans have gotten a decent man killed.
And I've had just about enough of your incompetence.
Listen, fella. I don't give two bits about you or this thirty-cent town...
But your problem isn't with me.
It's in the mines.

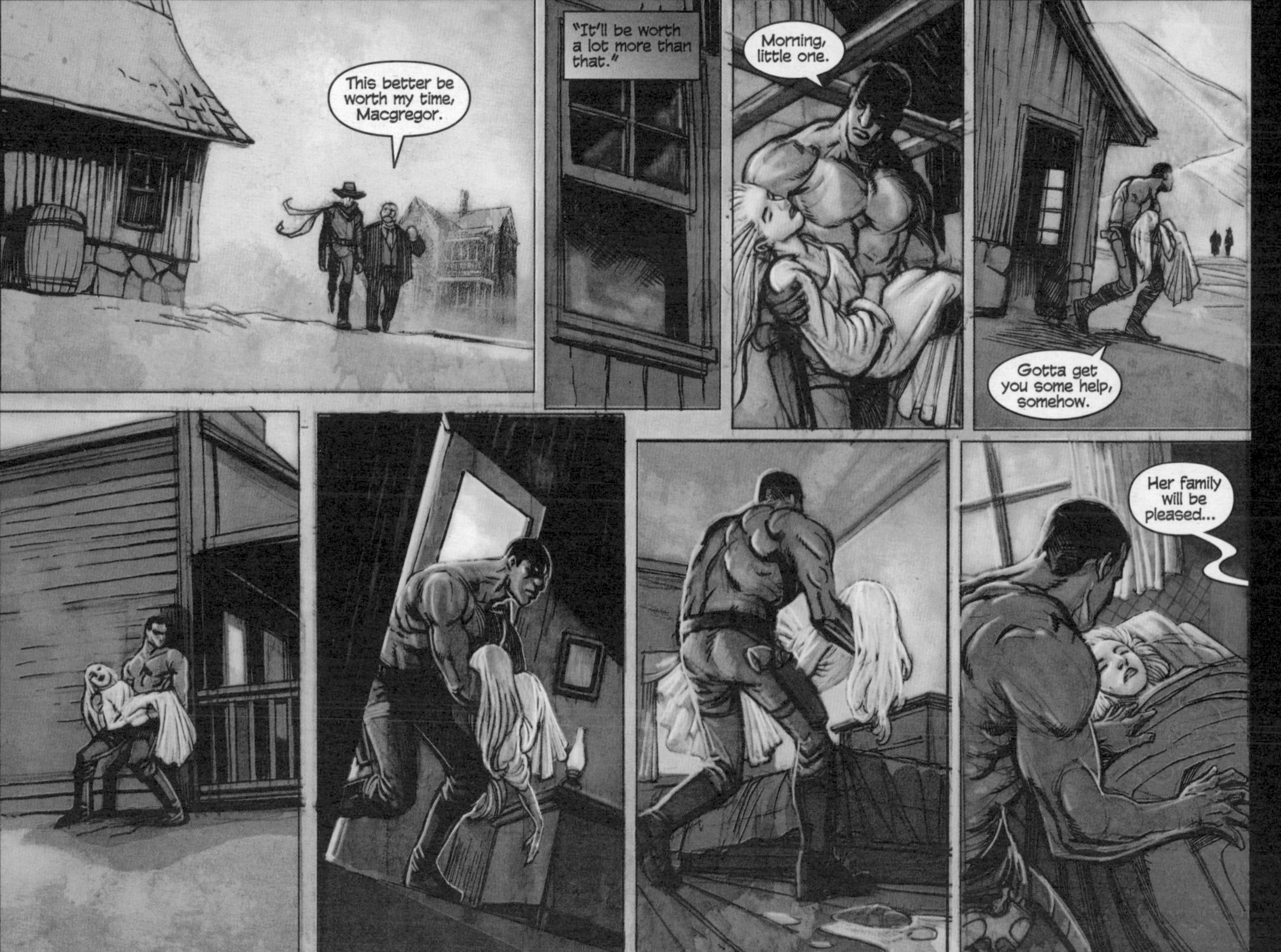
This better be worth my time, Macgregor.
"It'll be worth a lot more than that."
Morning, little one.
Gotta get you some help, somehow.
Her family will be pleased...

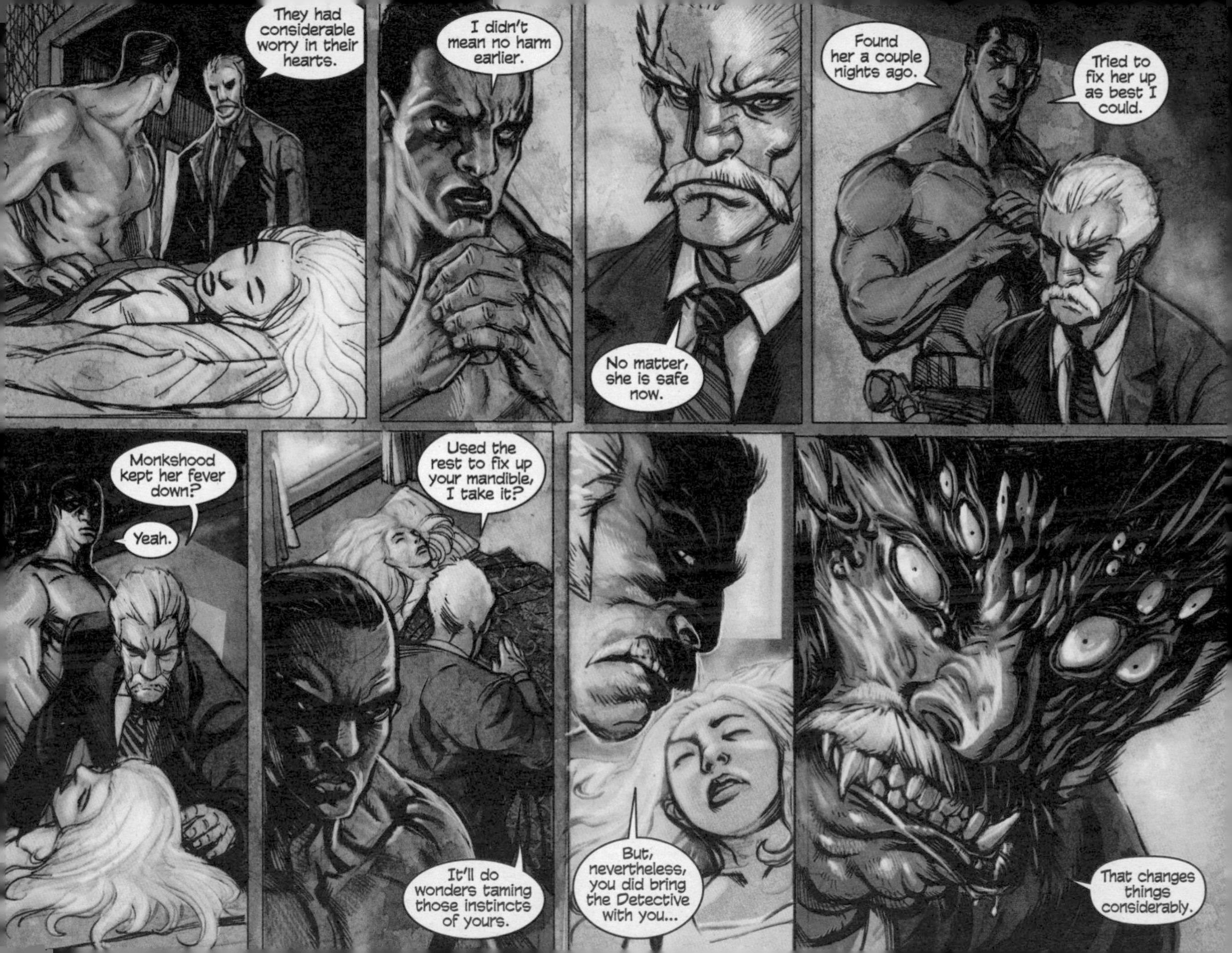
They had considerable worry in their hearts.
I didn't mean no harm earlier.
No matter, she is safe now.
Found her a couple nights ago.
Tried to fix her up as best I could.
Monkshood kept her fever down?
Yeah.
Used the rest to fix up your mandible, I take it?
It'll do wonders taming those instincts of yours.
But, nevertheless, you did bring the Detective with you...
That changes things considerably.

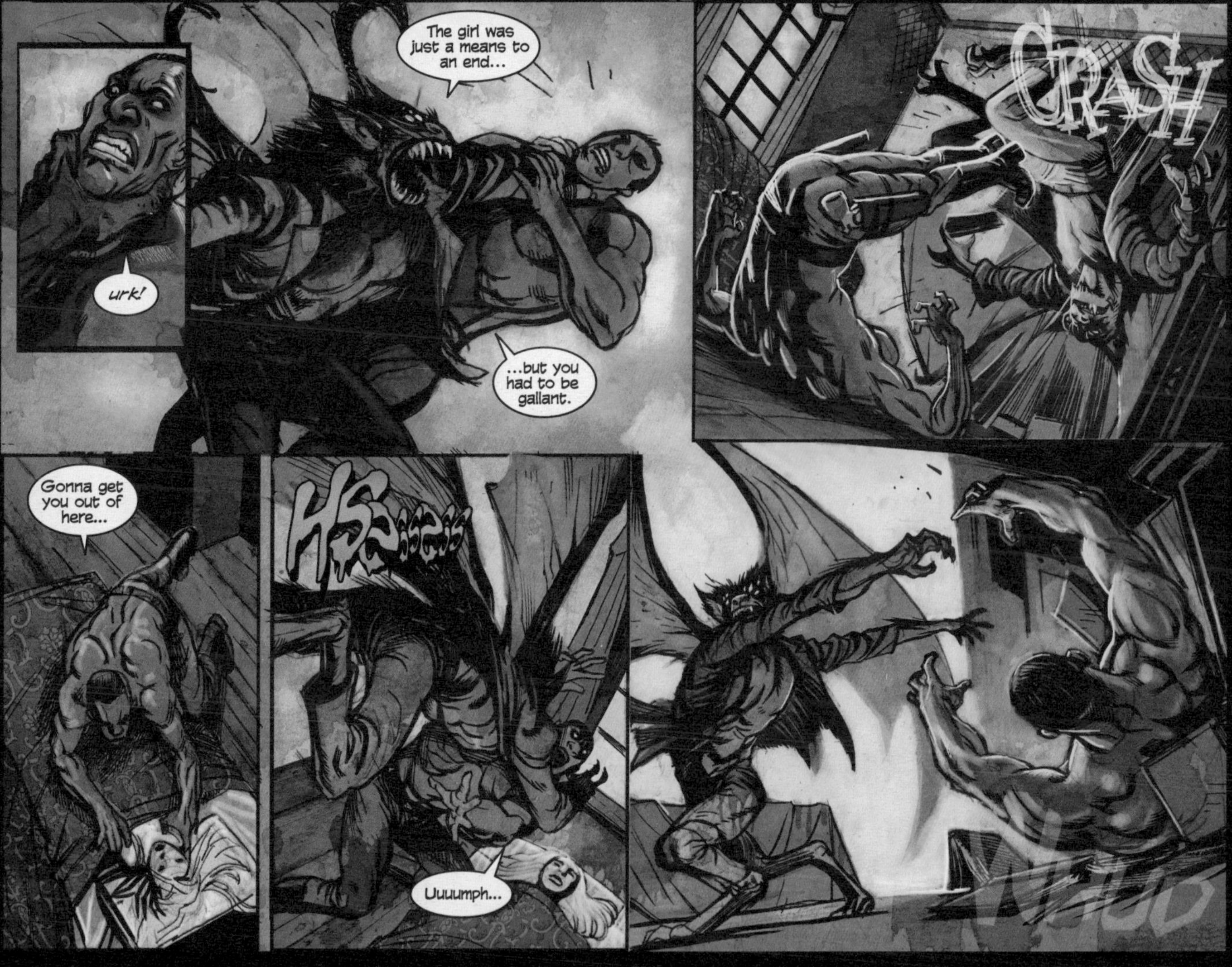
The girl was just a means to an end...
urk!
...but you had to be gallant.
CRASH
Gonna get you out of here...
Uuuumph...

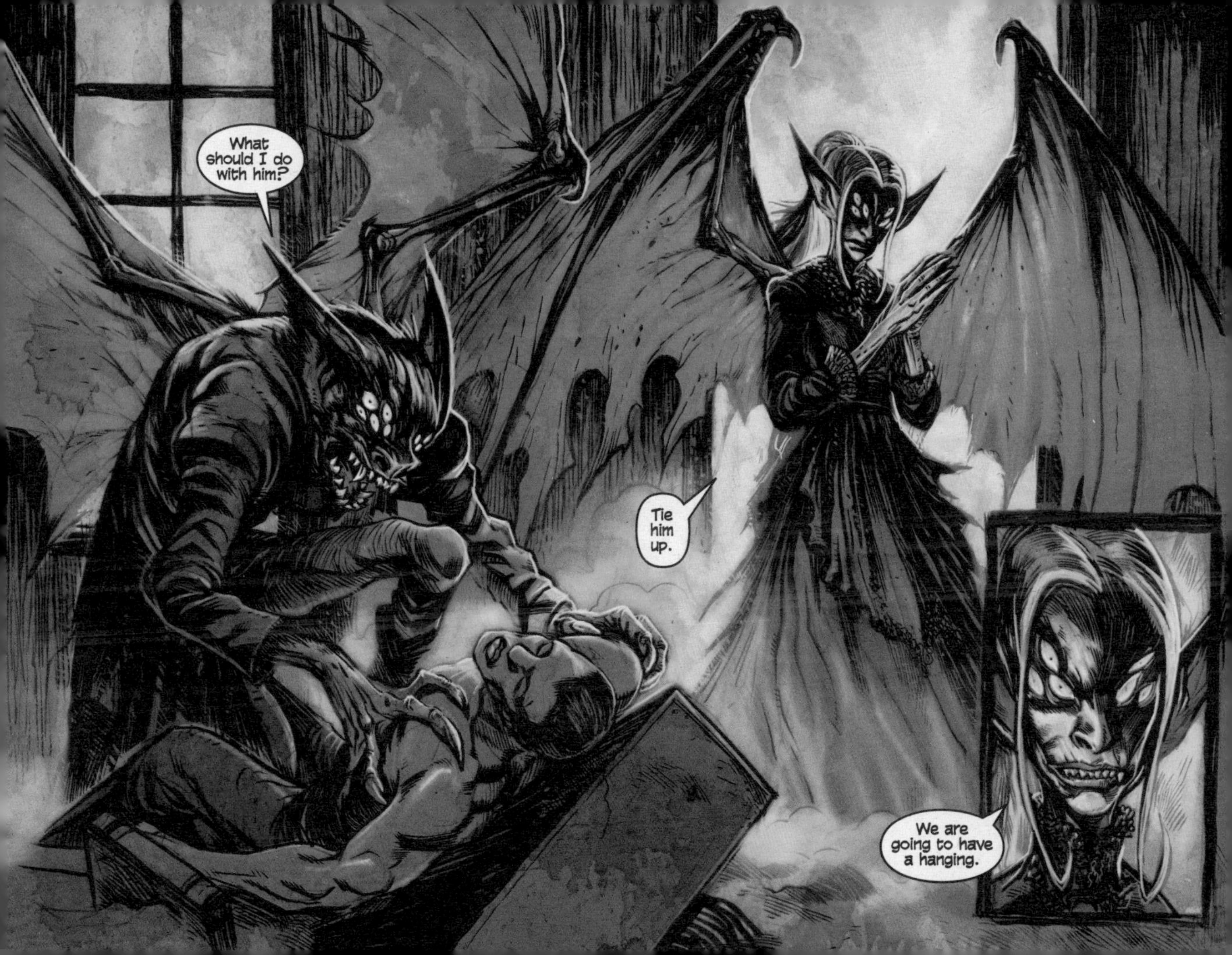
What should I do with him?
Tie him up.
We are going to have a hanging.

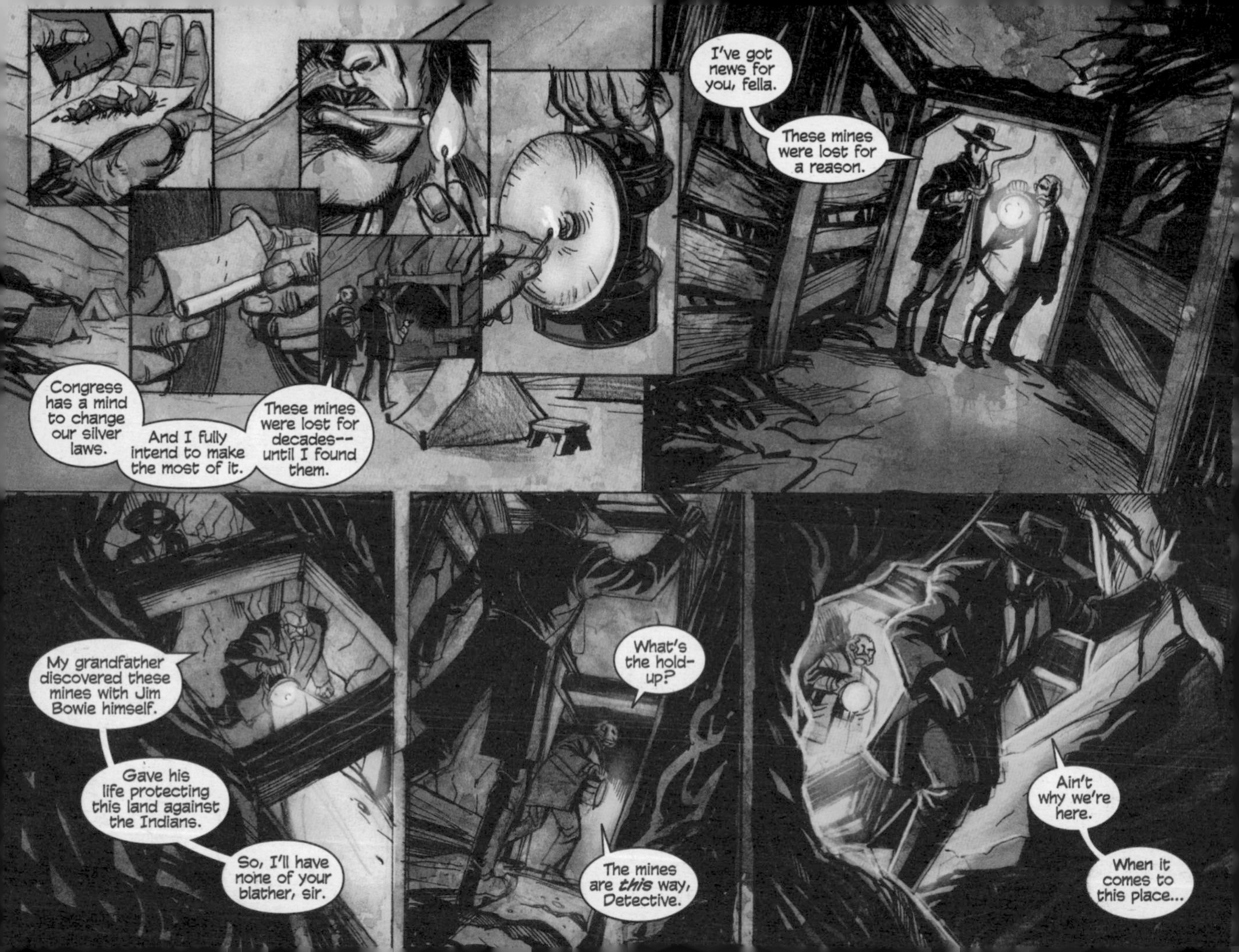
Congress has a mind to change our silver laws.
And I fully intend to make the most of it.
These mines were lost for decades--until I found them.
I've got news for you, fella.
These mines were lost for a reason.
My grandfather discovered these mines with Jim Bowie himself.
Gave his life protecting this land against the Indians.
So, I'll have none of your blather, sir.
What's the hold-up?
The mines are *this* way, Detective.
Ain't why we're here.
When it comes to this place...

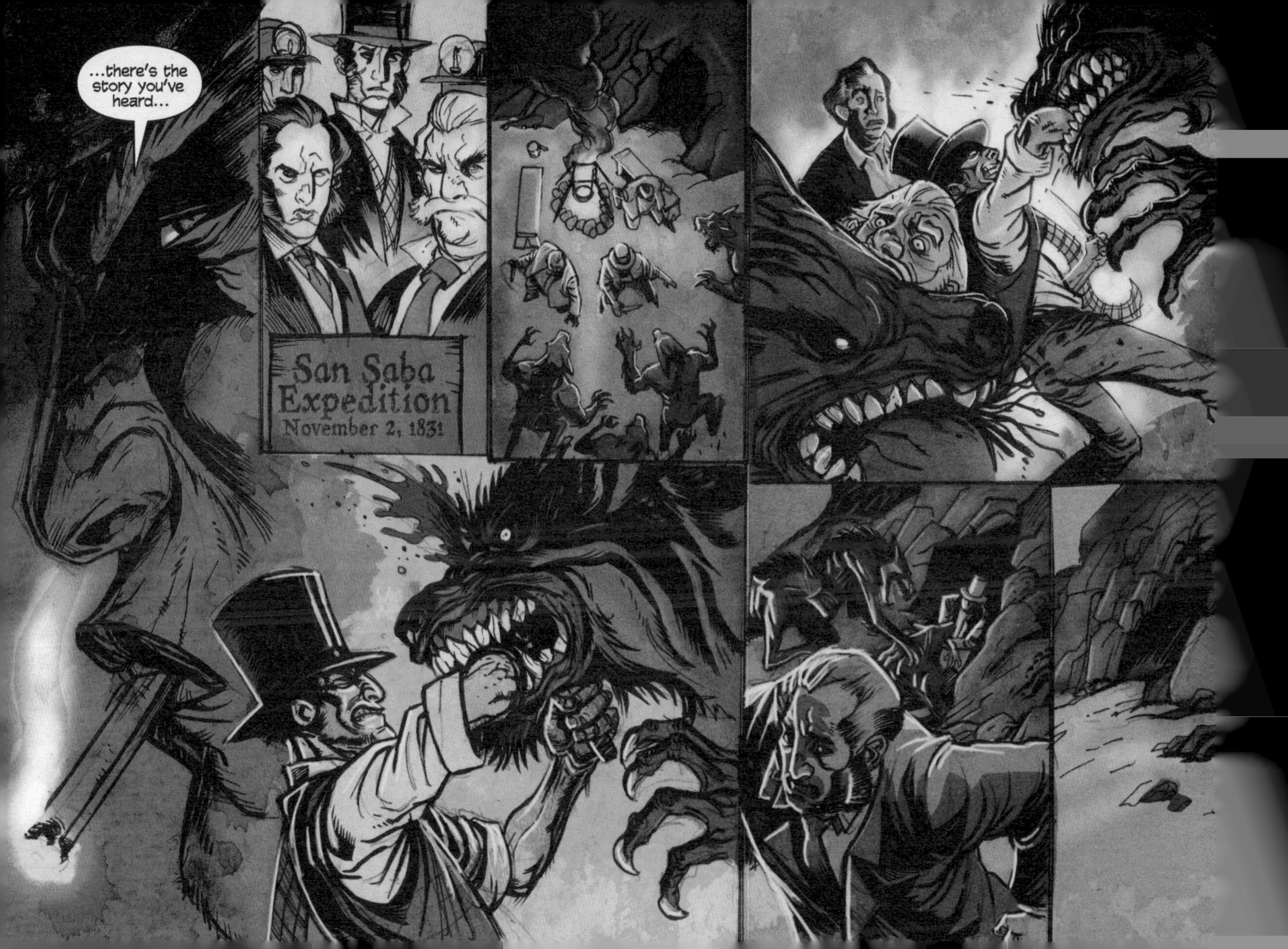
...there's the story you've heard...
San Saba Expedition November 2, 1831

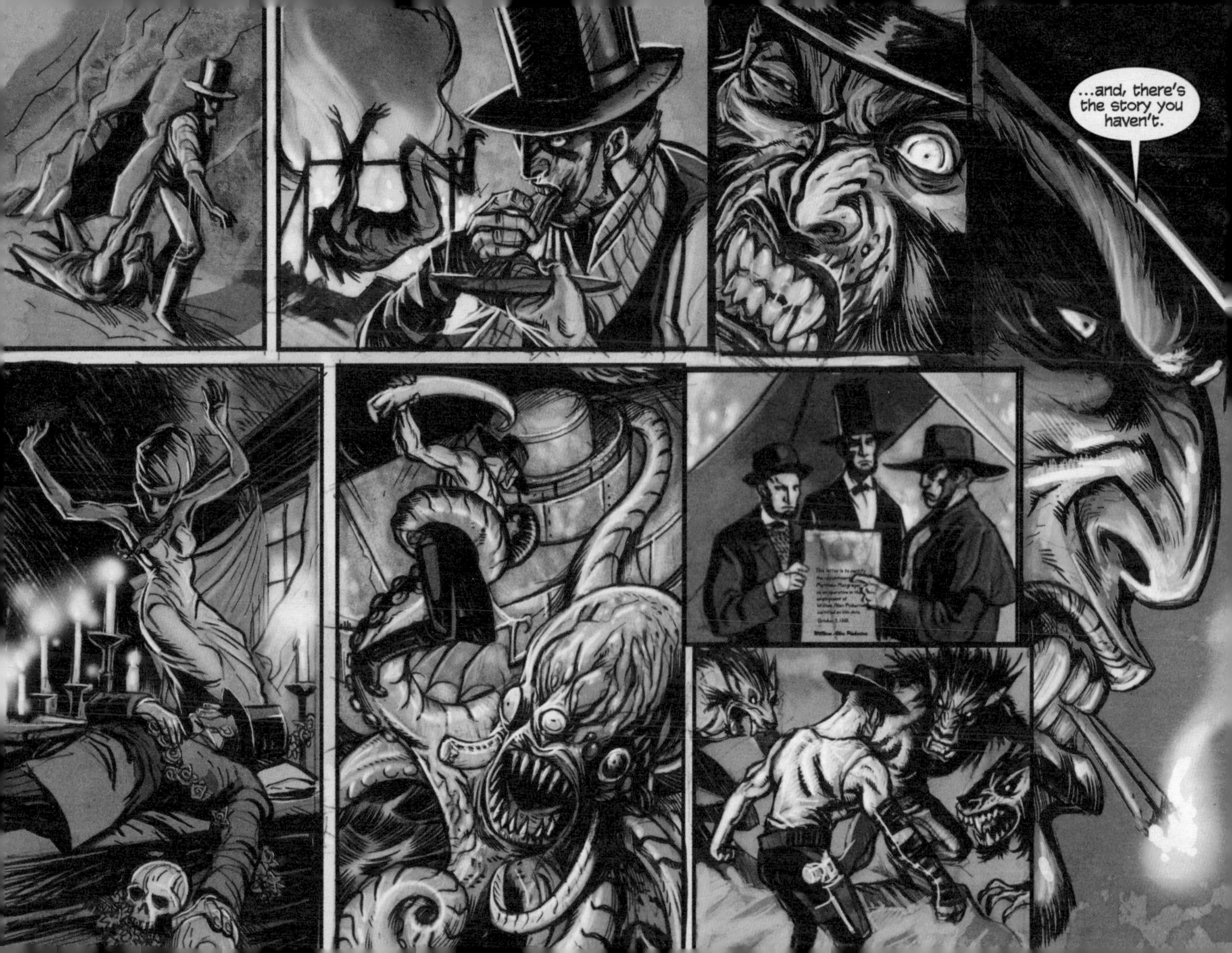
...and, there's the story you haven't.

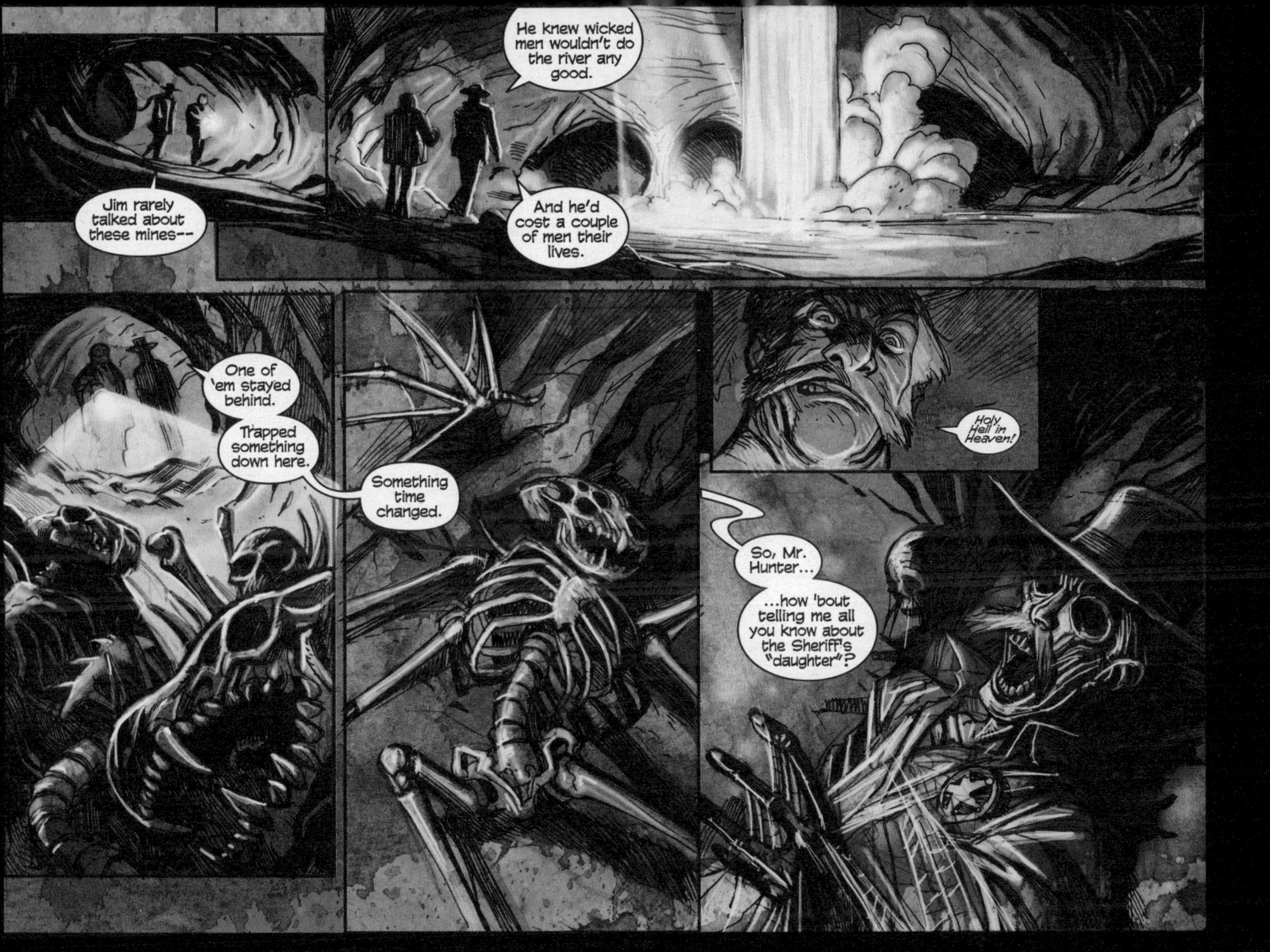
Jim rarely talked about these mines--
He knew wicked men wouldn't do the river any good.
And he'd cost a couple of men their lives.
One of 'em stayed behind.
Trapped something down here.
Something time changed.
Holy Hell in Heaven!
So, Mr. Hunter...
...how 'bout telling me all you know about the Sheriff's "daughter"?

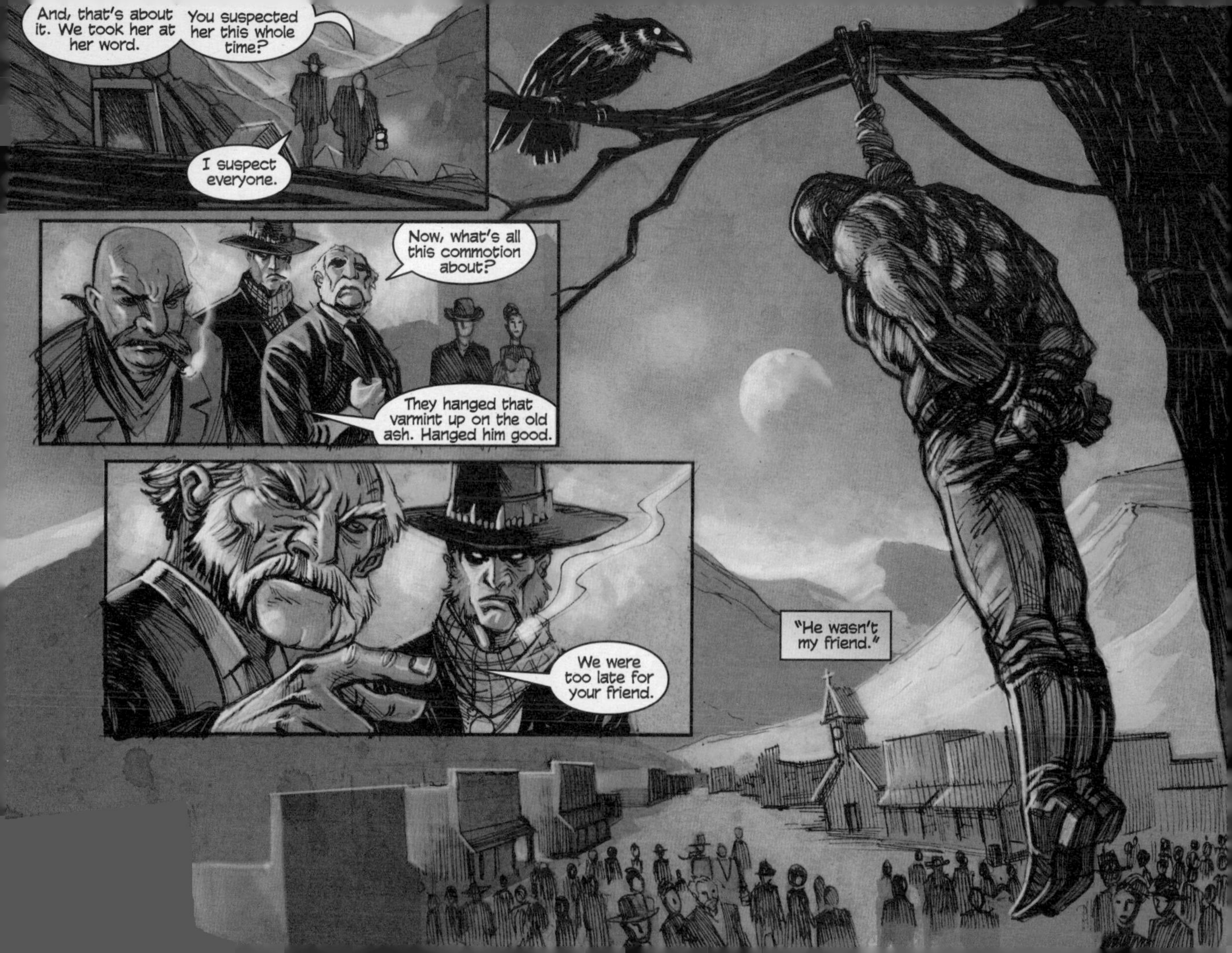
And, that's about it. We took her at her word.
You suspected her this whole time?
I suspect everyone.
Now, what's all this commotion about?
They hanged that varmint up on the old ash. Hanged him good.
We were too late for your friend.
"He wasn't my friend."

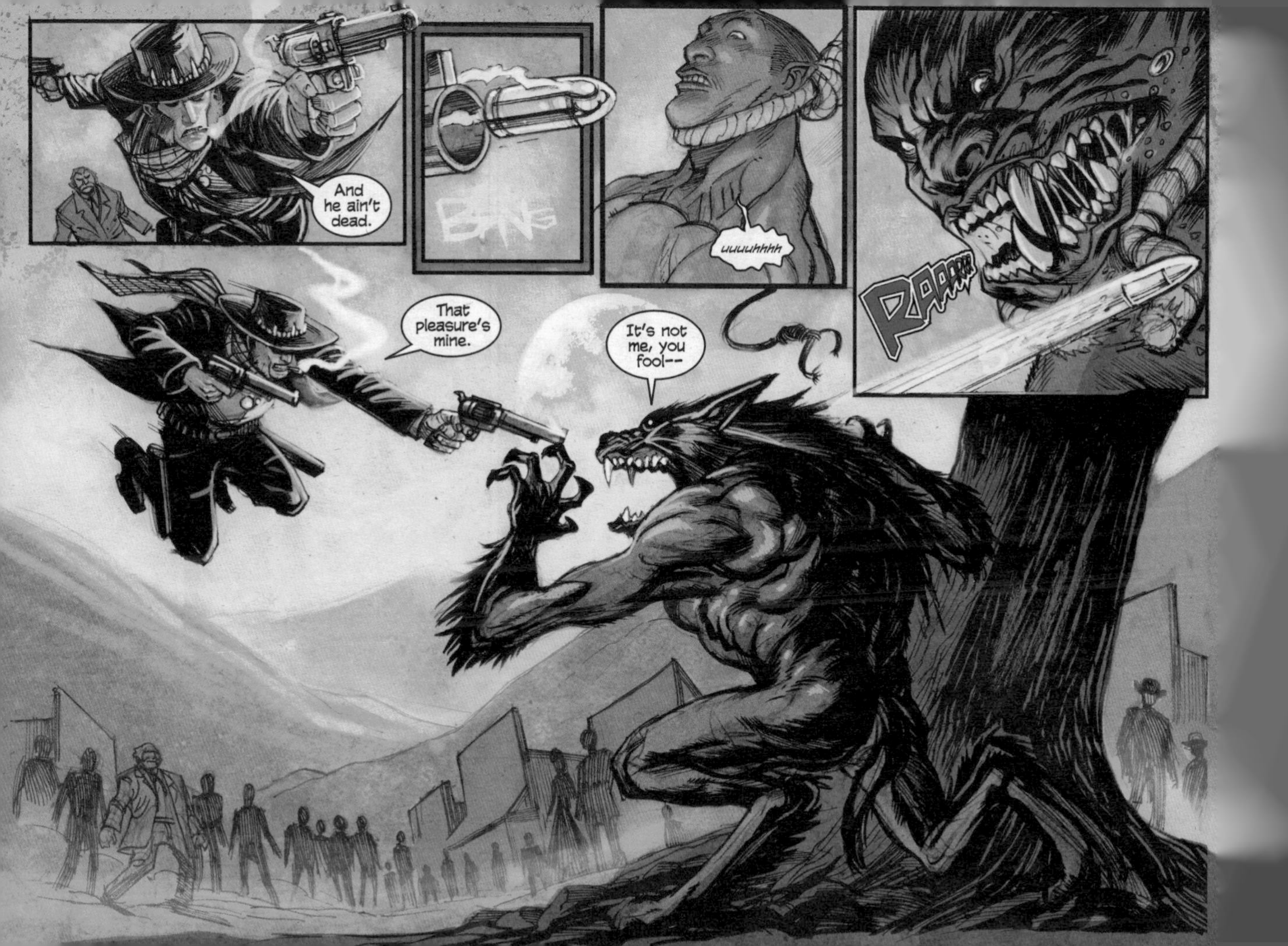
And he ain't dead.
BANG
uuuuhhhh
RAAARR
That pleasure's mine.
It's not me, you fool--

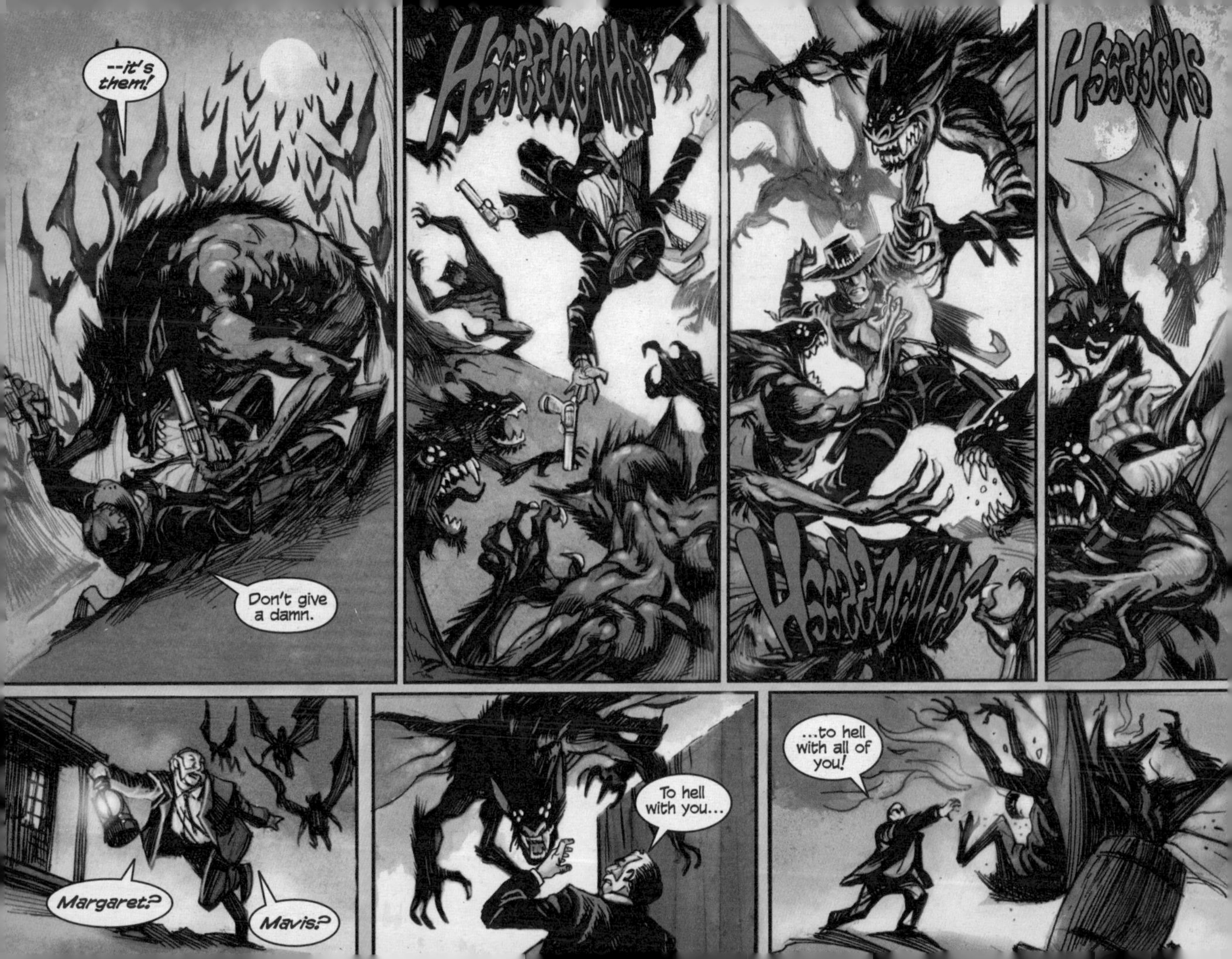
--it's them!
Don't give a damn.
HSSSCCHHS
HSSSCCHHS
HSSCCHS
Margaret?
Mavis?
To hell with you...
...to hell with all of you!

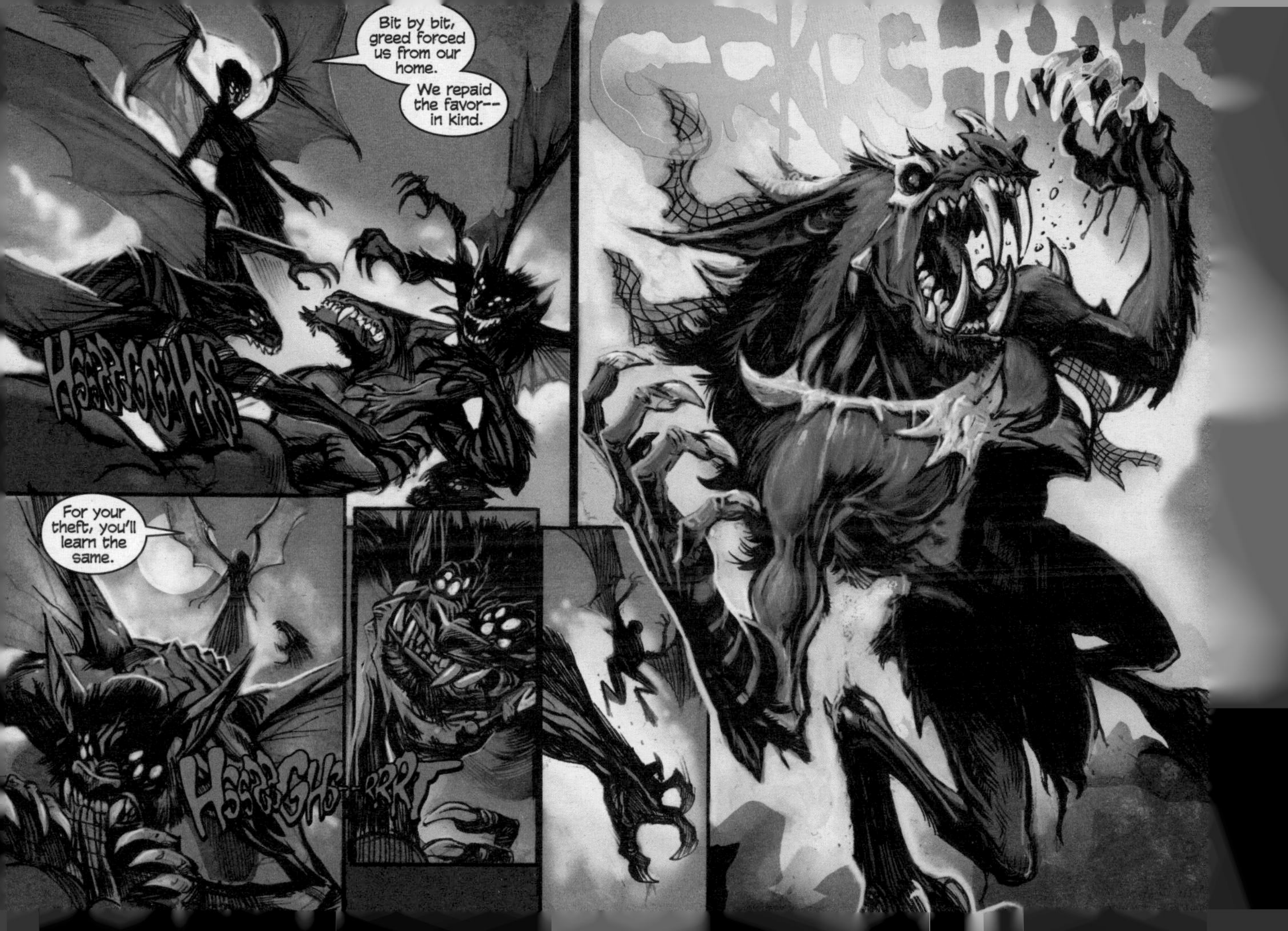
Bit by bit, greed forced us from our home.
We repaid the favor--in kind.
For your theft, you'll learn the same.

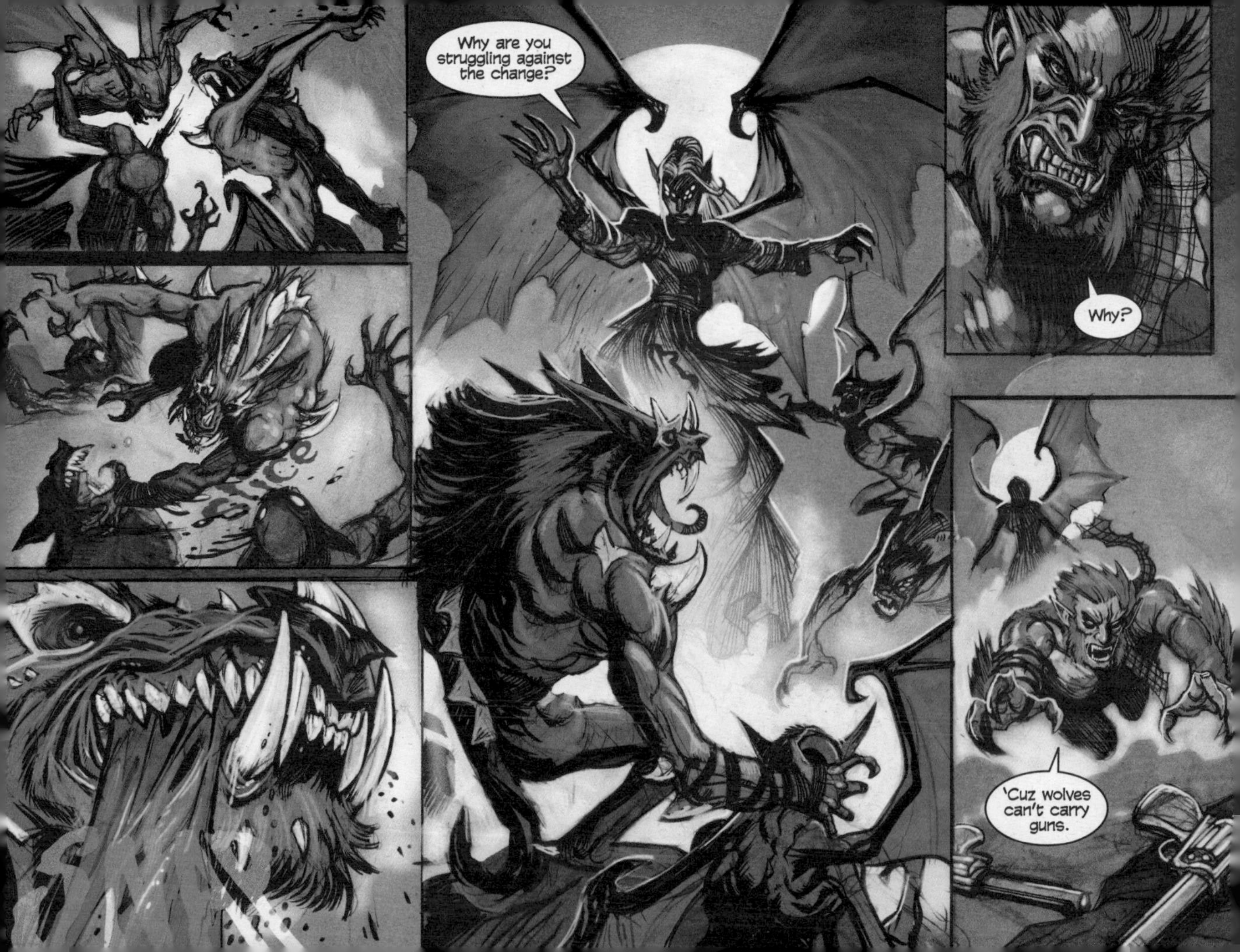
Why are you struggling against the change?
Why?
'Cuz wolves can't carry guns.

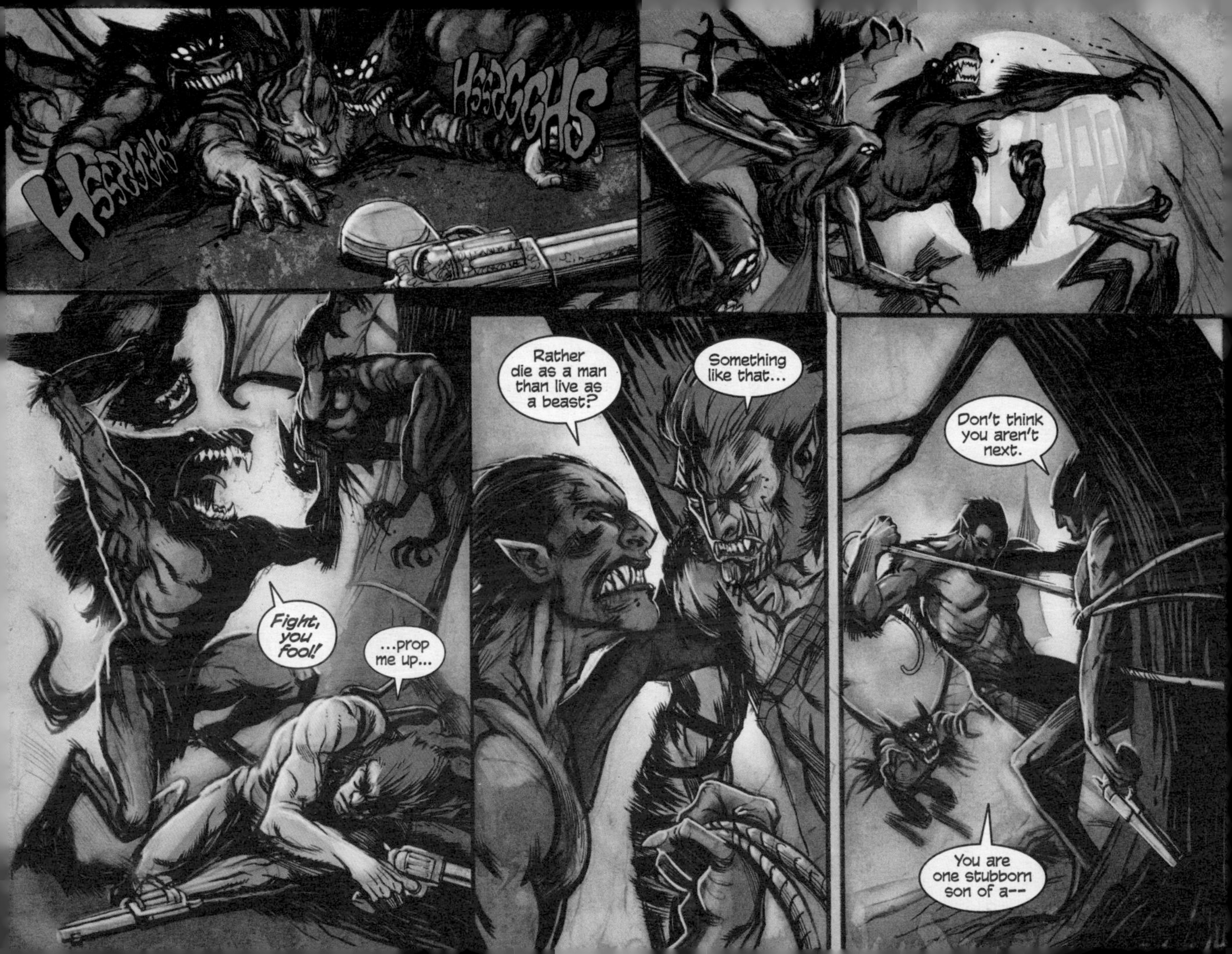
HSSSGGHS
HSSGGHS
Fight, you fool!
...prop me up...
Rather die as a man than live as a beast?
Something like that...
Don't think you aren't next.
You are one stubborn son of a--

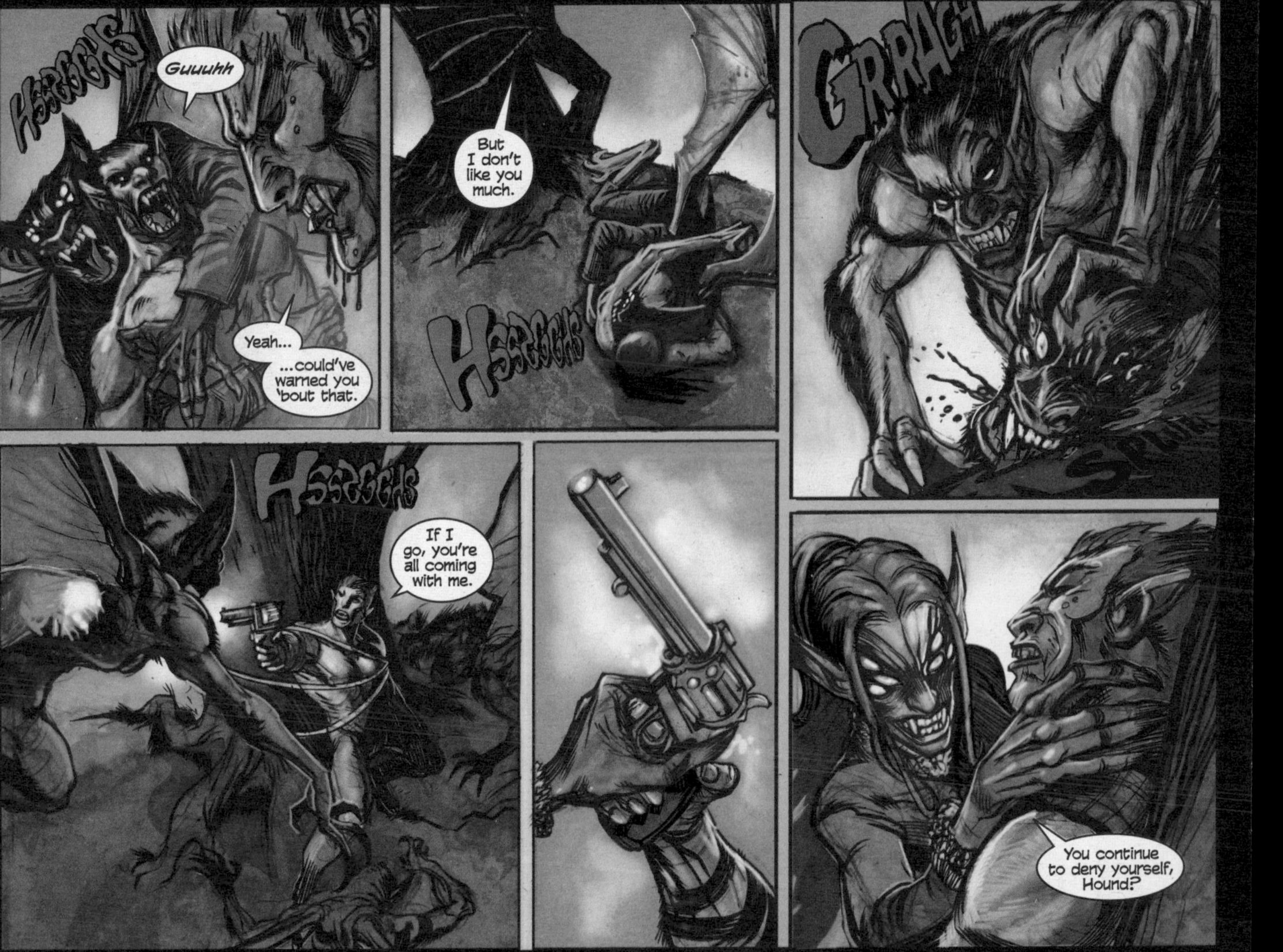

HSSSCCHS
Guuuhh
Yeah...
...could've warned you 'bout that.
But I don't like you much.
HSSSCCHS
GRRAGH
HSSSCCHS
If I go, you're all coming with me.
You continue to deny yourself, Hound?

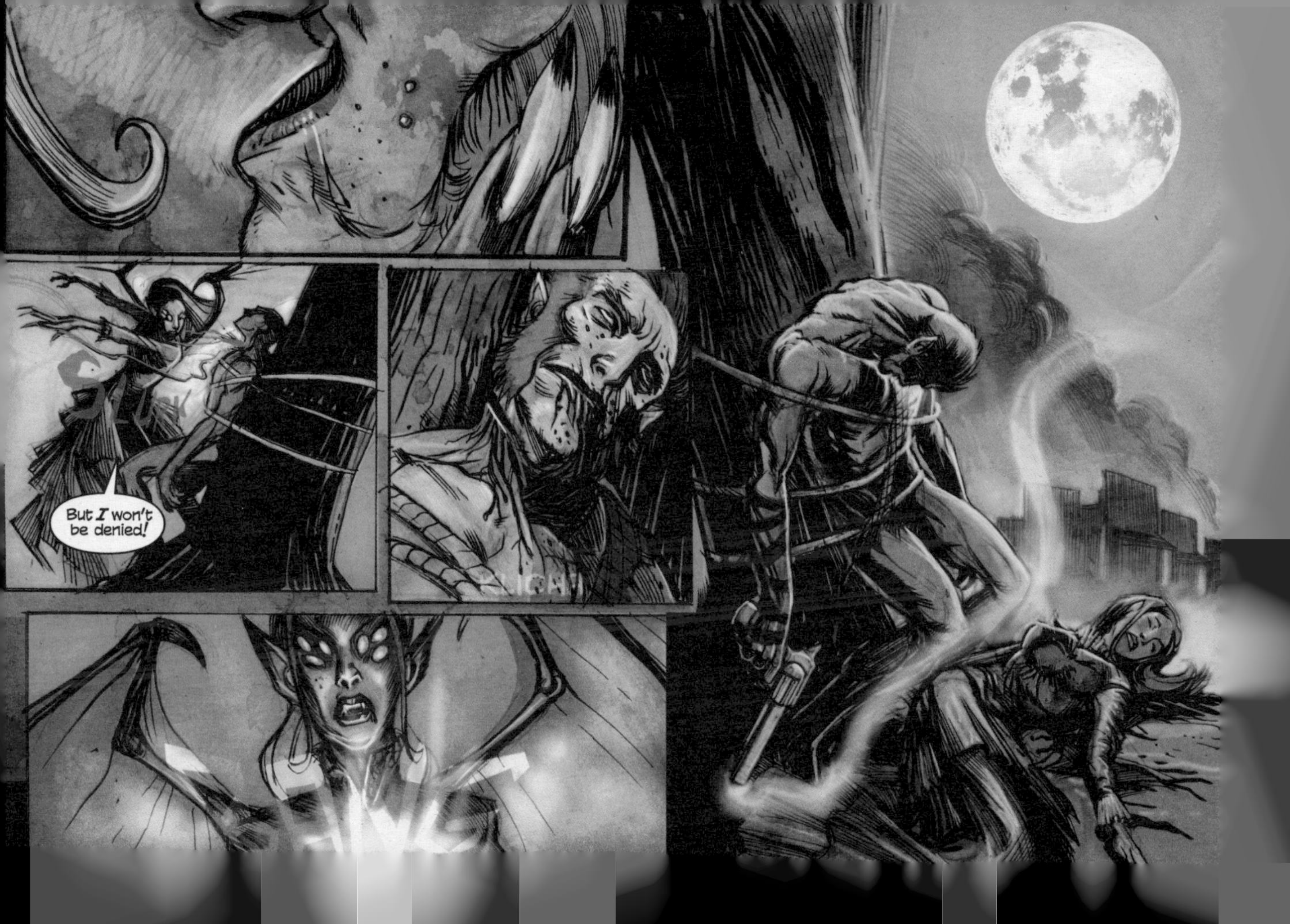

But I won't be denied!

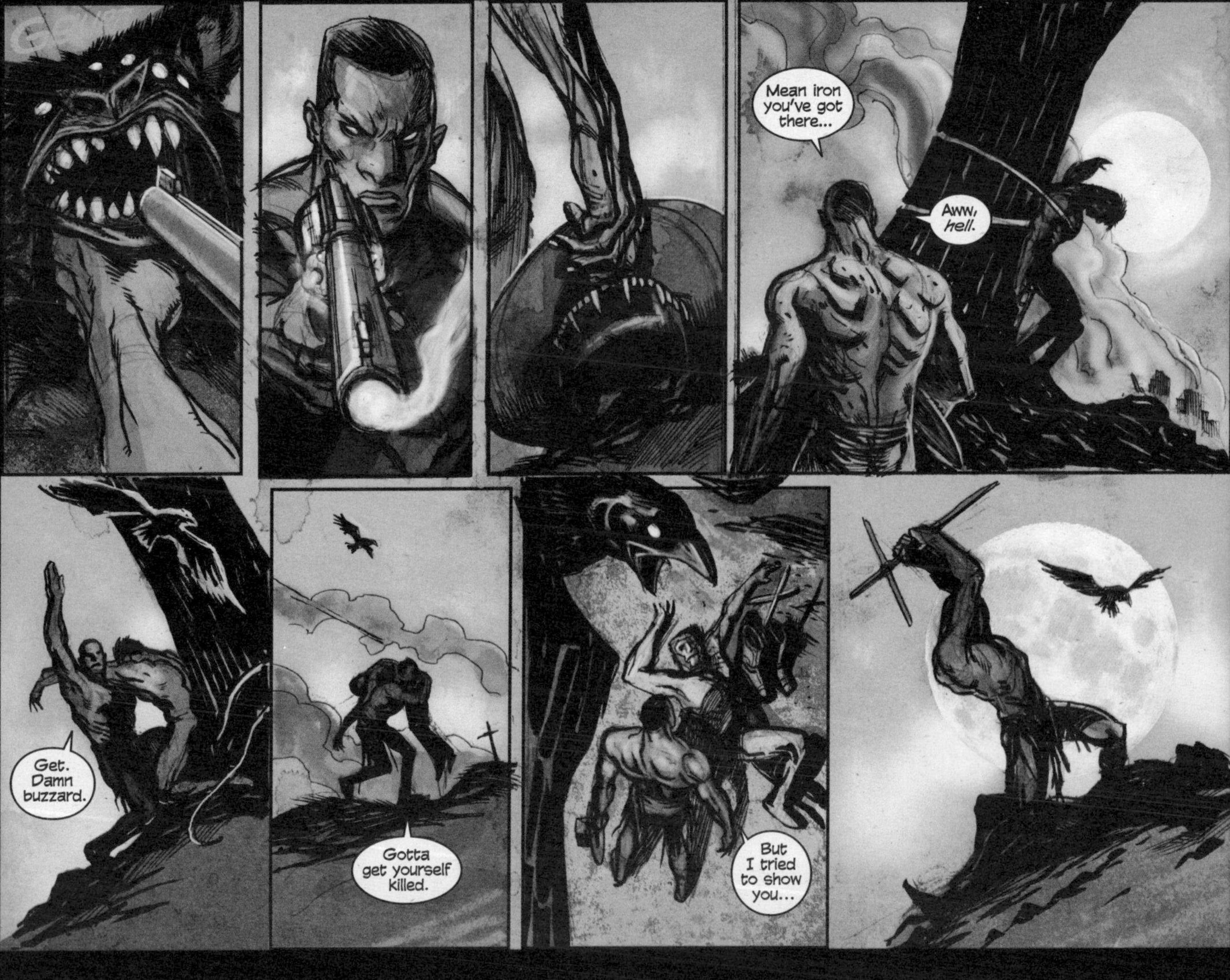
Mean iron you've got there...
Aww, *hell.*
Get. Damn buzzard.
Gotta get yourself killed.
But I tried to show you...

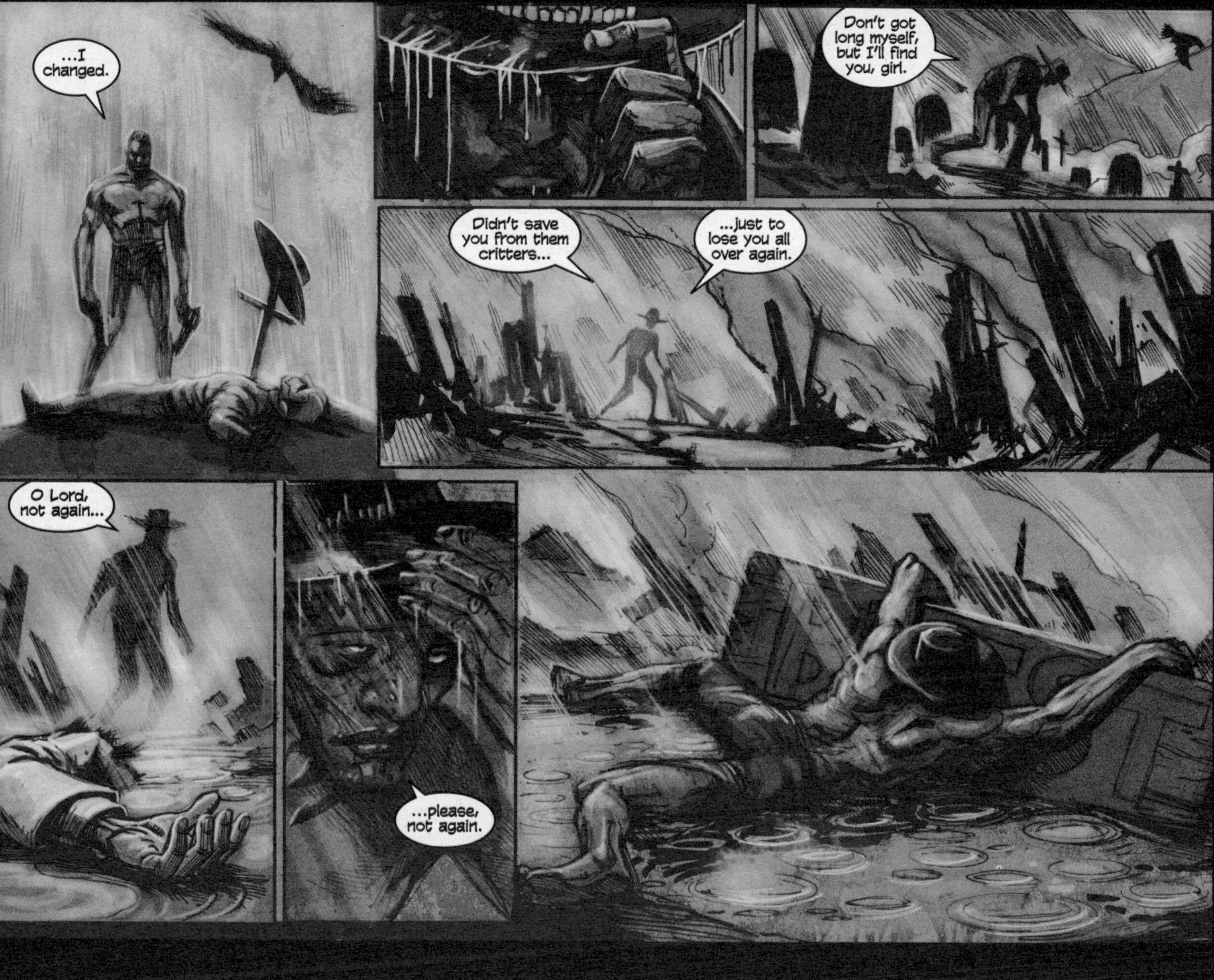
...I changed.
Don't got long myself, but I'll find you, girl.
Didn't save you from them critters...
...just to lose you all over again.
O Lord, not again...
...please, not again.

Heard whatcha done to my cousins.

This is my last courtesy. Pack your plunder and get.

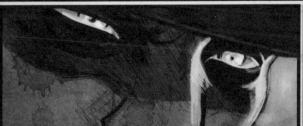

Ain't no tenderfoot gonna run out Marcus Sullivan.

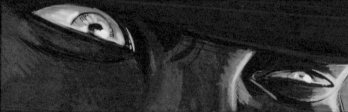

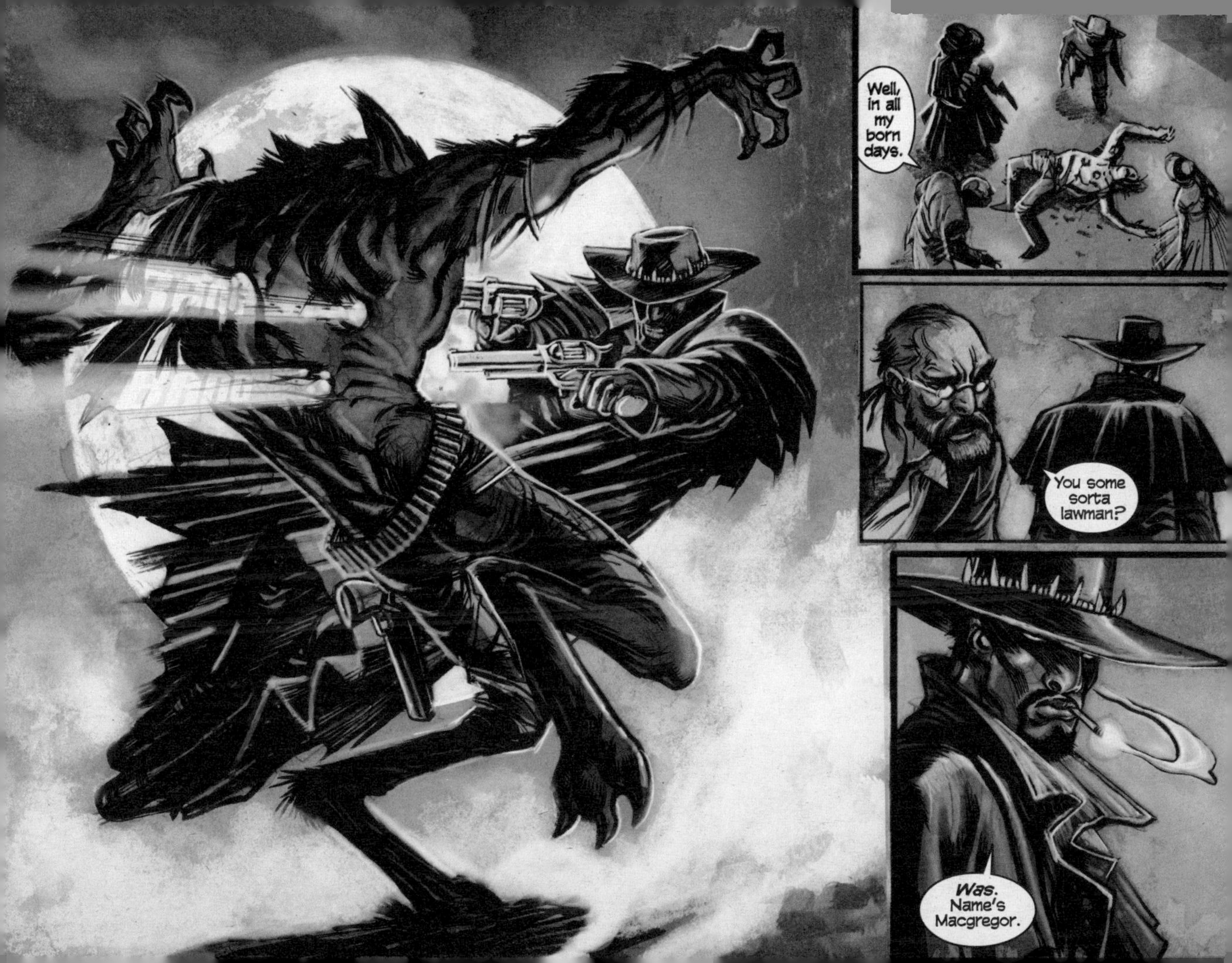
Well, in all my born days.
You some sorta lawman?
Was. Name's Macgregor.

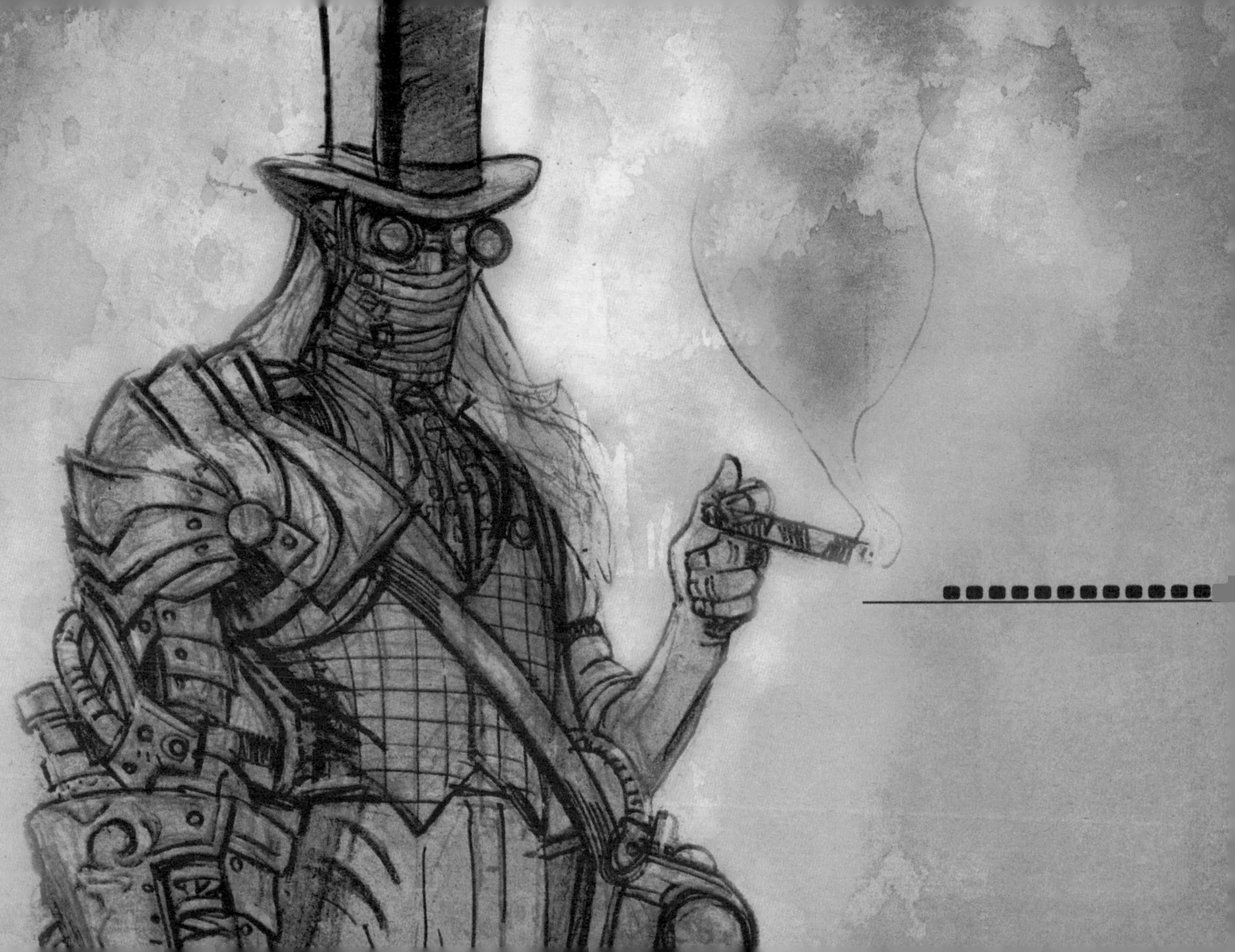

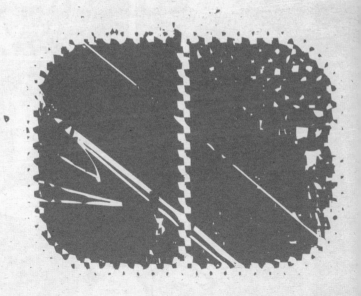

CHAPTER *2*

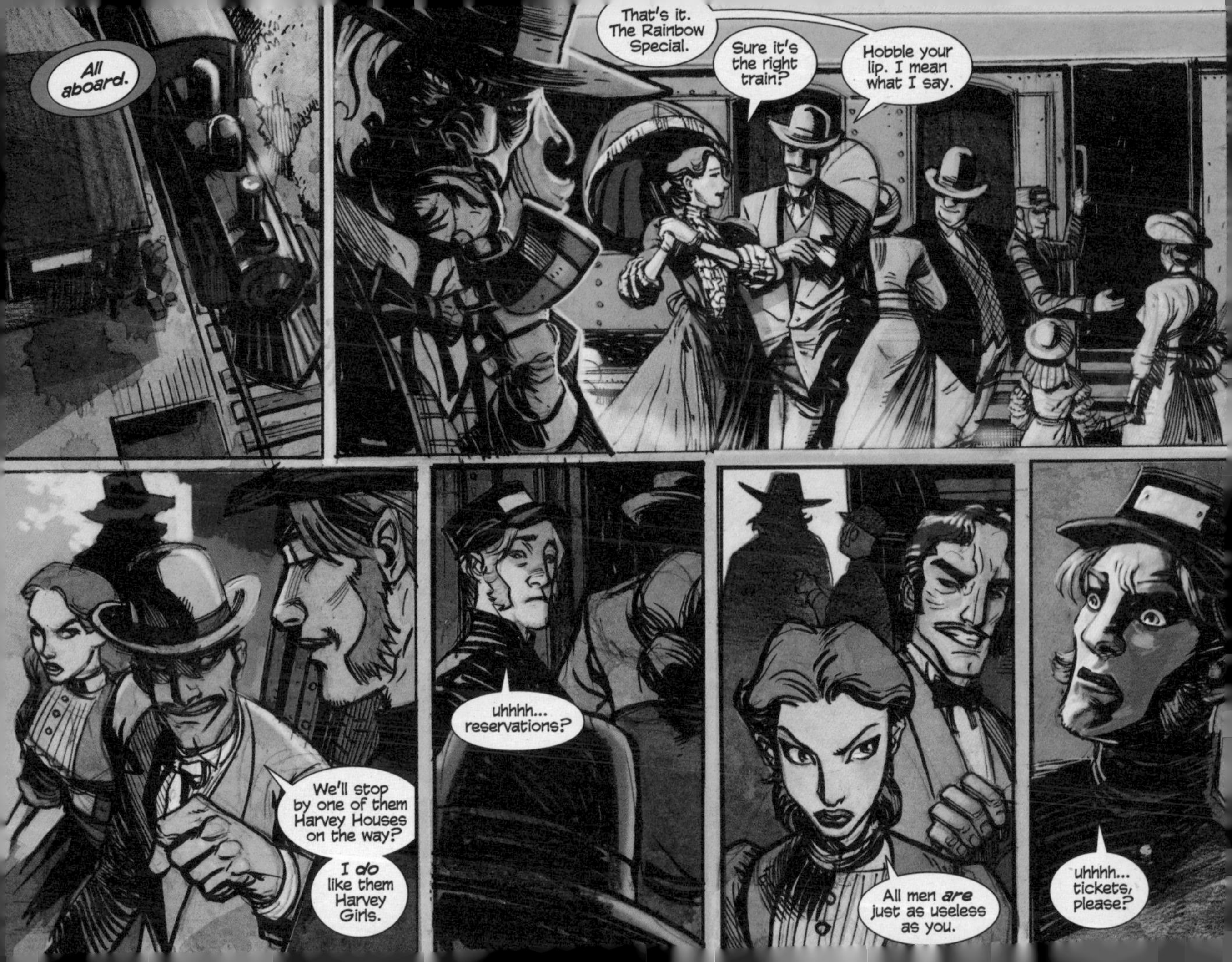
All aboard.
That's it. The Rainbow Special.
Sure it's the right train?
Hobble your lip. I mean what I say.
We'll stop by one of them Harvey Houses on the way?
I do like them Harvey Girls.
uhhhh... reservations?
All men are just as useless as you.
uhhhh... tickets, please?

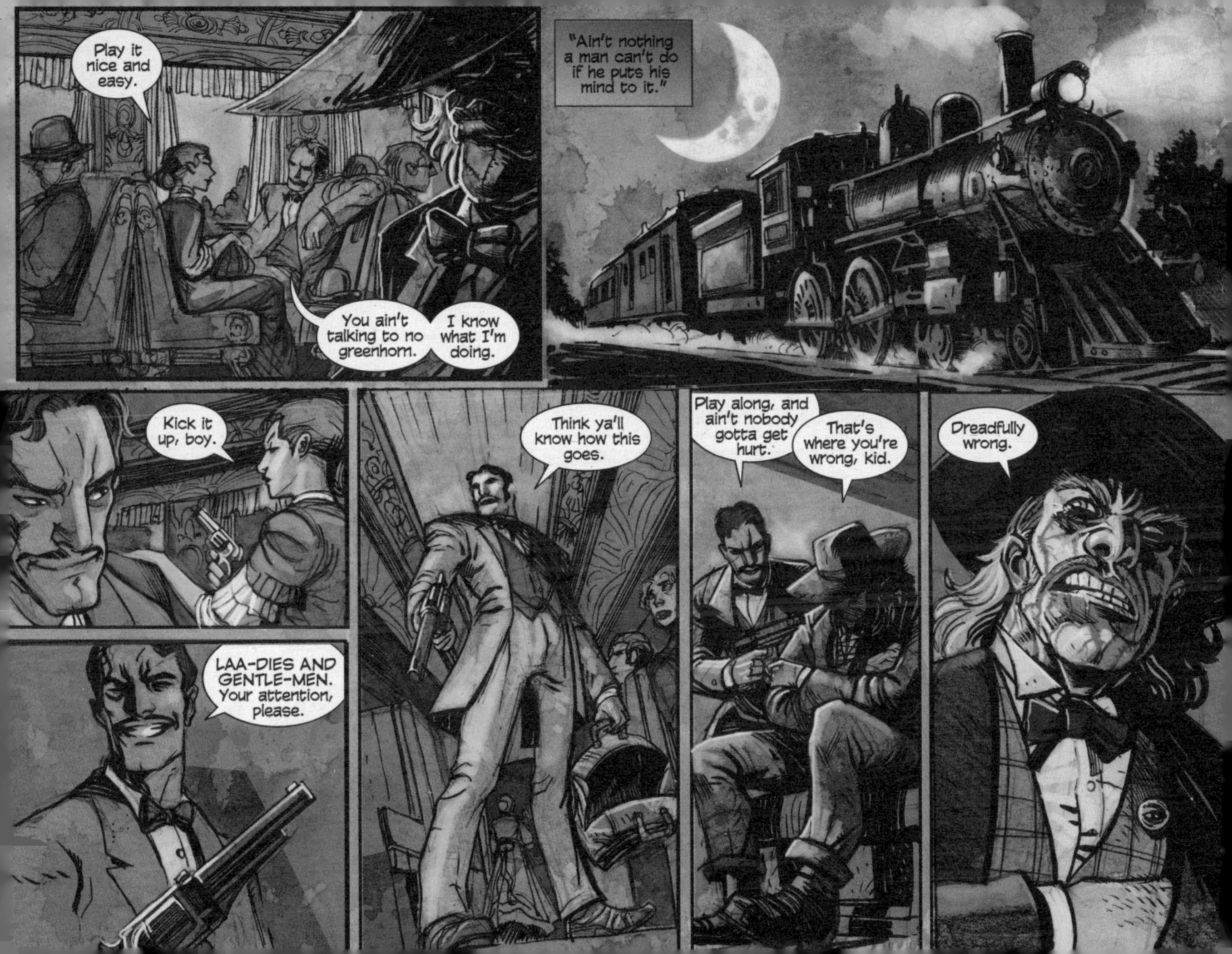
Play it nice and easy.
You ain't talking to no greenhorn.
I know what I'm doing.
"Ain't nothing a man can't do if he puts his mind to it."
Kick it up, boy.
LAA-DIES AND GENTLE-MEN. Your attention, please.
Think ya'll know how this goes.
Play along, and ain't nobody gotta get hurt.
That's where you're wrong, kid.
Dreadfully wrong.

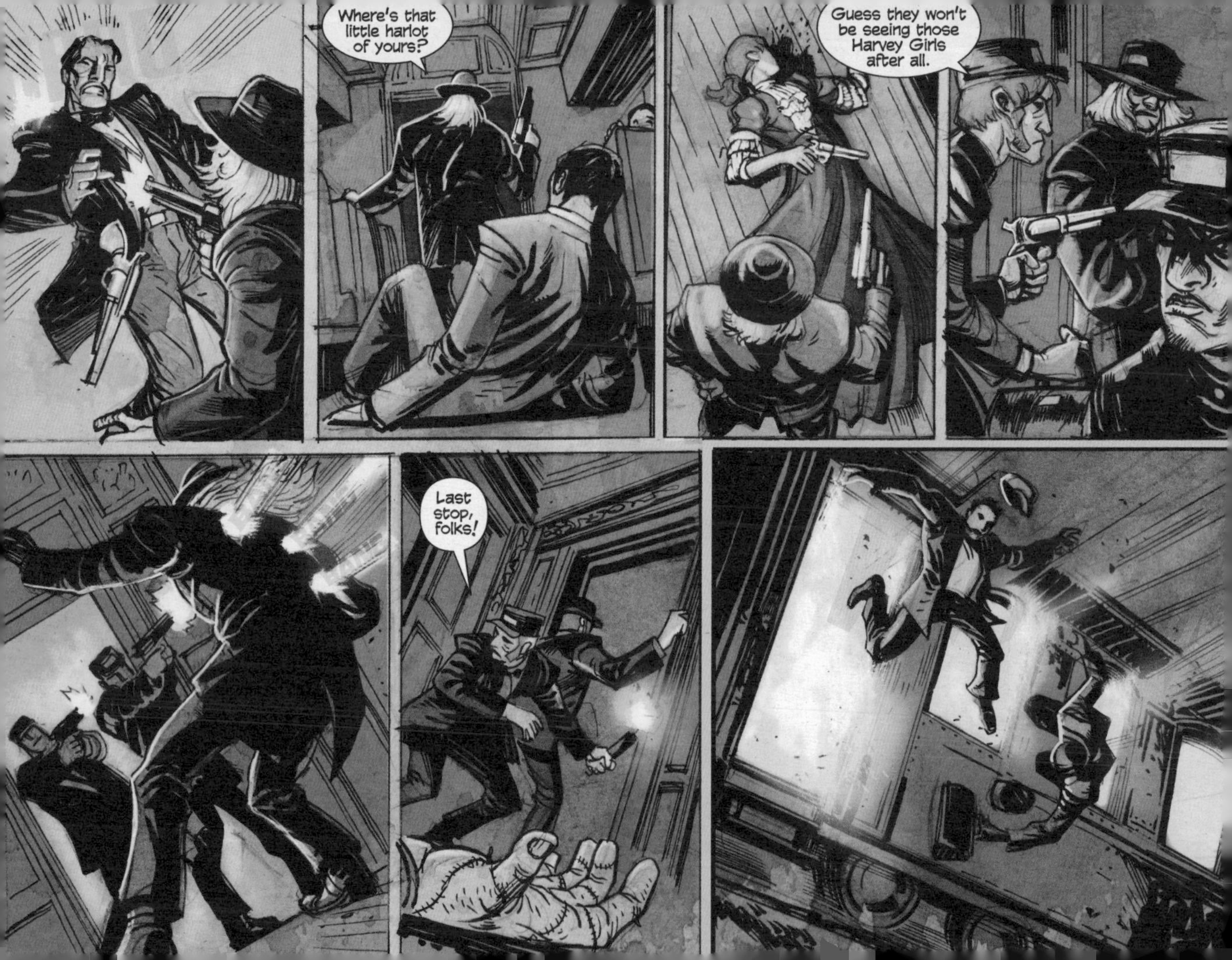
Where's that little harlot of yours?
Guess they won't be seeing those Harvey Girls after all.
Last stop, folks!

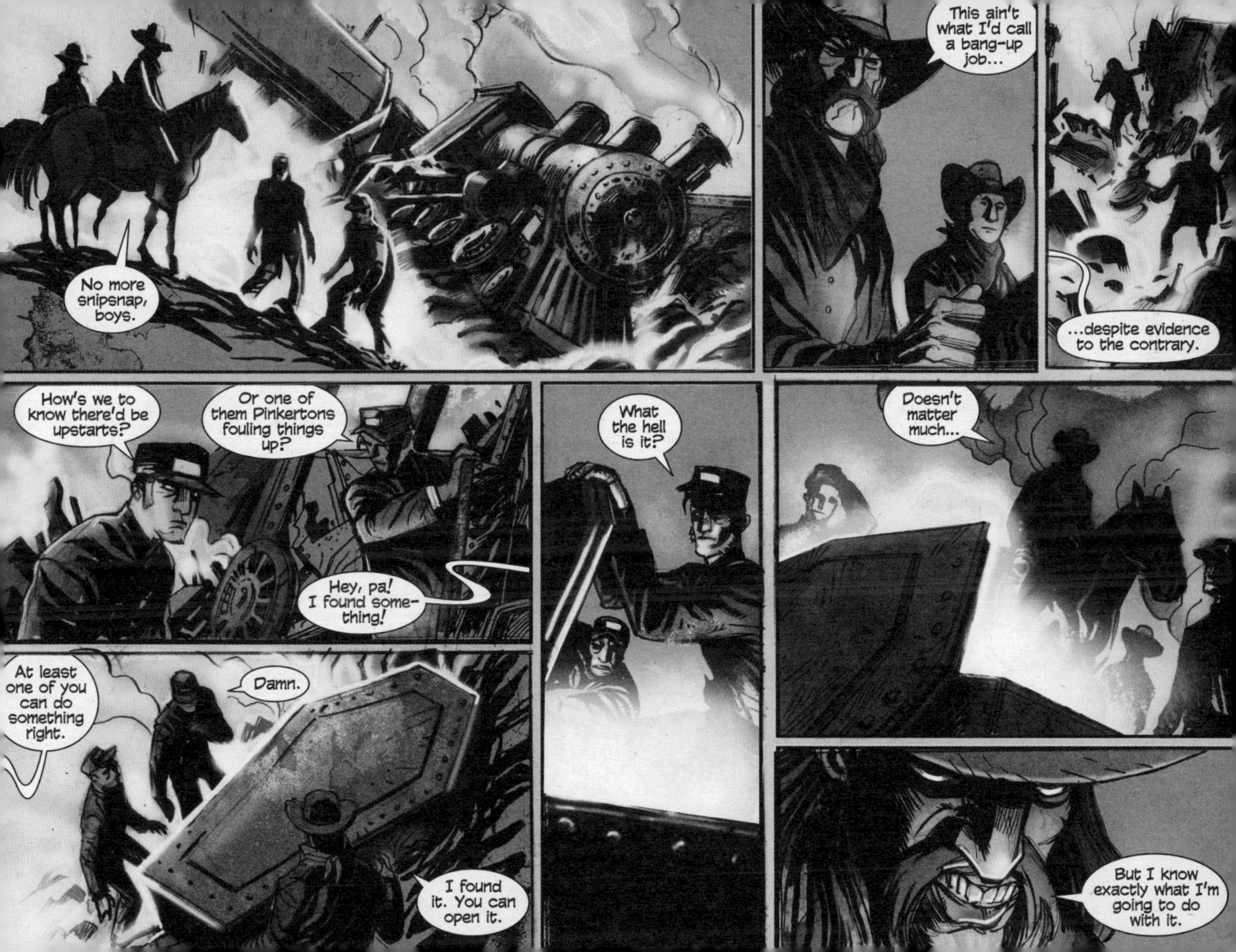
No more snipsnap, boys.
This ain't what I'd call a bang-up job...
...despite evidence to the contrary.
How's we to know there'd be upstarts?
Or one of them Pinkertons fouling things up?
Hey, pa! I found some-thing!
At least one of you can do something right.
Damn.
I found it. You can open it.
What the hell is it?
Doesn't matter much...
But I know exactly what I'm going to do with it.

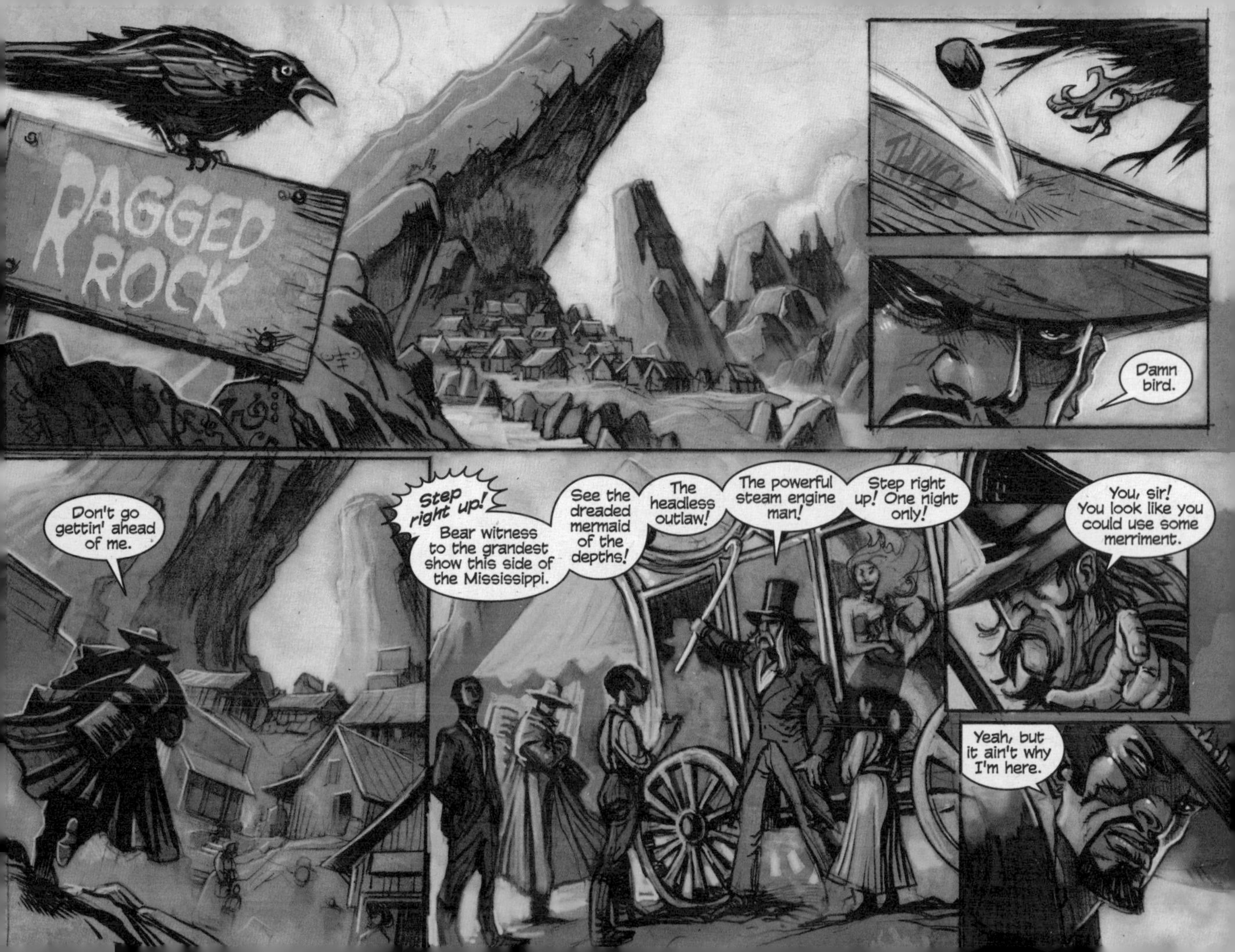
RAGGED ROCK
THUNK
Damn bird.
Don't go gettin' ahead of me.
Step right up!
Bear witness to the grandest show this side of the Mississippi.
See the dreaded mermaid of the depths!
The headless outlaw!
The powerful steam engine man!
Step right up! One night only!
You, sir! You look like you could use some merriment.
Yeah, but it ain't why I'm here.

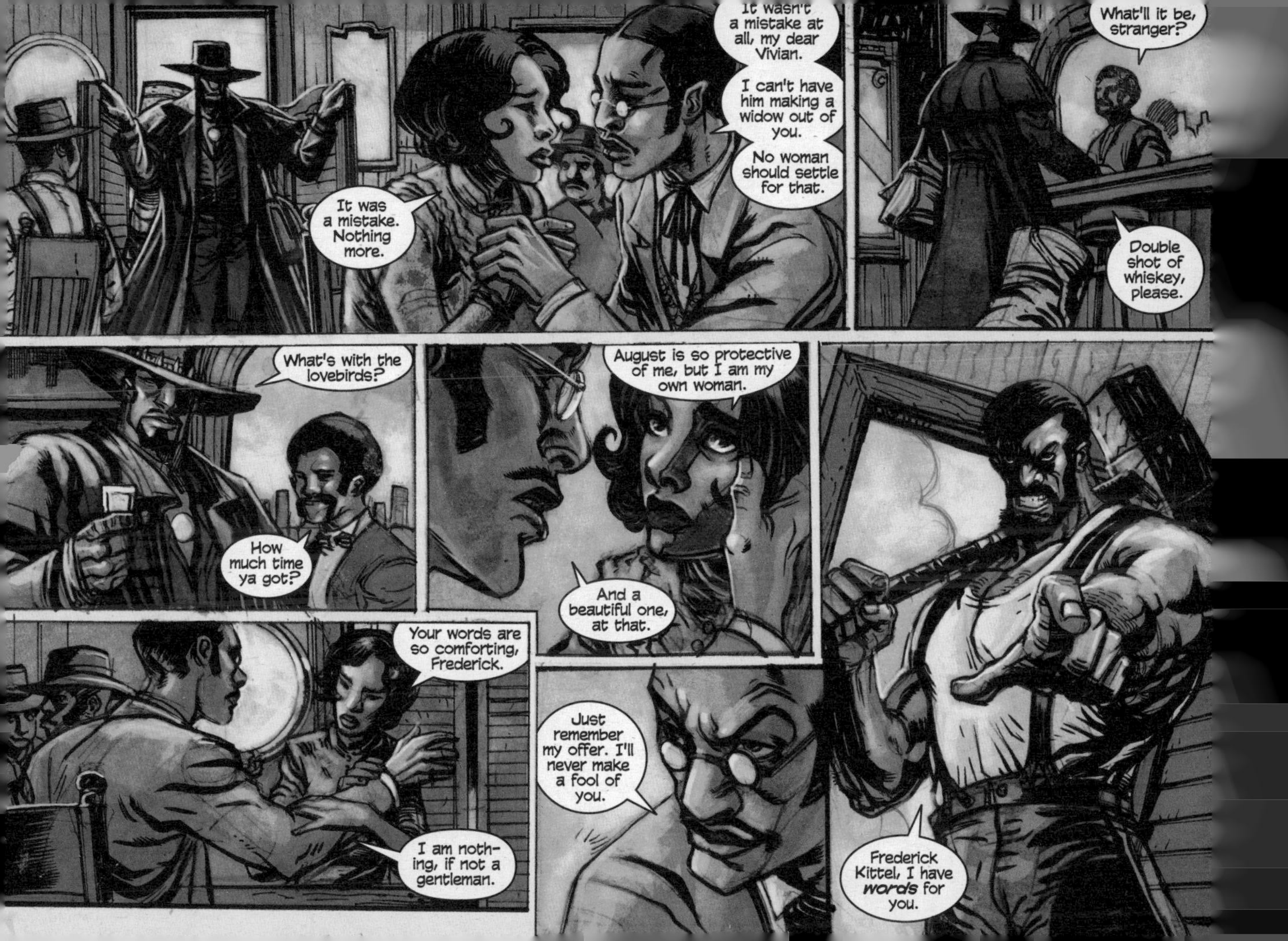
It was a mistake. Nothing more.
It wasn't a mistake at all, my dear Vivian.
I can't have him making a widow out of you.
No woman should settle for that.
What'll it be, stranger?
Double shot of whiskey, please.
What's with the lovebirds?
How much time ya got?
August is so protective of me, but I am my own woman.
And a beautiful one, at that.
Your words are so comforting, Frederick.
I am nothing, if not a gentleman.
Just remember my offer. I'll never make a fool of you.
Frederick Kittel, I have *words* for you.

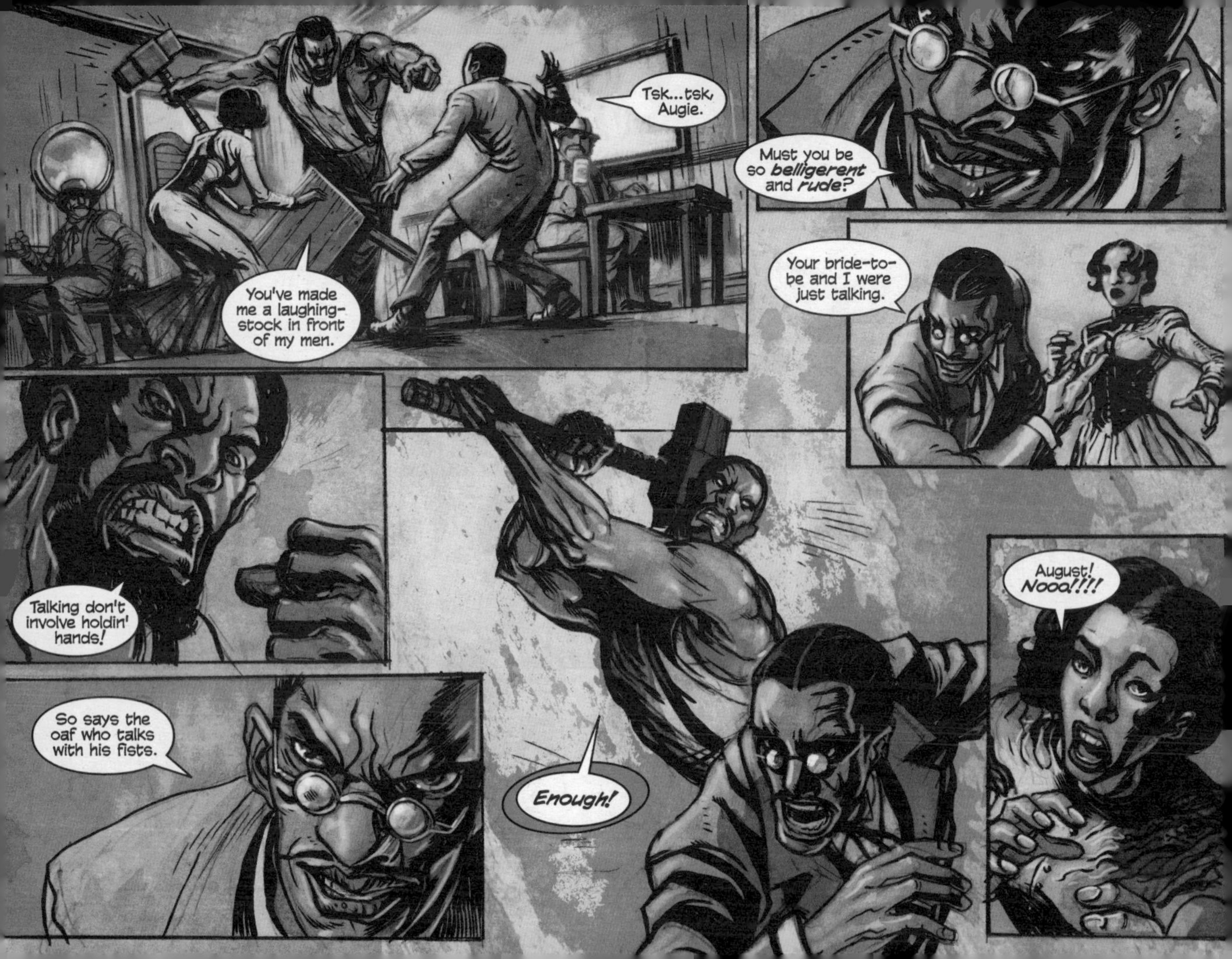
You've made me a laughing-stock in front of my men.
Tsk...tsk, Augie.
Must you be so belligerent and rude?
Your bride-to-be and I were just talking.
Talking don't involve holdin' hands!
So says the oaf who talks with his fists.
Enough!
August! Nooo!!!!

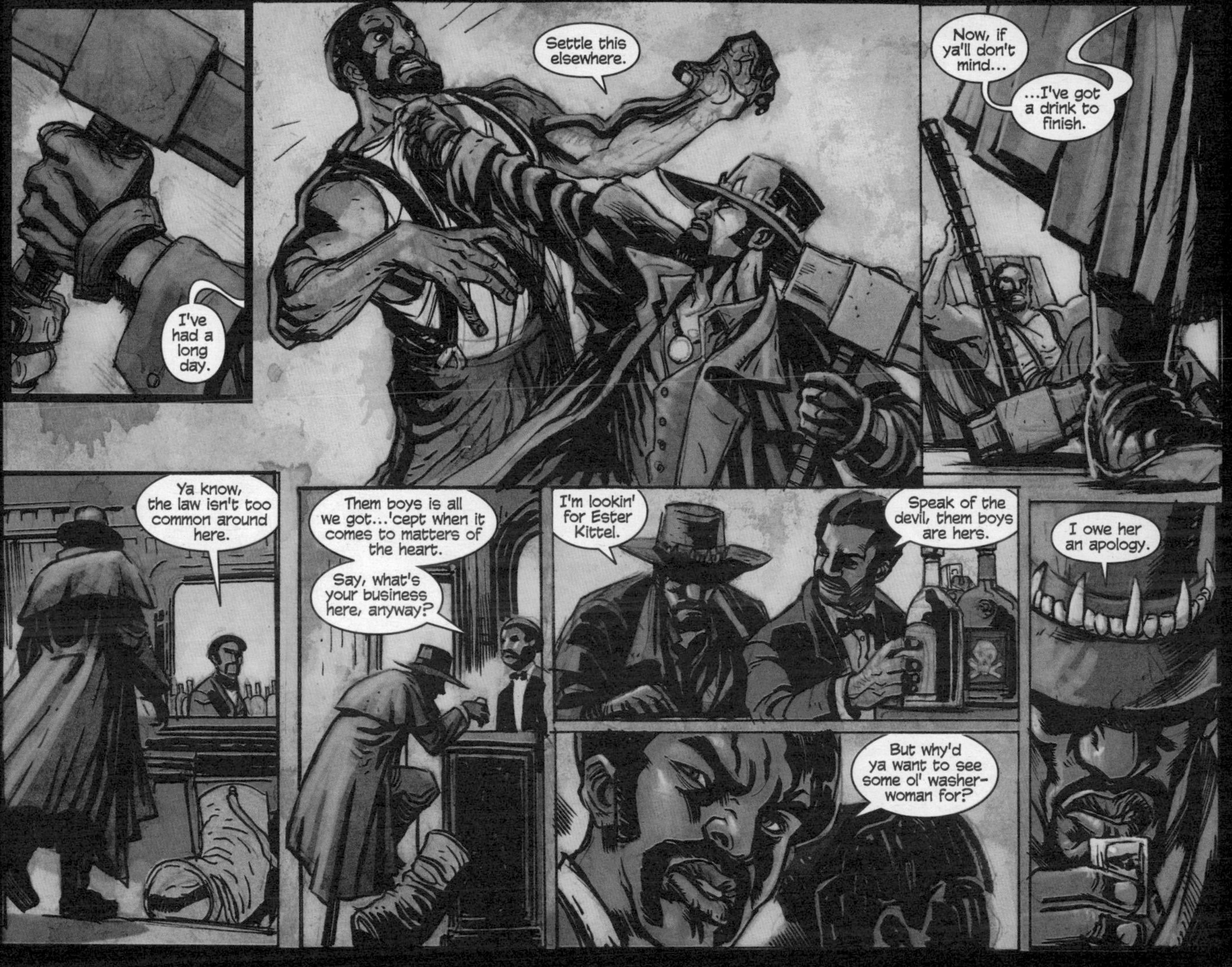
I've had a long day.
Settle this elsewhere.
Now, if ya'll don't mind...
...I've got a drink to finish.
Ya know, the law isn't too common around here.
Them boys is all we got...'cept when it comes to matters of the heart.
Say, what's your business here, anyway?
I'm lookin' for Ester Kittel.
Speak of the devil, them boys are hers.
But why'd ya want to see some ol' washer-woman for?
I owe her an apology.

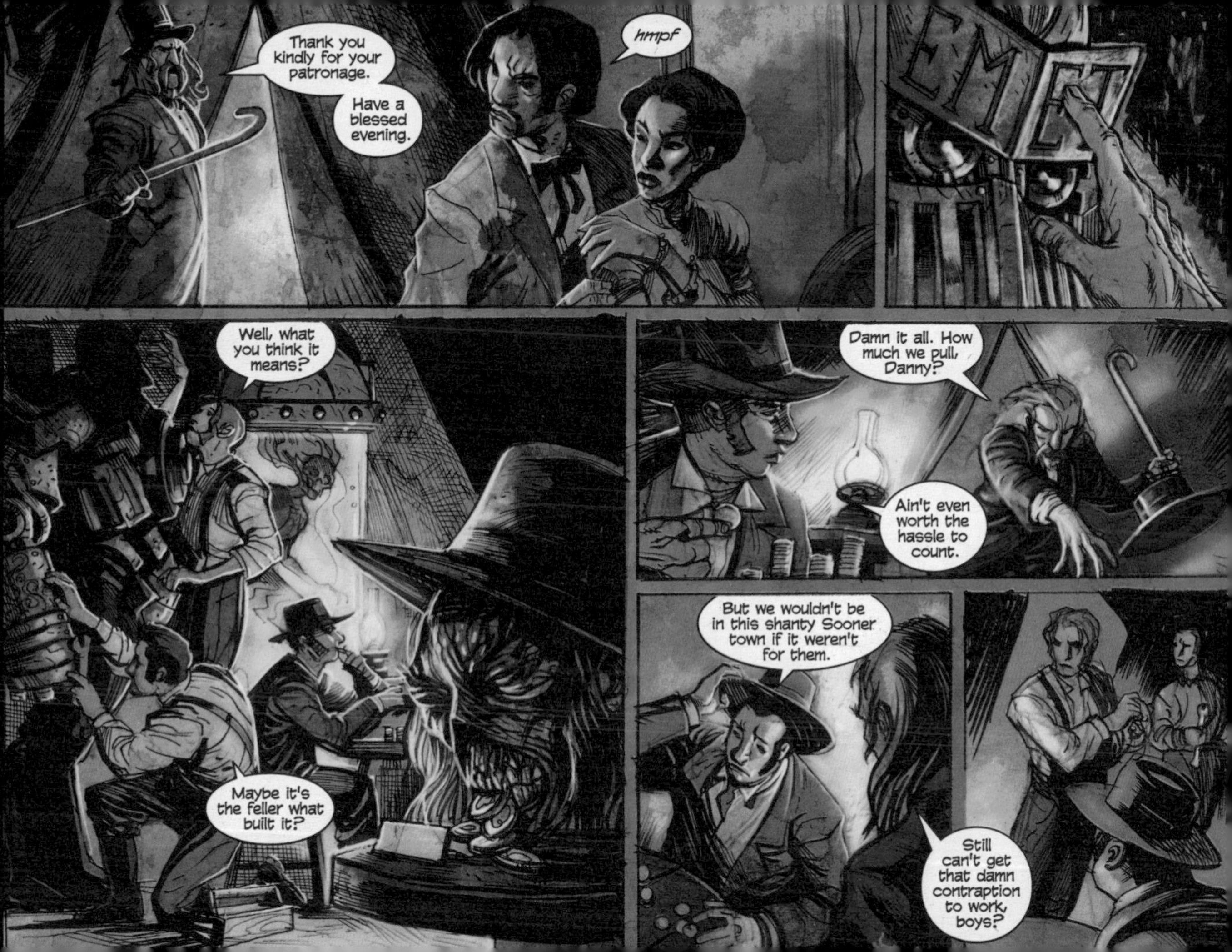
Thank you kindly for your patronage.
Have a blessed evening.
hmpf
EMET
Well, what you think it means?
Maybe it's the feller what built it?
Damn it all. How much we pull, Danny?
Ain't even worth the hassle to count.
But we wouldn't be in this shanty Sooner town if it weren't for them.
Still can't get that damn contraption to work, boys?

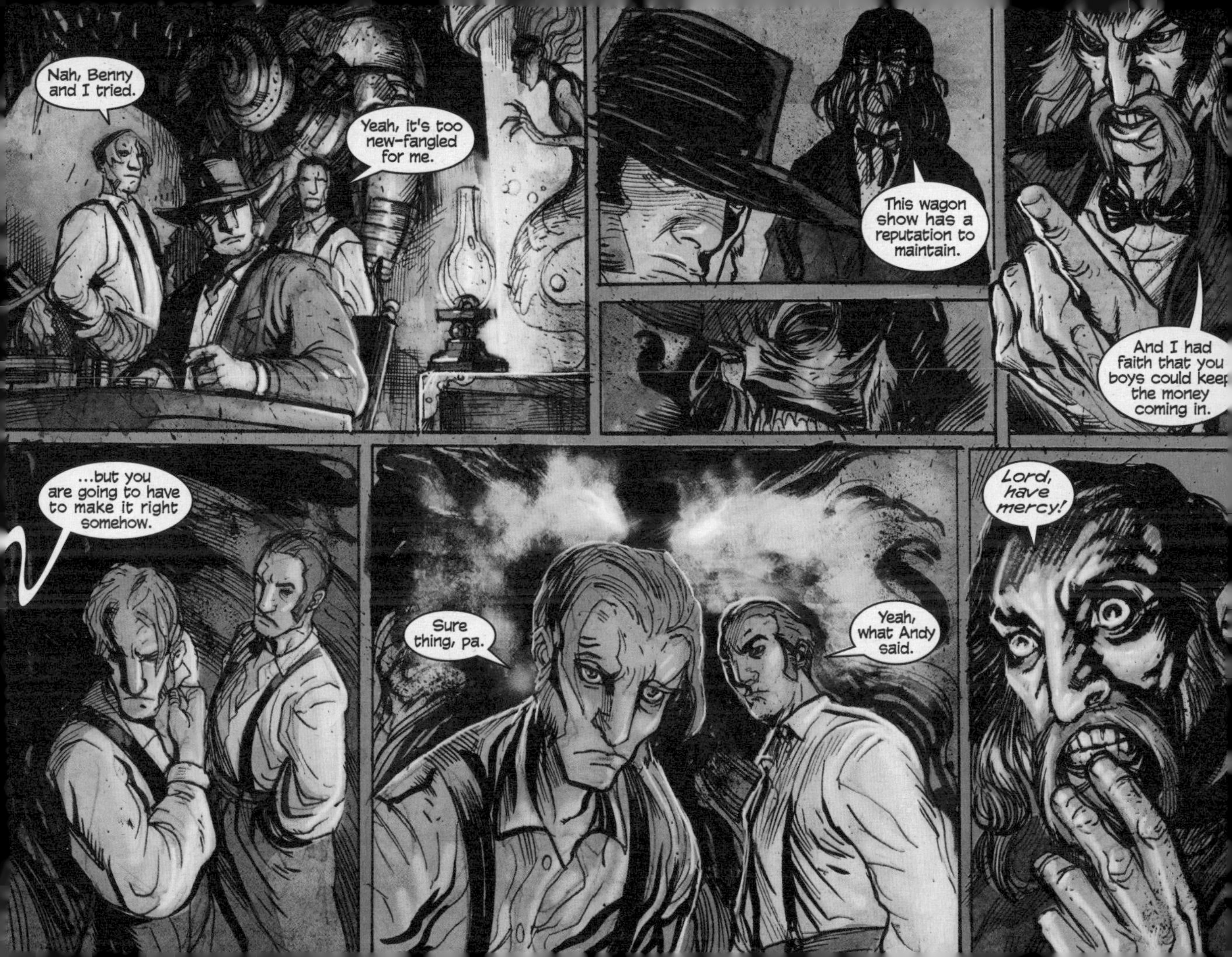
Nah, Benny and I tried.
Yeah, it's too new-fangled for me.
This wagon show has a reputation to maintain.
And I had faith that you boys could keep the money coming in.
...but you are going to have to make it right somehow.
Sure thing, pa.
Yeah, what Andy said.
Lord, have mercy!

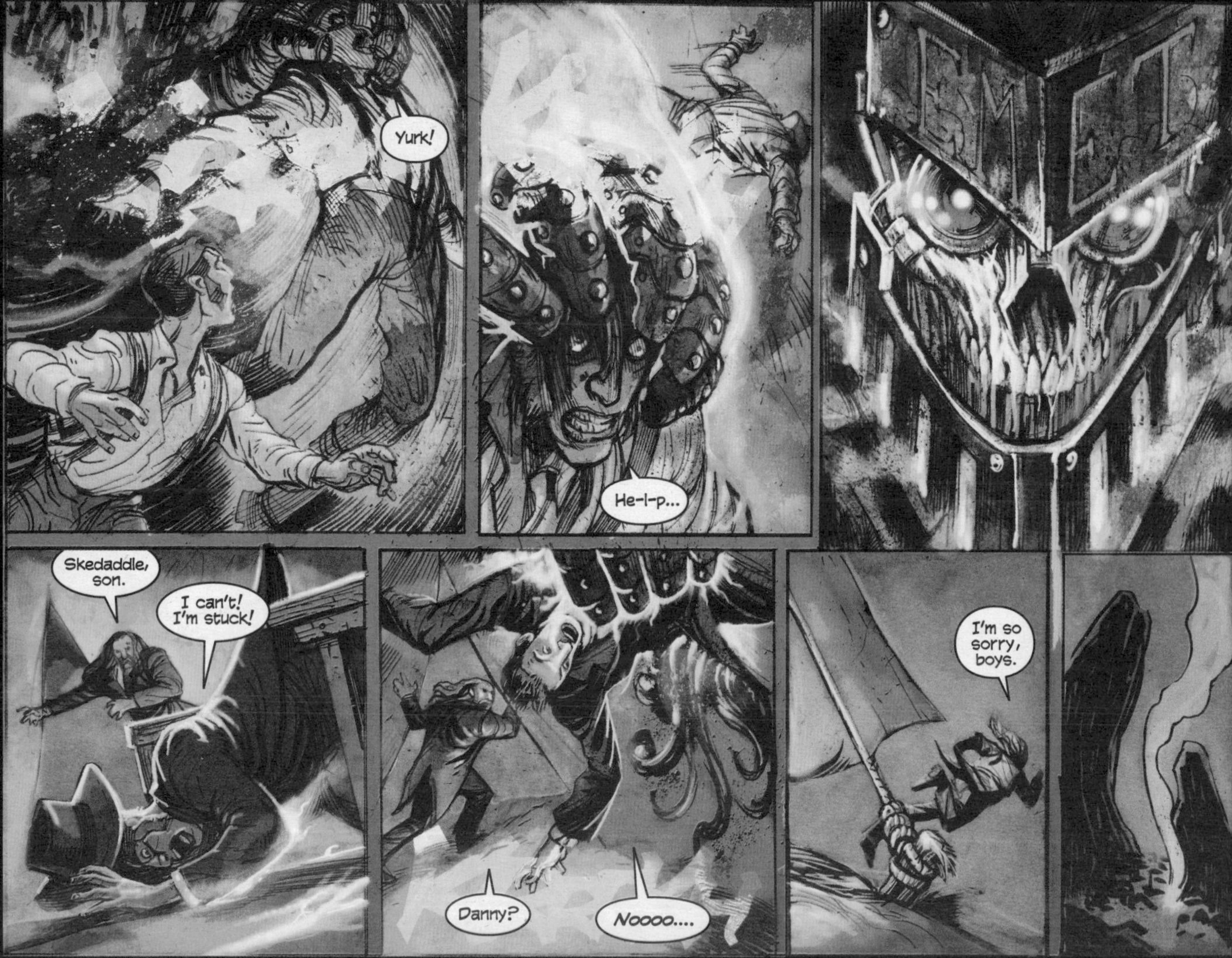
Yurk!
He-l-p...
Skedaddle, son.
I can't! I'm stuck!
Danny?
Noooo....
I'm so sorry, boys.

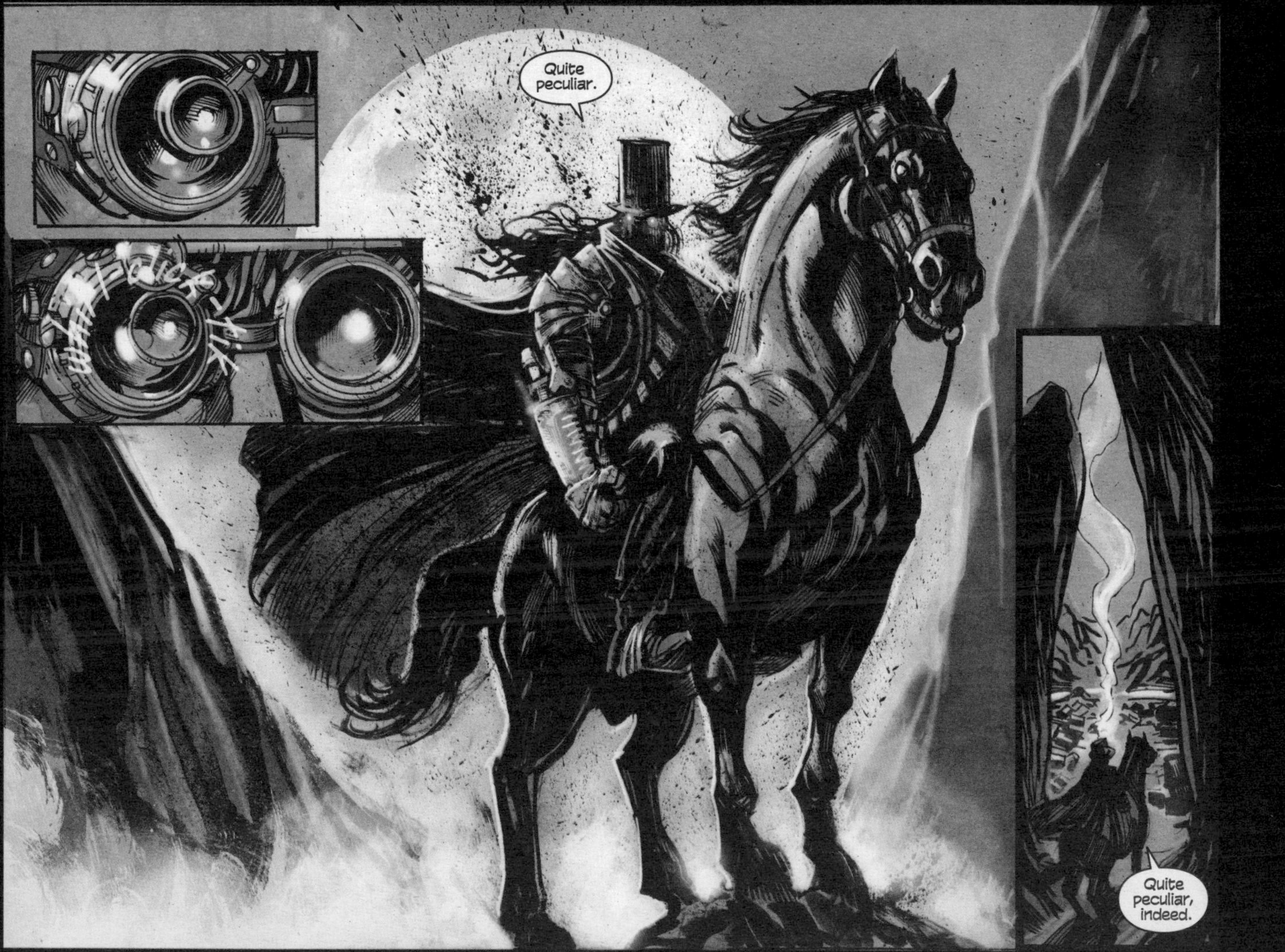
Quite peculiar.
Quite peculiar, indeed.

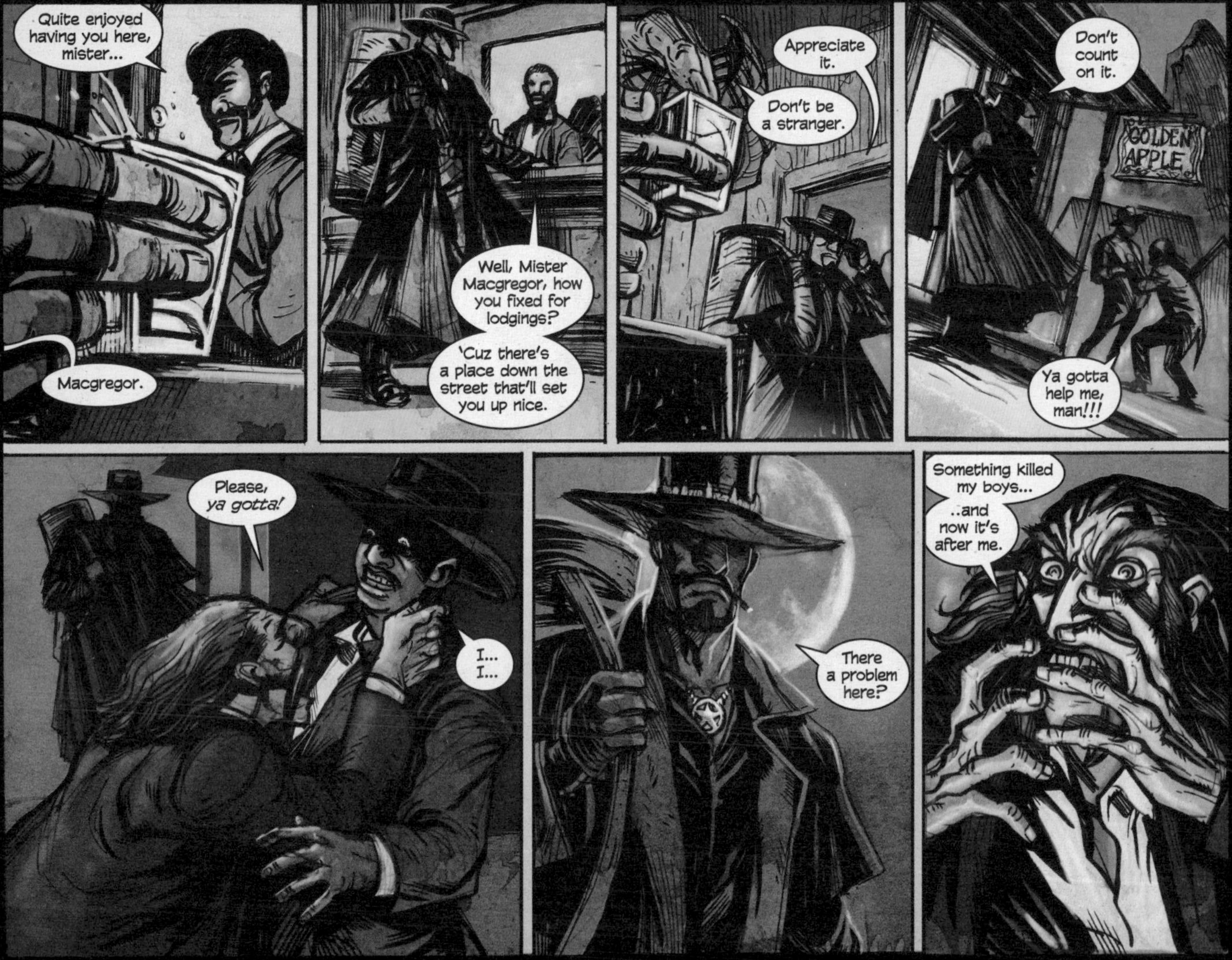
Quite enjoyed having you here, mister...
Macgregor.
Well, Mister Macgregor, how you fixed for lodgings?
'Cuz there's a place down the street that'll set you up nice.
Appreciate it.
Don't be a stranger.
Don't count on it.
GOLDEN APPLE
Ya gotta help me, man!!!
Please, *ya gotta!*
I... I...
There a problem here?
Something killed my boys...
..and now it's after me.

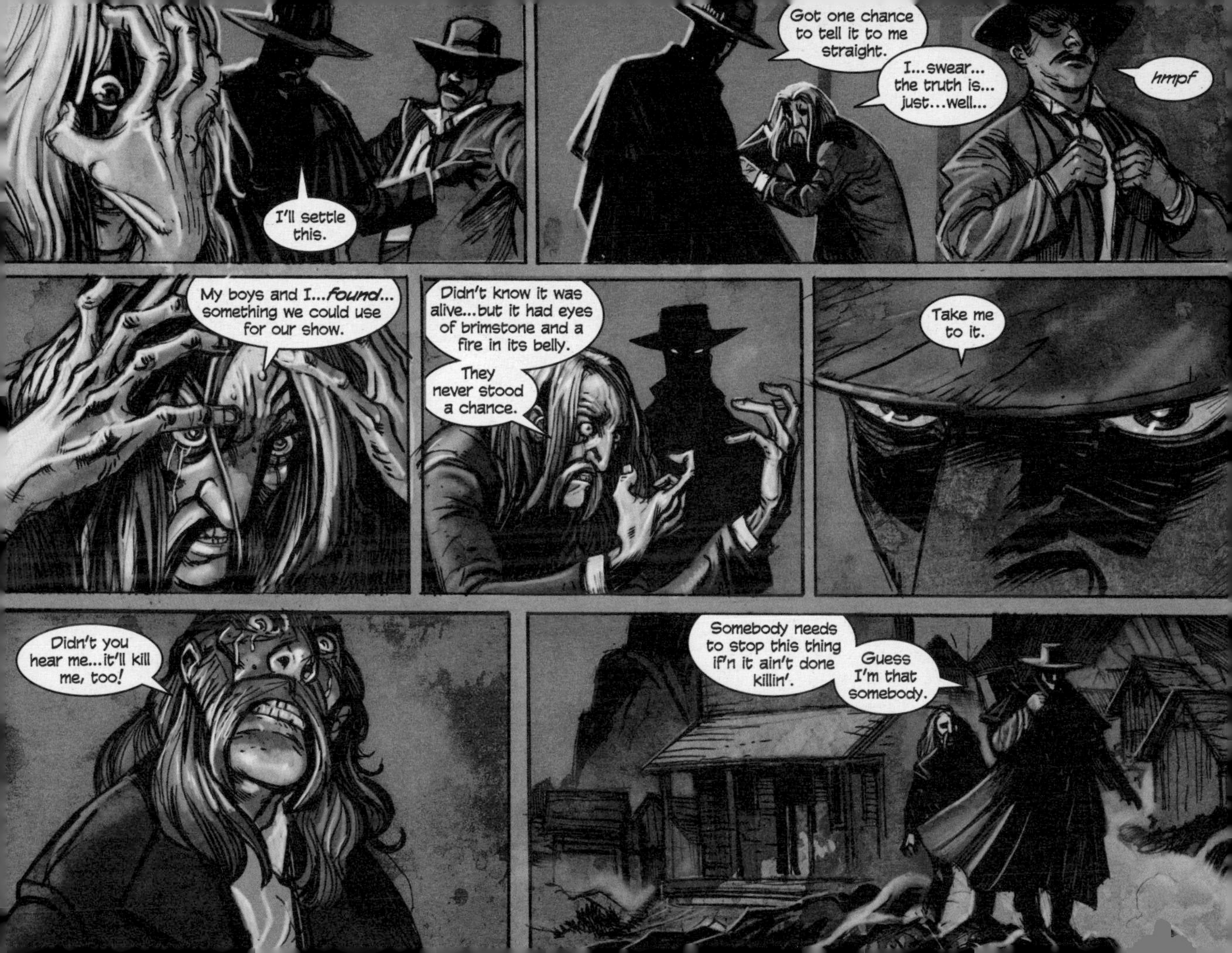
I'll settle this.
Got one chance to tell it to me straight.
I...swear... the truth is... just...well...
hmpf
My boys and I...*found*... something we could use for our show.
Didn't know it was alive...but it had eyes of brimstone and a fire in its belly.
They never stood a chance.
Take me to it.
Didn't you hear me...it'll kill me, too!
Somebody needs to stop this thing if'n it ain't done killin'.
Guess I'm that somebody.

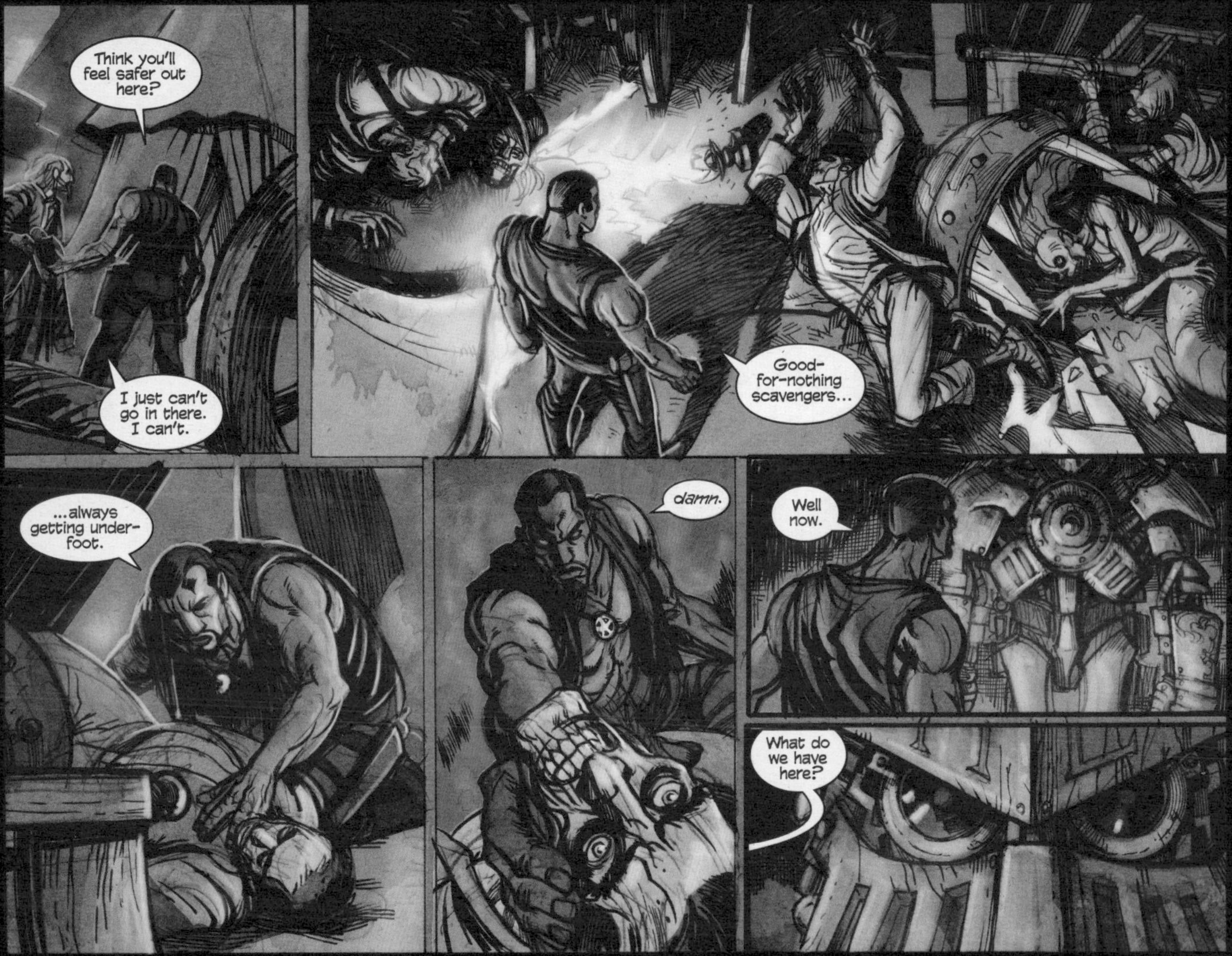
Think you'll feel safer out here?
I just can't go in there. I can't.
Good-for-nothing scavengers...
...always getting under-foot.
damn.
Well now.
What do we have here?

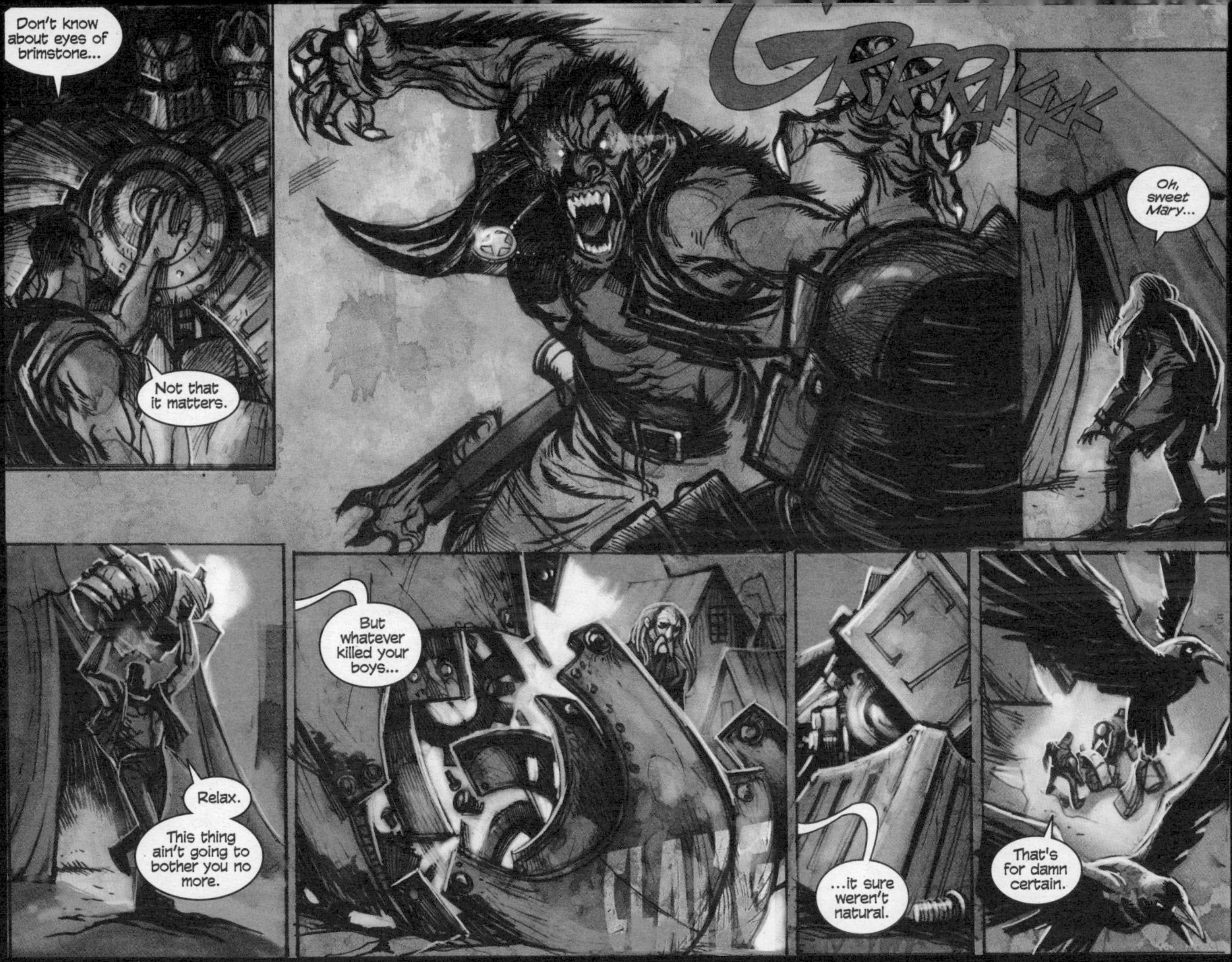

Don't know about eyes of brimstone...
Not that it matters.
GRRRAKKK
Oh, sweet Mary...
Relax.
This thing ain't going to bother you no more.
But whatever killed your boys...
...it sure weren't natural.
That's for damn certain.

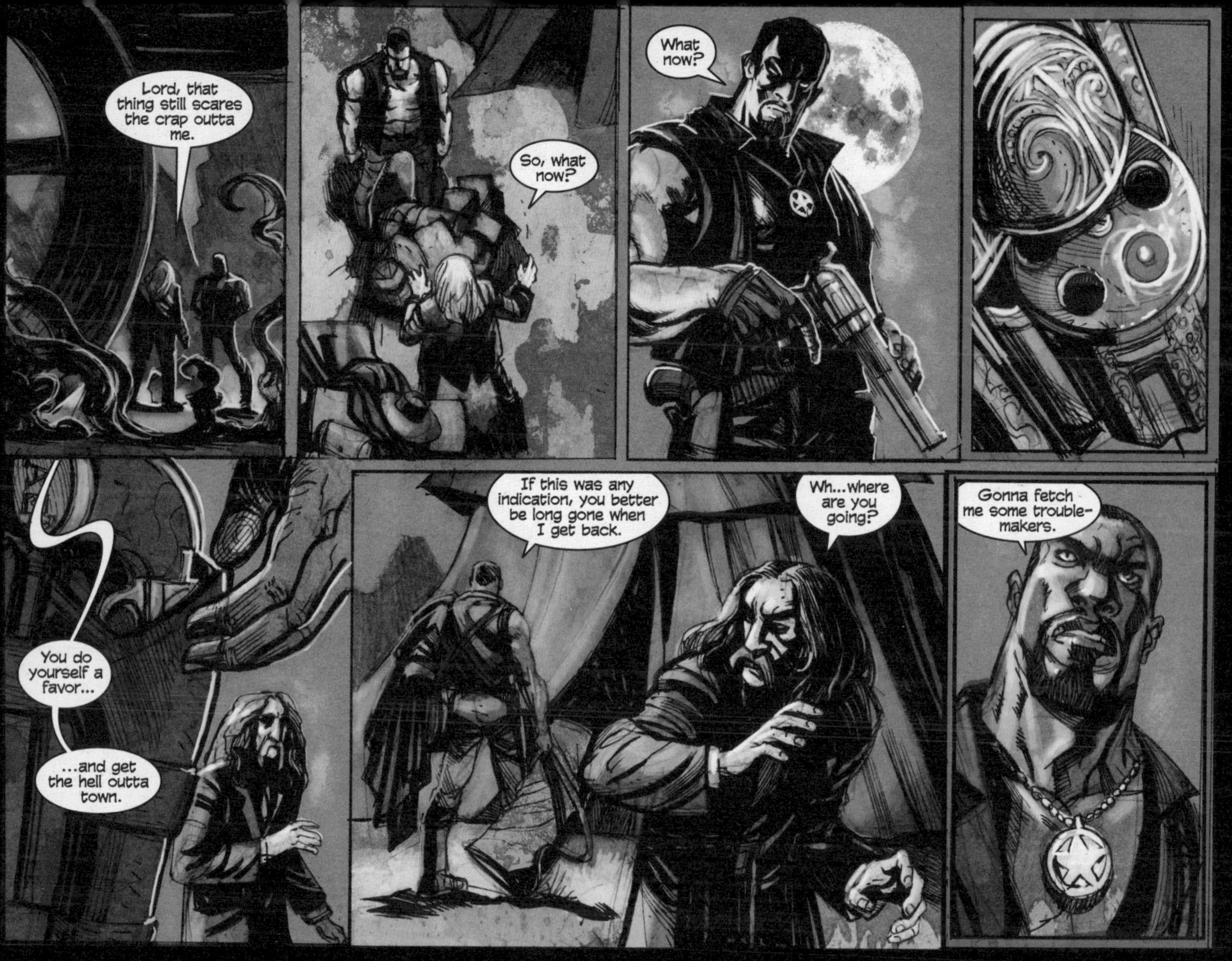
Lord, that thing still scares the crap outta me.
So, what now?
What now?
You do yourself a favor...
...and get the hell outta town.
If this was any indication, you better be long gone when I get back.
Wh...where are you going?
Gonna fetch me some trouble-makers.

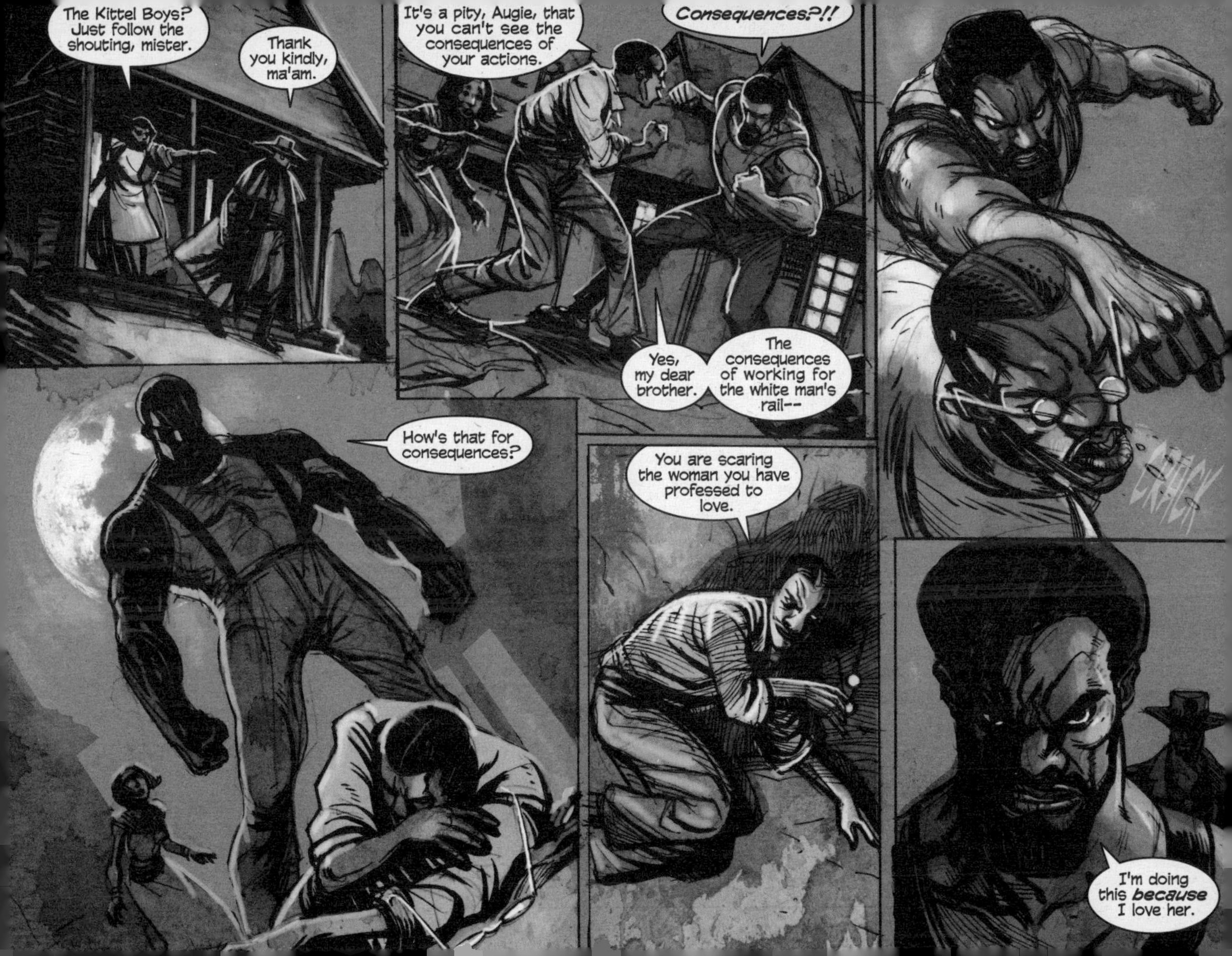
The Kittel Boys? Just follow the shouting, mister.
Thank you kindly, ma'am.
It's a pity, Augie, that you can't see the consequences of your actions.
Consequences?!!
Yes, my dear brother.
The consequences of working for the white man's rail--
CRACK
How's that for consequences?
You are scaring the woman you have professed to love.
I'm doing this *because* I love her.

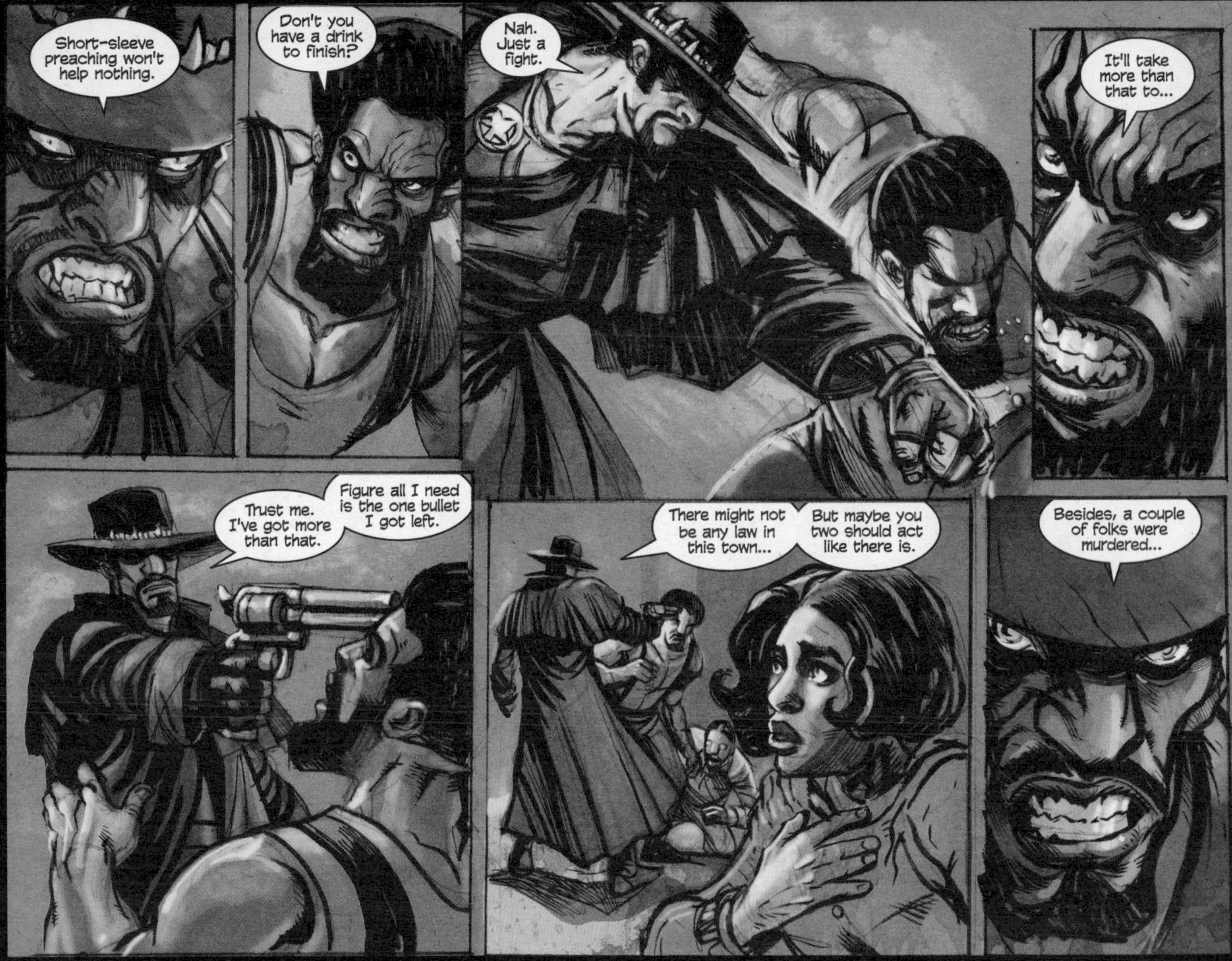
Short-sleeve preaching won't help nothing.
Don't you have a drink to finish?
Nah. Just a fight.
It'll take more than that to...
Trust me. I've got more than that.
Figure all I need is the one bullet I got left.
There might not be any law in this town...
But maybe you two should act like there is.
Besides, a couple of folks were murdered...

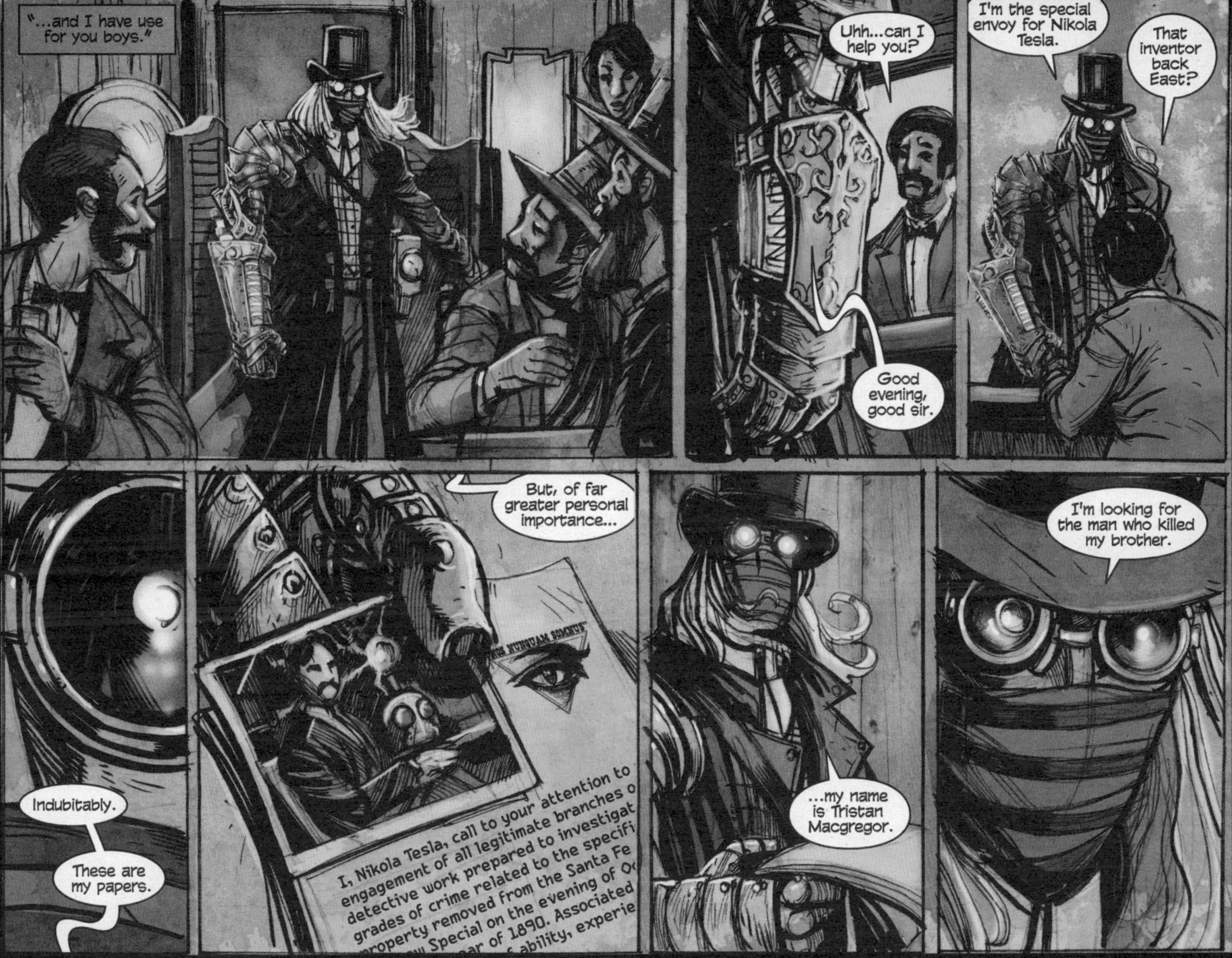
"...and I have use for you boys."
Uhh...can I help you?
Good evening, good sir.
I'm the special envoy for Nikola Tesla.
That inventor back East?
Indubitably.
These are my papers.
But, of far greater personal importance...
I, Nikola Tesla, call to your attention to
engagement of all legitimate branches
detective work prepared to investigat
grades of crime related to the specifi
property removed from the Santa Fe
Special on the evening of
of 1890. Associated
...my name is Tristan Macgregor.
I'm looking for the man who killed my brother.

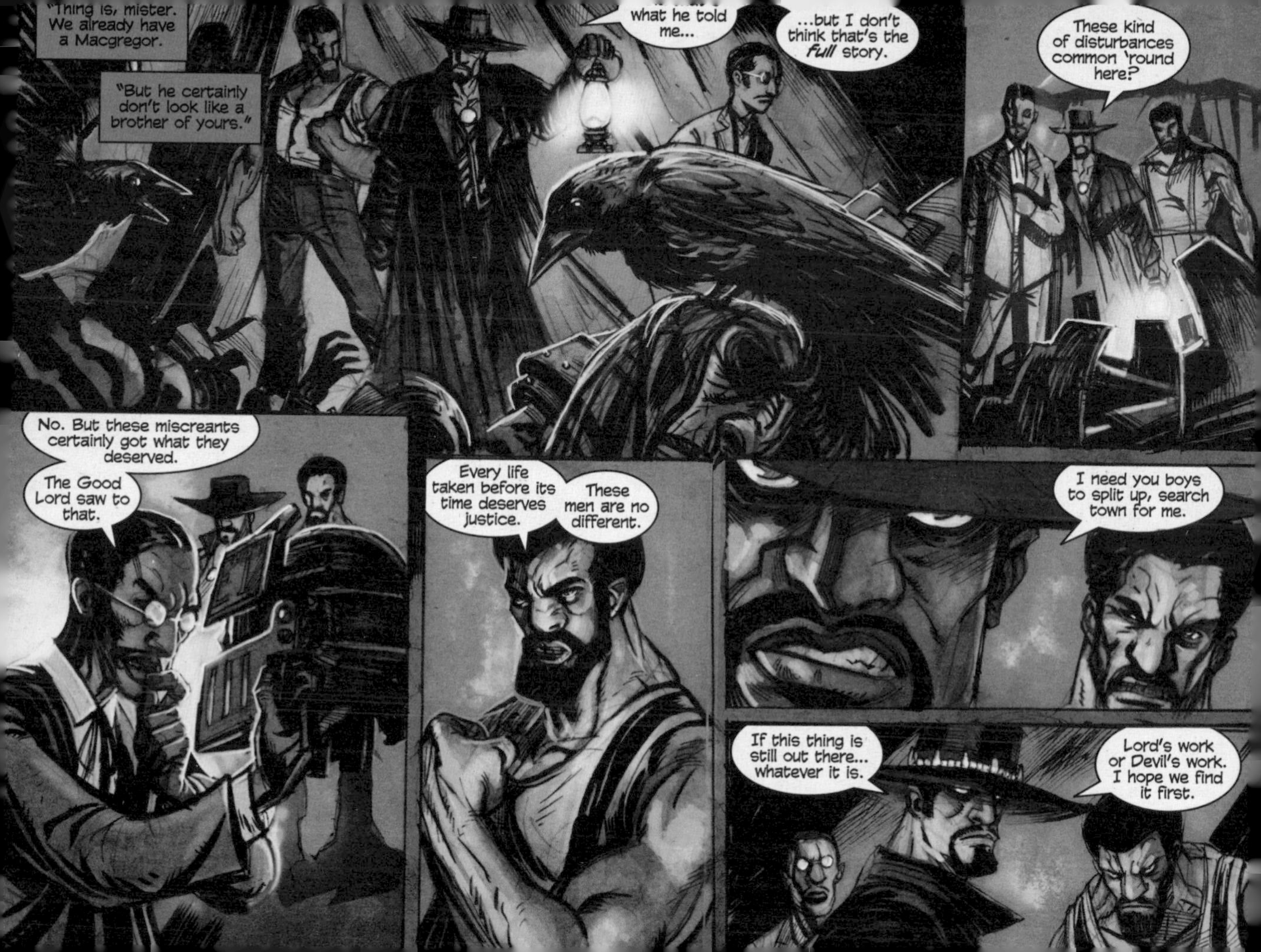
"Thing is, mister. We already have a Macgregor.
"But he certainly don't look like a brother of yours."
what he told me...
...but I don't think that's the *full* story.
These kind of disturbances common 'round here?
No. But these miscreants certainly got what they deserved.
The Good Lord saw to that.
Every life taken before its time deserves justice.
These men are no different.
I need you boys to split up, search town for me.
If this thing is still out there... whatever it is.
Lord's work or Devil's work. I hope we find it first.

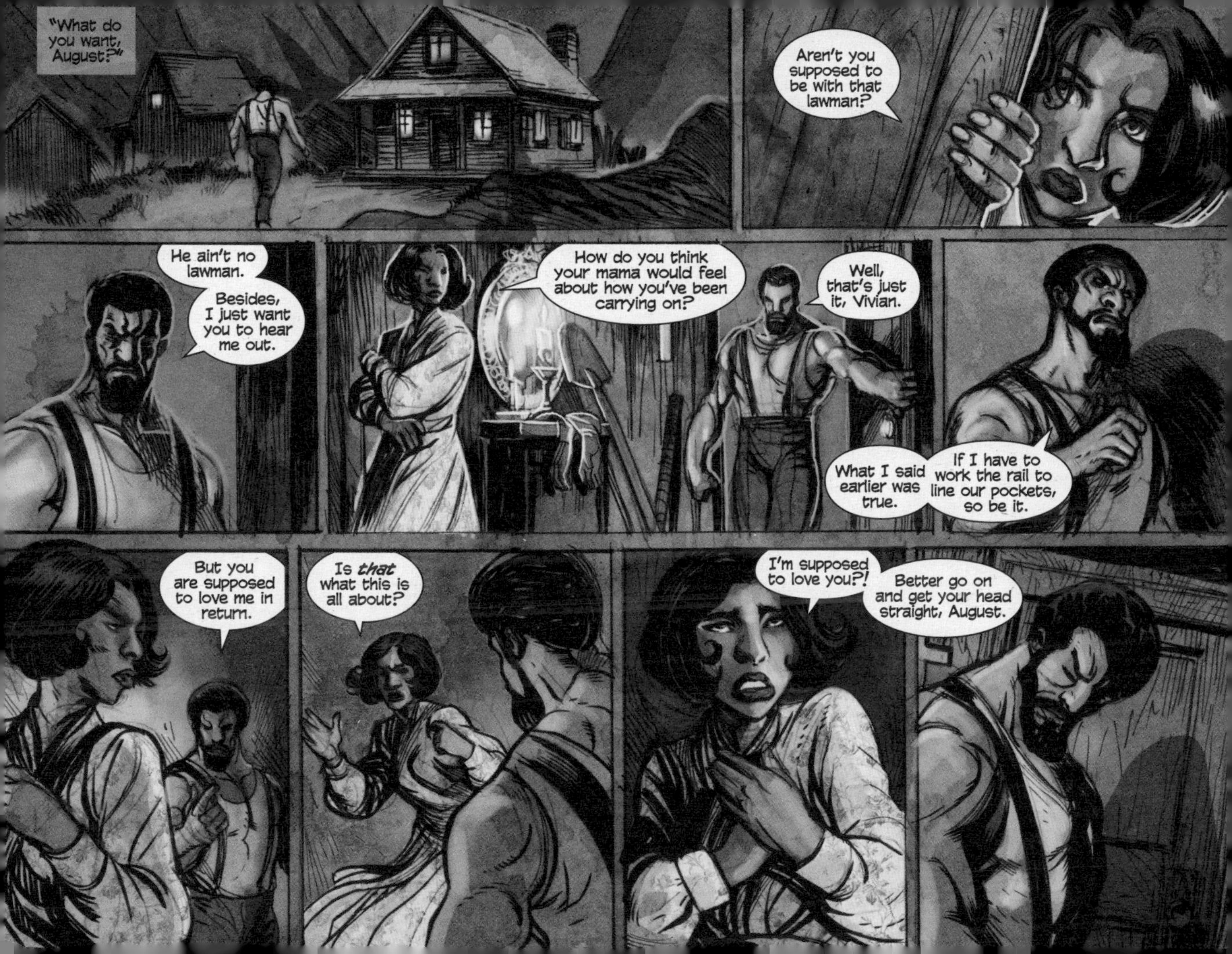
"What do you want, August?"
Aren't you supposed to be with that lawman?
He ain't no lawman.
Besides, I just want you to hear me out.
How do you think your mama would feel about how you've been carrying on?
Well, that's just it, Vivian.
What I said earlier was true.
If I have to work the rail to line our pockets, so be it.
But you are supposed to love me in return.
Is *that* what this is all about?
I'm supposed to love you?!
Better go on and get your head straight, August.

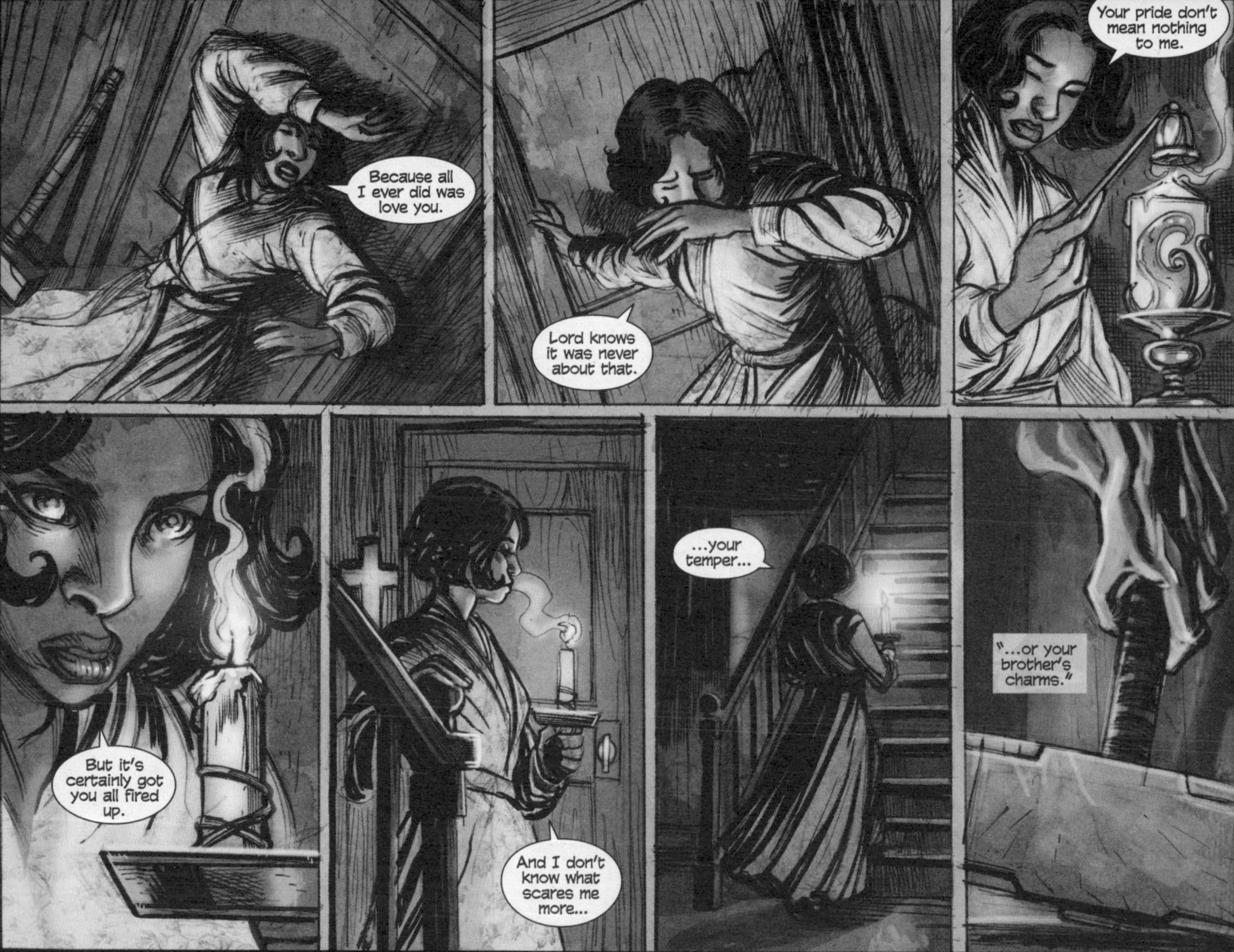
Because all I ever did was love you.
Lord knows it was never about that.
Your pride don't mean nothing to me.
But it's certainly got you all fired up.
And I don't know what scares me more...
...your temper...
"...or your brother's charms."

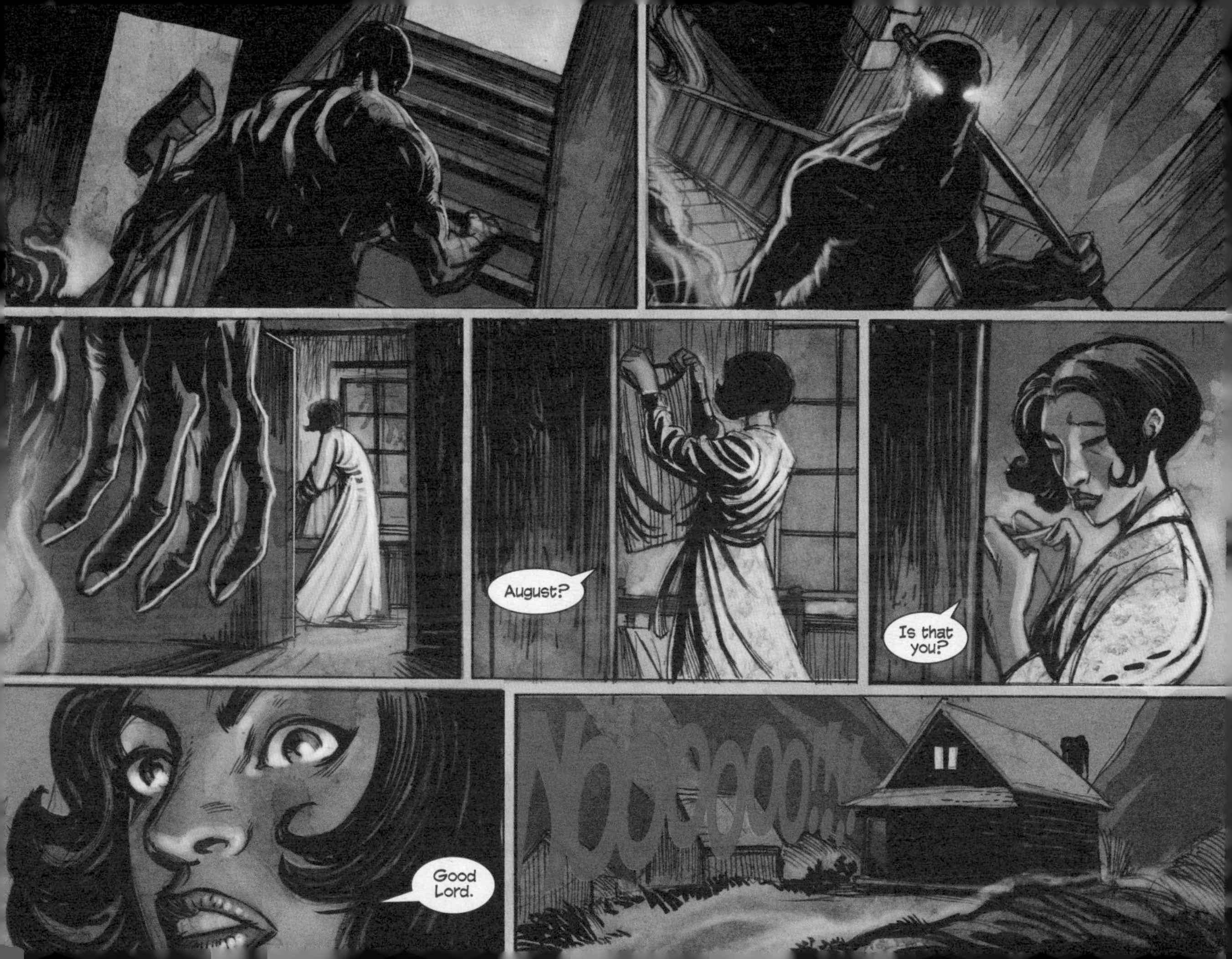
August?
Is that you?
Good Lord.

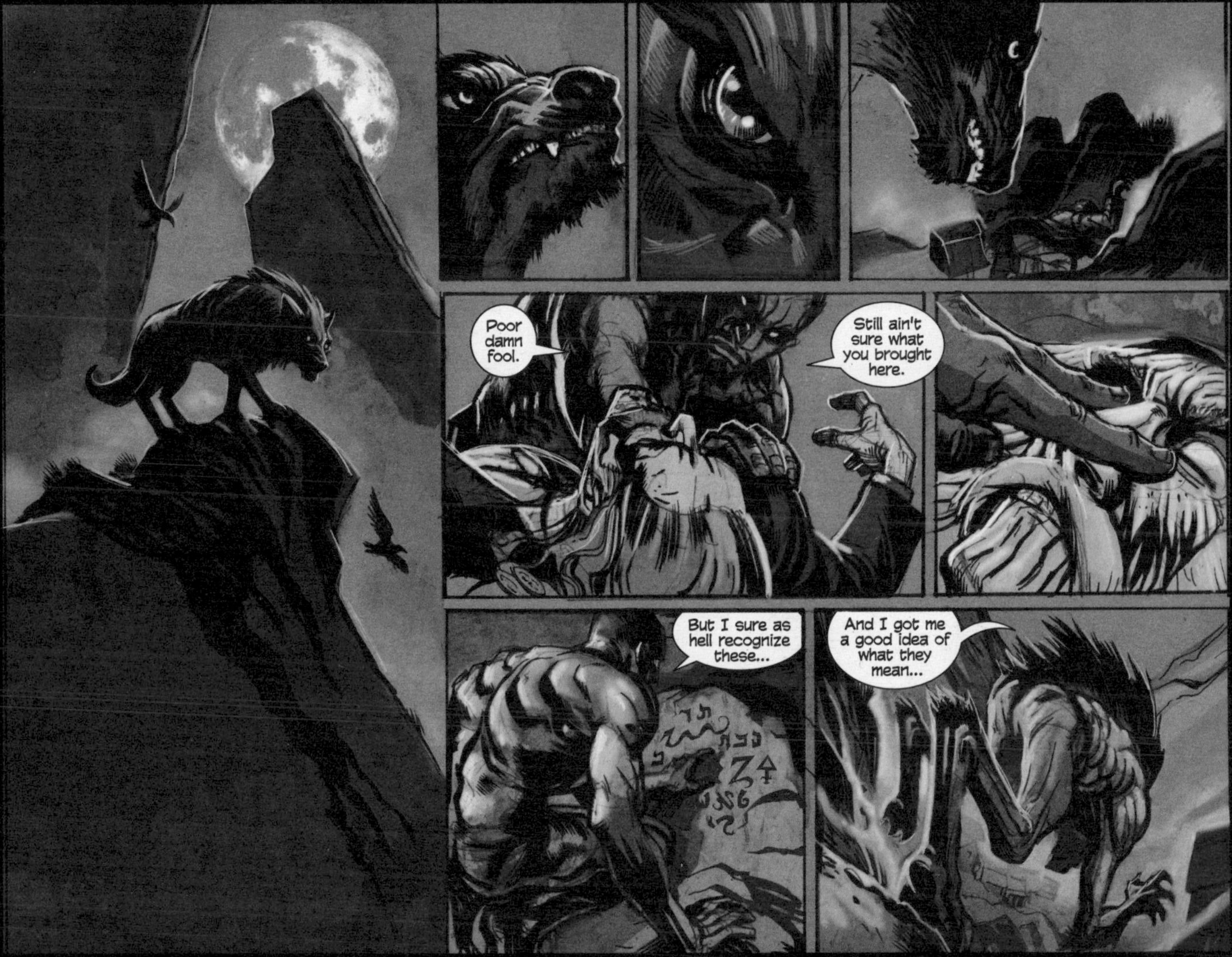
Poor damn fool.
Still ain't sure what you brought here.
But I sure as hell recognize these...
And I got me a good idea of what they mean...

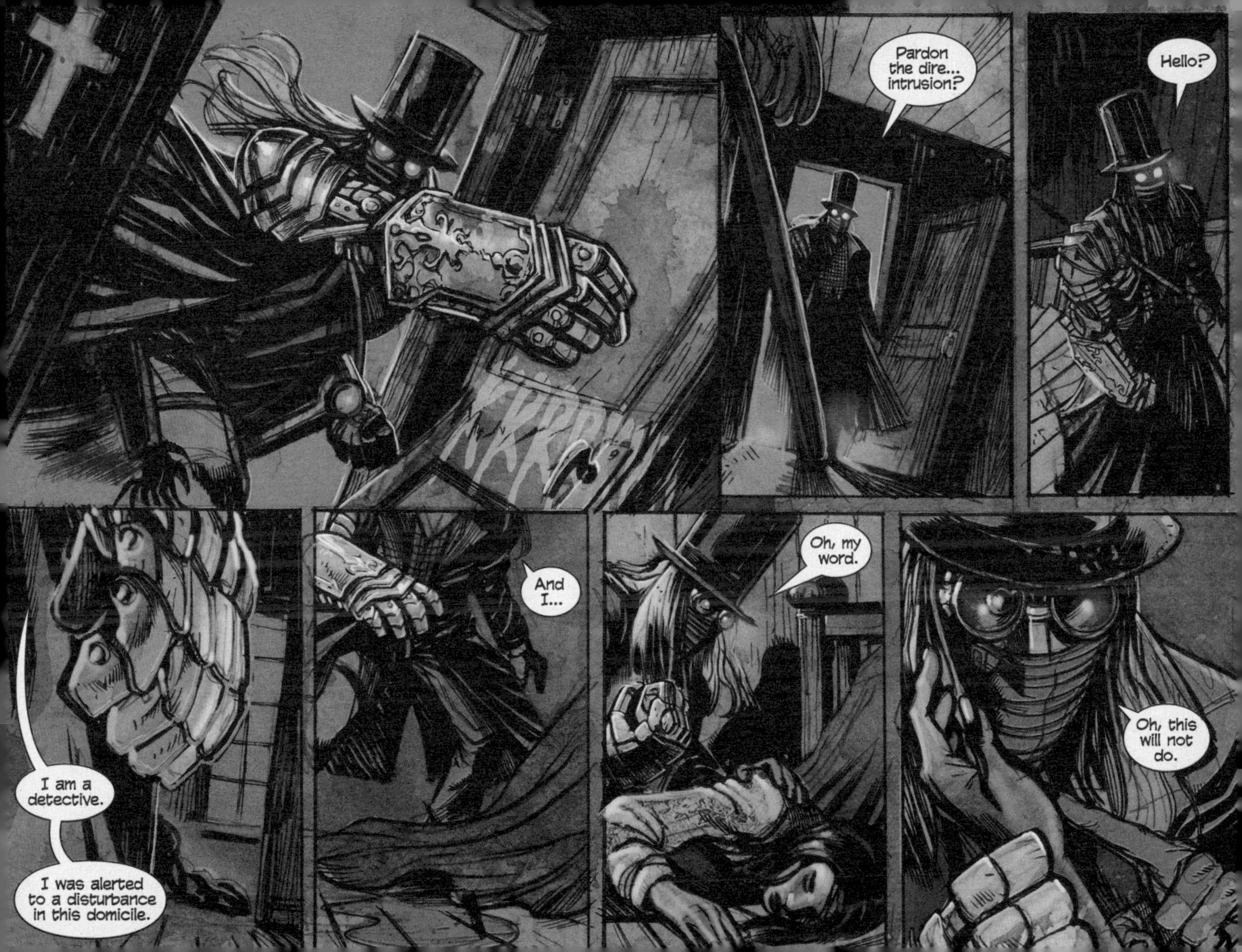

Pardon the dire... intrusion?
Hello?
I am a detective.
I was alerted to a disturbance in this domicile.
And I...
Oh, my word.
Oh, this will not do.

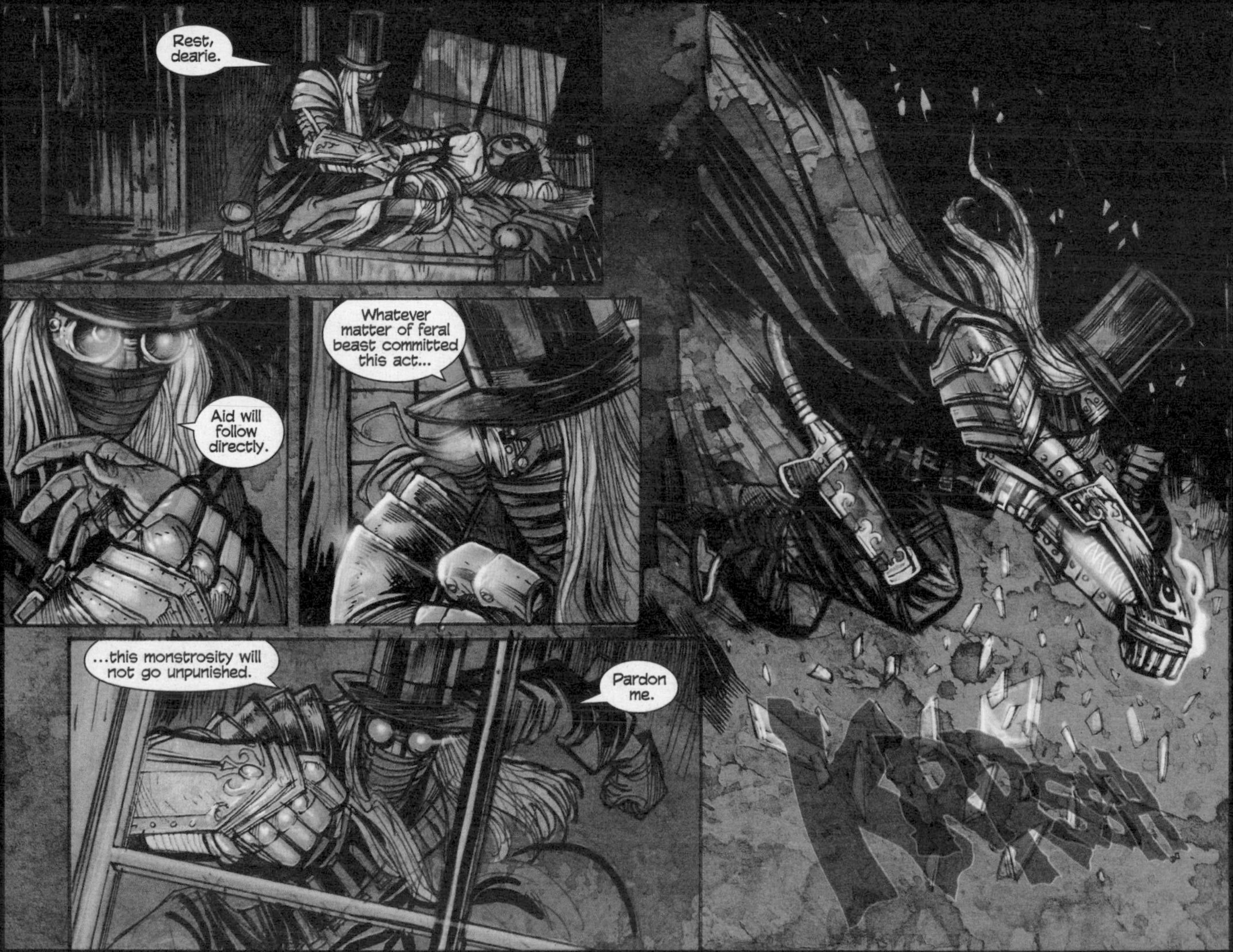
Rest, dearie.
Aid will follow directly.
Whatever matter of feral beast committed this act...
...this monstrosity will not go unpunished.
Pardon me.

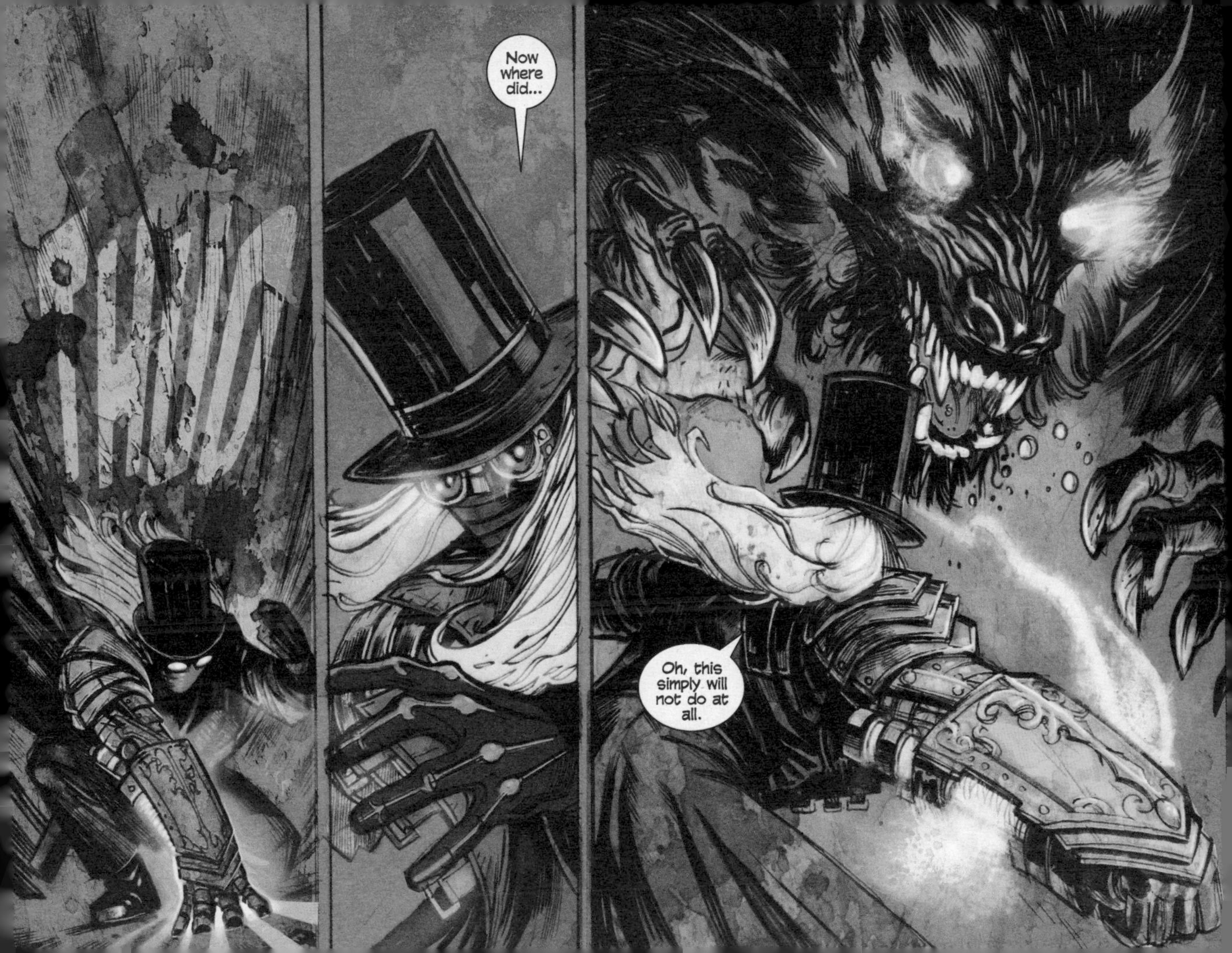
Now where did...
Oh, this simply will not do at all.

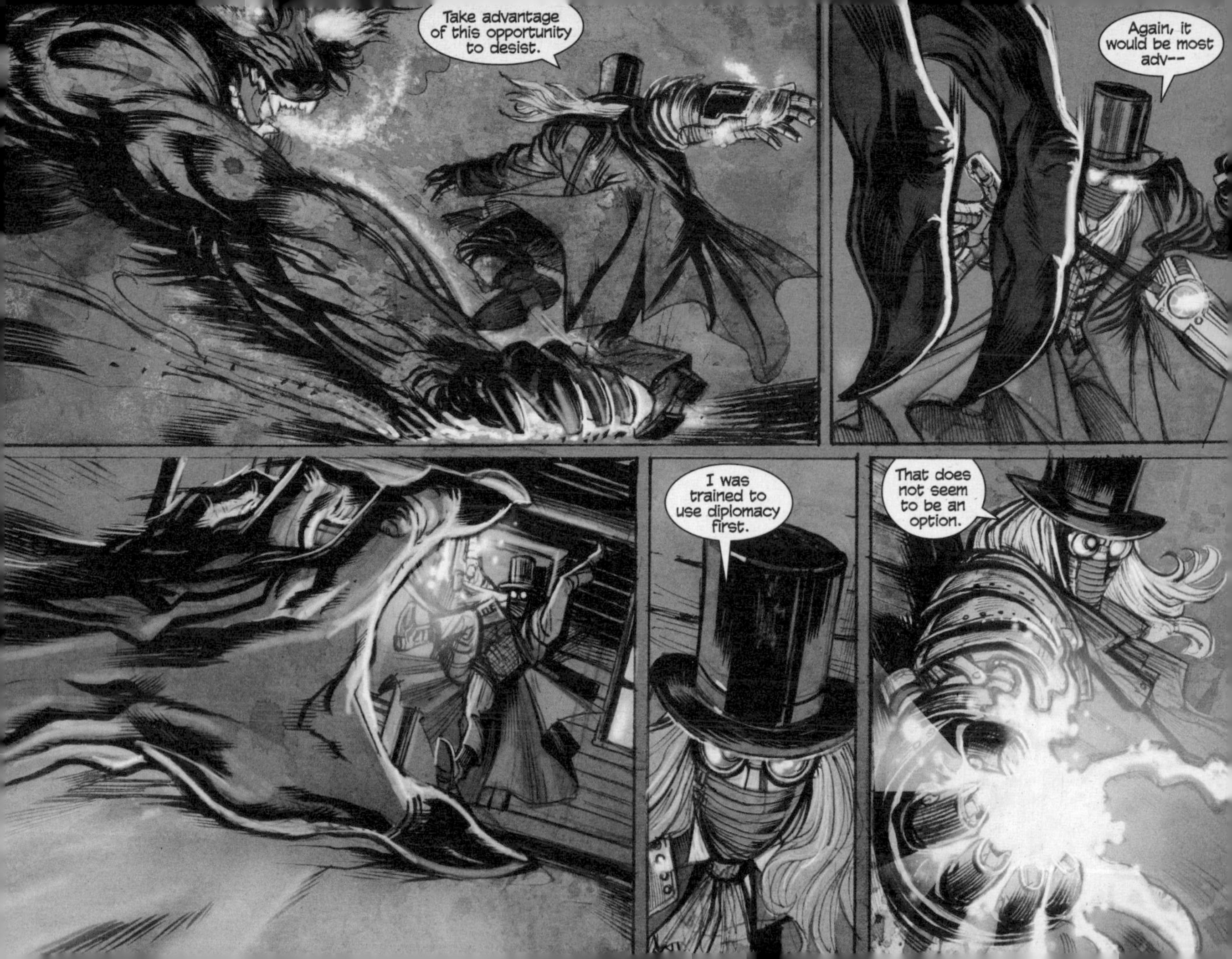
Take advantage of this opportunity to desist.
Again, it would be most adv--
I was trained to use diplomacy first.
That does not seem to be an option.

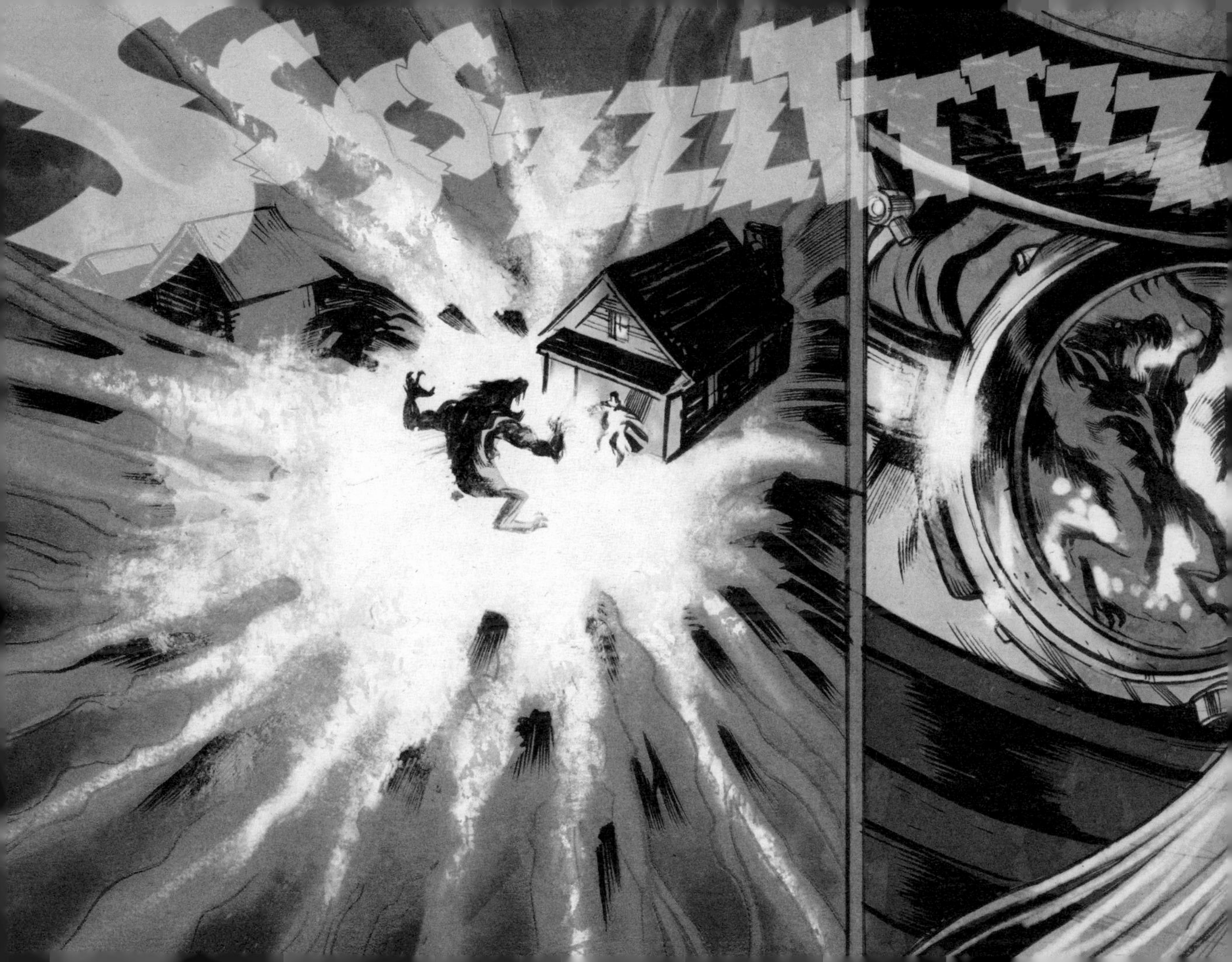
SSSZZZT

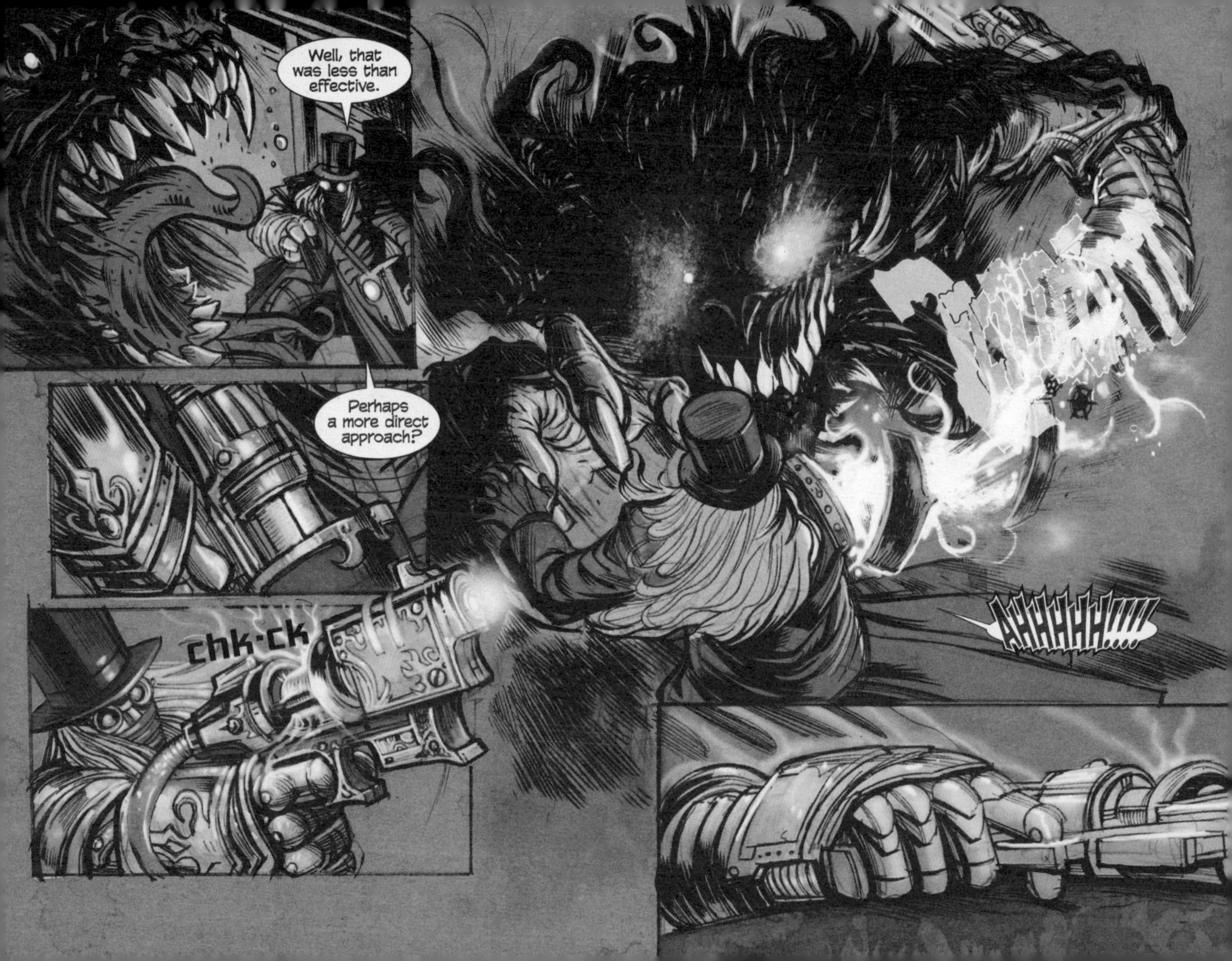
Well, that was less than effective.
Perhaps a more direct approach?
chk-ck
AHHHHH!!!!

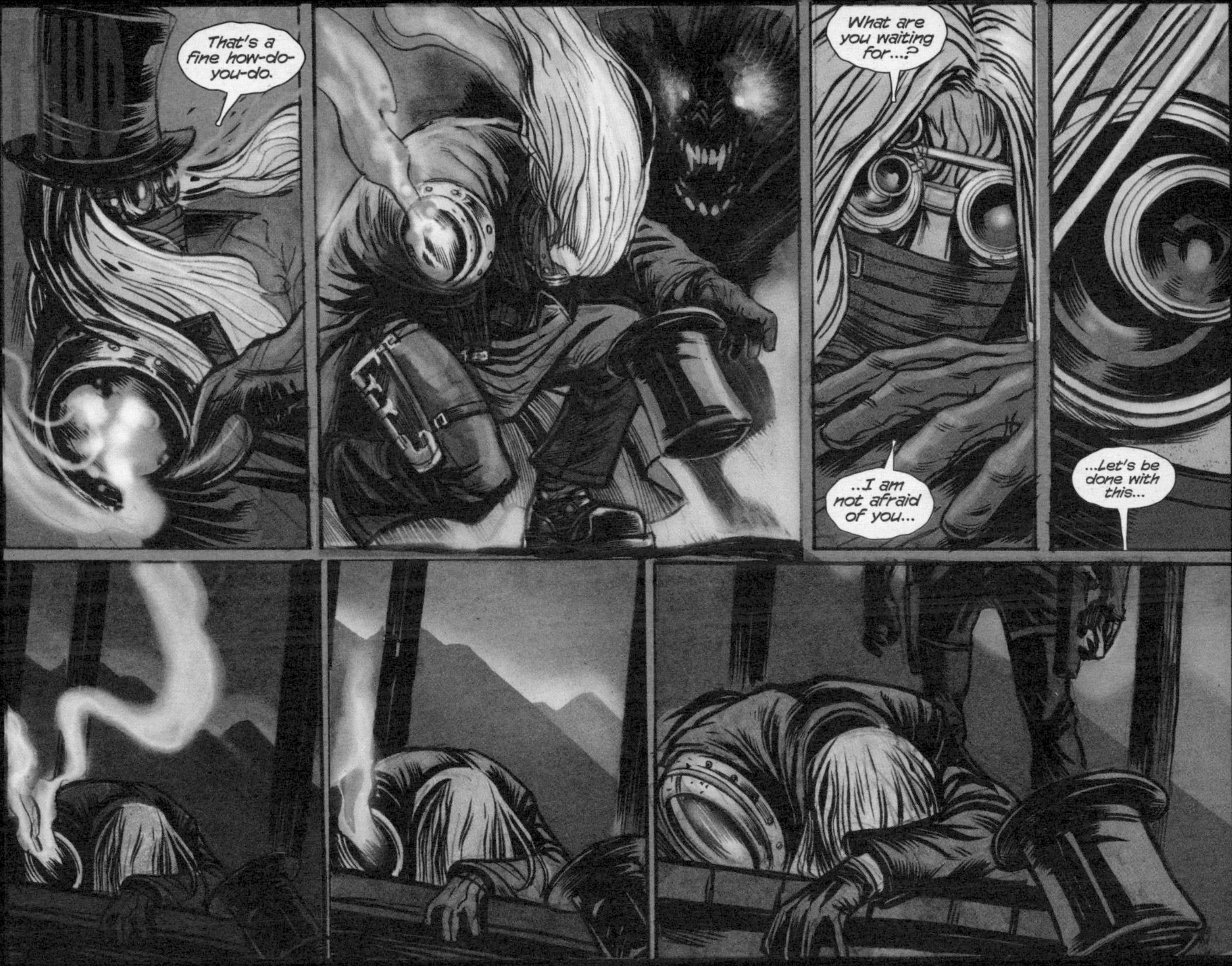
That's a fine how-do-you-do.
What are you waiting for...?
...I am not afraid of you...
...Let's be done with this...

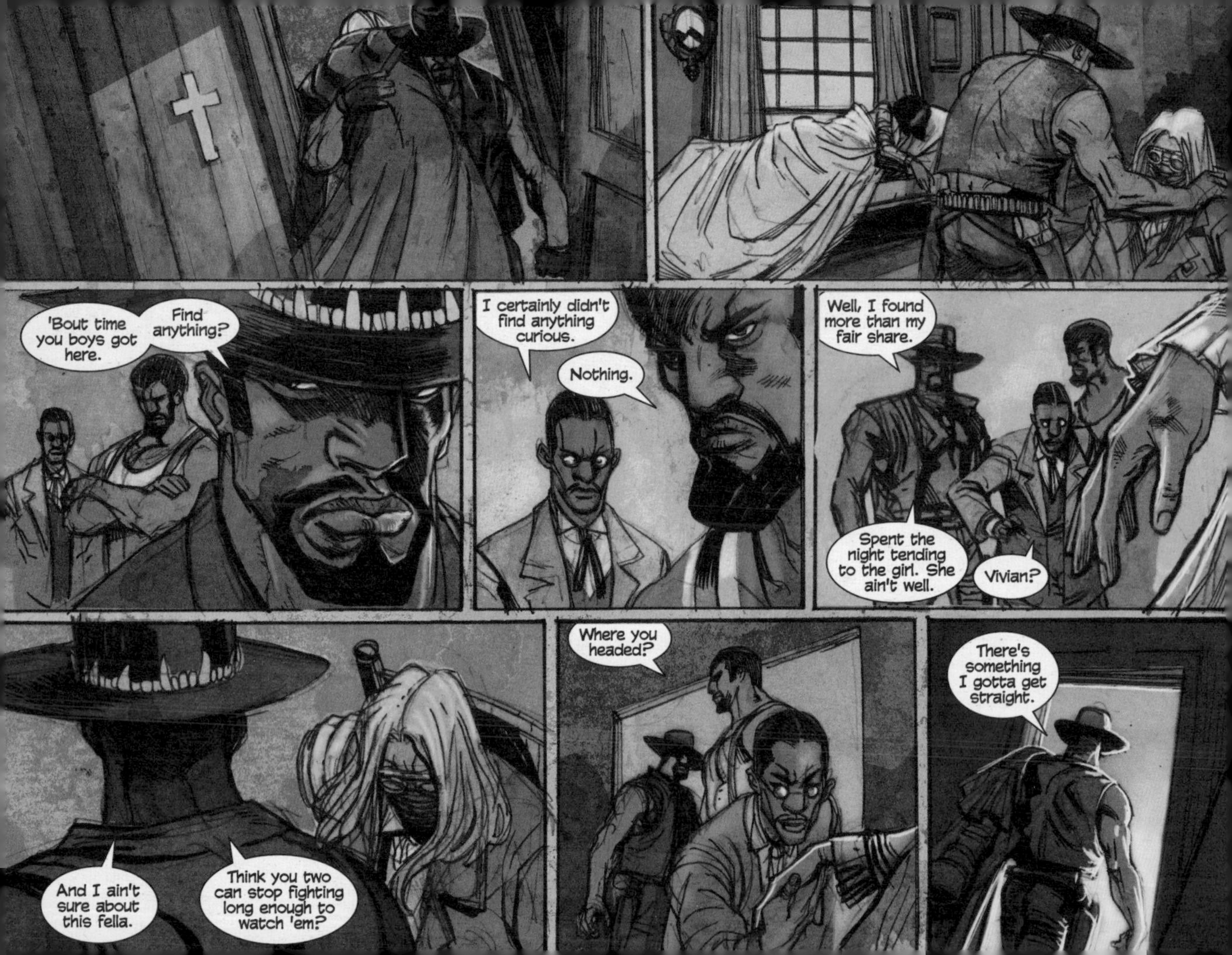
'Bout time you boys got here.
Find anything?
I certainly didn't find anything curious.
Nothing.
Well, I found more than my fair share.
Spent the night tending to the girl. She ain't well.
Vivian?
And I ain't sure about this fella.
Think you two can stop fighting long enough to watch 'em?
Where you headed?
There's something I gotta get straight.

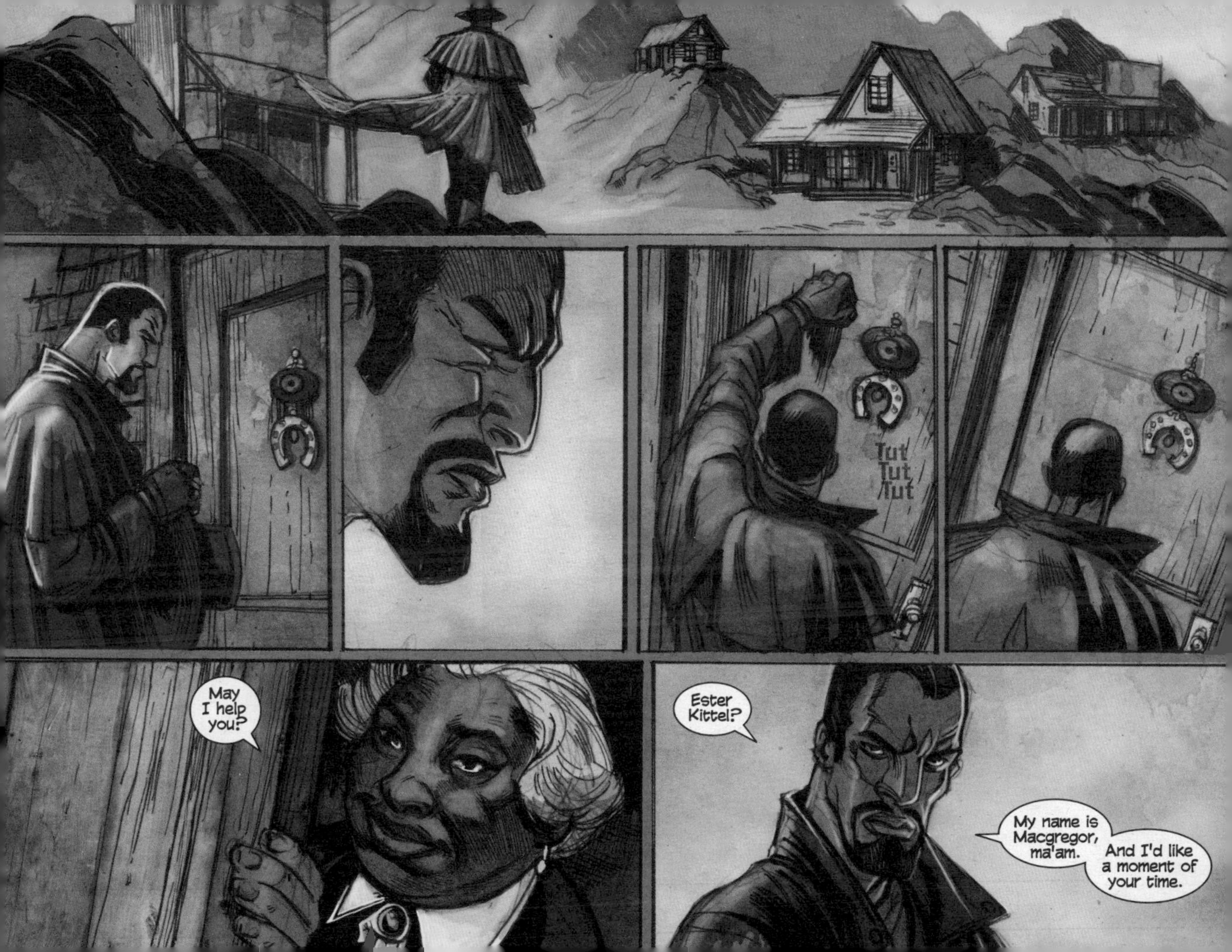
Tut
Tut
Tut
May I help you?
Ester Kittel?
My name is Macgregor, ma'am.
And I'd like a moment of your time.

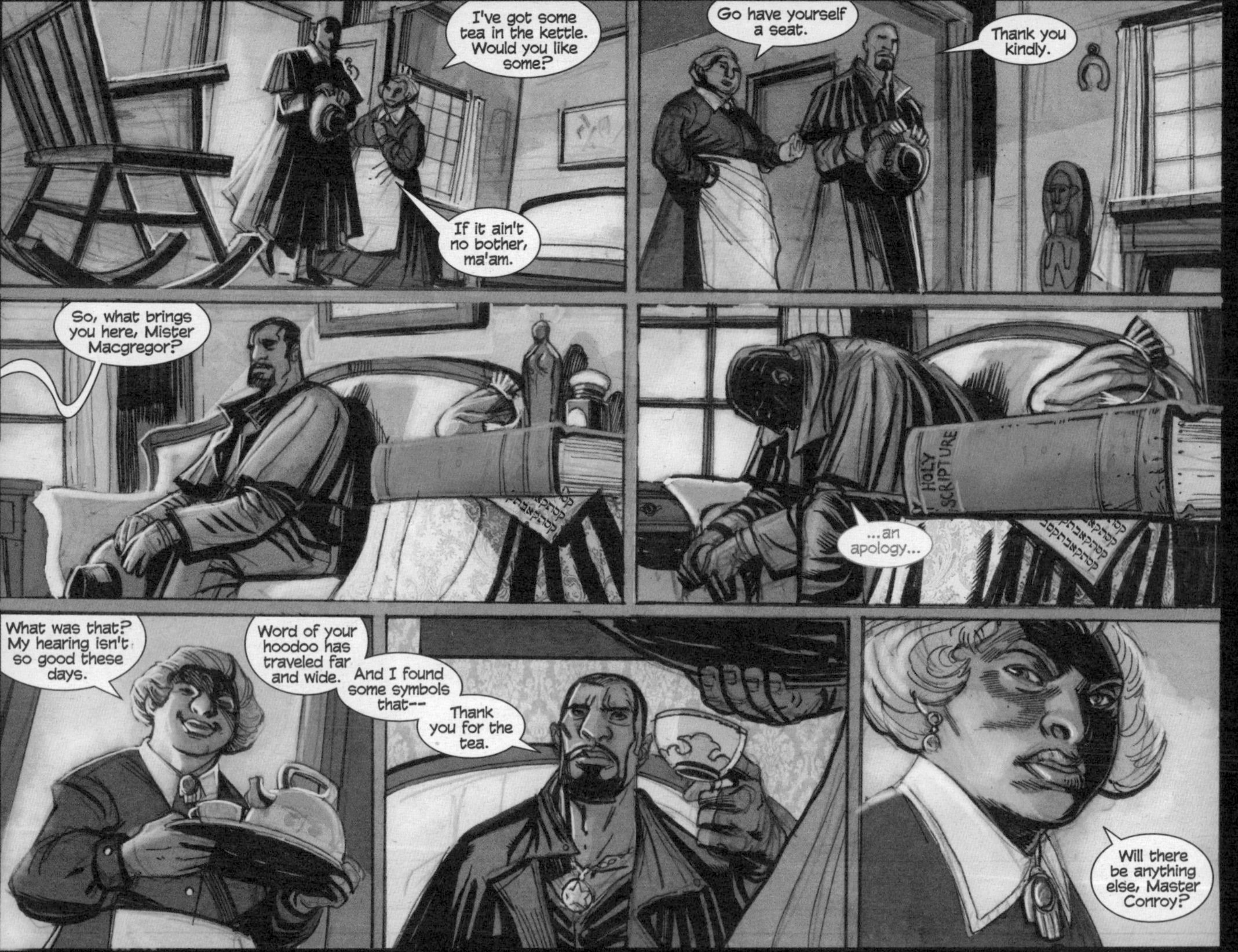
I've got some tea in the kettle. Would you like some?
If it ain't no bother, ma'am.
Go have yourself a seat.
Thank you kindly.
So, what brings you here, Mister Macgregor?
...an apology...
HOLY SCRIPTURE
What was that? My hearing isn't so good these days.
Word of your hoodoo has traveled far and wide.
And I found some symbols that--
Thank you for the tea.
Will there be anything else, Master Conroy?

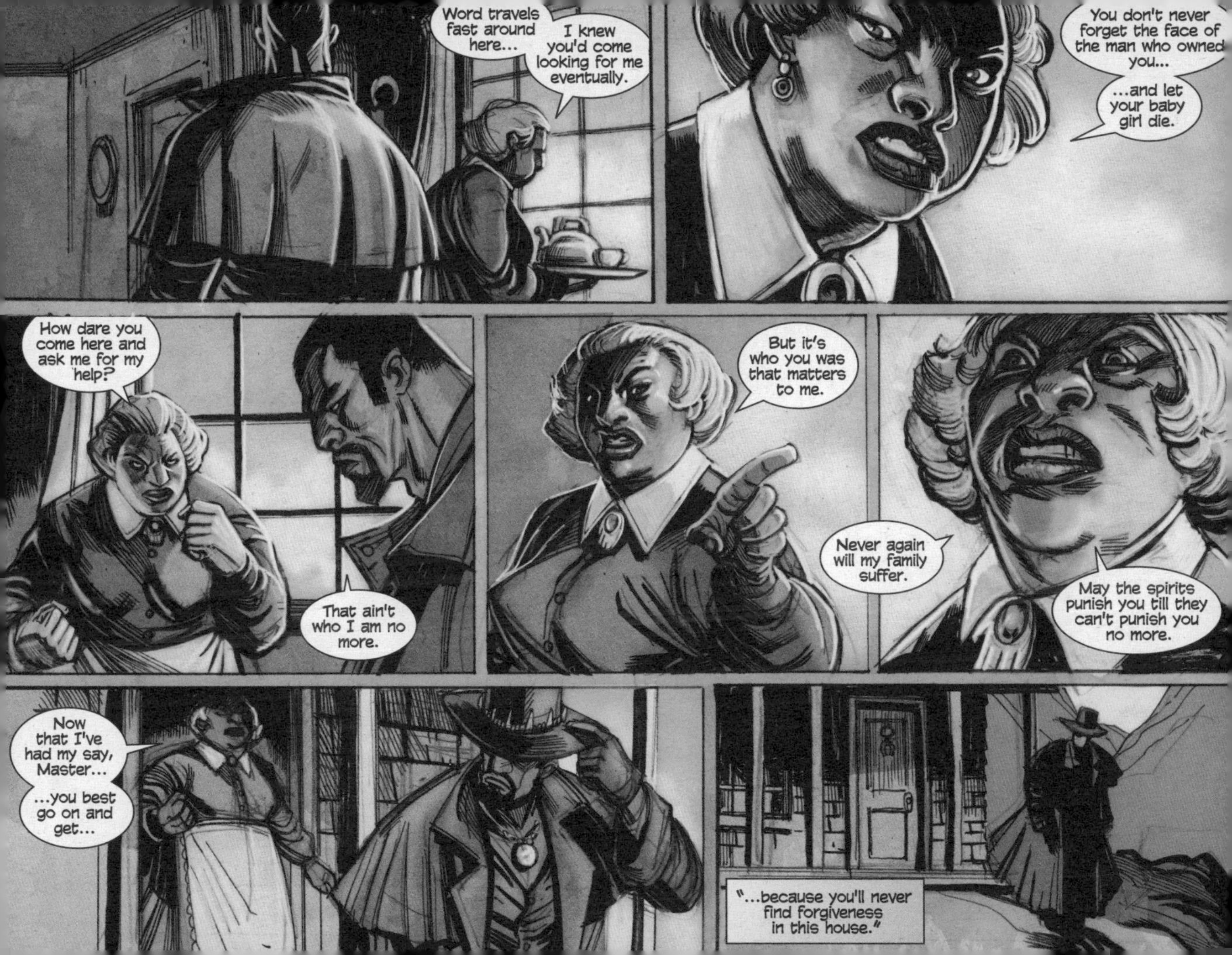
Word travels fast around here...
I knew you'd come looking for me eventually.
You don't never forget the face of the man who owned you...
...and let your baby girl die.
How dare you come here and ask me for my help?
That ain't who I am no more.
But it's who you was that matters to me.
Never again will my family suffer.
May the spirits punish you till they can't punish you no more.
Now that I've had my say, Master...
...you best go on and get...
"...because you'll never find forgiveness in this house."

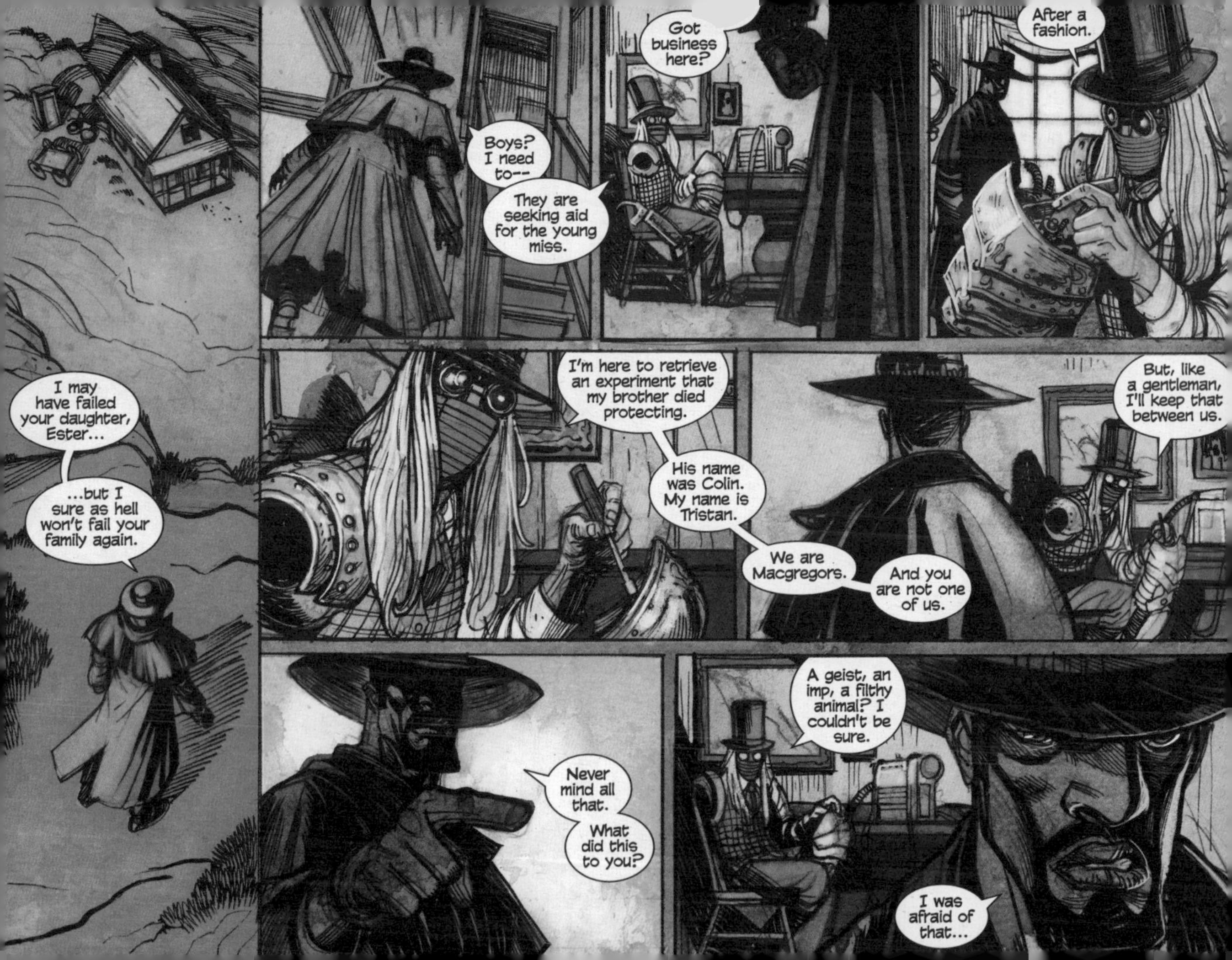
Boys? I need to--
They are seeking aid for the young miss.
Got business here?
After a fashion.
I may have failed your daughter, Ester...
...but I sure as hell won't fail your family again.
I'm here to retrieve an experiment that my brother died protecting.
His name was Colin. My name is Tristan.
We are Macgregors.
And you are not one of us.
But, like a gentleman, I'll keep that between us.
Never mind all that.
What did this to you?
A geist, an imp, a filthy animal? I couldn't be sure.
I was afraid of that...

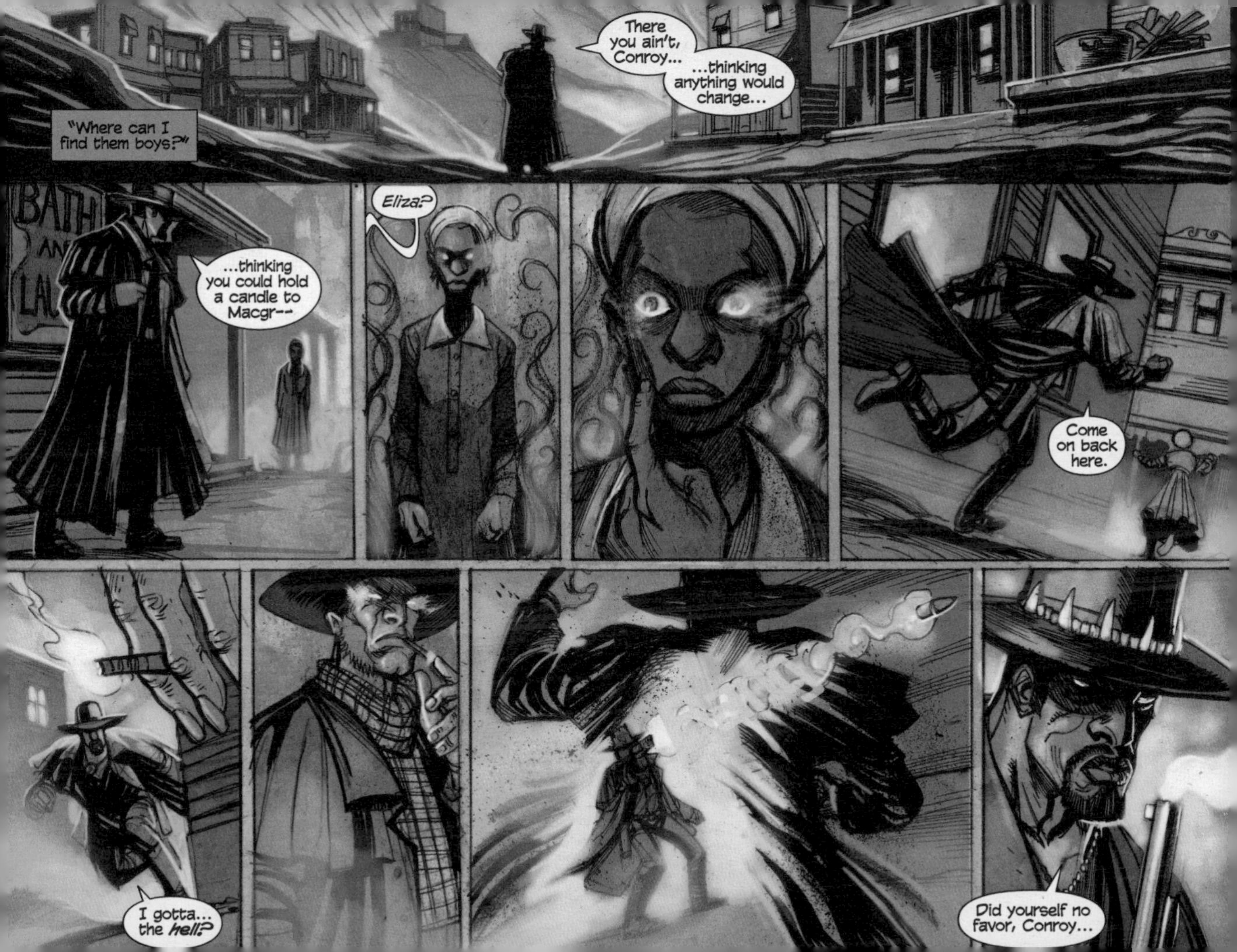
"Where can I find them boys?"
There you ain't, Conroy...
...thinking anything would change...
...thinking you could hold a candle to Macgr--
Eliza?
Come on back here.
I gotta... the *hell?*
Did yourself no favor, Conroy...

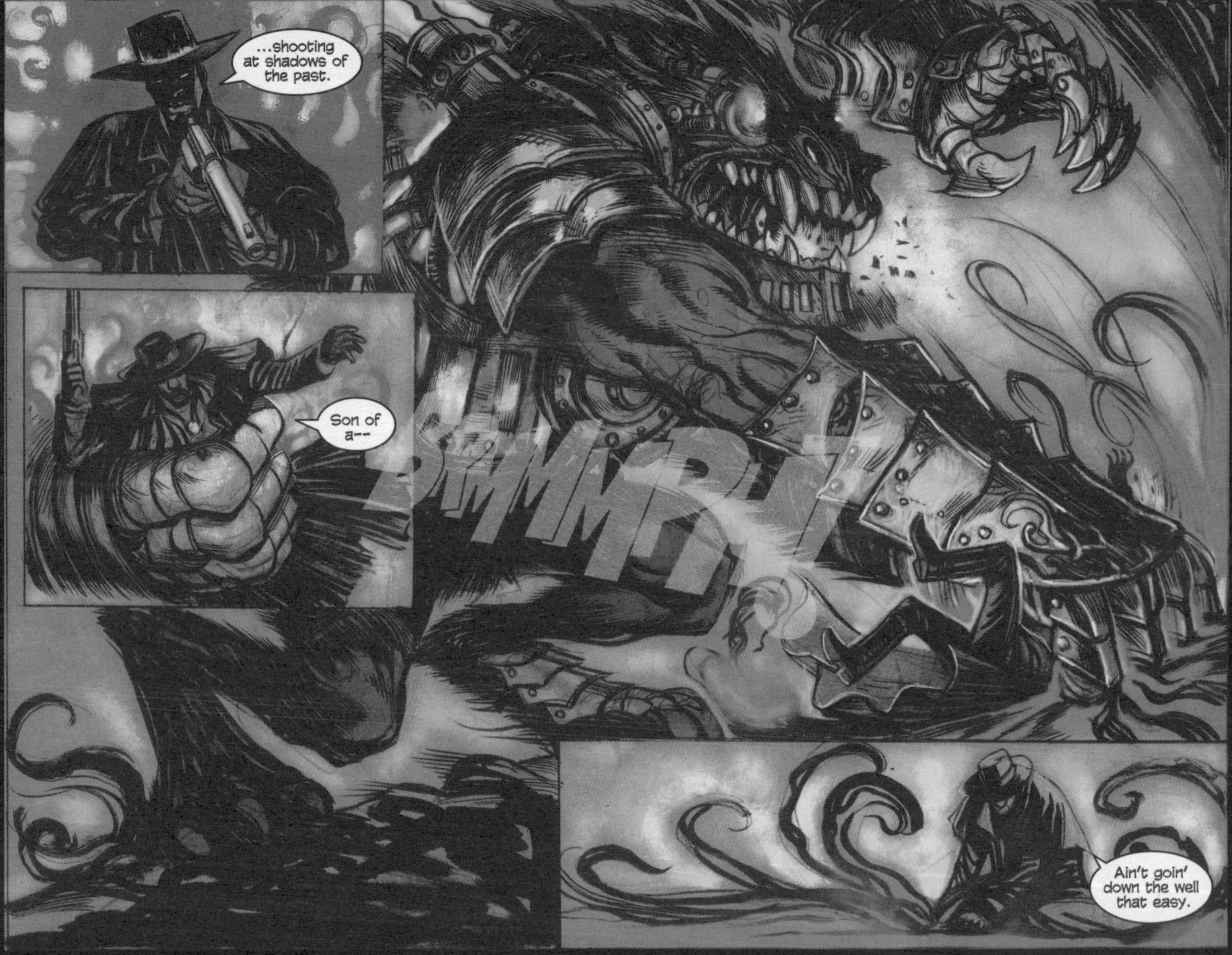
...shooting at shadows of the past.
Son of a--
Ain't goin' down the well that easy.

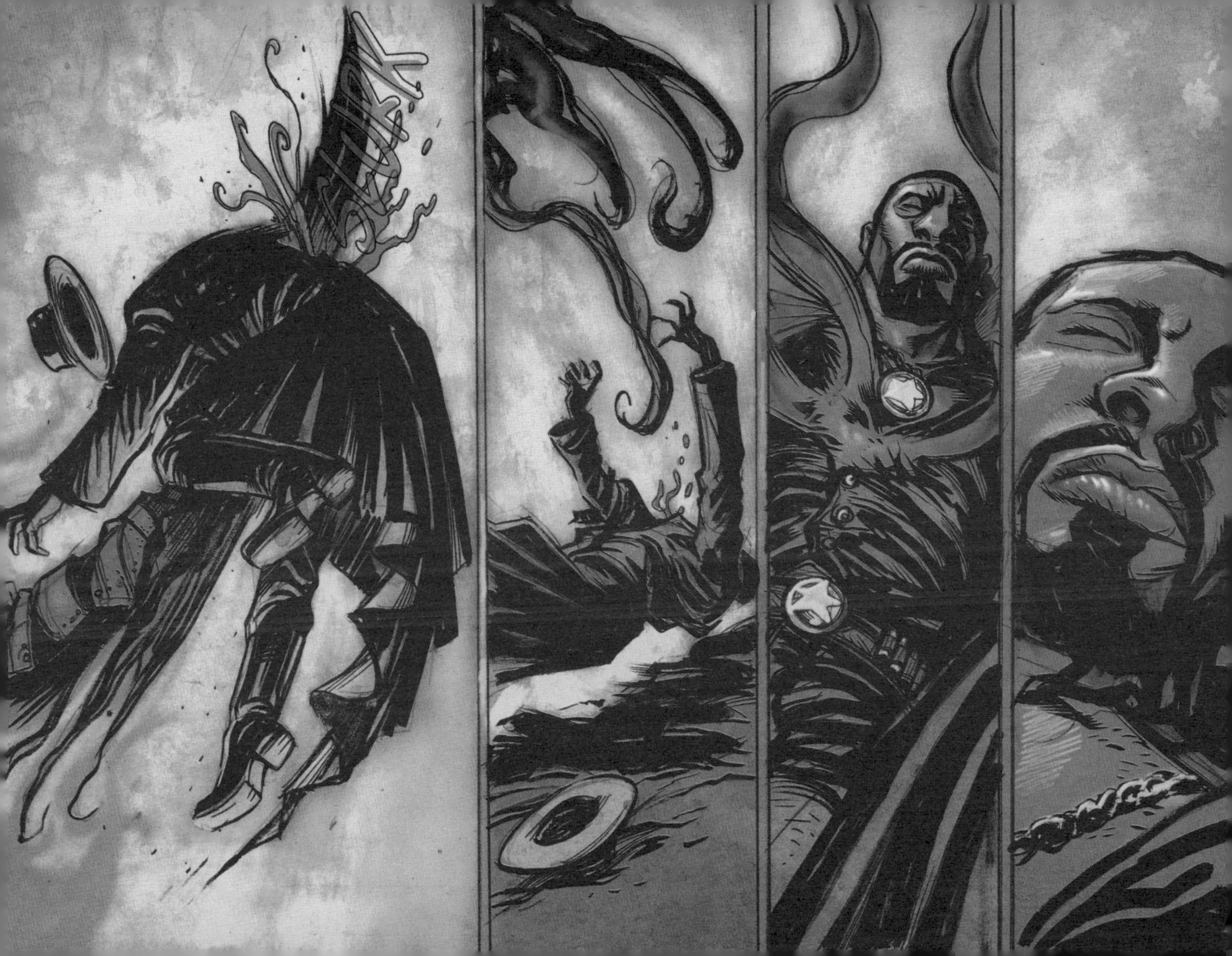

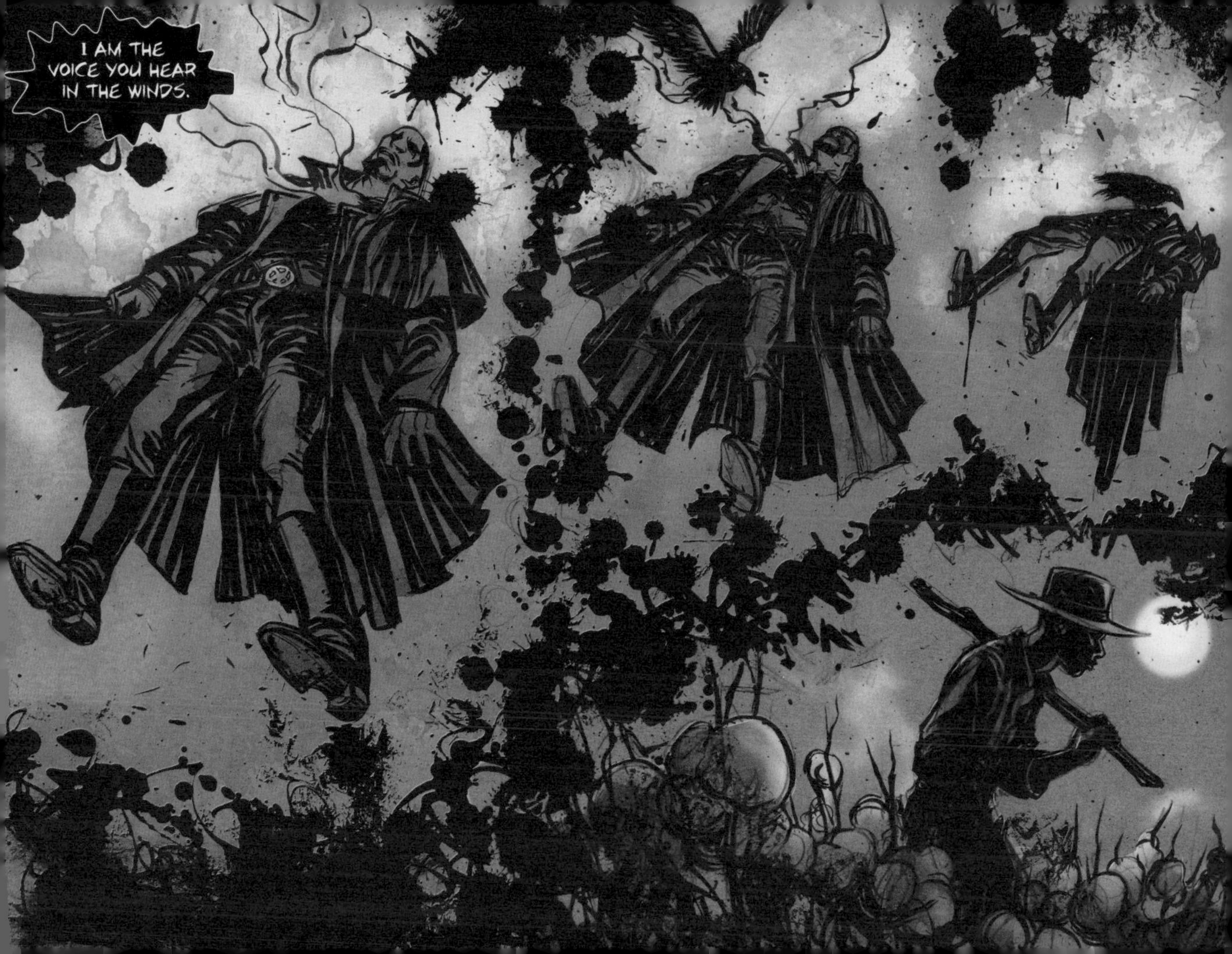
I AM THE VOICE YOU HEAR IN THE WINDS.

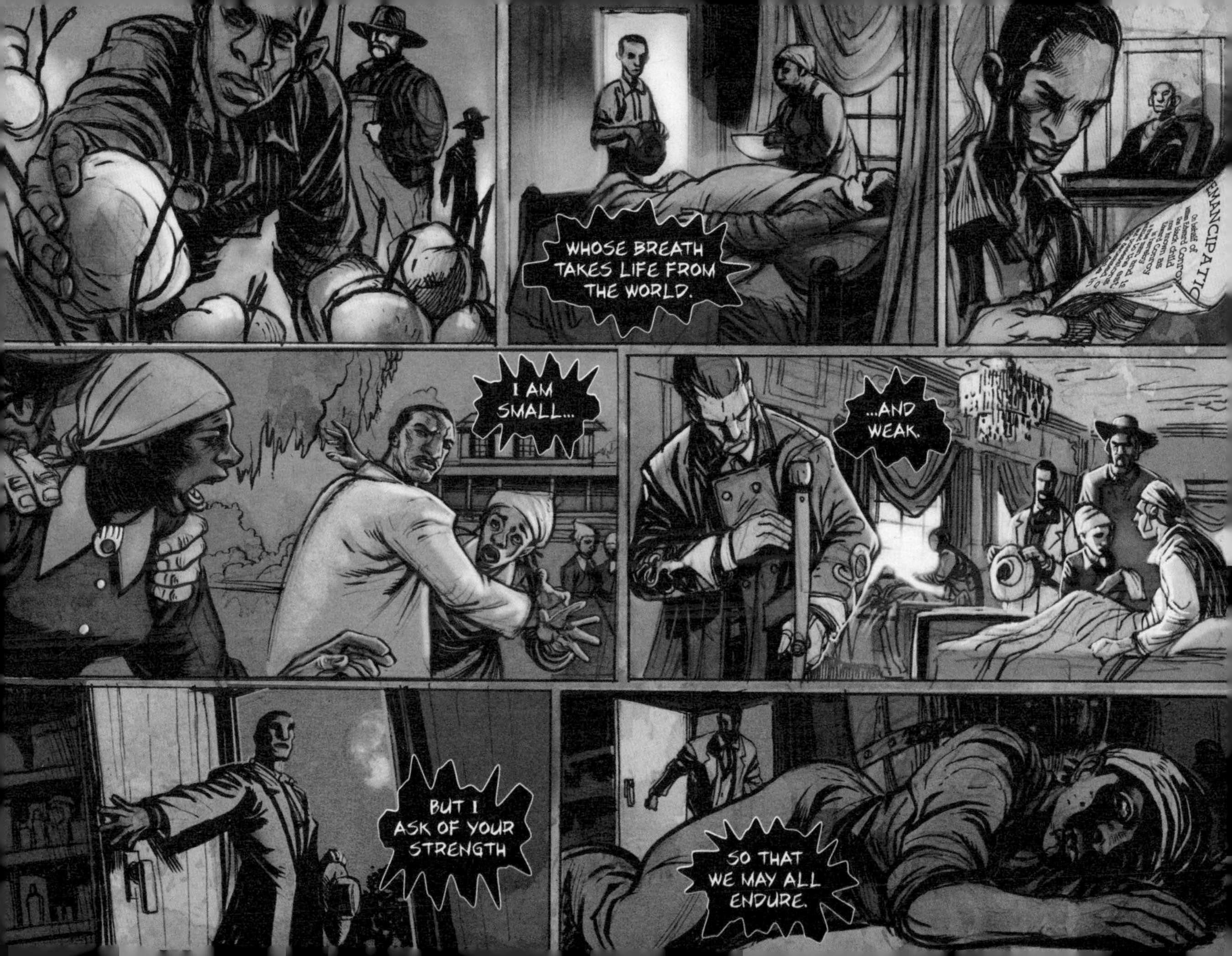
WHOSE BREATH TAKES LIFE FROM THE WORLD.
I AM SMALL...
...AND WEAK.
BUT I ASK OF YOUR STRENGTH
SO THAT WE MAY ALL ENDURE.

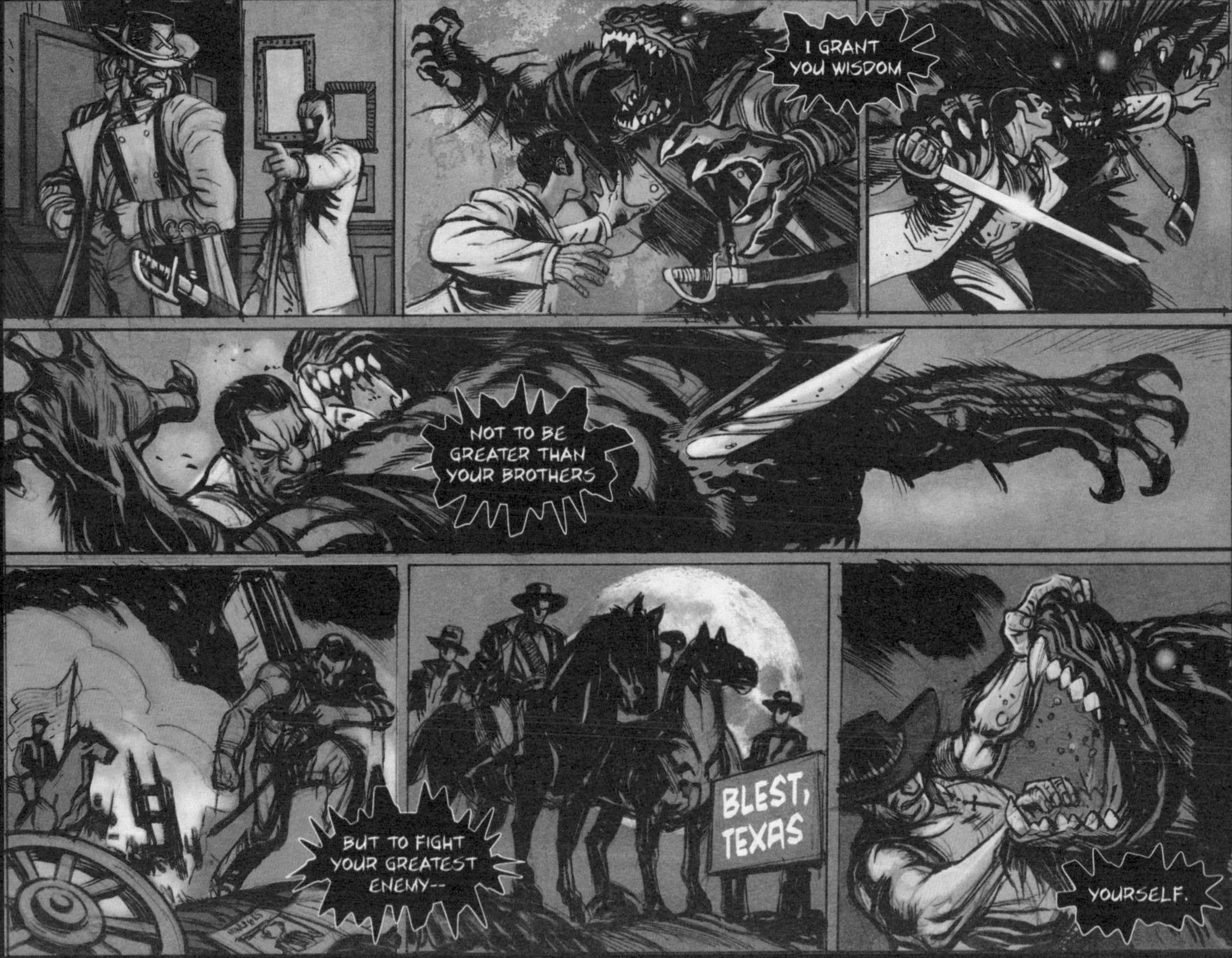
I GRANT YOU WISDOM
NOT TO BE GREATER THAN YOUR BROTHERS
BUT TO FIGHT YOUR GREATEST ENEMY--
BLEST, TEXAS
YOURSELF.

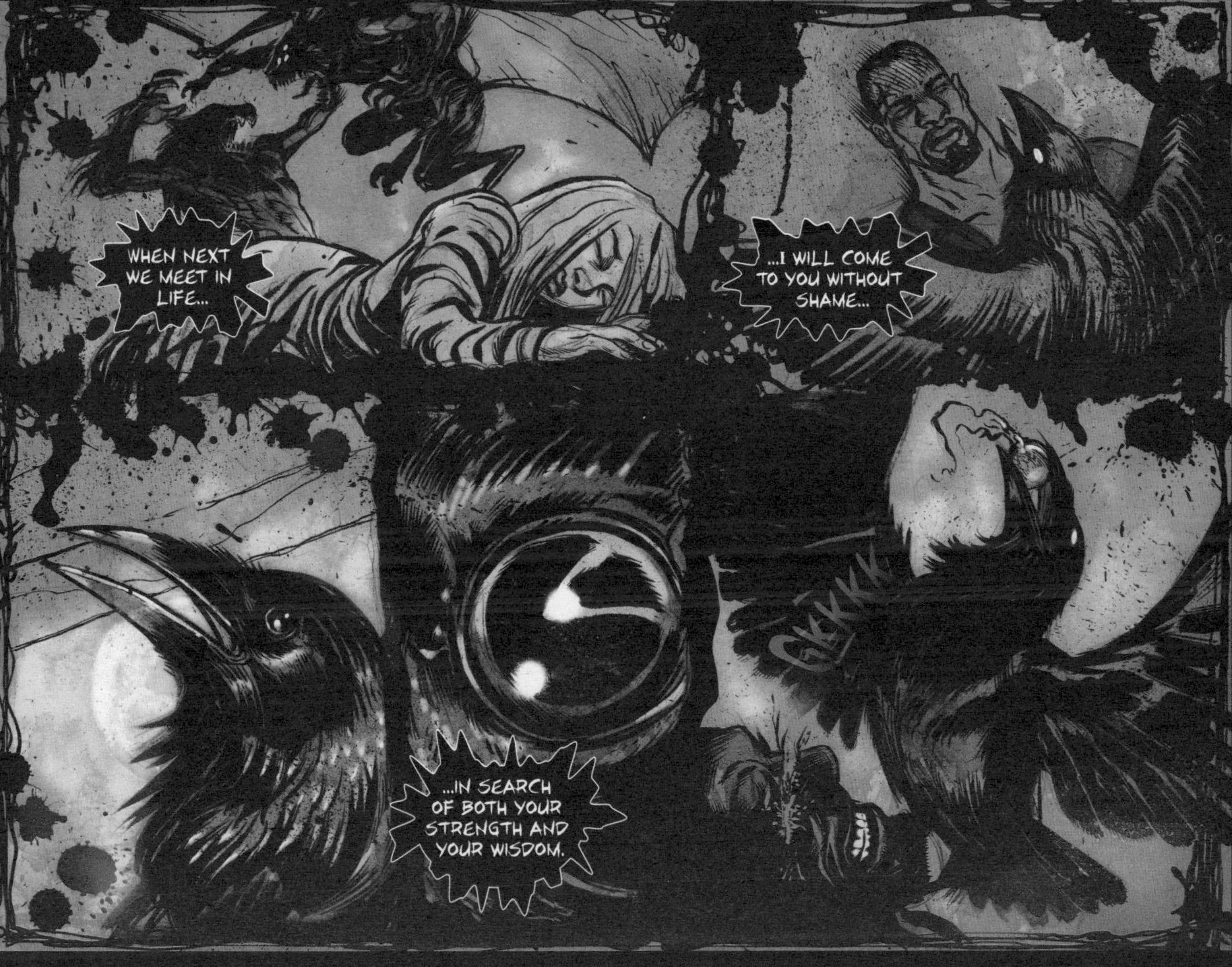
WHEN NEXT WE MEET IN LIFE...
...I WILL COME TO YOU WITHOUT SHAME...
...IN SEARCH OF BOTH YOUR STRENGTH AND YOUR WISDOM.
GKKKK

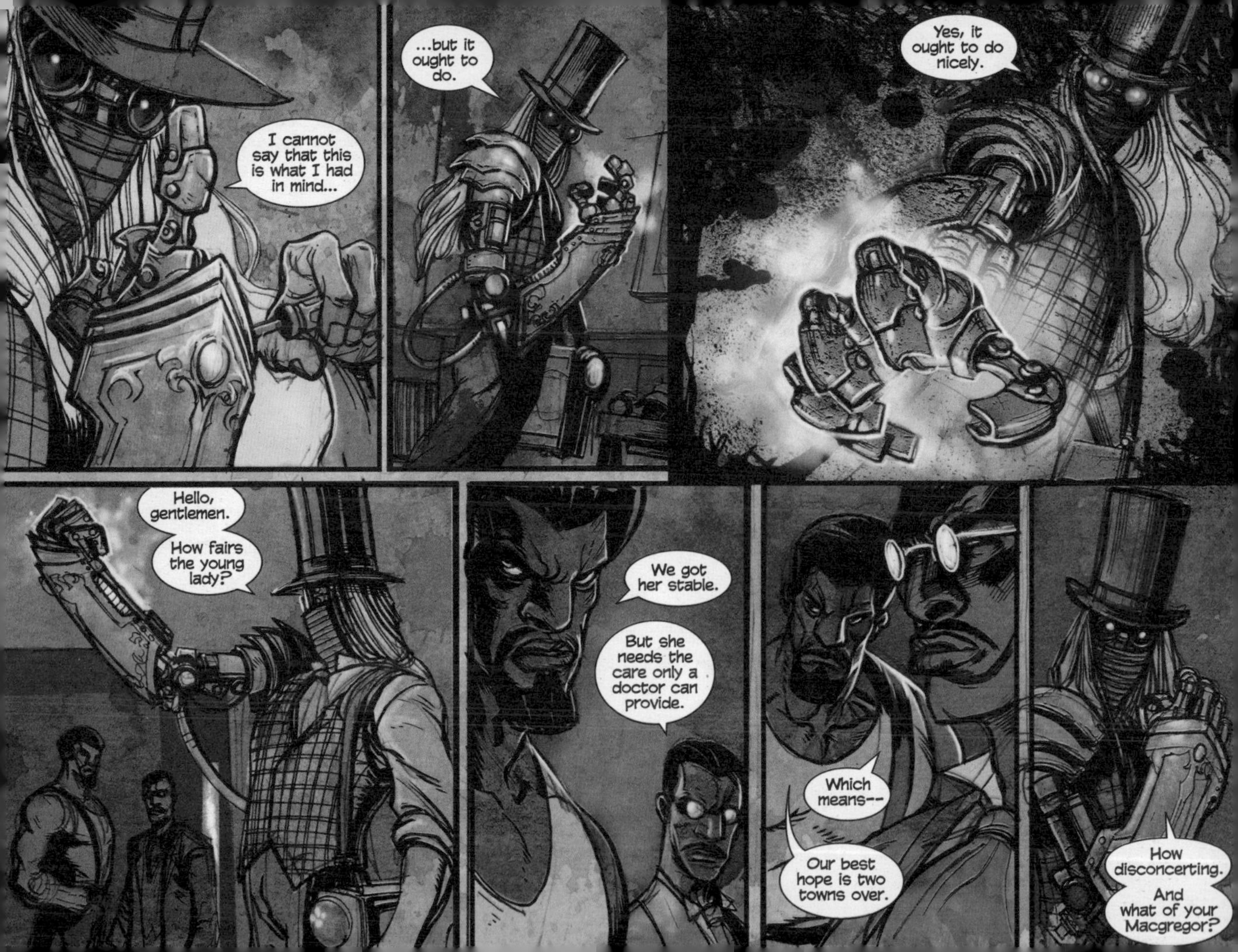
I cannot say that this is what I had in mind...
...but it ought to do.
Yes, it ought to do nicely.
Hello, gentlemen.
How fairs the young lady?
We got her stable.
But she needs the care only a doctor can provide.
Which means--
Our best hope is two towns over.
How disconcerting.
And what of your Macgregor?

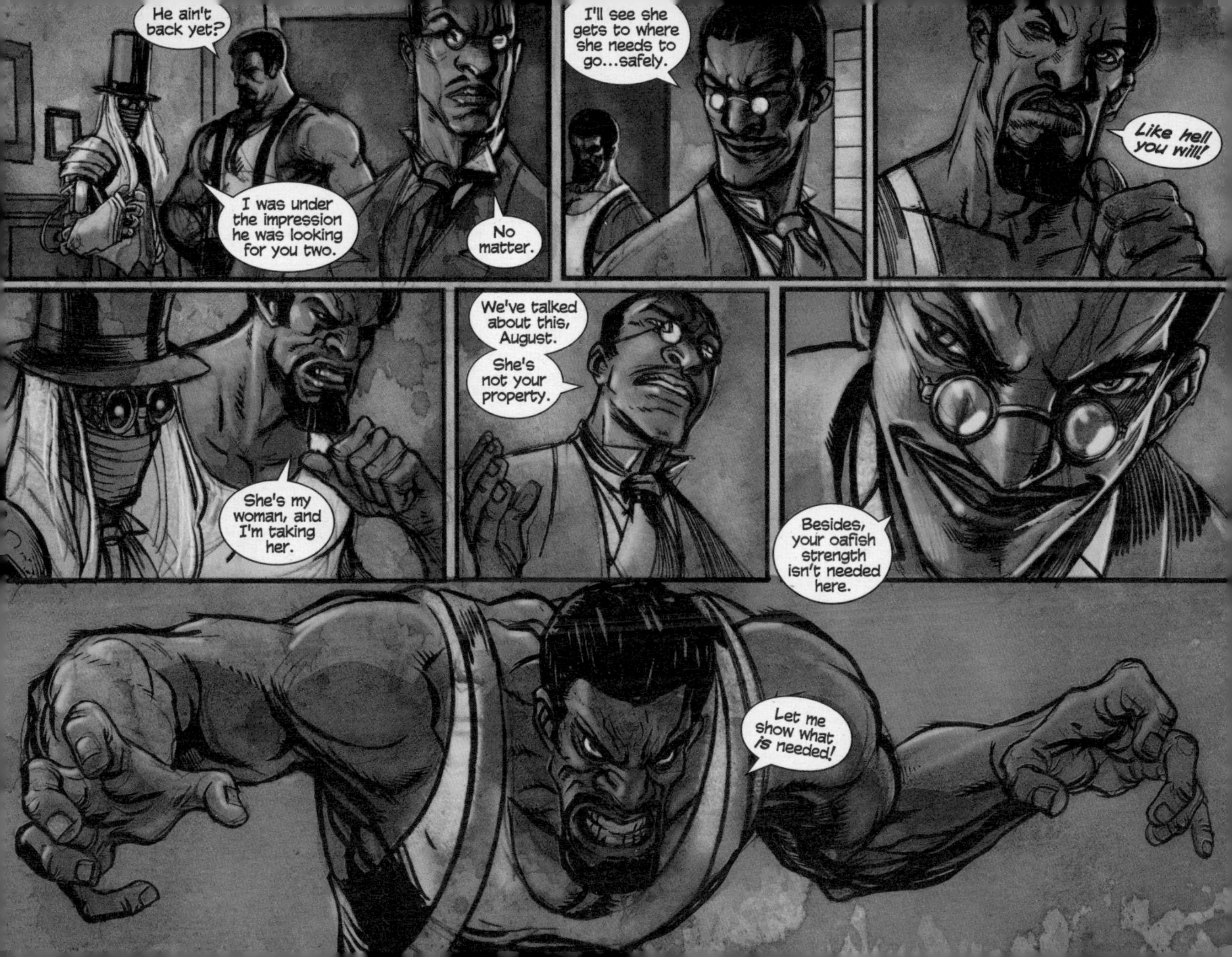
He ain't back yet?
I was under the impression he was looking for you two.
No matter.
I'll see she gets to where she needs to go...safely.
Like hell you will!
She's my woman, and I'm taking her.
We've talked about this, August.
She's not your property.
Besides, your oafish strength isn't needed here.
Let me show what *is* needed!

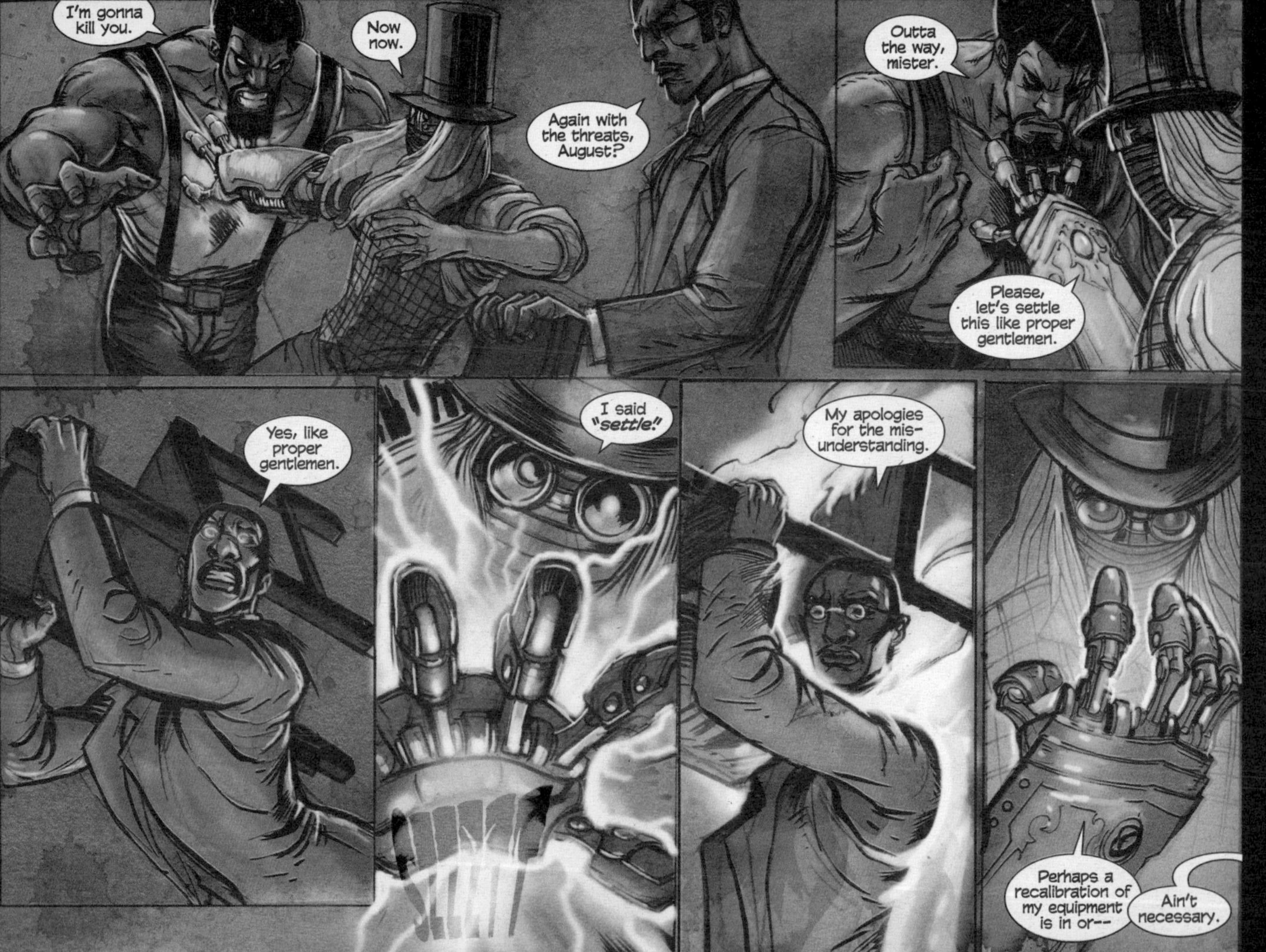
I'm gonna kill you.
Now now.
Again with the threats, August?
Outta the way, mister.
Please, let's settle this like proper gentlemen.
Yes, like proper gentlemen.
I said "settle!"
My apologies for the mis-understanding.
Perhaps a recalibration of my equipment is in or--
Ain't necessary.

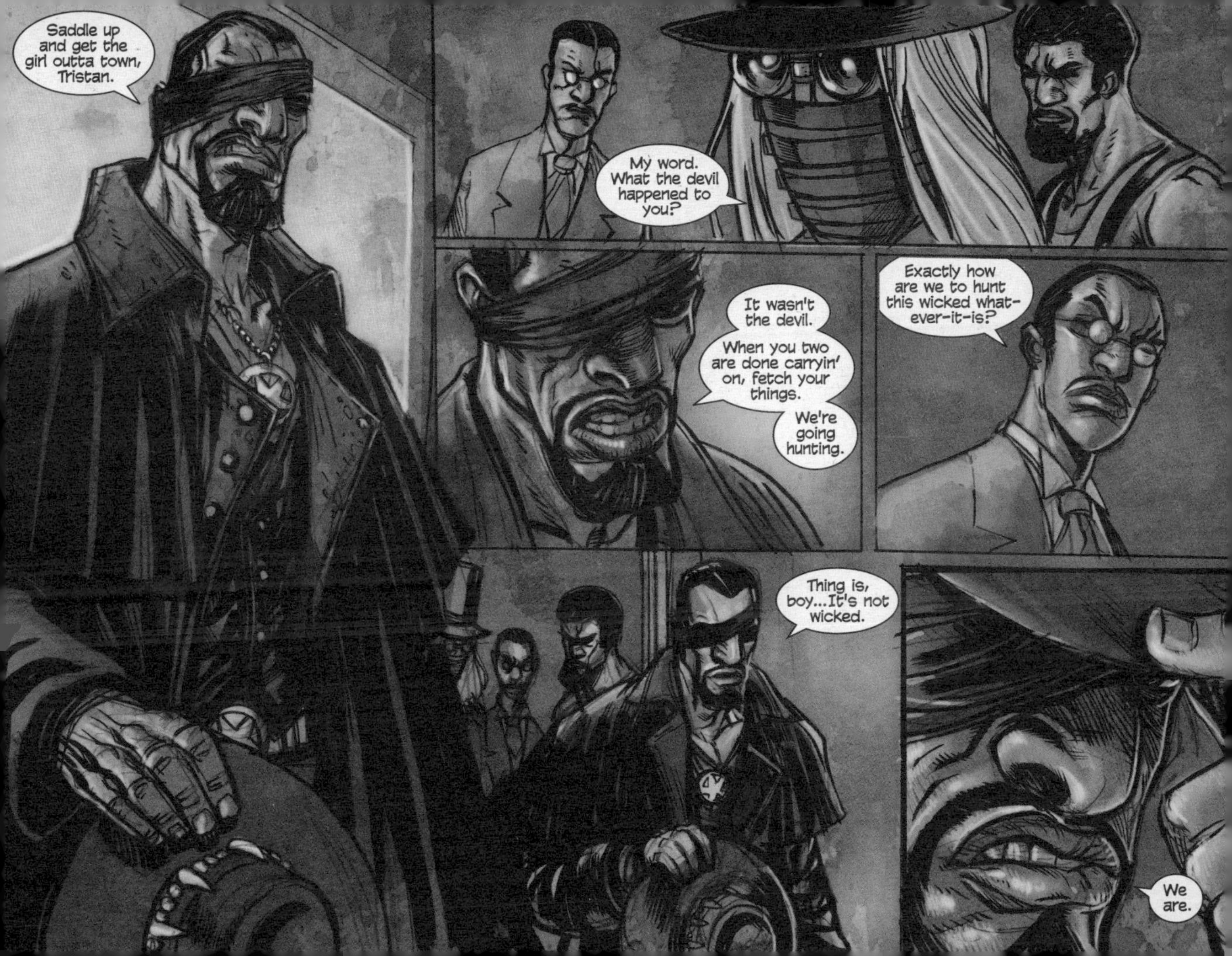
Saddle up and get the girl outta town, Tristan.
My word. What the devil happened to you?
It wasn't the devil.
When you two are done carryin' on, fetch your things.
We're going hunting.
Exactly how are we to hunt this wicked what-ever-it-is?
Thing is, boy...It's not wicked.
We are.

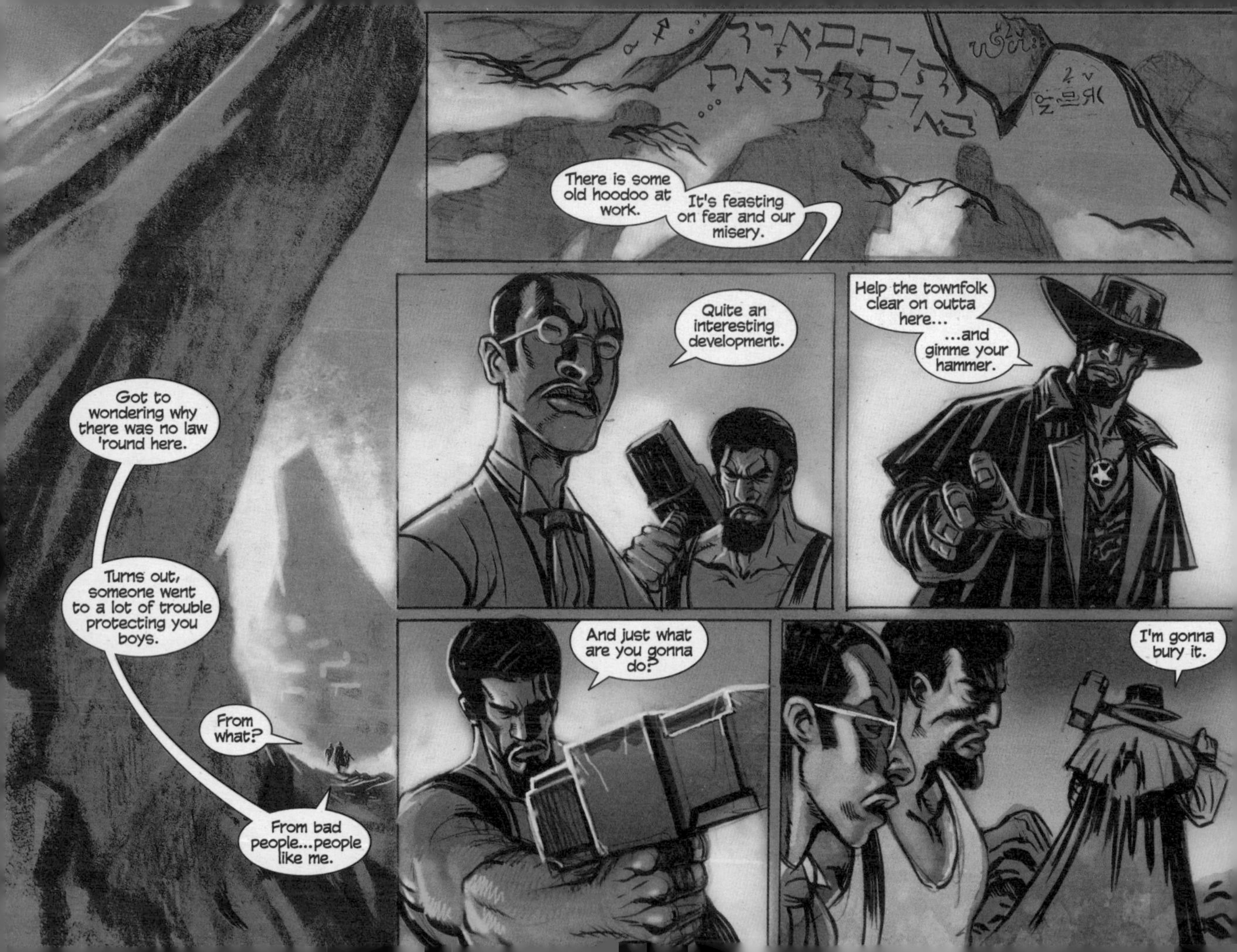
There is some old hoodoo at work.
It's feasting on fear and our misery.
Got to wondering why there was no law 'round here.
Turns out, someone went to a lot of trouble protecting you boys.
From what?
From bad people...people like me.
Quite an interesting development.
Help the townfolk clear on outta here...
...and gimme your hammer.
And just what are you gonna do?
I'm gonna bury it.

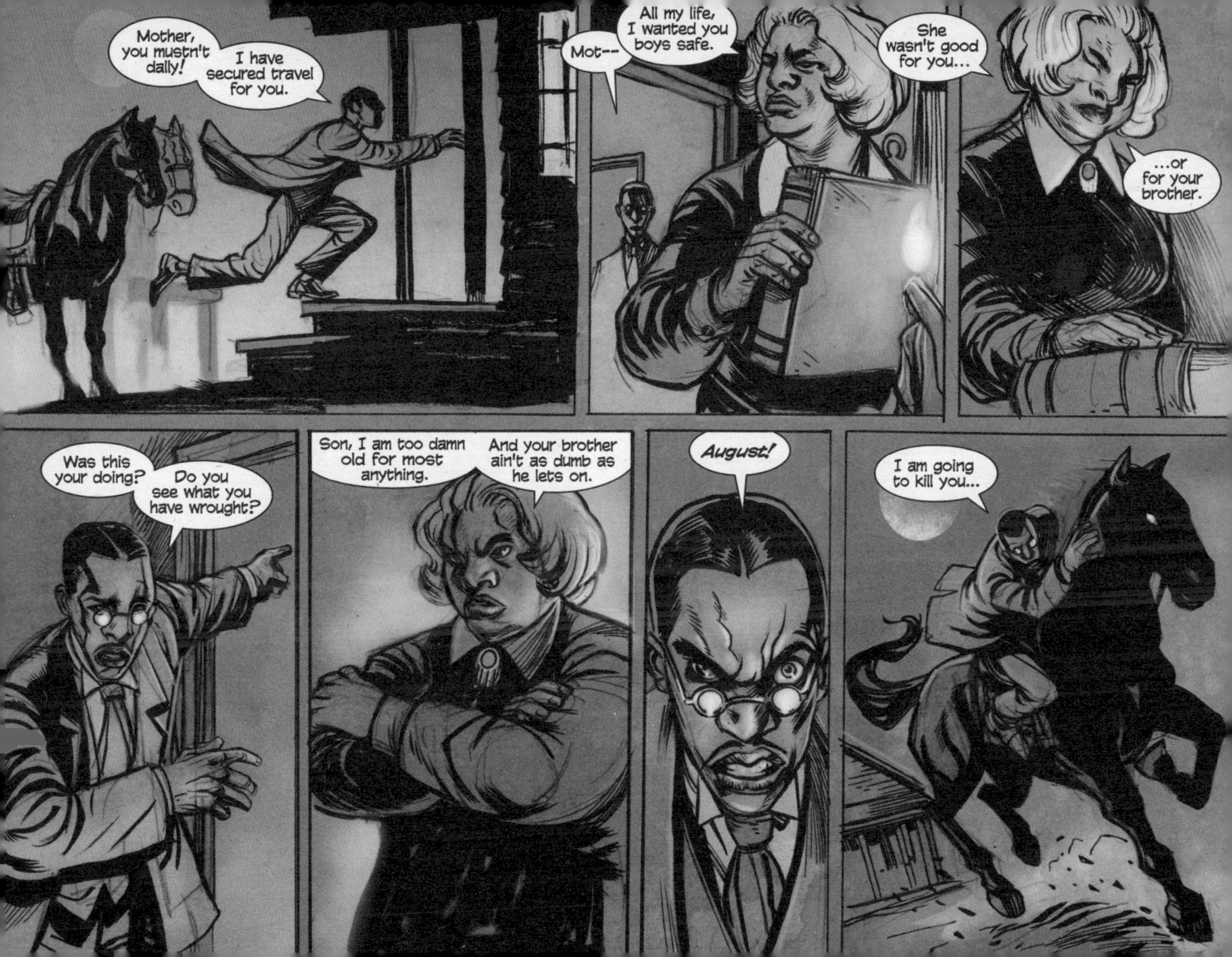

Mother, you mustn't dally!
I have secured travel for you.
Mot--
All my life, I wanted you boys safe.
She wasn't good for you...
...or for your brother.
Was this your doing?
Do you see what you have wrought?
Son, I am too damn old for most anything.
And your brother ain't as dumb as he lets on.
August!
I am going to kill you...

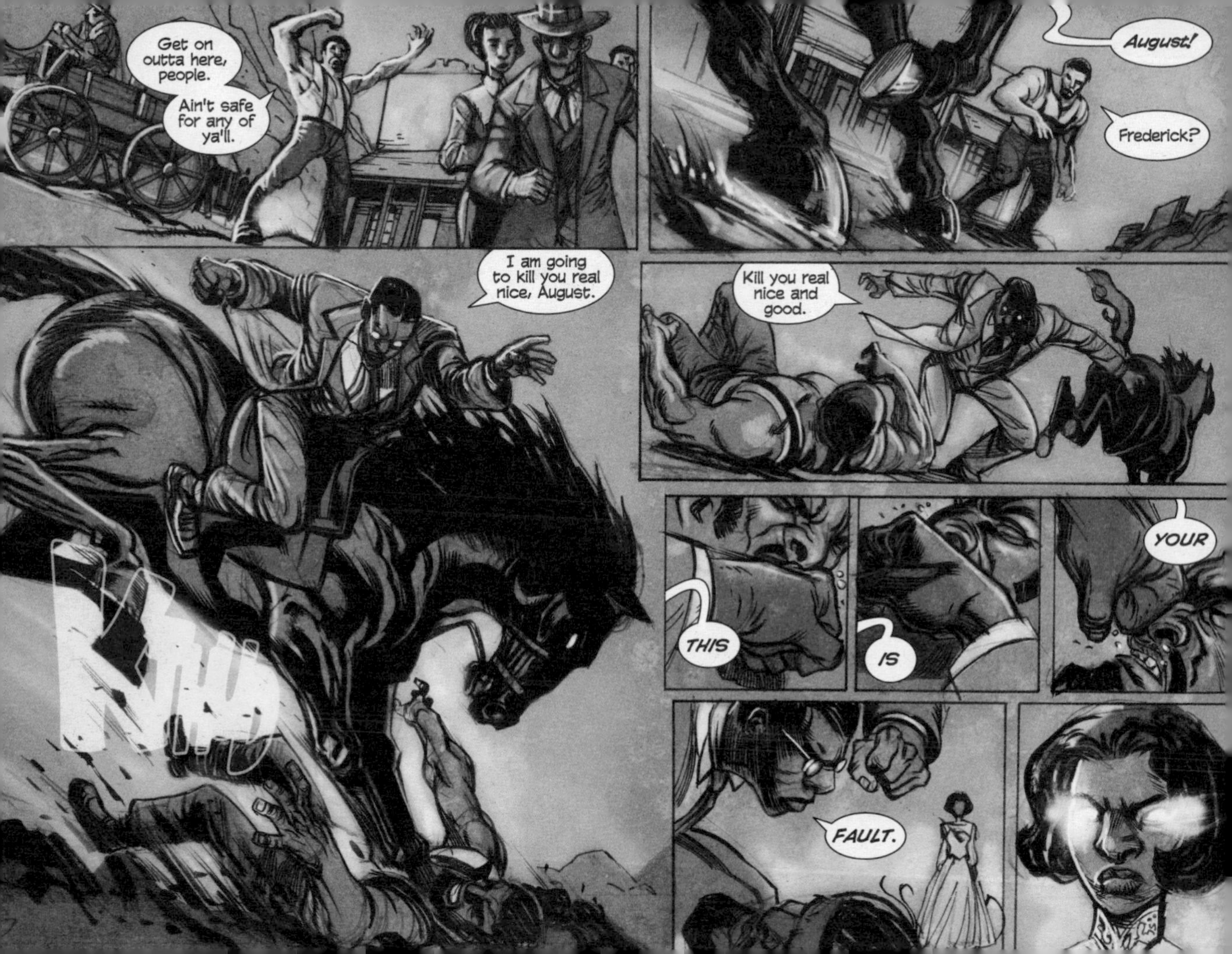

Get on outta here, people.
Ain't safe for any of ya'll.
August!
Frederick?
I am going to kill you real nice, August.
Kill you real nice and good.
THIS
IS
YOUR
FAULT.

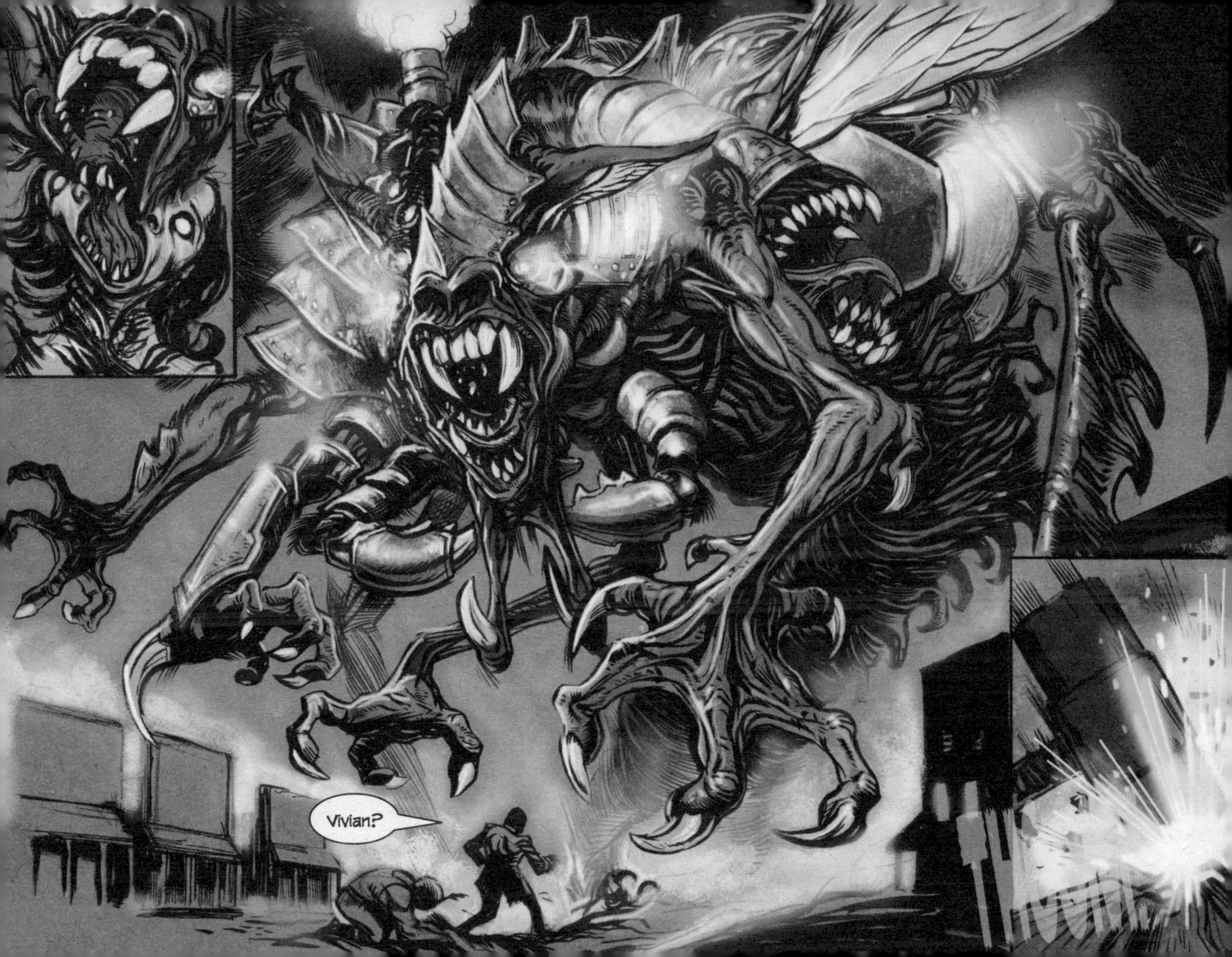
Vivian?

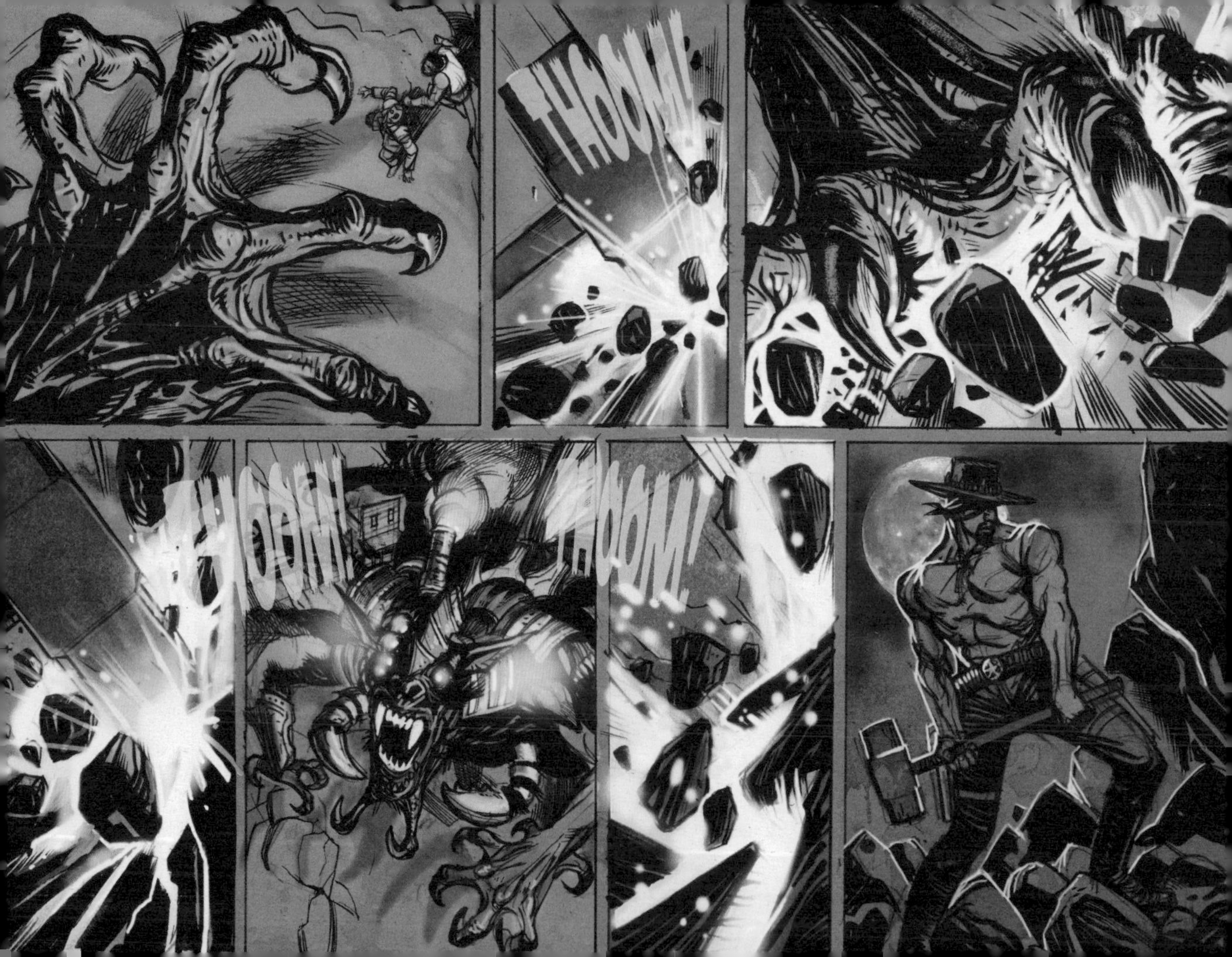
THOOM!
THOOM!
THOOM!

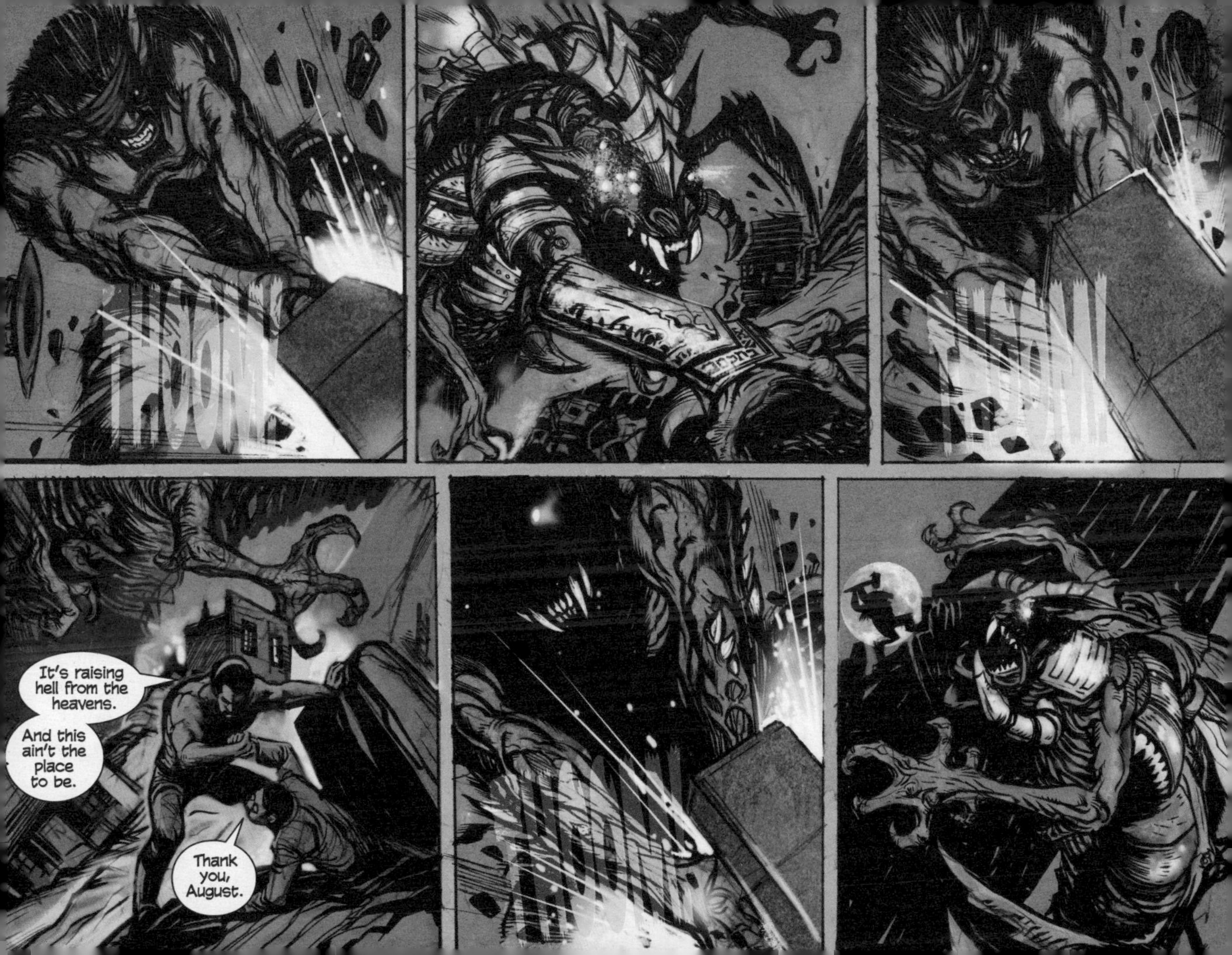
It's raising hell from the heavens.
And this ain't the place to be.
Thank you, August.

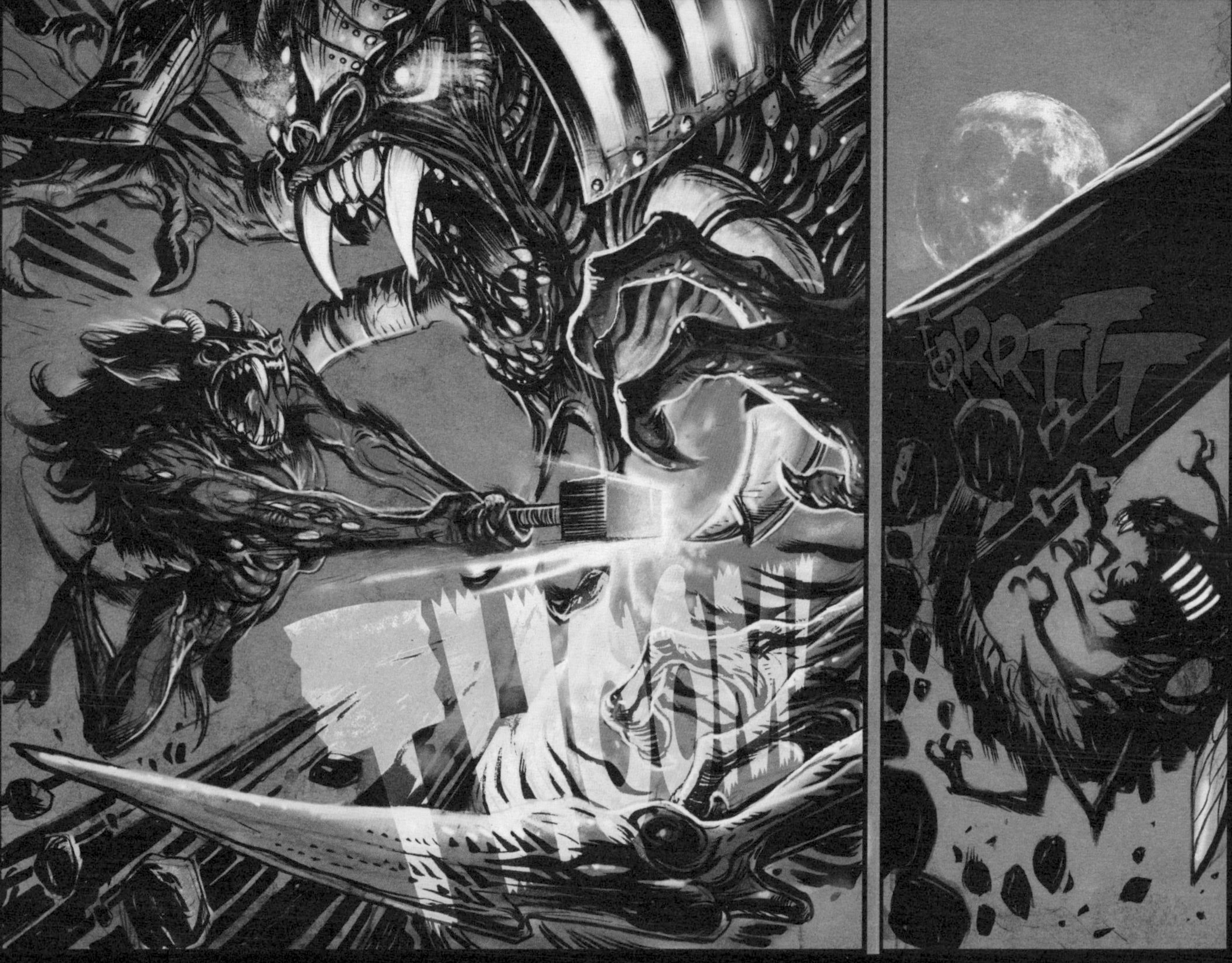
BRRTTT

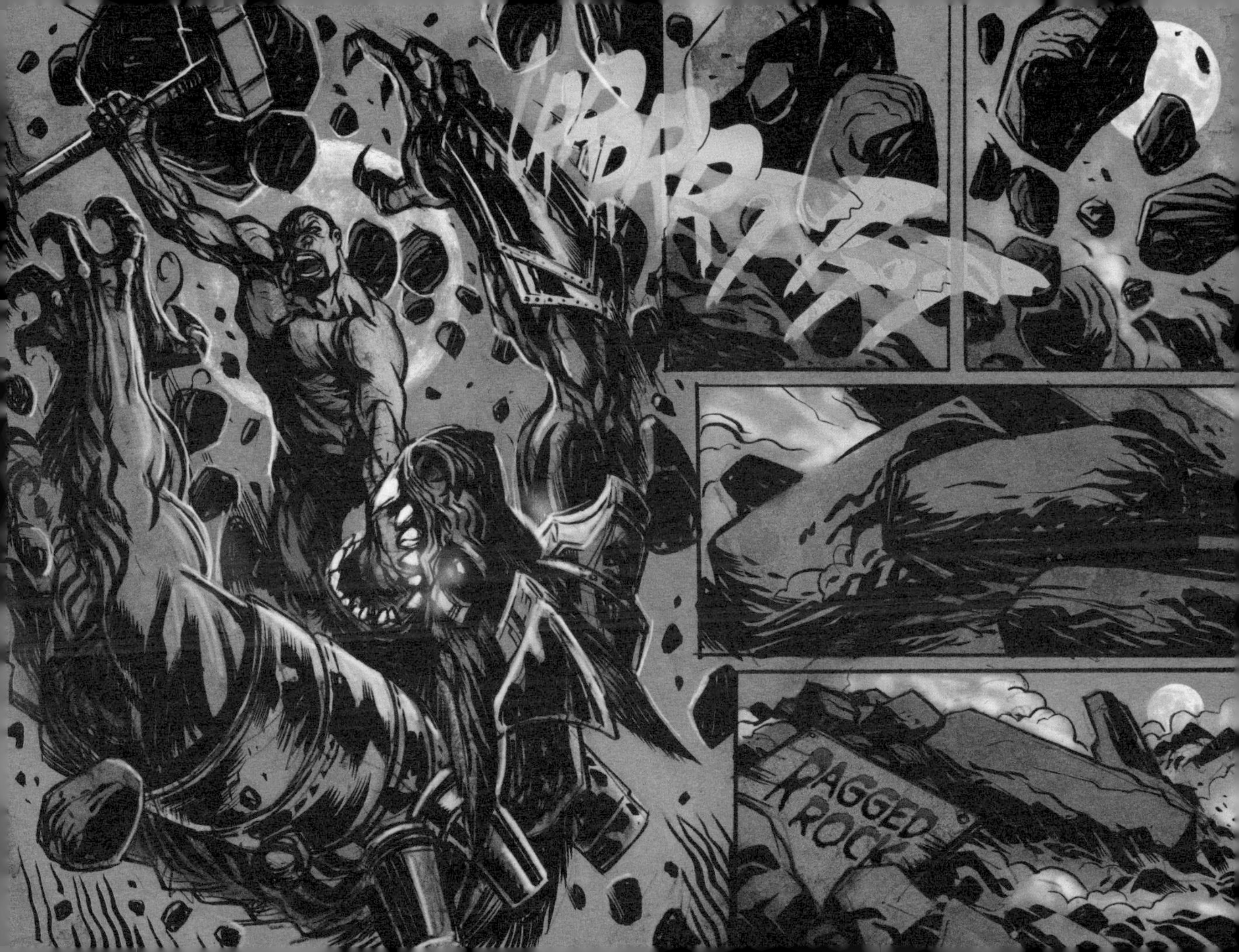
RAGGED ROCK

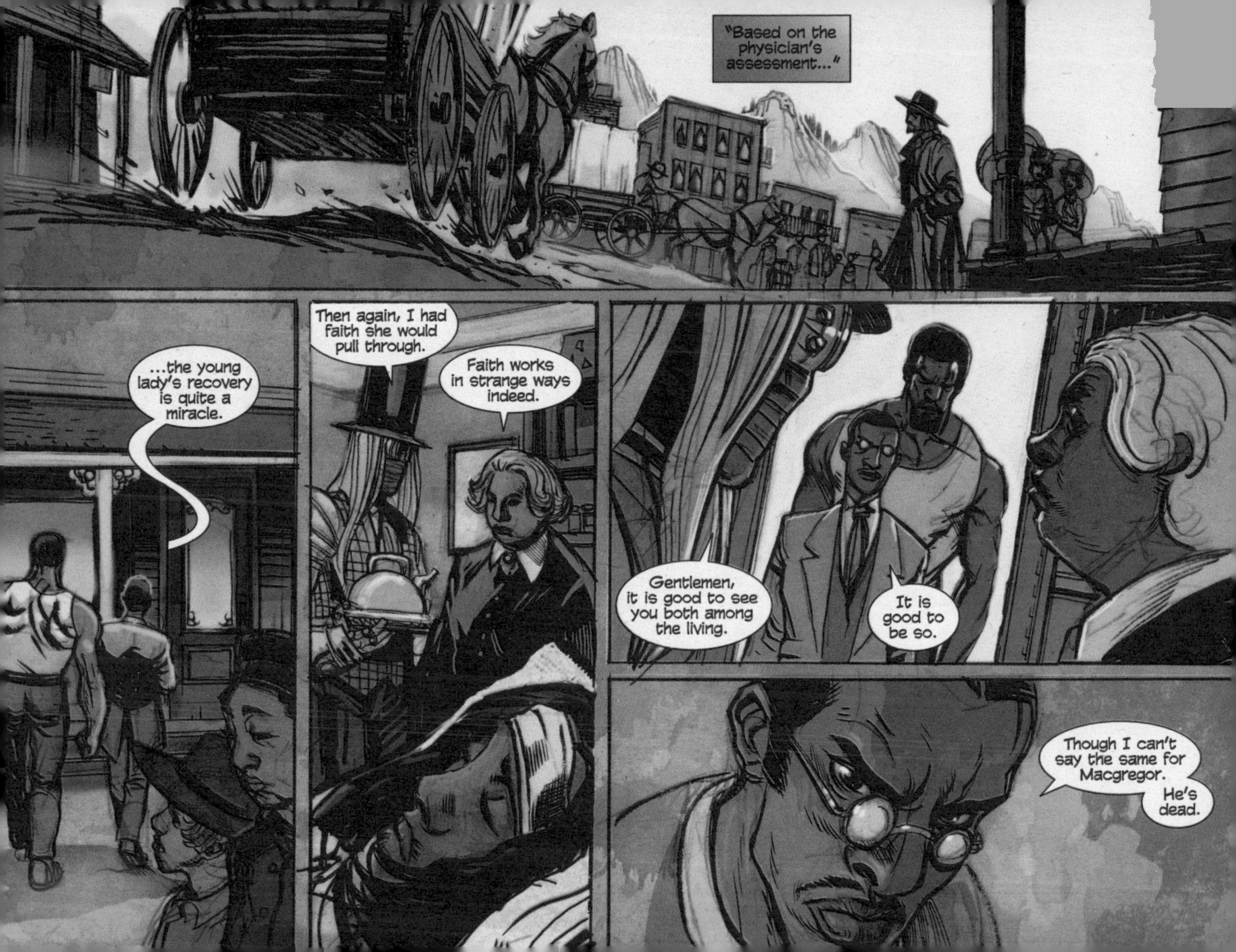
"Based on the physician's assessment..."
...the young lady's recovery is quite a miracle.
Then again, I had faith she would pull through.
Faith works in strange ways indeed.
Gentlemen, it is good to see you both among the living.
It is good to be so.
Though I can't say the same for Macgregor.
He's dead.

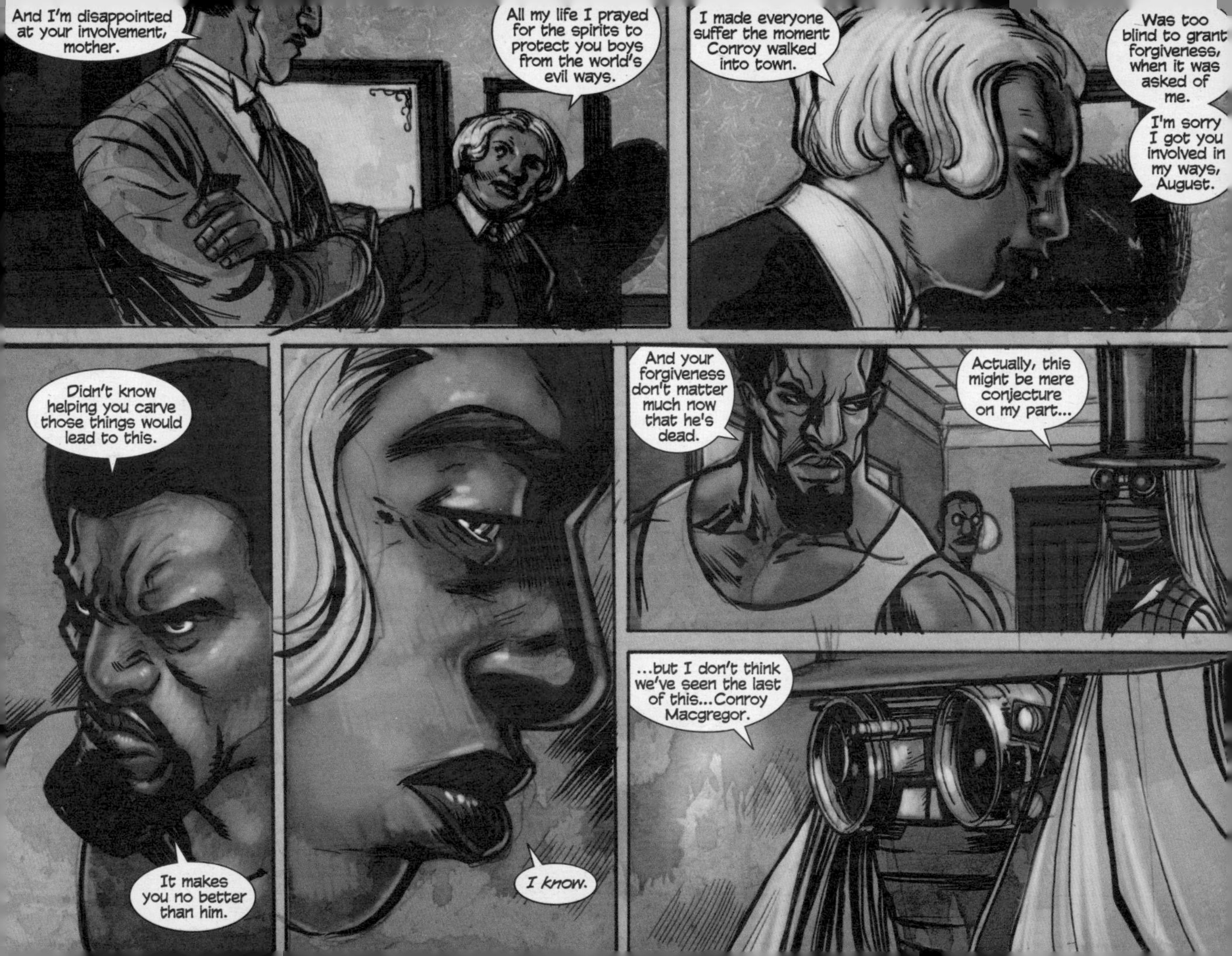
And I'm disappointed at your involvement, mother.
All my life I prayed for the spirits to protect you boys from the world's evil ways.
I made everyone suffer the moment Conroy walked into town.
Was too blind to grant forgiveness, when it was asked of me.
I'm sorry I got you involved in my ways, August.
Didn't know helping you carve those things would lead to this.
It makes you no better than him.
I know.
And your forgiveness don't matter much now that he's dead.
Actually, this might be mere conjecture on my part...
...but I don't think we've seen the last of this...Conroy Macgregor.

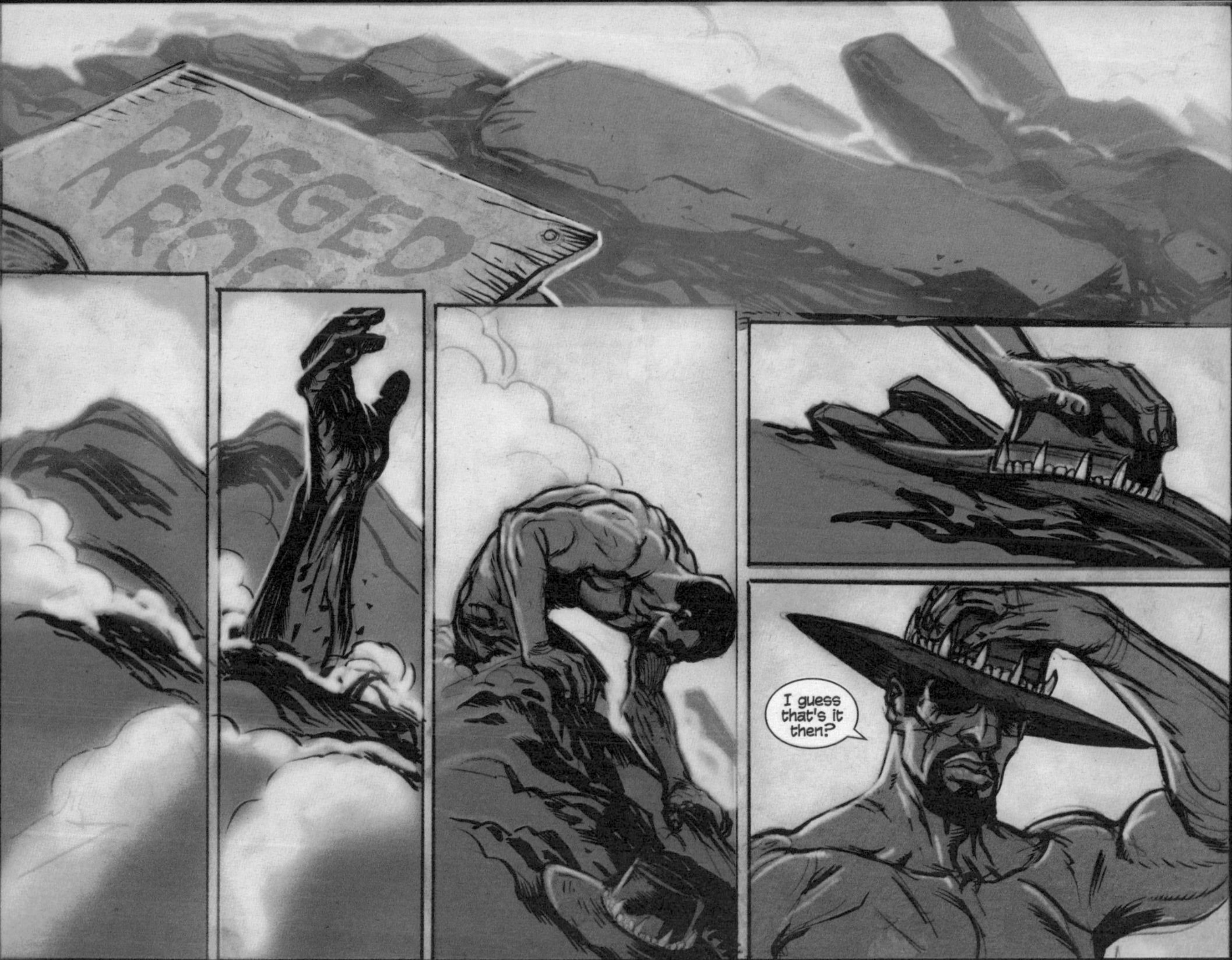
RAGGED
I guess that's it then?

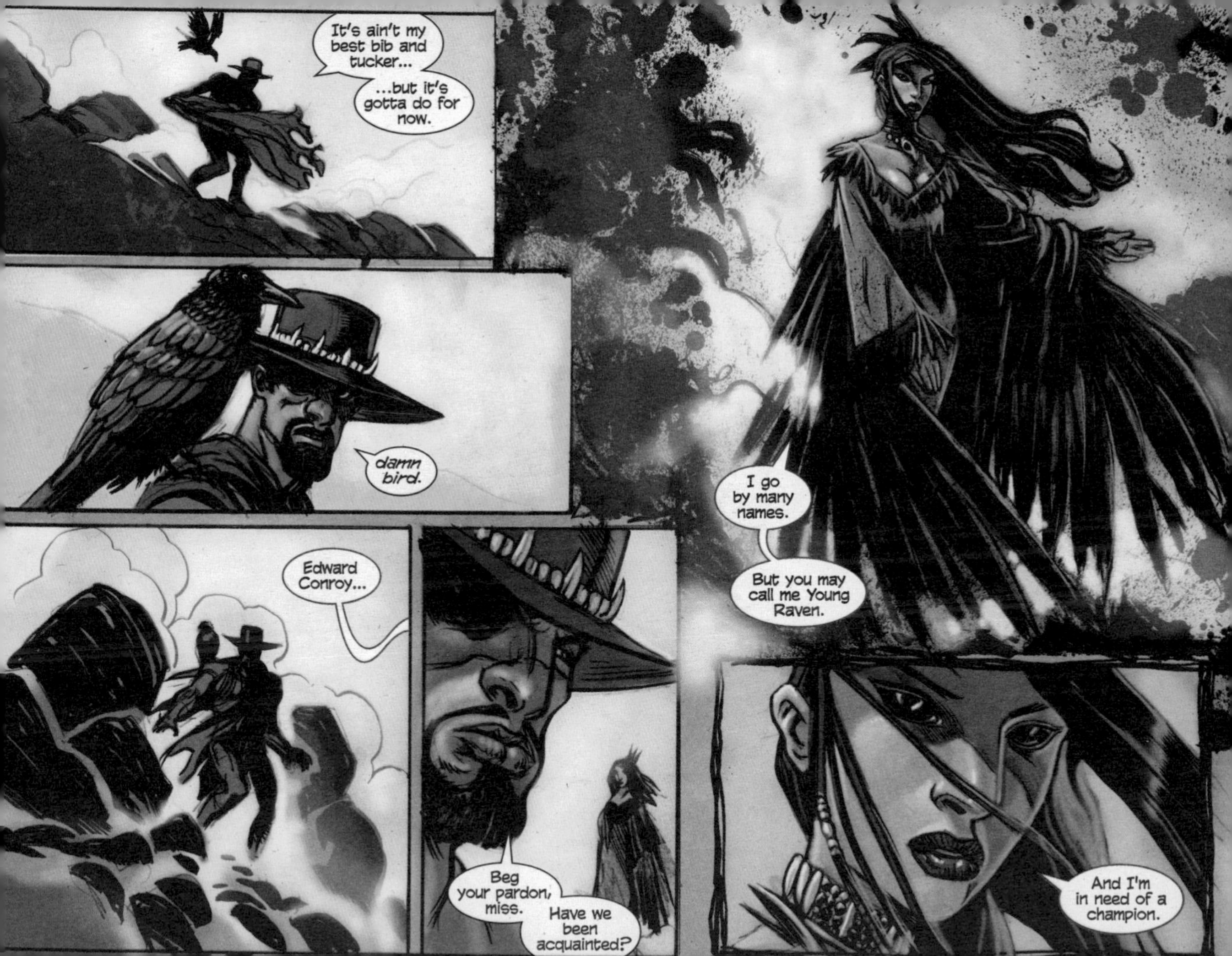
It's ain't my best bib and tucker...
...but it's gotta do for now.
damn bird.
Edward Conroy...
Beg your pardon, miss.
Have we been acquainted?
I go by many names.
But you may call me Young Raven.
And I'm in need of a champion.

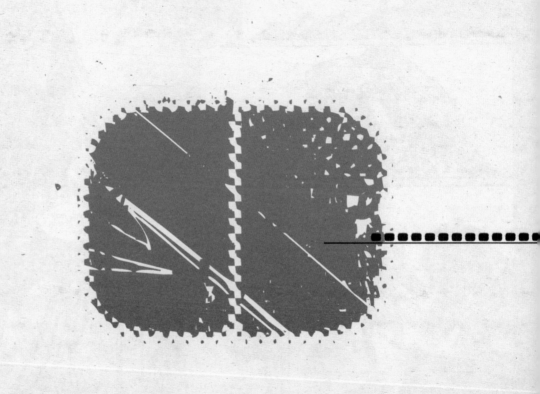

CHAPTER 3

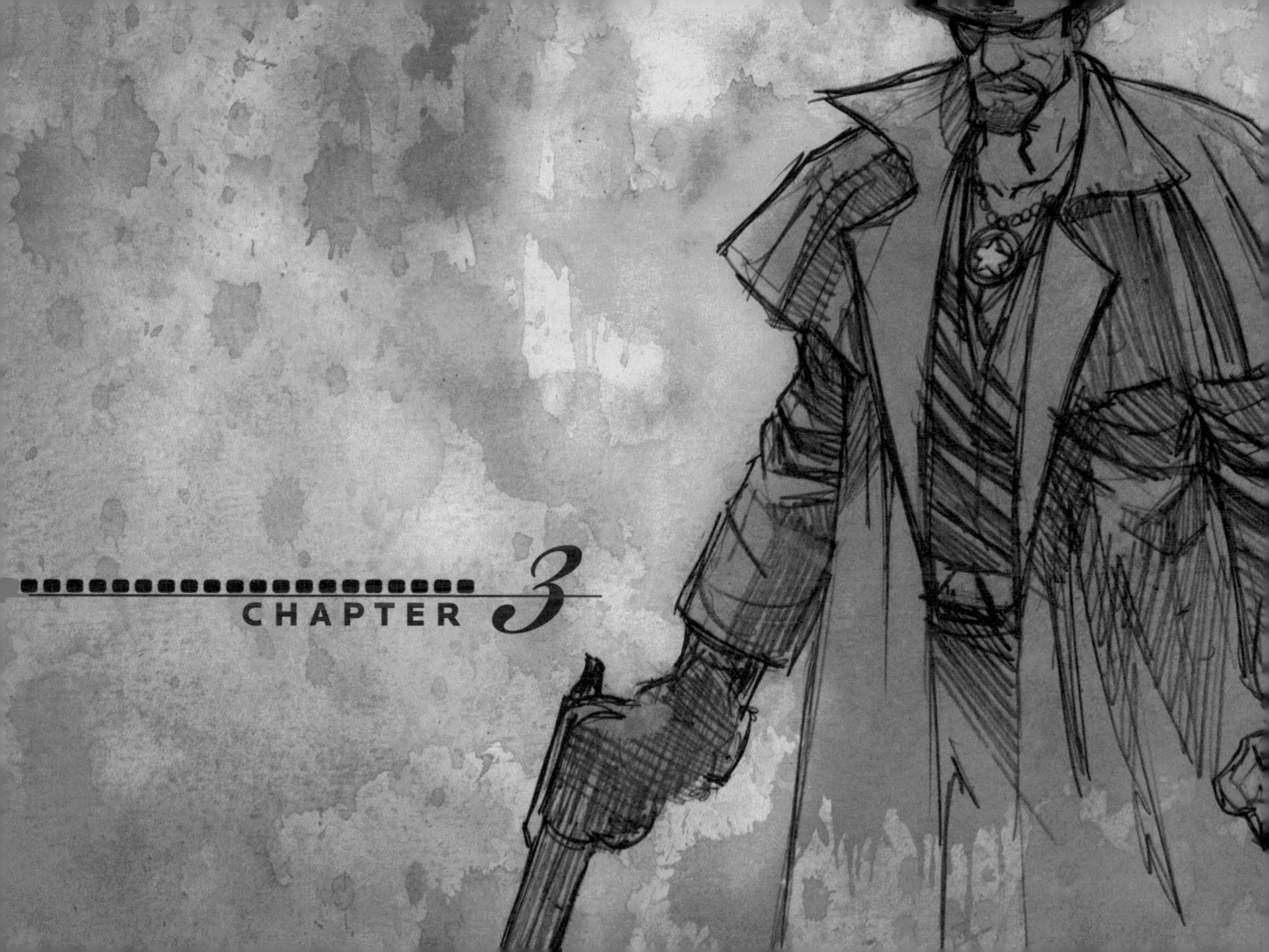

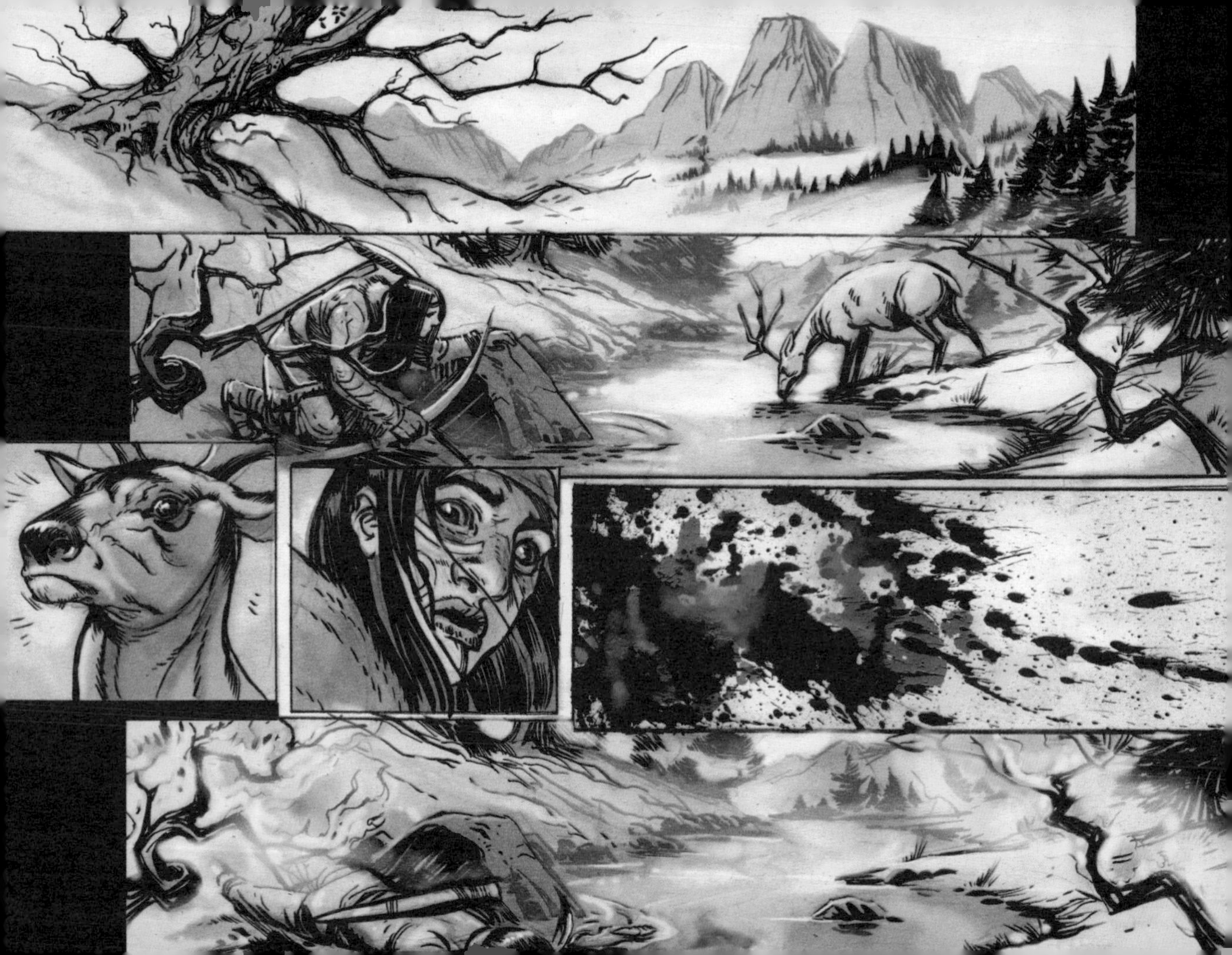

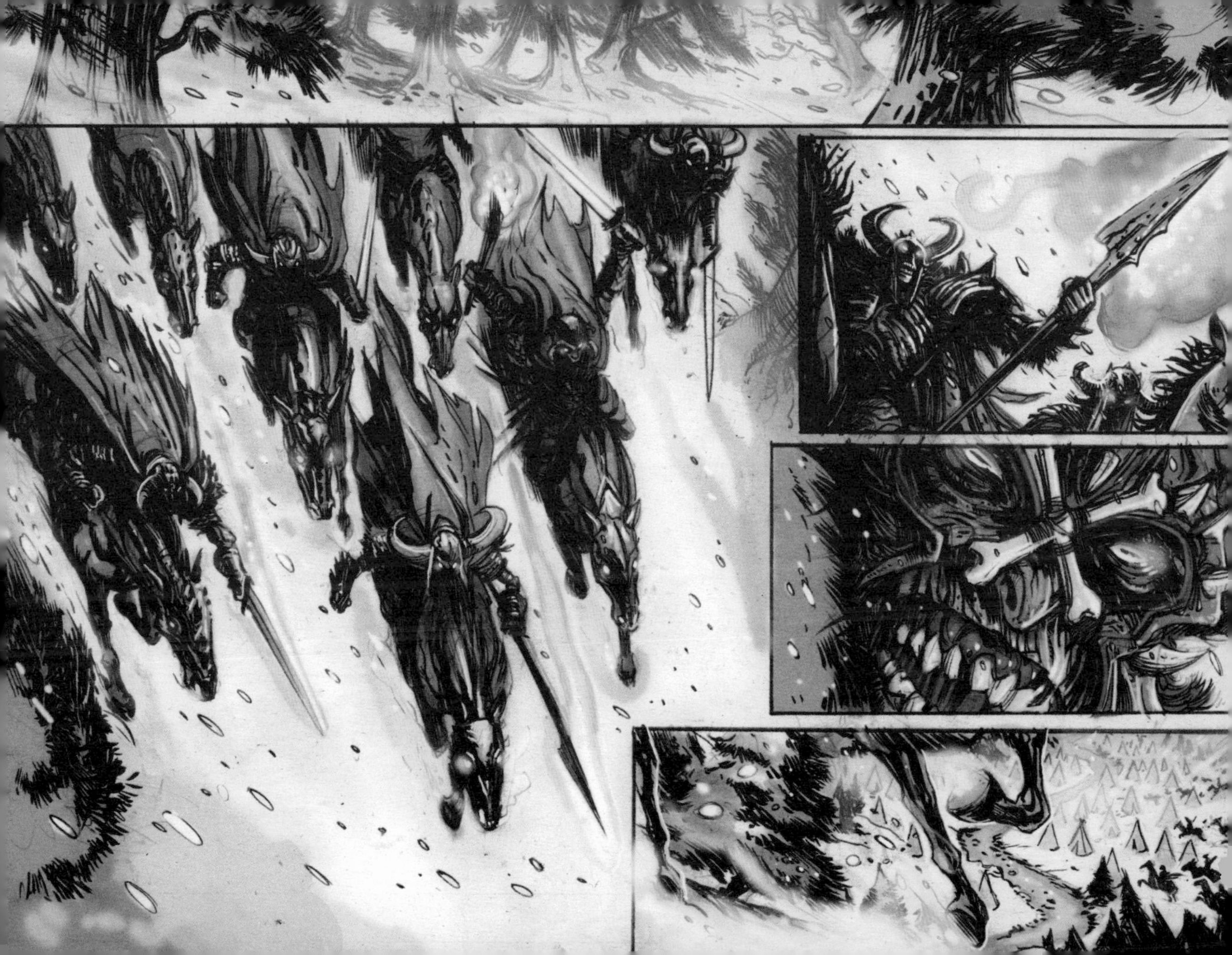

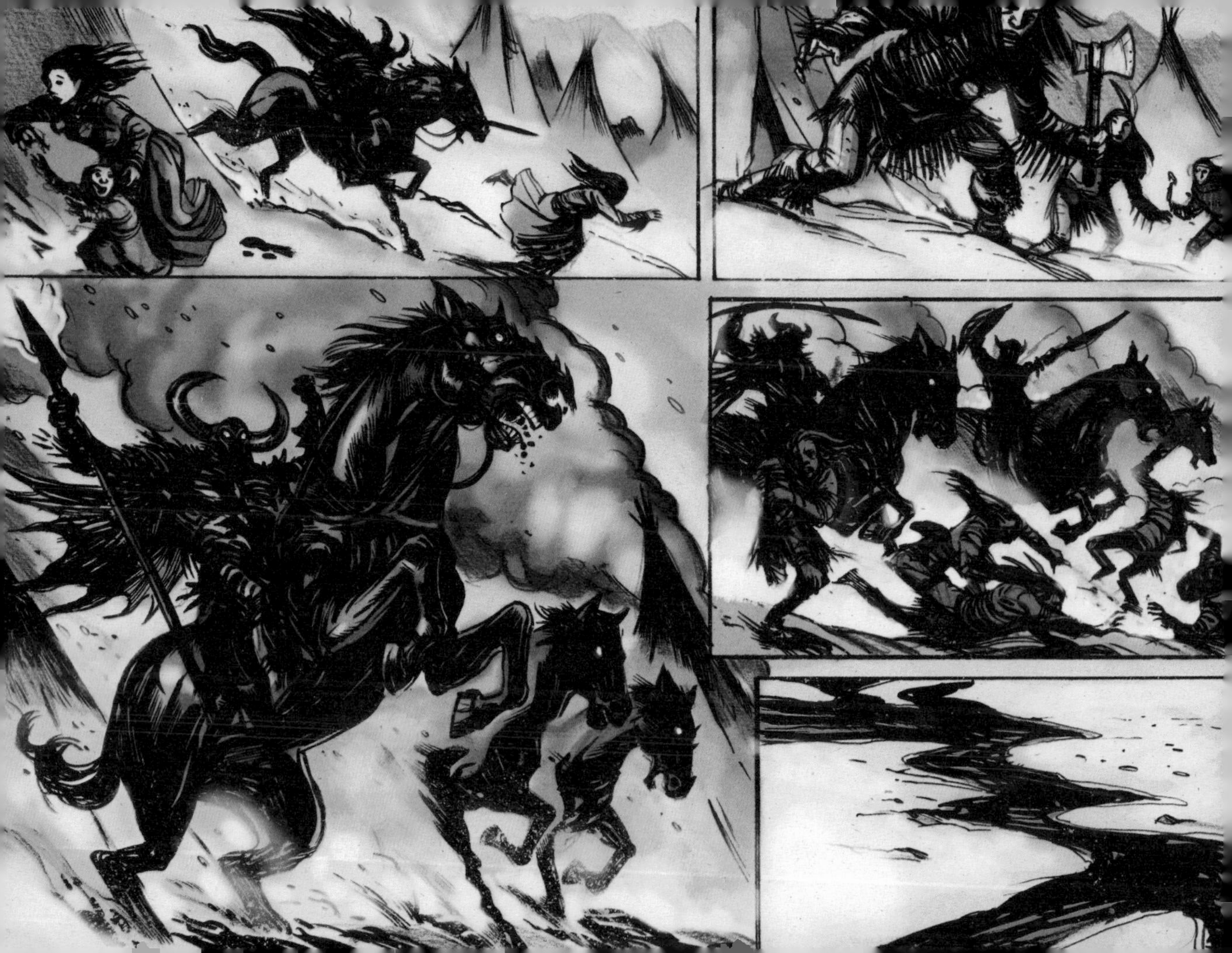

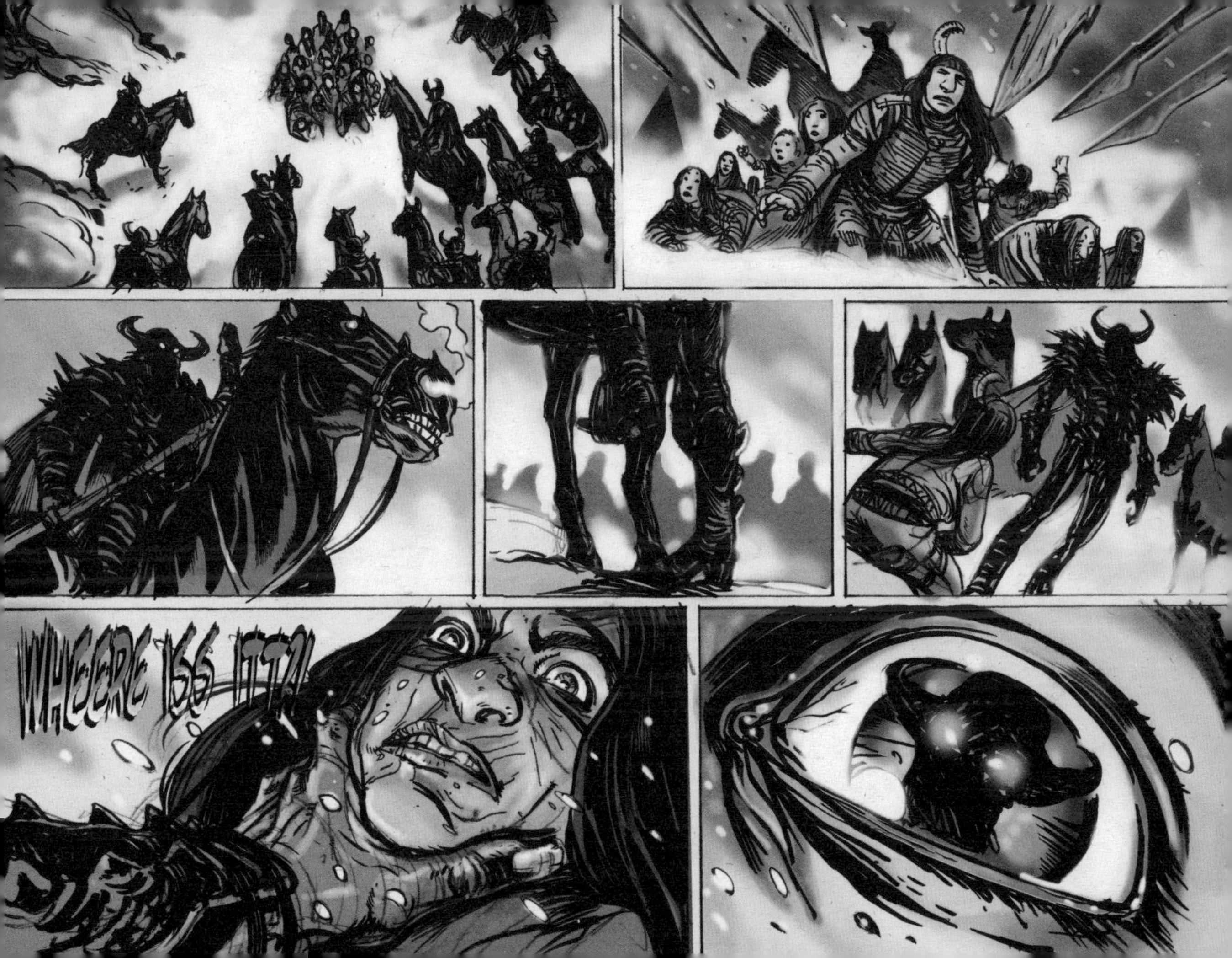
WHEERE ISS ITT?!

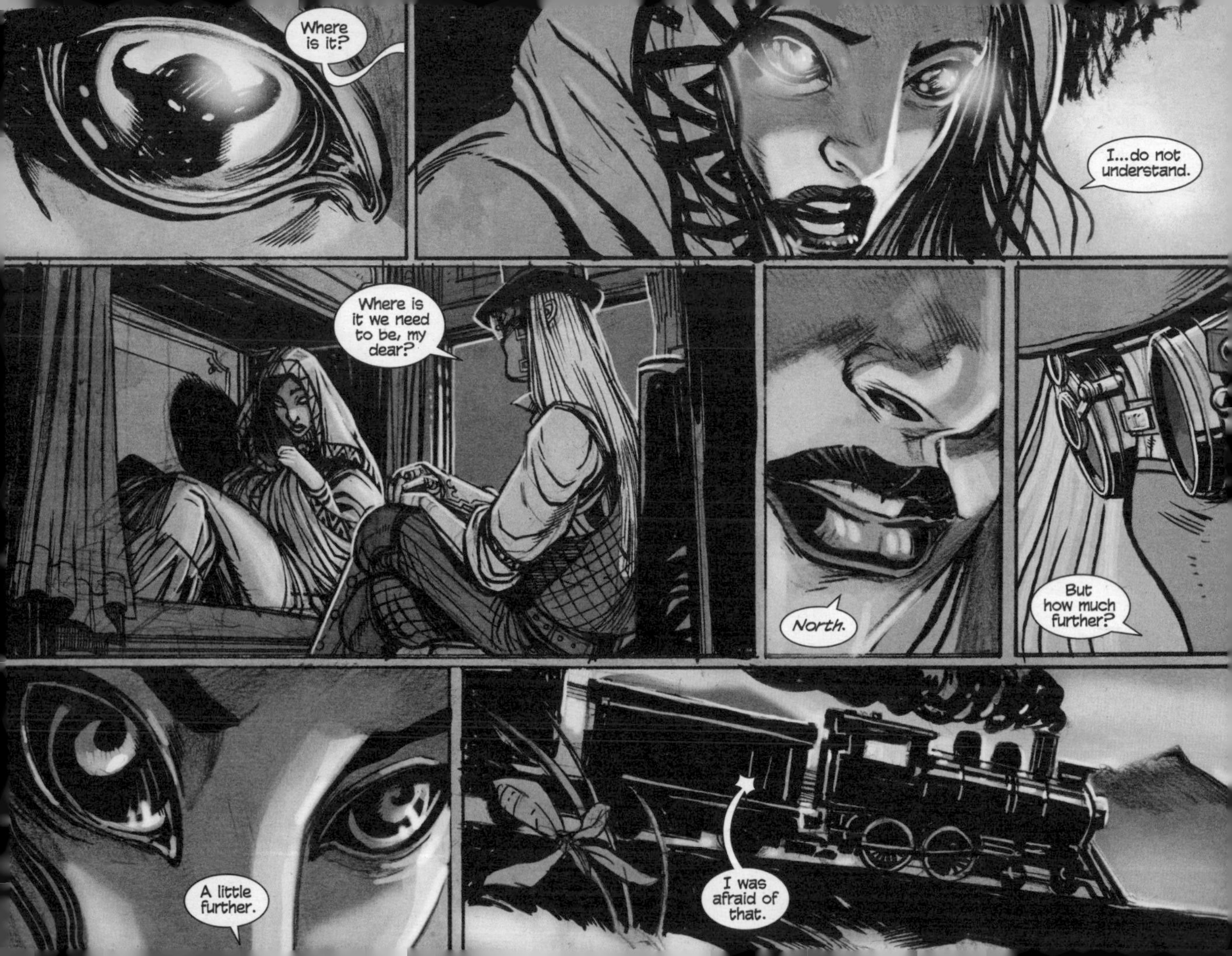
Where is it?
I...do not understand.
Where is it we need to be, my dear?
North.
But how much further?
A little further.
I was afraid of that.

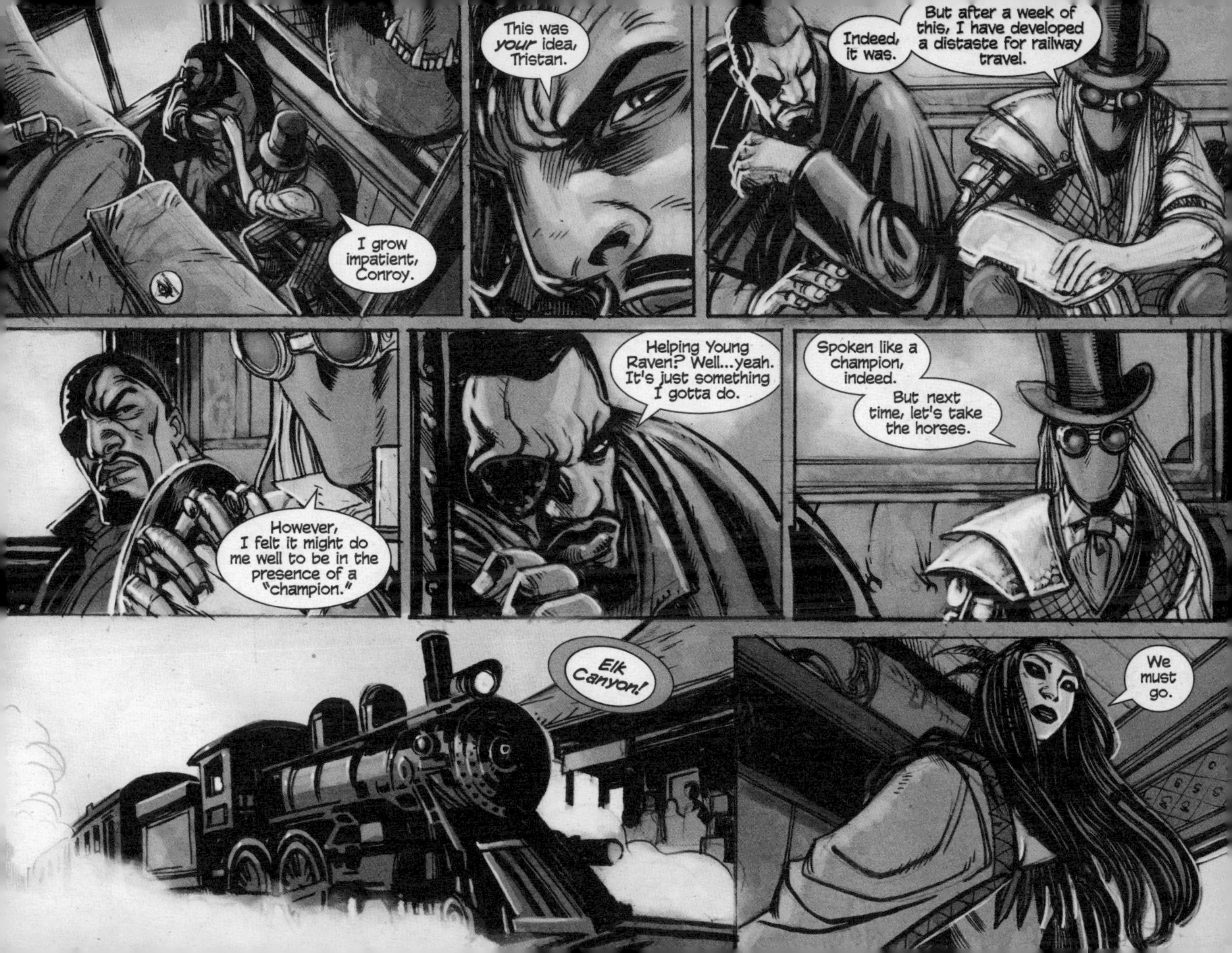
I grow impatient, Conroy.
This was *your* idea, Tristan.
Indeed, it was.
But after a week of this, I have developed a distaste for railway travel.
However, I felt it might do me well to be in the presence of a "champion."
Helping Young Raven? Well...yeah. It's just something I gotta do.
Spoken like a champion, indeed.
But next time, let's take the horses.
Elk Canyon!
We must go.

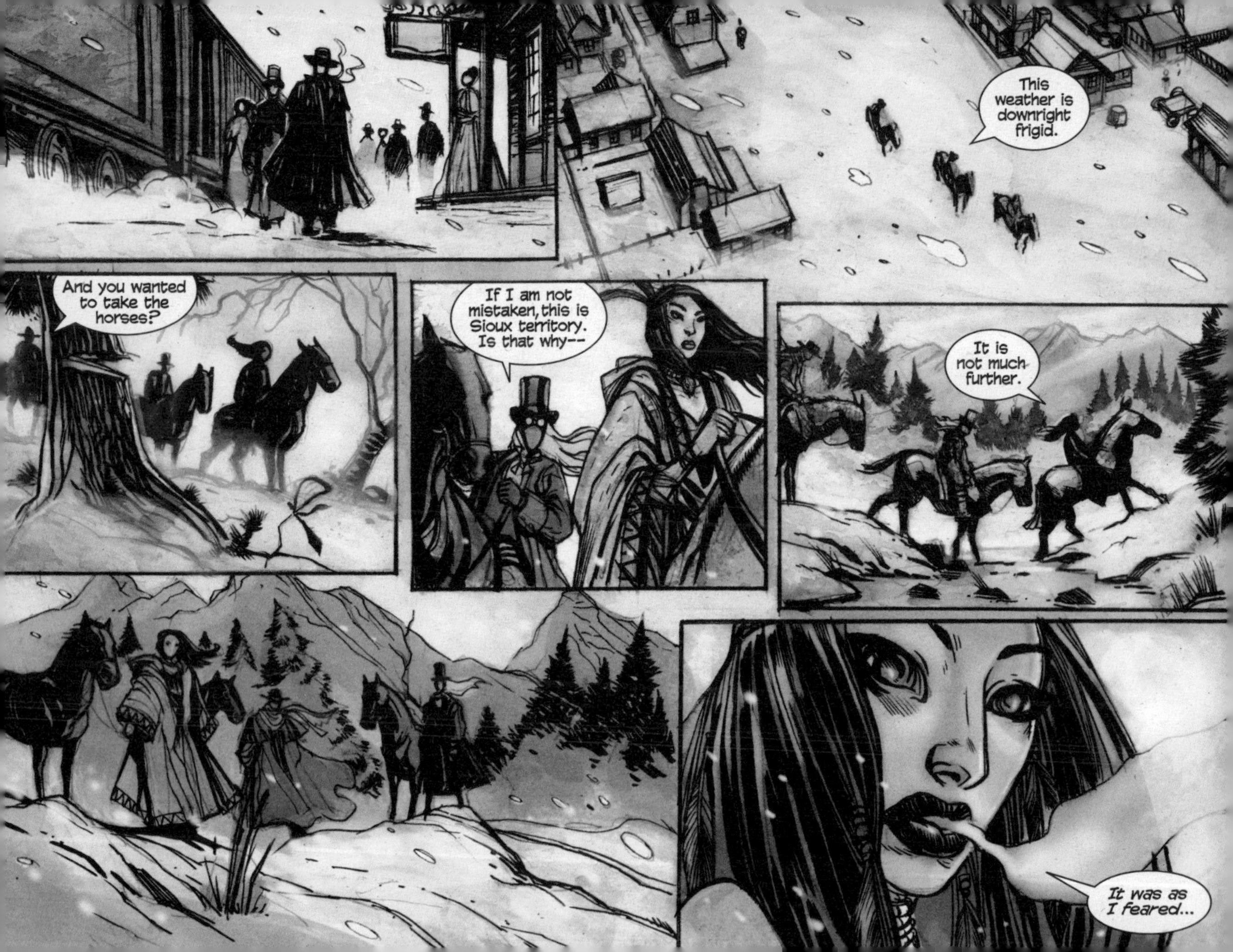
This weather is downright frigid.
And you wanted to take the horses?
If I am not mistaken, this is Sioux territory. Is that why--
It is not much further.
It was as I feared...

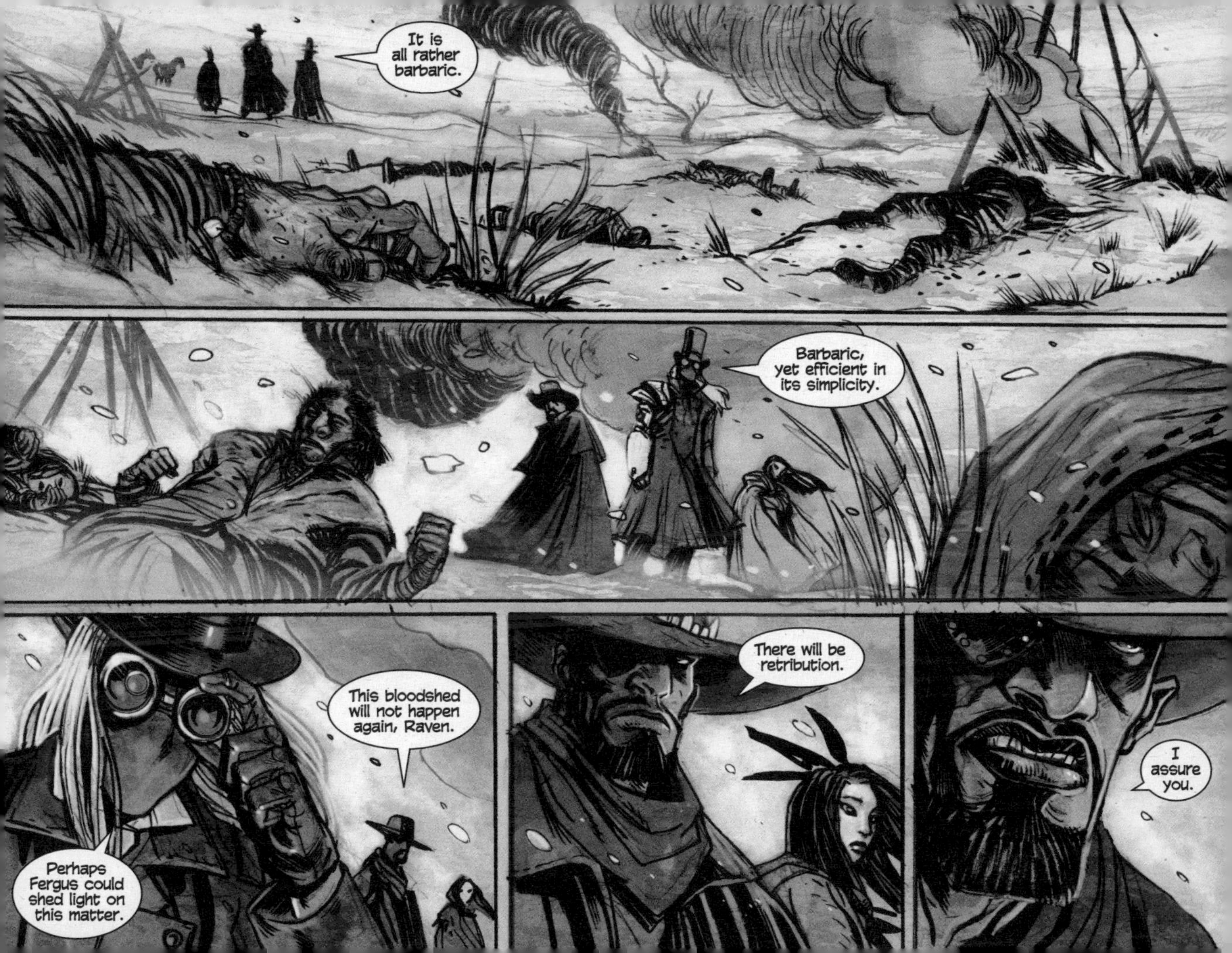
It is all rather barbaric.
Barbaric, yet efficient in its simplicity.
Perhaps Fergus could shed light on this matter.
This bloodshed will not happen again, Raven.
There will be retribution.
I assure you.

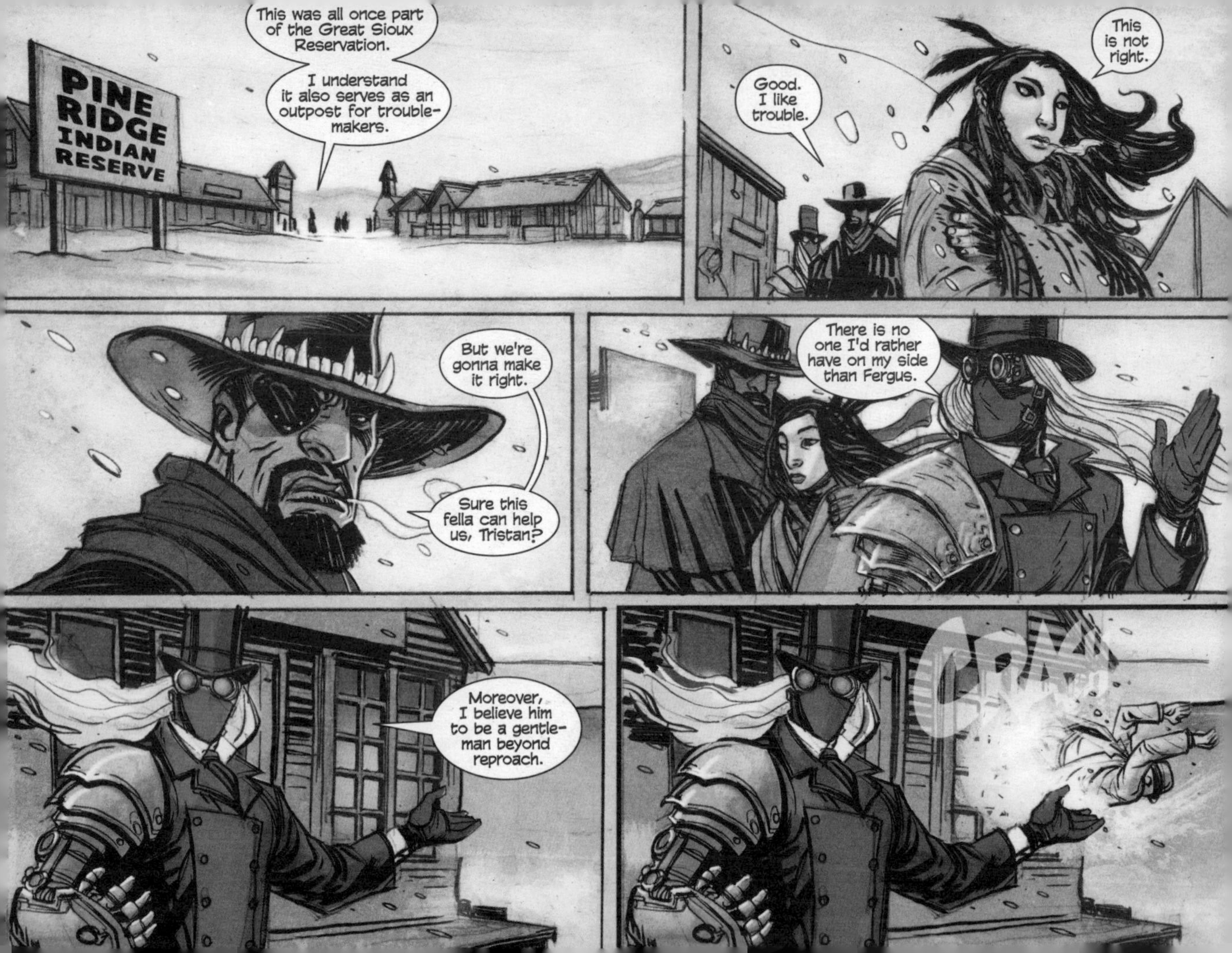
PINE RIDGE INDIAN RESERVE
This was all once part of the Great Sioux Reservation.
I understand it also serves as an outpost for trouble-makers.
Good. I like trouble.
This is not right.
But we're gonna make it right.
Sure this fella can help us, Tristan?
There is no one I'd rather have on my side than Fergus.
Moreover, I believe him to be a gentle-man beyond reproach.

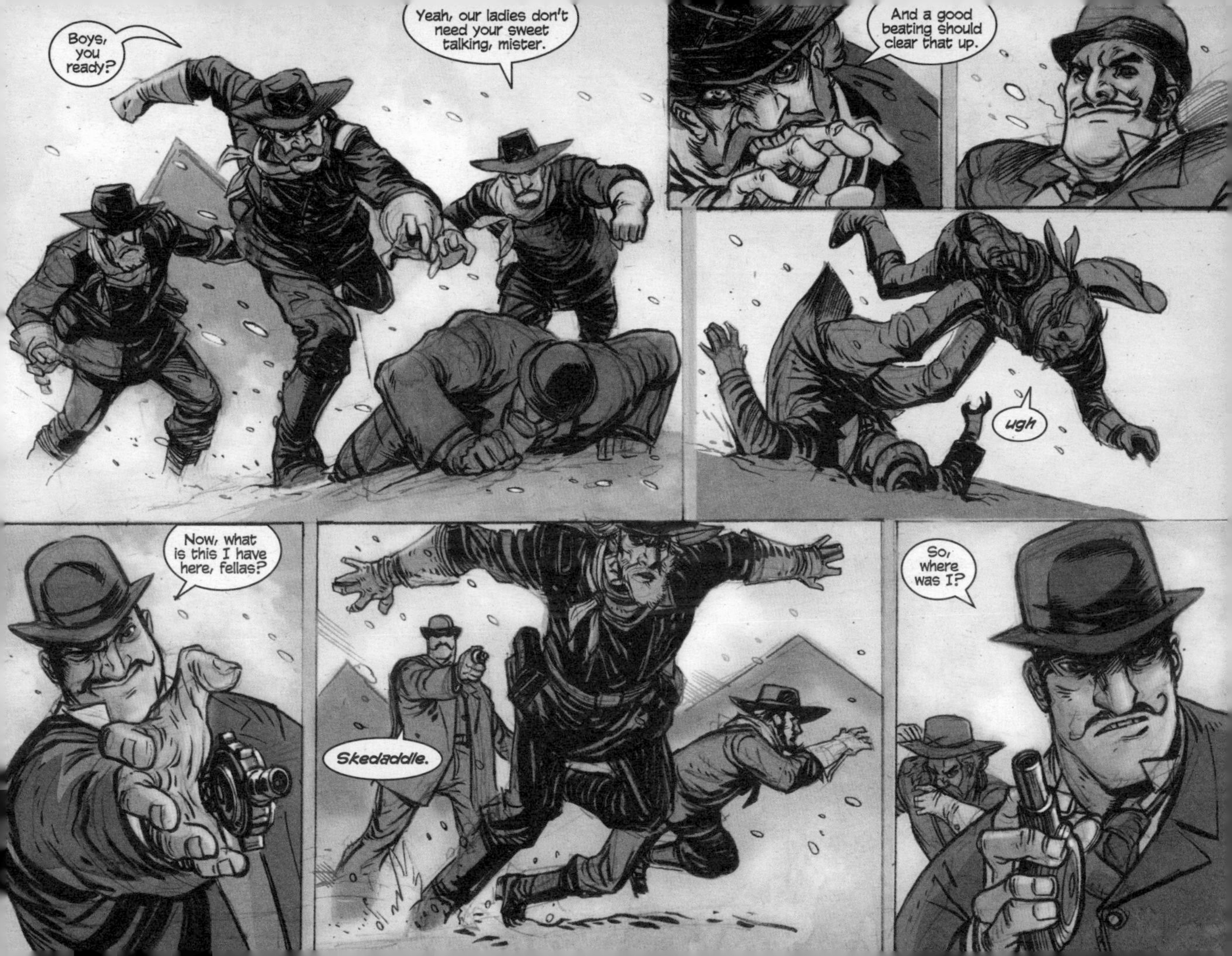
Boys, you ready?
Yeah, our ladies don't need your sweet talking, mister.
And a good beating should clear that up.
ugh
Now, what is this I have here, fellas?
Skedaddle.
So, where was I?

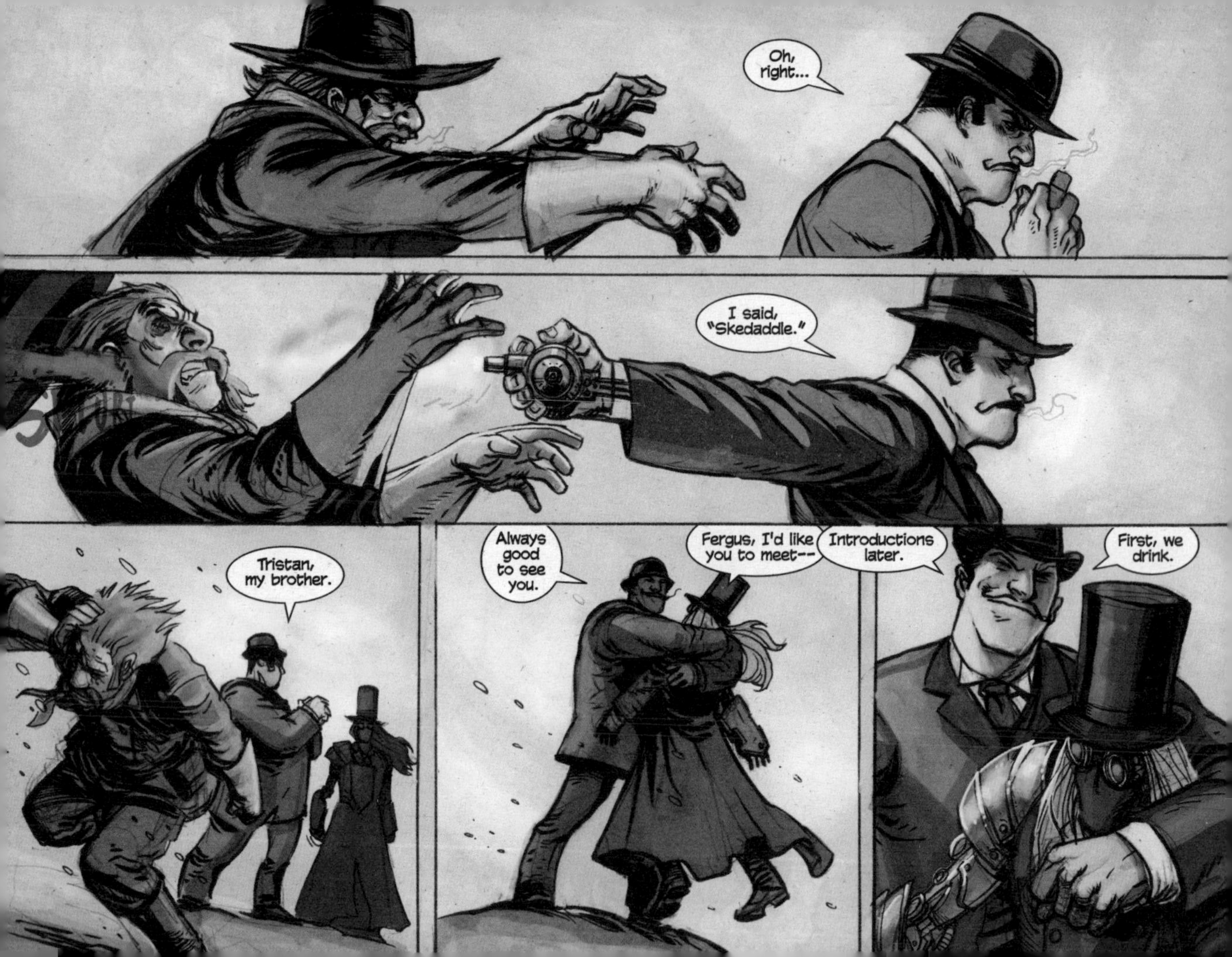
Oh, right...
I said, "Skedaddle."
Tristan, my brother.
Always good to see you.
Fergus, I'd like you to meet--
Introductions later.
First, we drink.

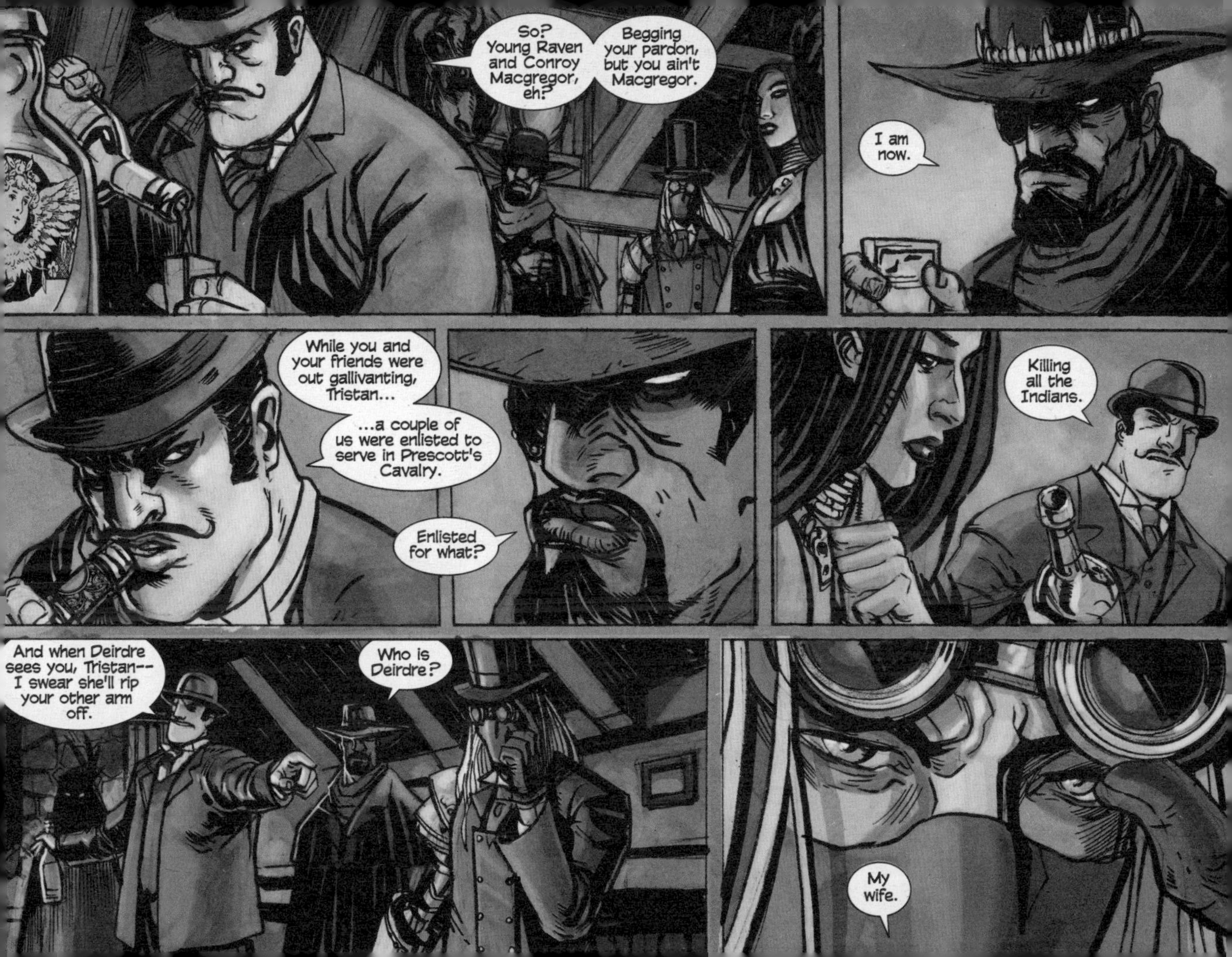
So? Young Raven and Conroy Macgregor, eh?
Begging your pardon, but you ain't Macgregor.
I am now.
While you and your friends were out gallivanting, Tristan...
...a couple of us were enlisted to serve in Prescott's Cavalry.
Enlisted for what?
Killing all the Indians.
And when Deirdre sees you, Tristan-- I swear she'll rip your other arm off.
Who is Deirdre?
My wife.

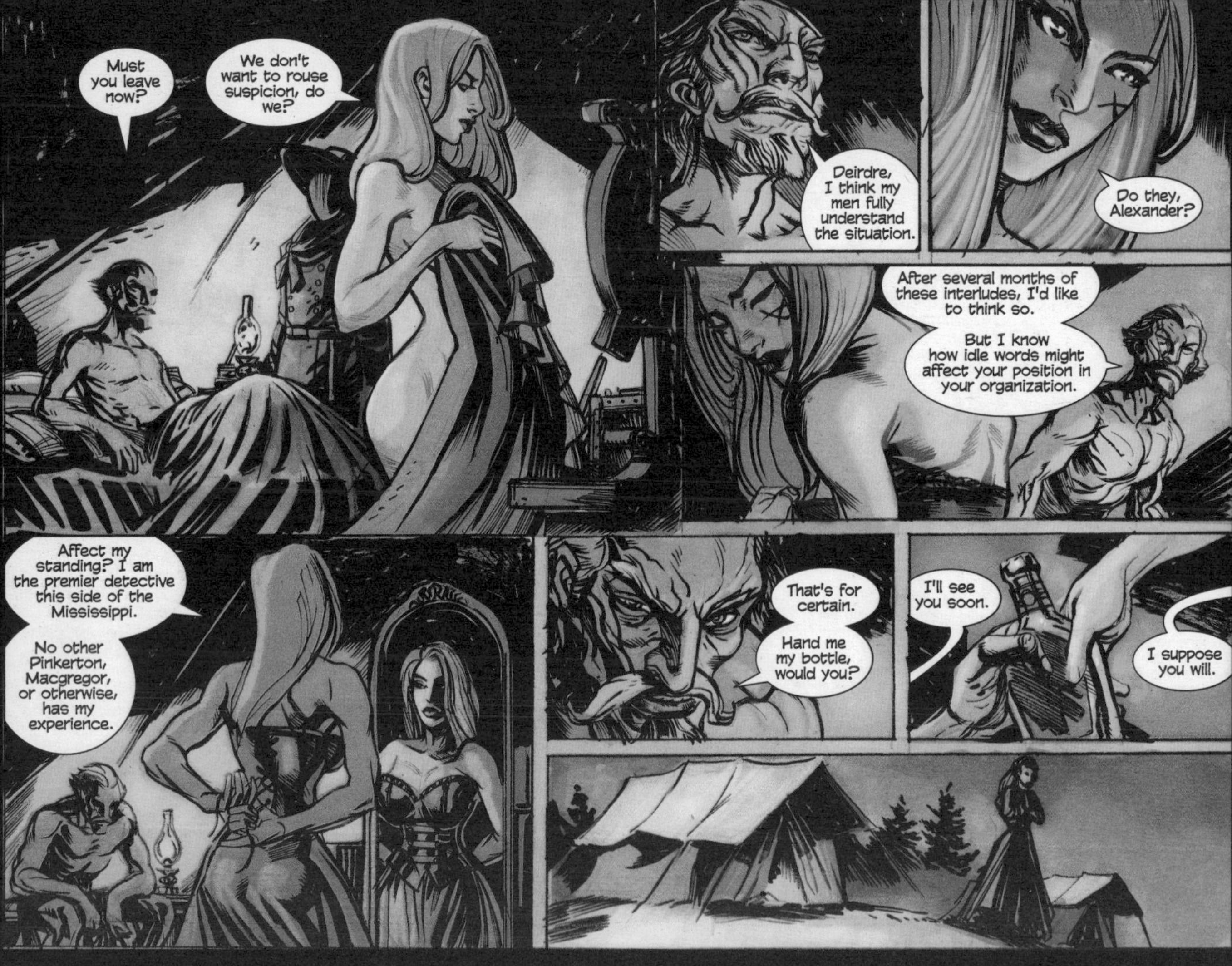
Must you leave now?
We don't want to rouse suspicion, do we?
Deirdre, I think my men fully understand the situation.
Do they, Alexander?
After several months of these interludes, I'd like to think so.
But I know how idle words might affect your position in your organization.
Affect my standing? I am the premier detective this side of the Mississippi.
No other Pinkerton, Macgregor, or otherwise, has my experience.
That's for certain.
Hand me my bottle, would you?
I'll see you soon.
I suppose you will.

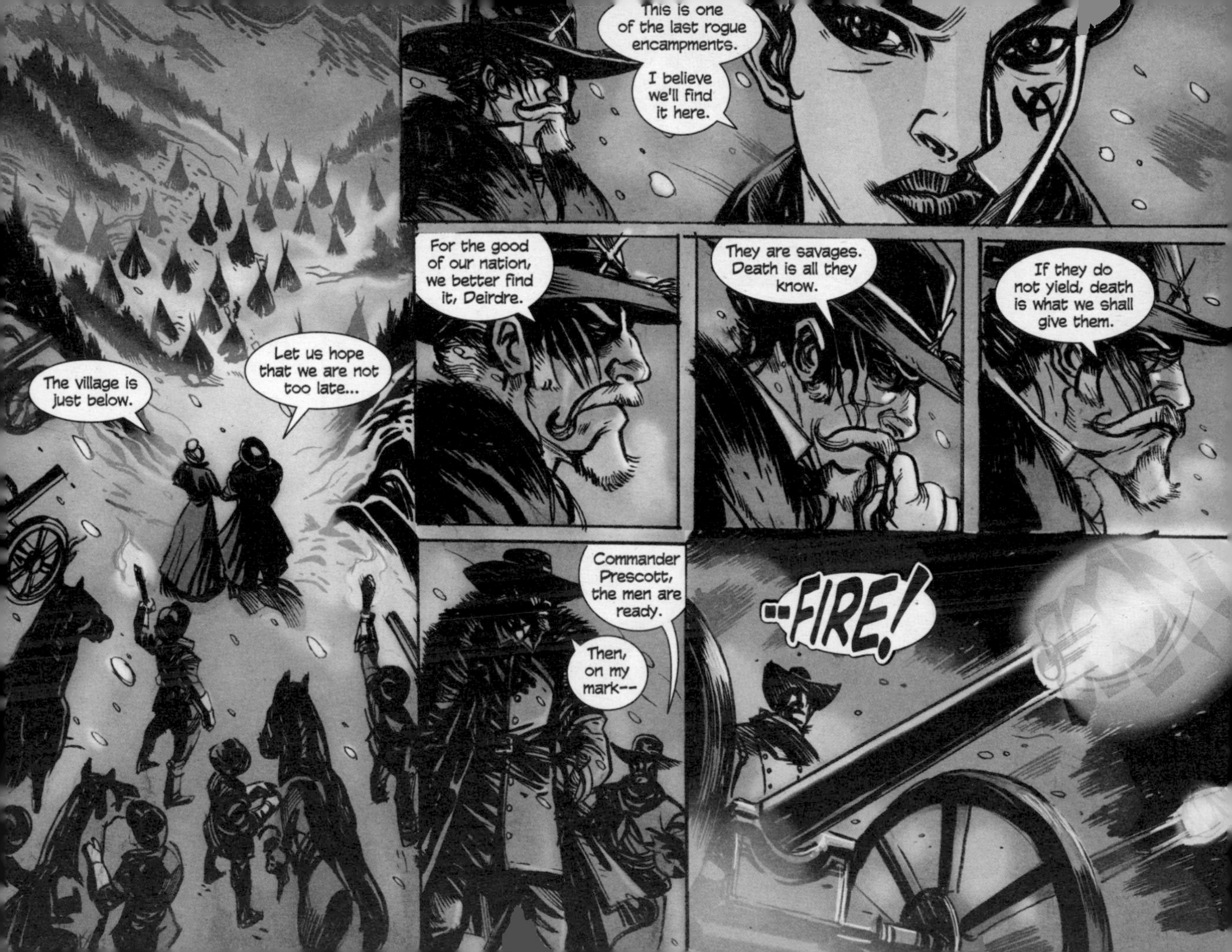
The village is just below.
Let us hope that we are not too late...
This is one of the last rogue encampments.
I believe we'll find it here.
For the good of our nation, we better find it, Deirdre.
They are savages. Death is all they know.
If they do not yield, death is what we shall give them.
Commander Prescott, the men are ready.
Then, on my mark--
--FIRE!

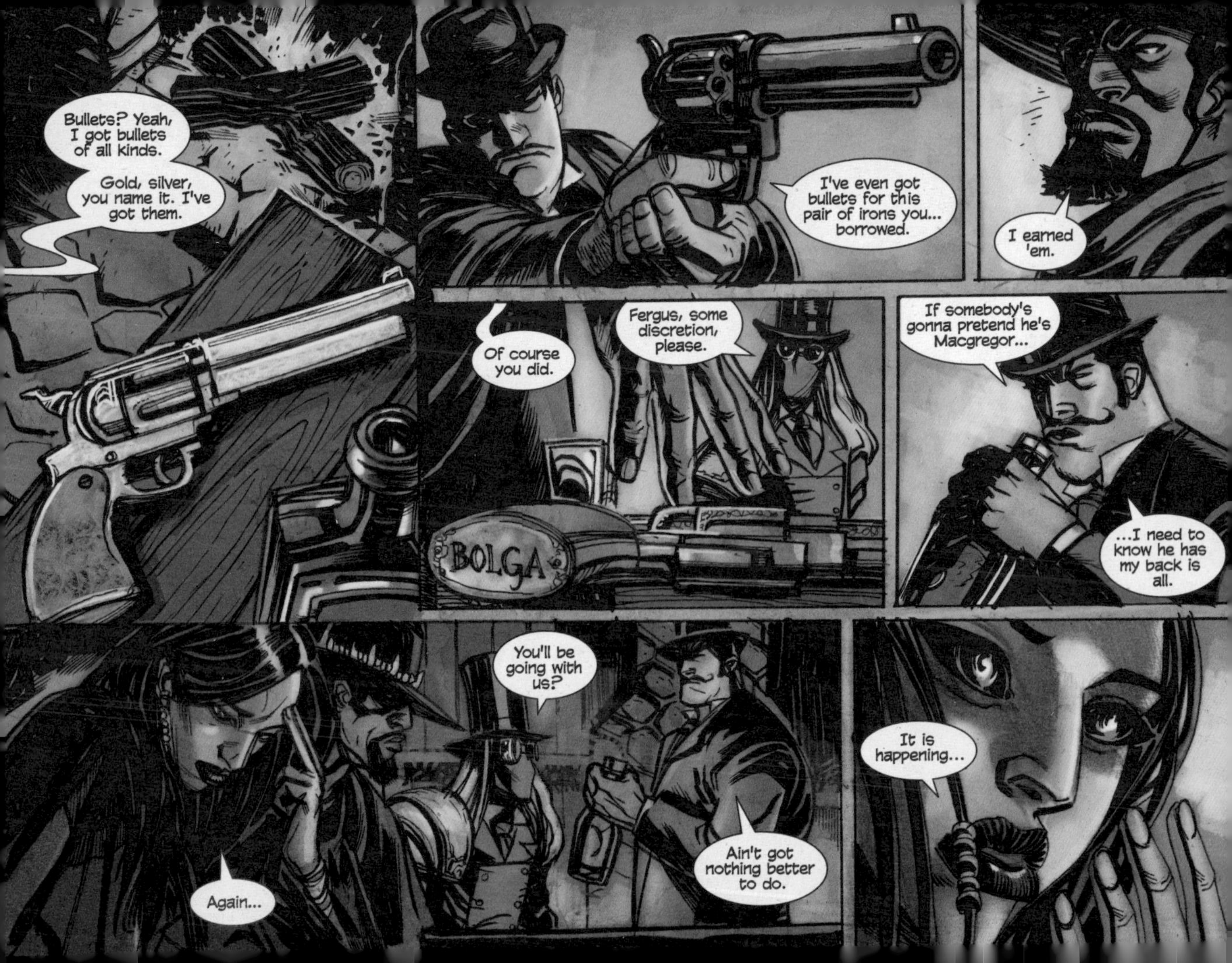

Bullets? Yeah, I got bullets of all kinds.
Gold, silver, you name it. I've got them.
I've even got bullets for this pair of irons you... borrowed.
I earned 'em.
Of course you did.
Fergus, some discretion, please.
BOLGA
If somebody's gonna pretend he's Macgregor...
...I need to know he has my back is all.
Again...
You'll be going with us?
Ain't got nothing better to do.
It is happening...

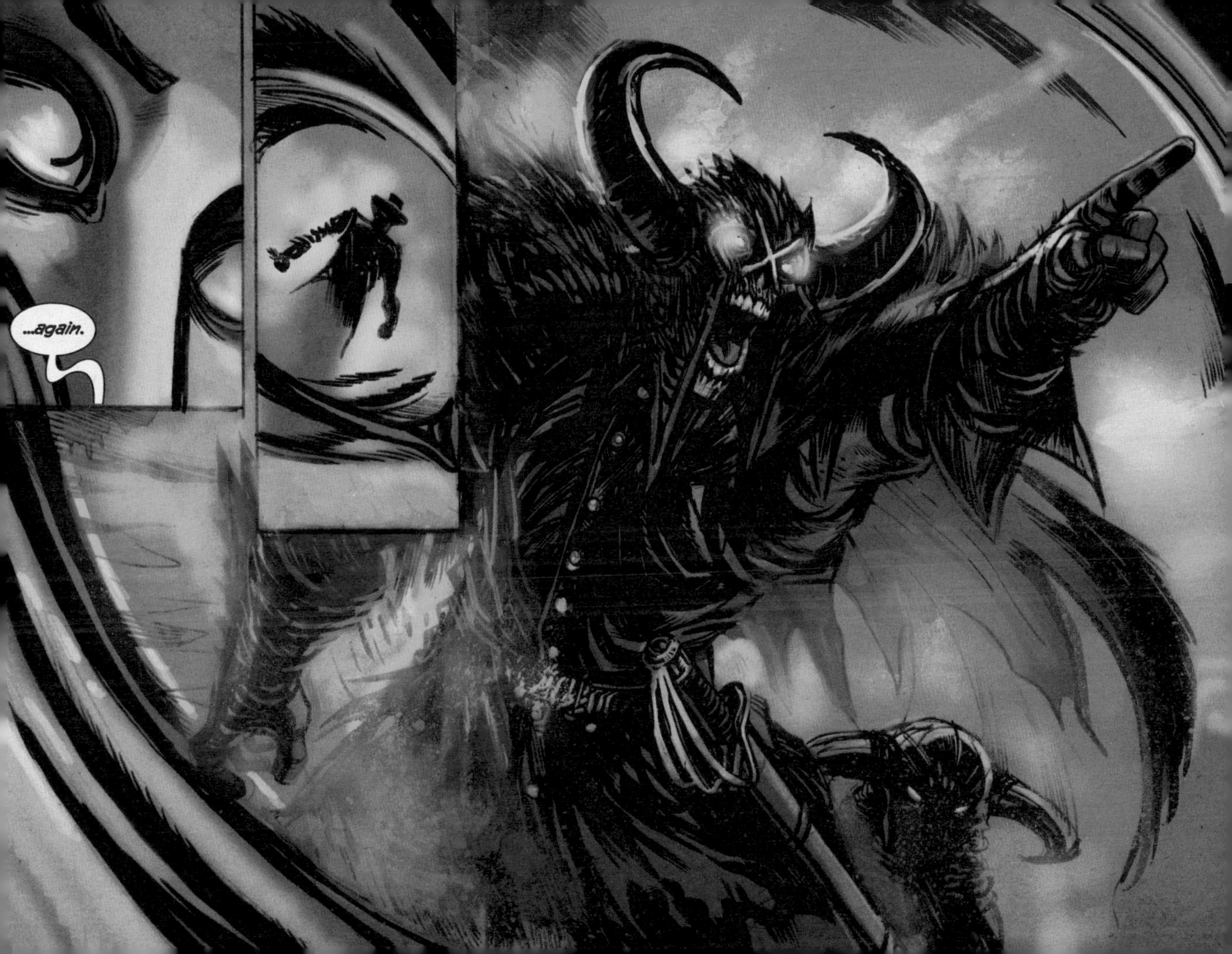
...again.

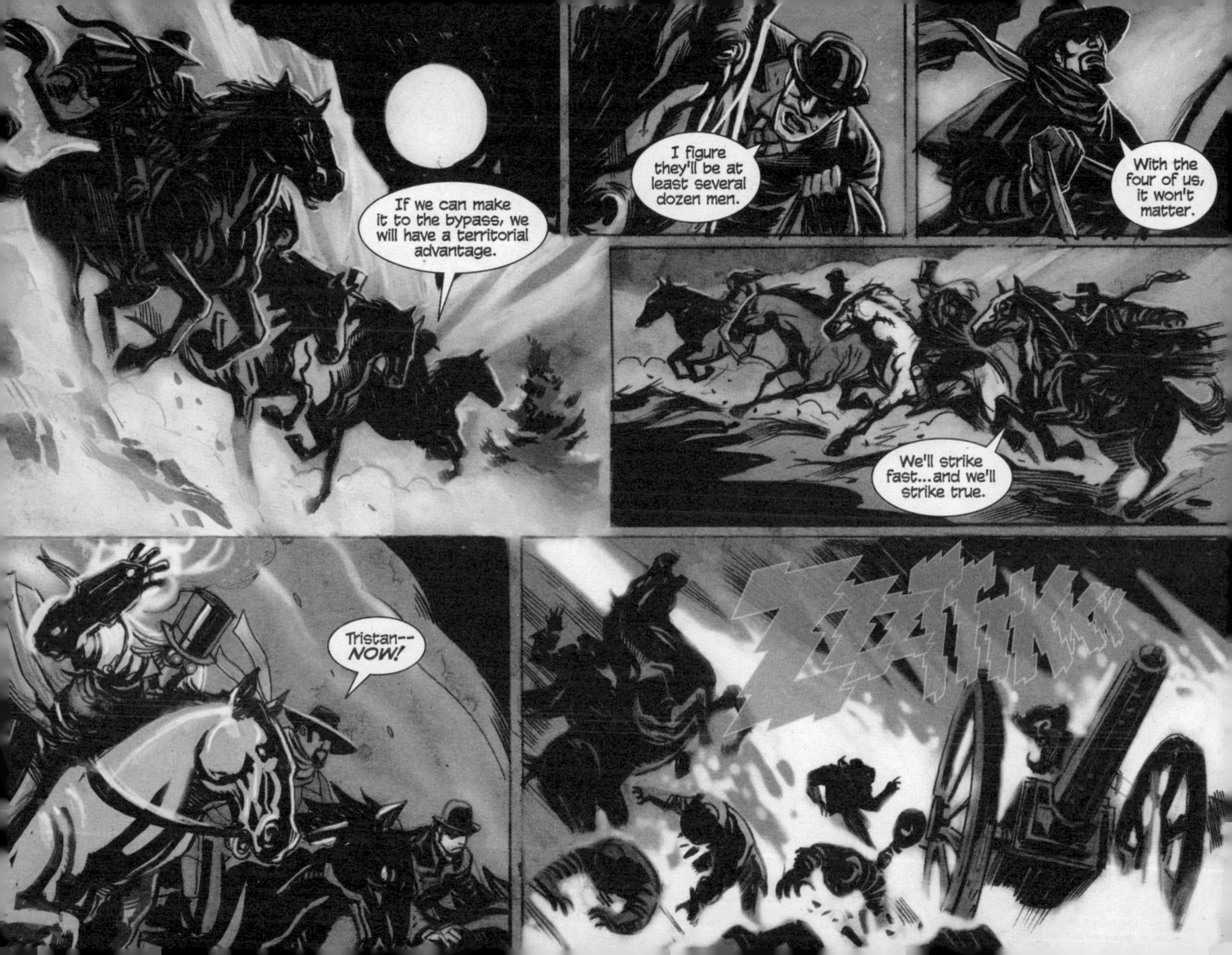
If we can make it to the bypass, we will have a territorial advantage.
I figure they'll be at least several dozen men.
With the four of us, it won't matter.
We'll strike fast...and we'll strike true.
Tristan-- NOW!
ZZZTTTKKK

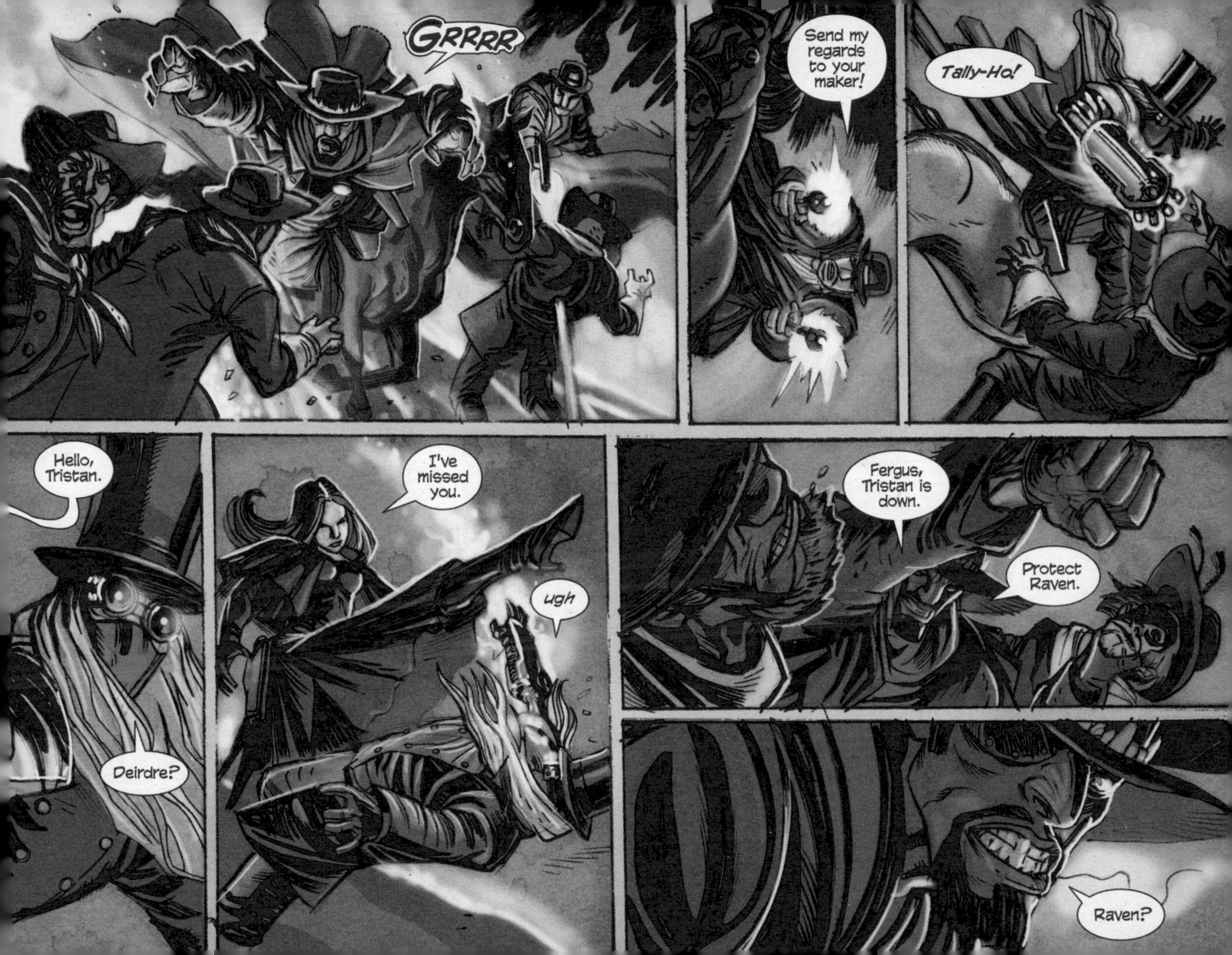
GRRRR
Send my regards to your maker!
Tally-Ho!
Hello, Tristan.
Deirdre?
I've missed you.
ugh
Fergus, Tristan is down.
Protect Raven.
Raven?

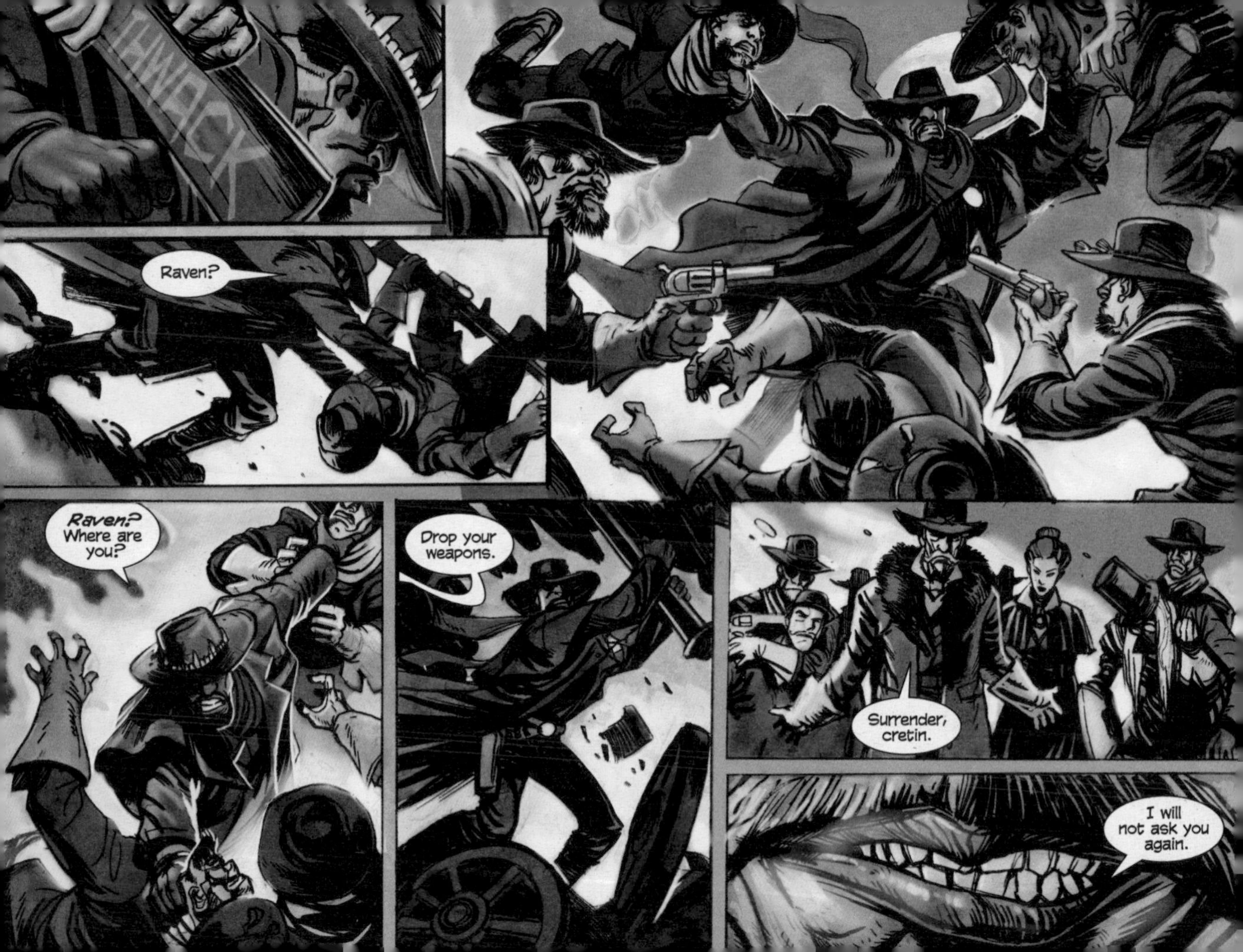
Raven?
Raven? Where are you?
Drop your weapons.
Surrender, cretin.
I will not ask you again.

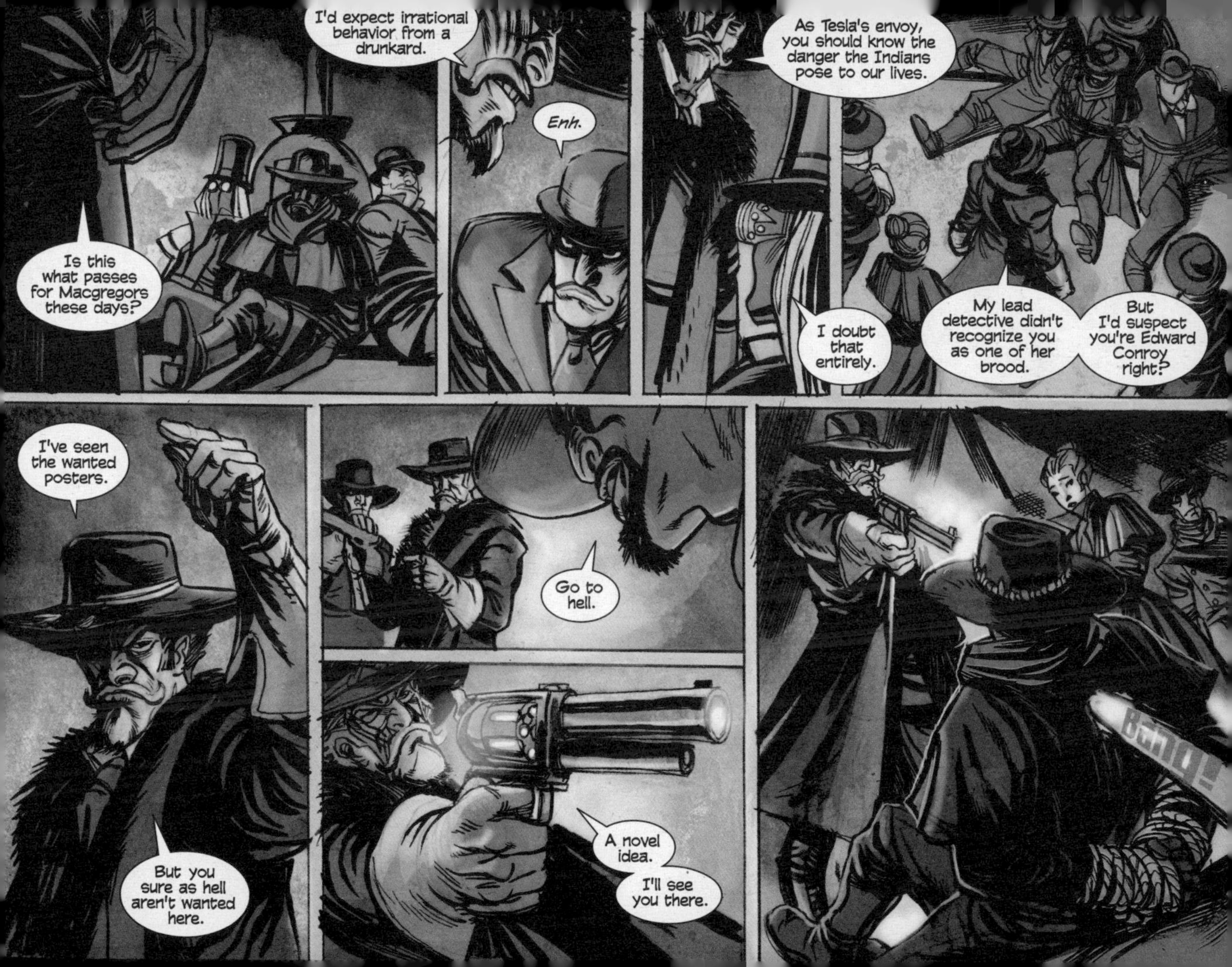
Is this what passes for Macgregors these days?
I'd expect irrational behavior from a drunkard.
Enh.
As Tesla's envoy, you should know the danger the Indians pose to our lives.
I doubt that entirely.
My lead detective didn't recognize you as one of her brood.
But I'd suspect you're Edward Conroy right?
I've seen the wanted posters.
But you sure as hell aren't wanted here.
Go to hell.
A novel idea.
I'll see you there.
Bang!

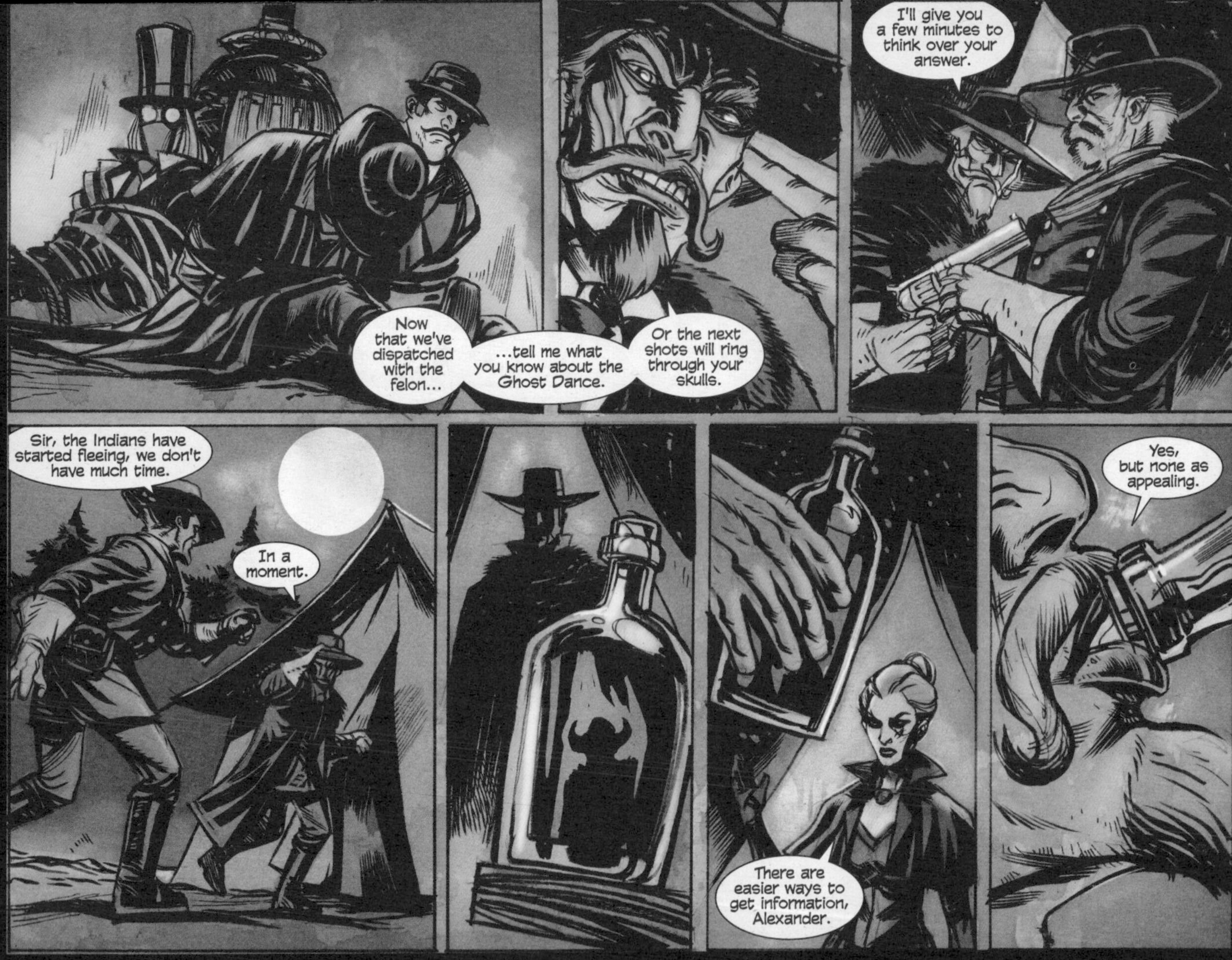
Now that we've dispatched with the felon...
...tell me what you know about the Ghost Dance.
Or the next shots will ring through your skulls.
I'll give you a few minutes to think over your answer.
Sir, the Indians have started fleeing, we don't have much time.
In a moment.
There are easier ways to get information, Alexander.
Yes, but none as appealing.

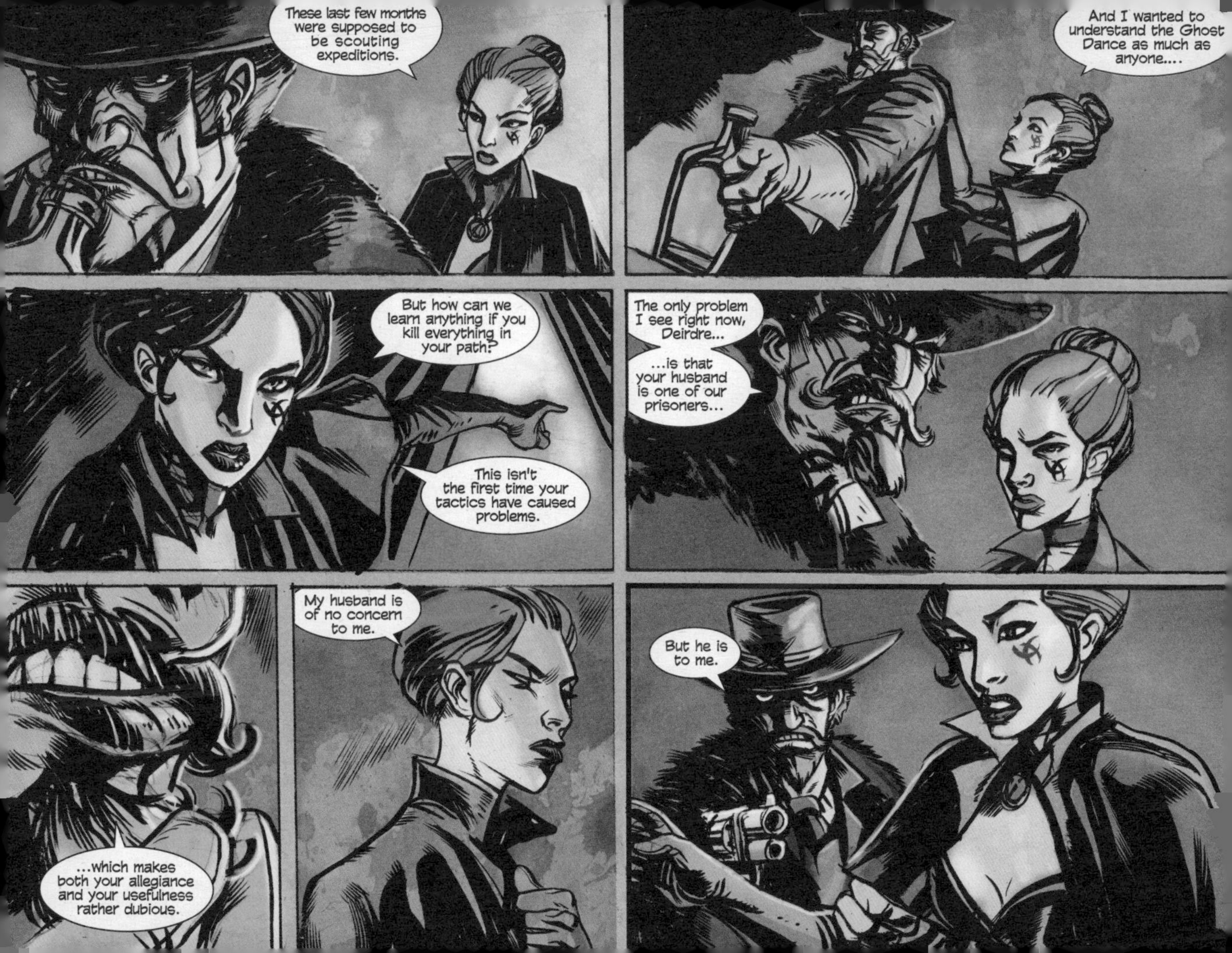
These last few months were supposed to be scouting expeditions.
And I wanted to understand the Ghost Dance as much as anyone....
But how can we learn anything if you kill everything in your path?
This isn't the first time your tactics have caused problems.
The only problem I see right now, Deirdre...
...is that your husband is one of our prisoners...
...which makes both your allegiance and your usefulness rather dubious.
My husband is of no concern to me.
But he is to me.

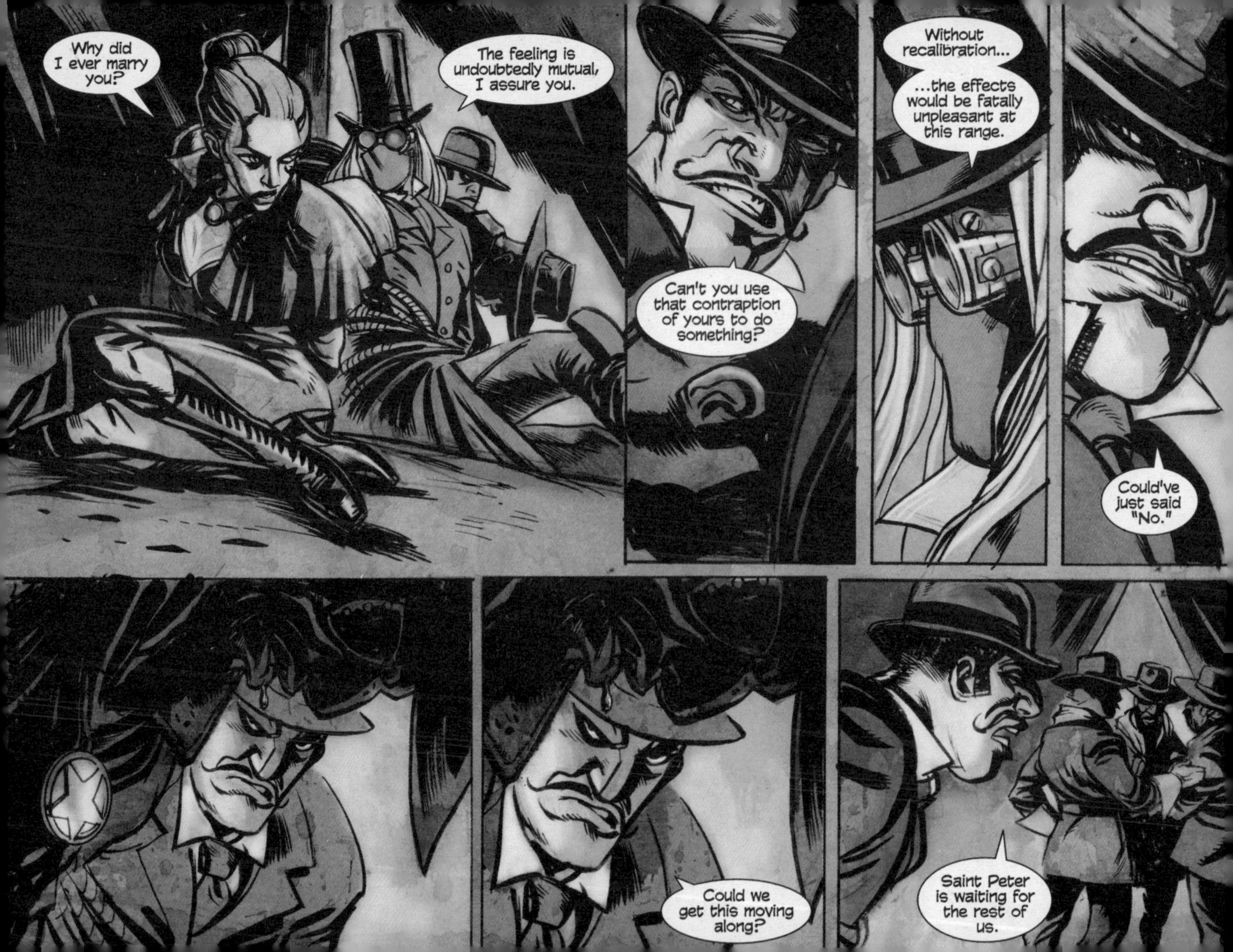
Why did I ever marry you?
The feeling is undoubtedly mutual, I assure you.
Can't you use that contraption of yours to do something?
Without recalibration...
...the effects would be fatally unpleasant at this range.
Could've just said "No."
Could we get this moving along?
Saint Peter is waiting for the rest of us.

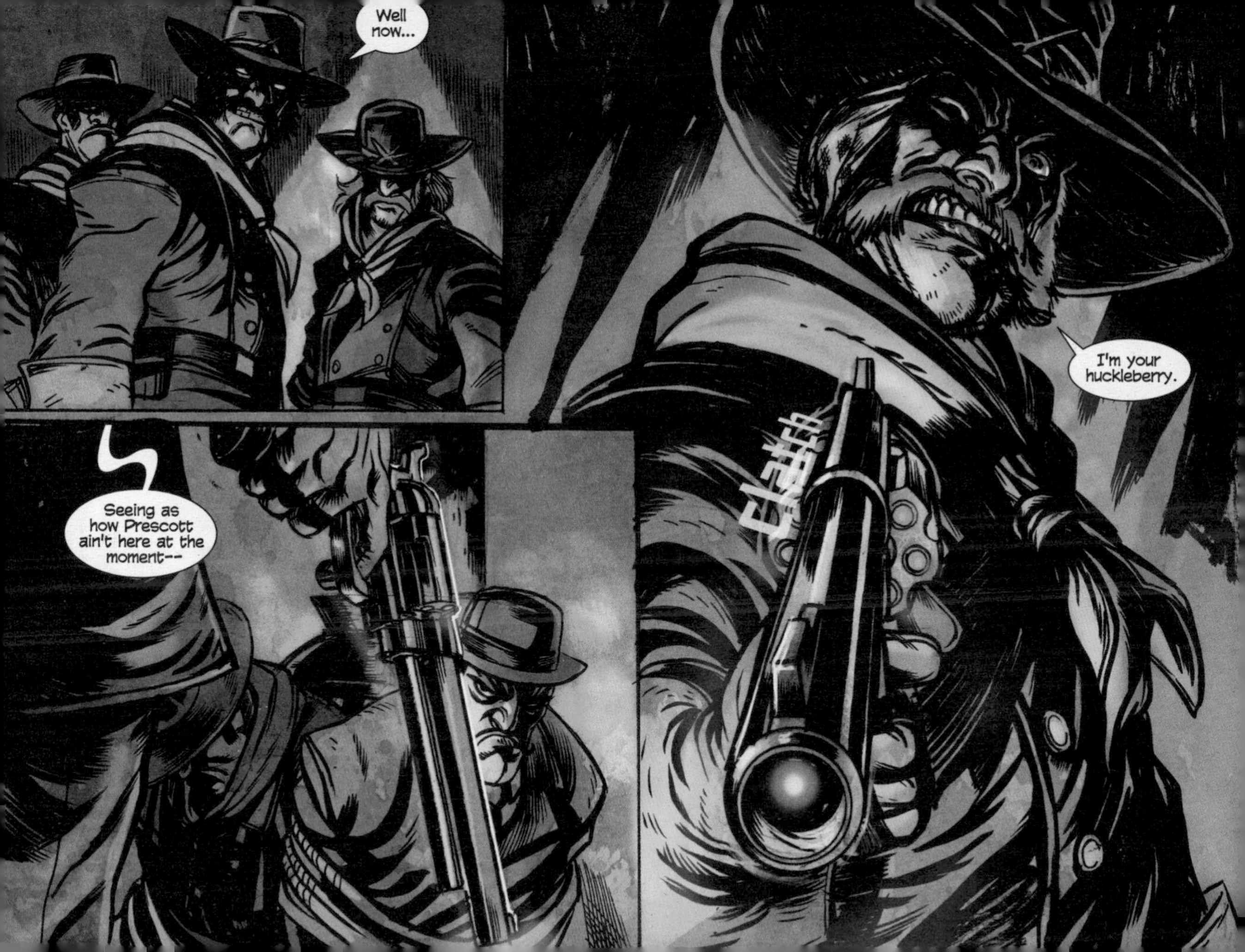
Well now...
Seeing as how Prescott ain't here at the moment--
I'm your huckleberry.
clatch

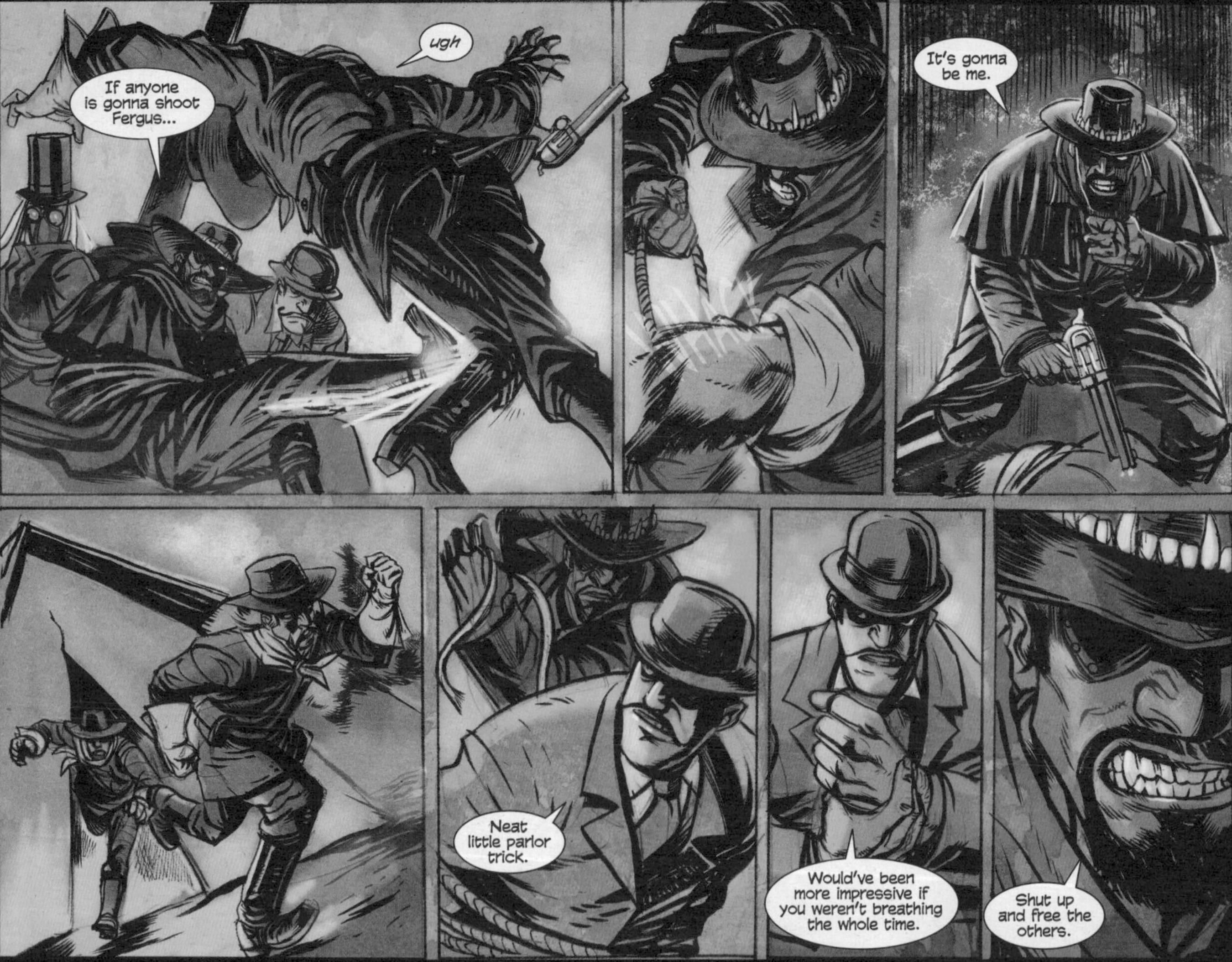
ugh
If anyone is gonna shoot Fergus...
It's gonna be me.
Neat little parlor trick.
Would've been more impressive if you weren't breathing the whole time.
Shut up and free the others.

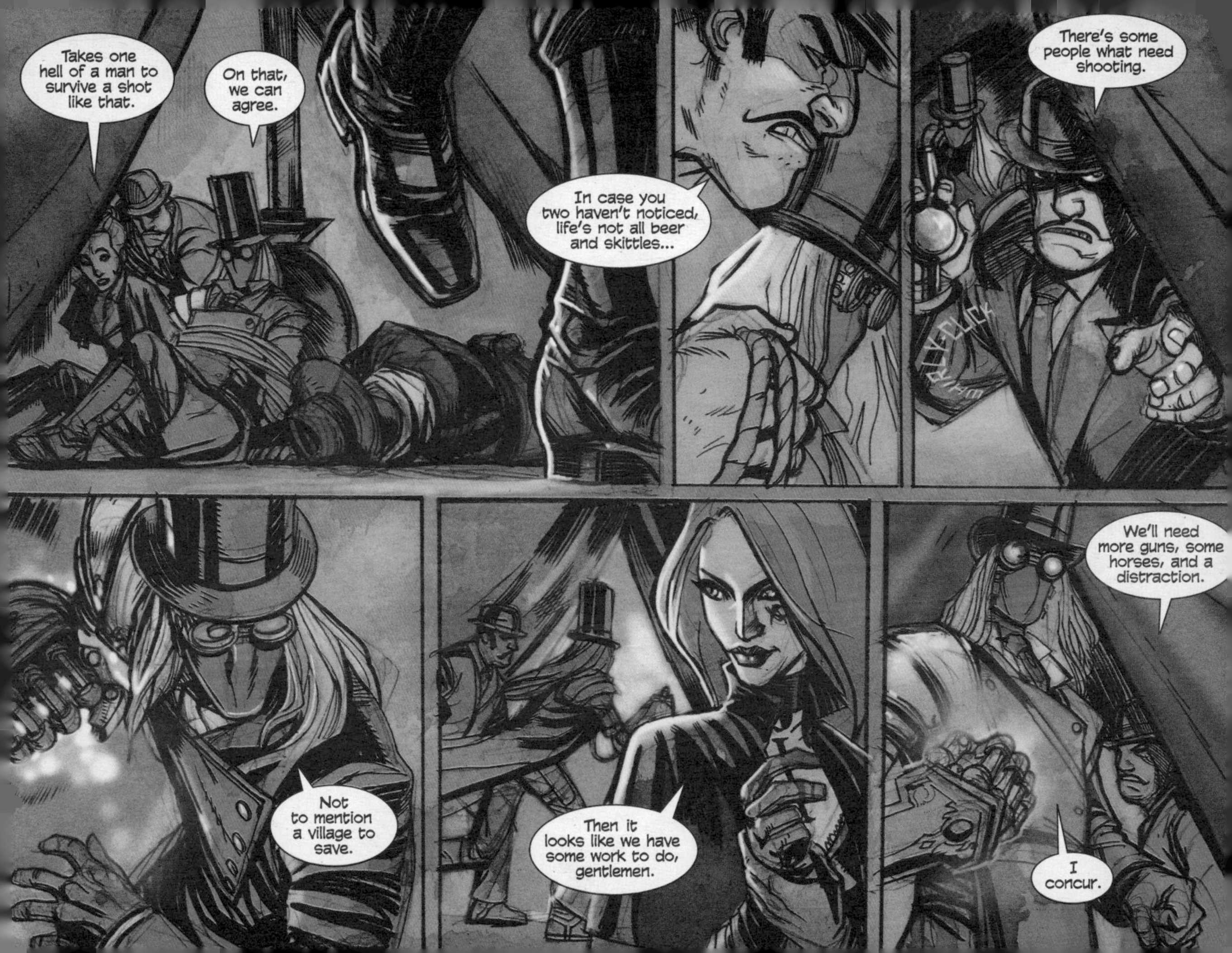
Takes one hell of a man to survive a shot like that.
On that, we can agree.
In case you two haven't noticed, life's not all beer and skittles...
There's some people what need shooting.
Not to mention a village to save.
Then it looks like we have some work to do, gentlemen.
We'll need more guns, some horses, and a distraction.
I concur.

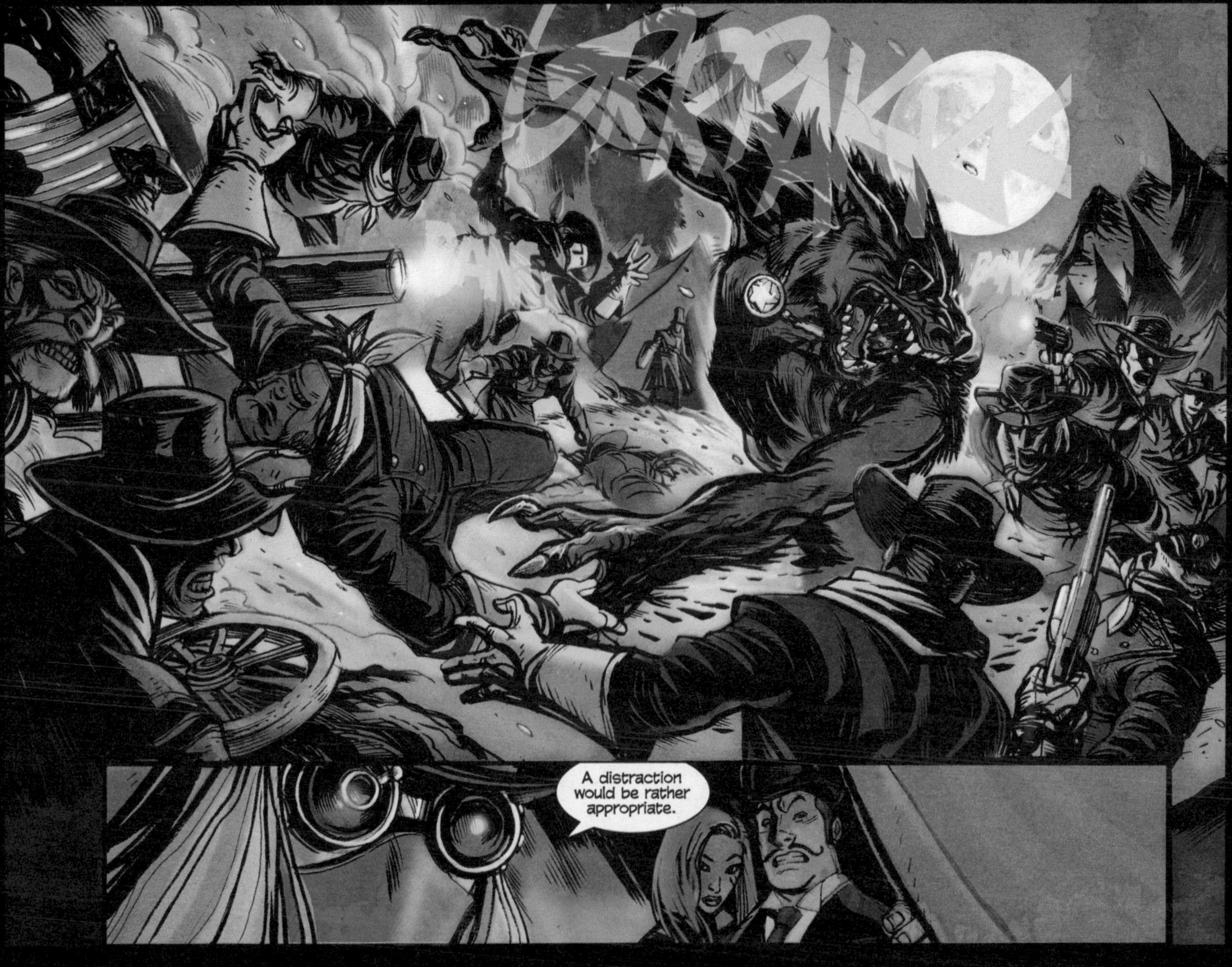
A distraction would be rather appropriate.

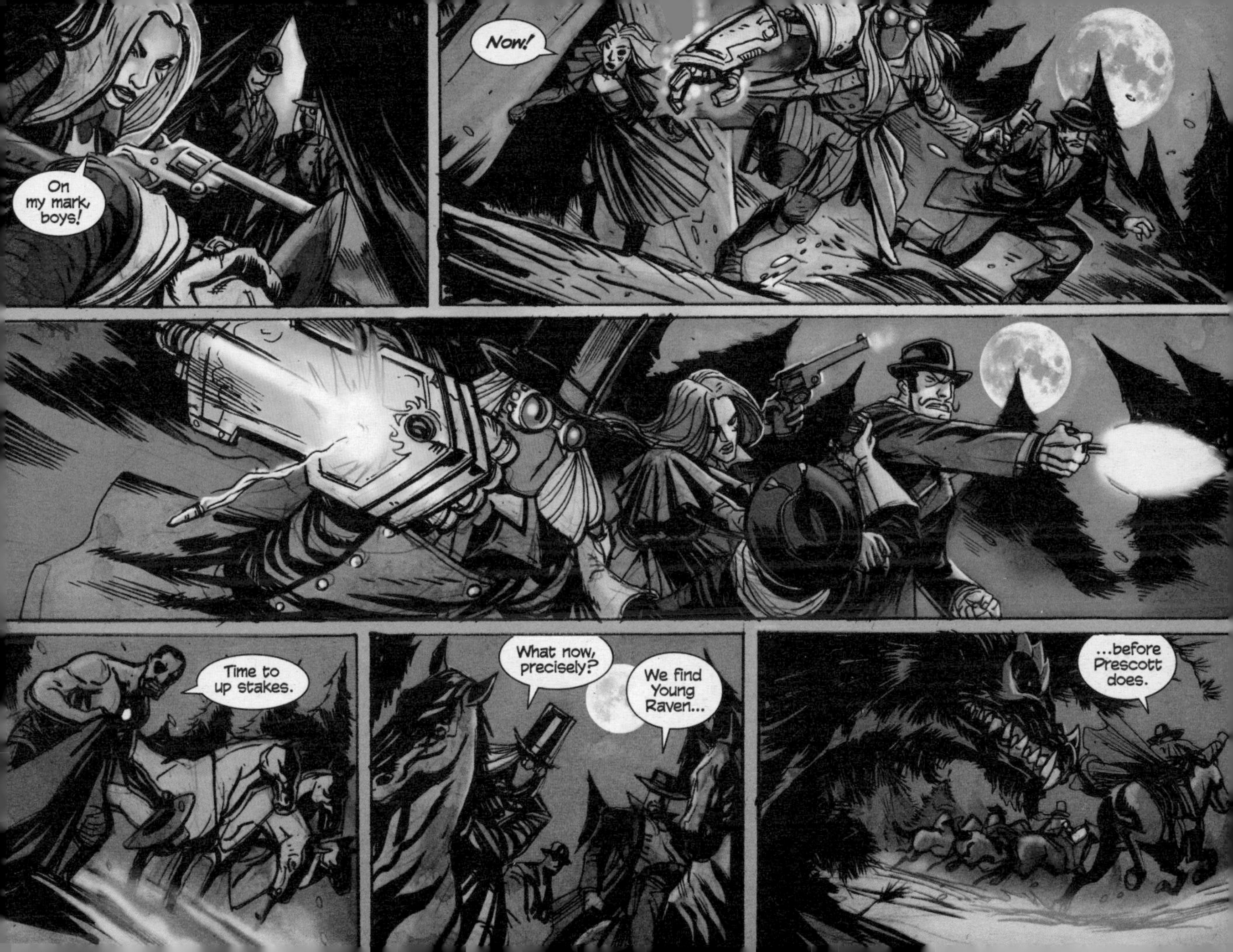
On my mark, boys!
Now!
Time to up stakes.
What now, precisely?
We find Young Raven...
...before Prescott does.

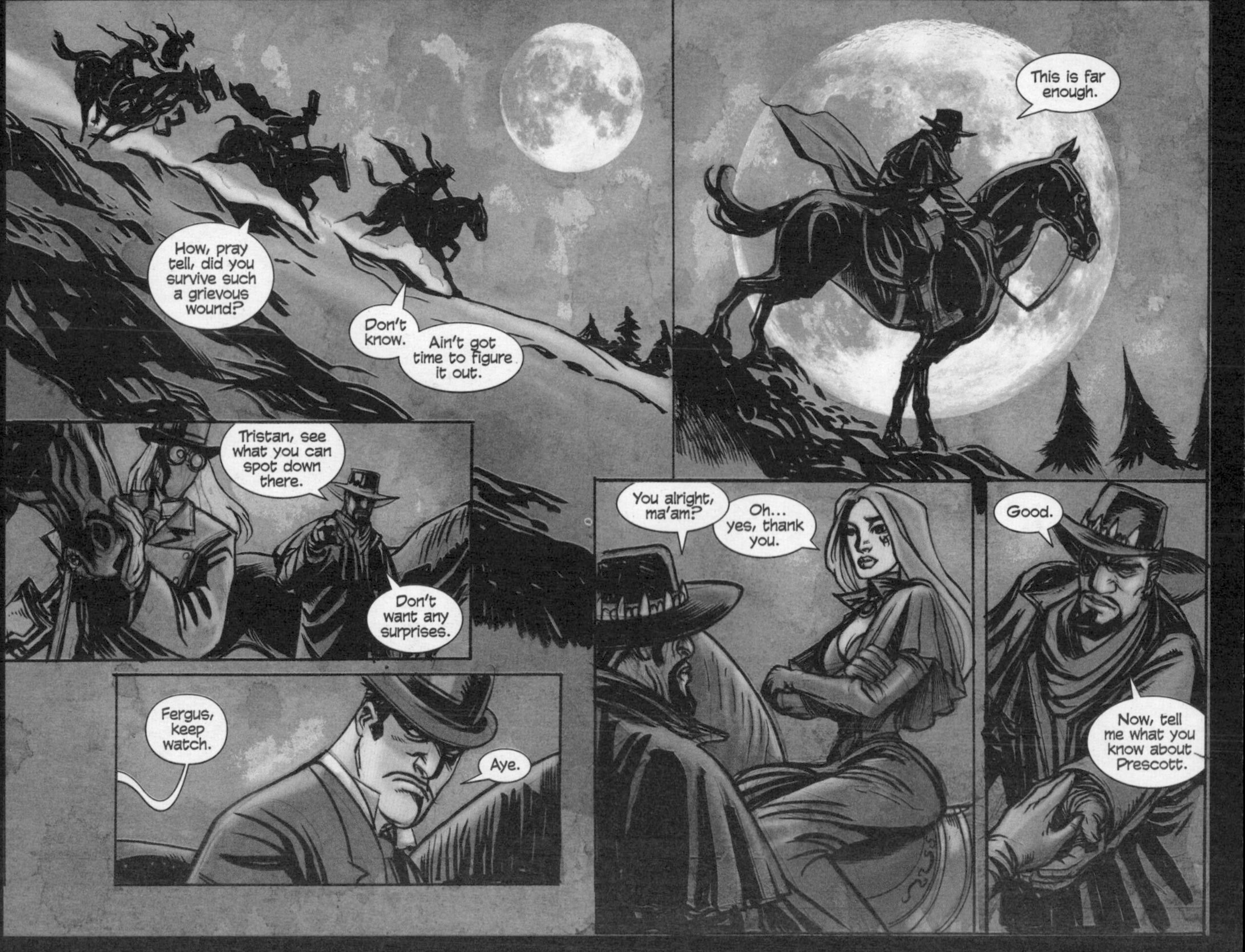
How, pray tell, did you survive such a grievous wound?
Don't know.
Ain't got time to figure it out.
This is far enough.
Tristan, see what you can spot down there.
Don't want any surprises.
Fergus, keep watch.
Aye.
You alright, ma'am?
Oh... yes, thank you.
Good.
Now, tell me what you know about Prescott.

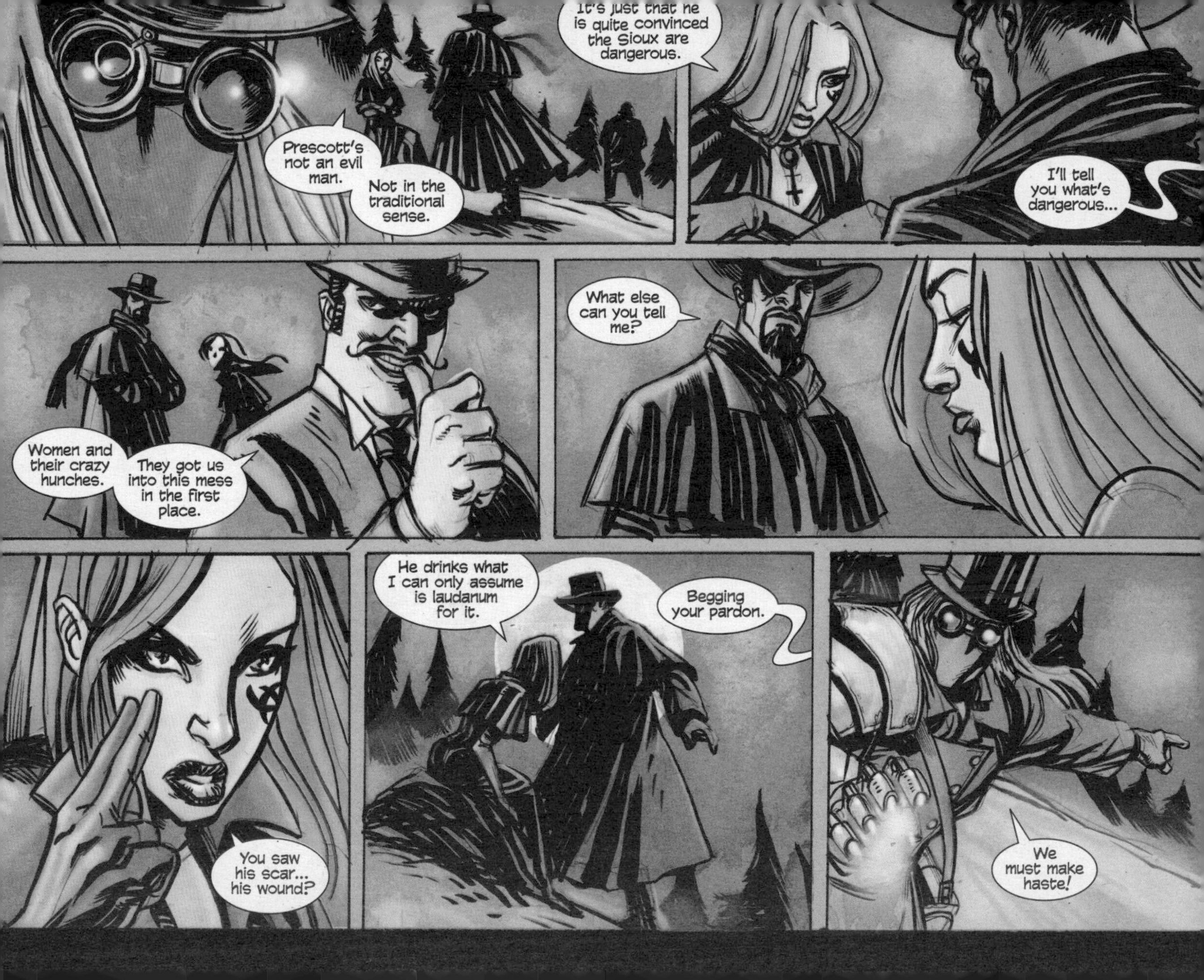
It's just that he is quite convinced the Sioux are dangerous.
Prescott's not an evil man.
Not in the traditional sense.
I'll tell you what's dangerous...
Women and their crazy hunches.
They got us into this mess in the first place.
What else can you tell me?
You saw his scar... his wound?
He drinks what I can only assume is laudanum for it.
Begging your pardon.
We must make haste!

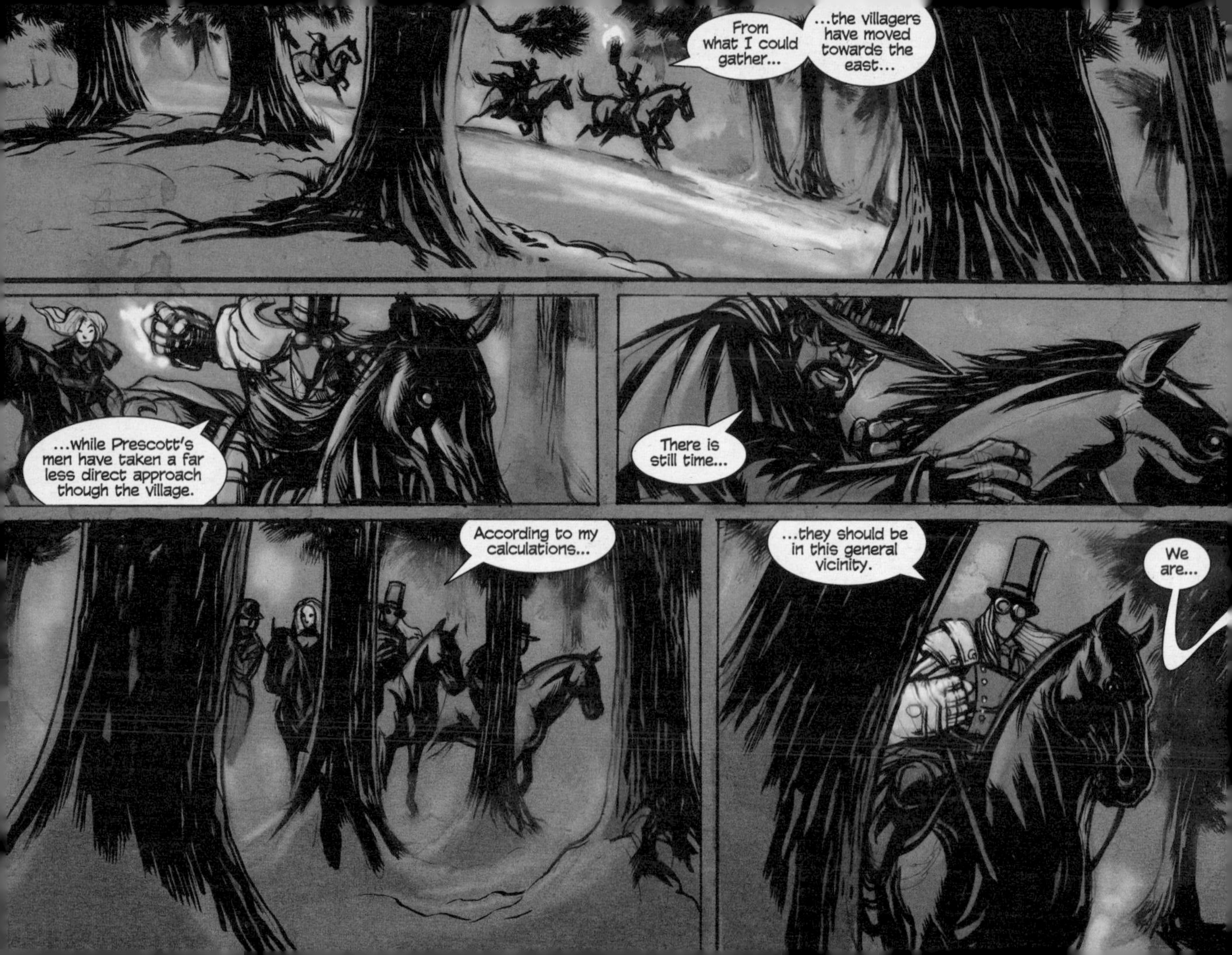
From what I could gather...
...the villagers have moved towards the east...
...while Prescott's men have taken a far less direct approach though the village.
There is still time...
According to my calculations...
...they should be in this general vicinity.
We are...

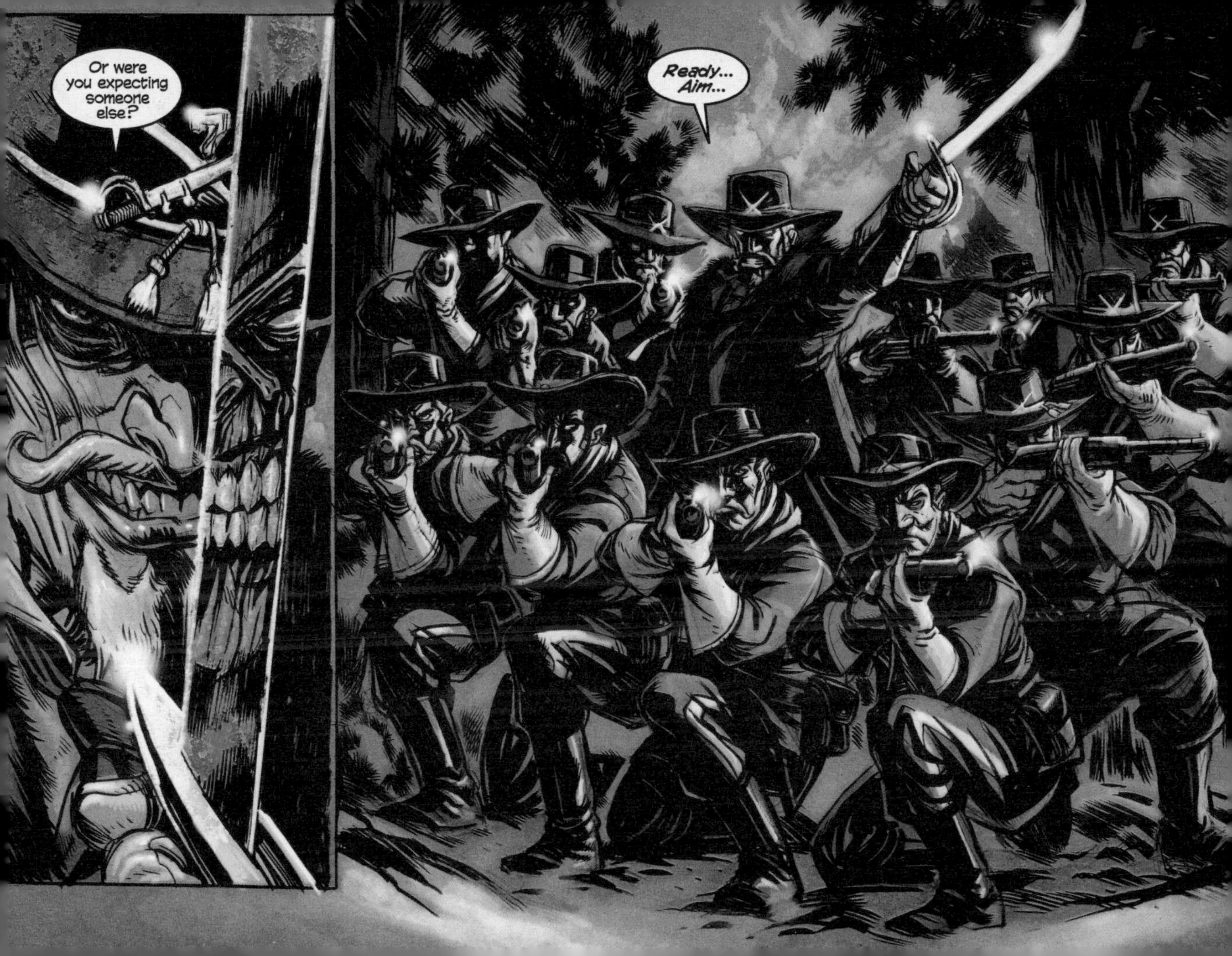
Or were you expecting someone else?
Ready... Aim...

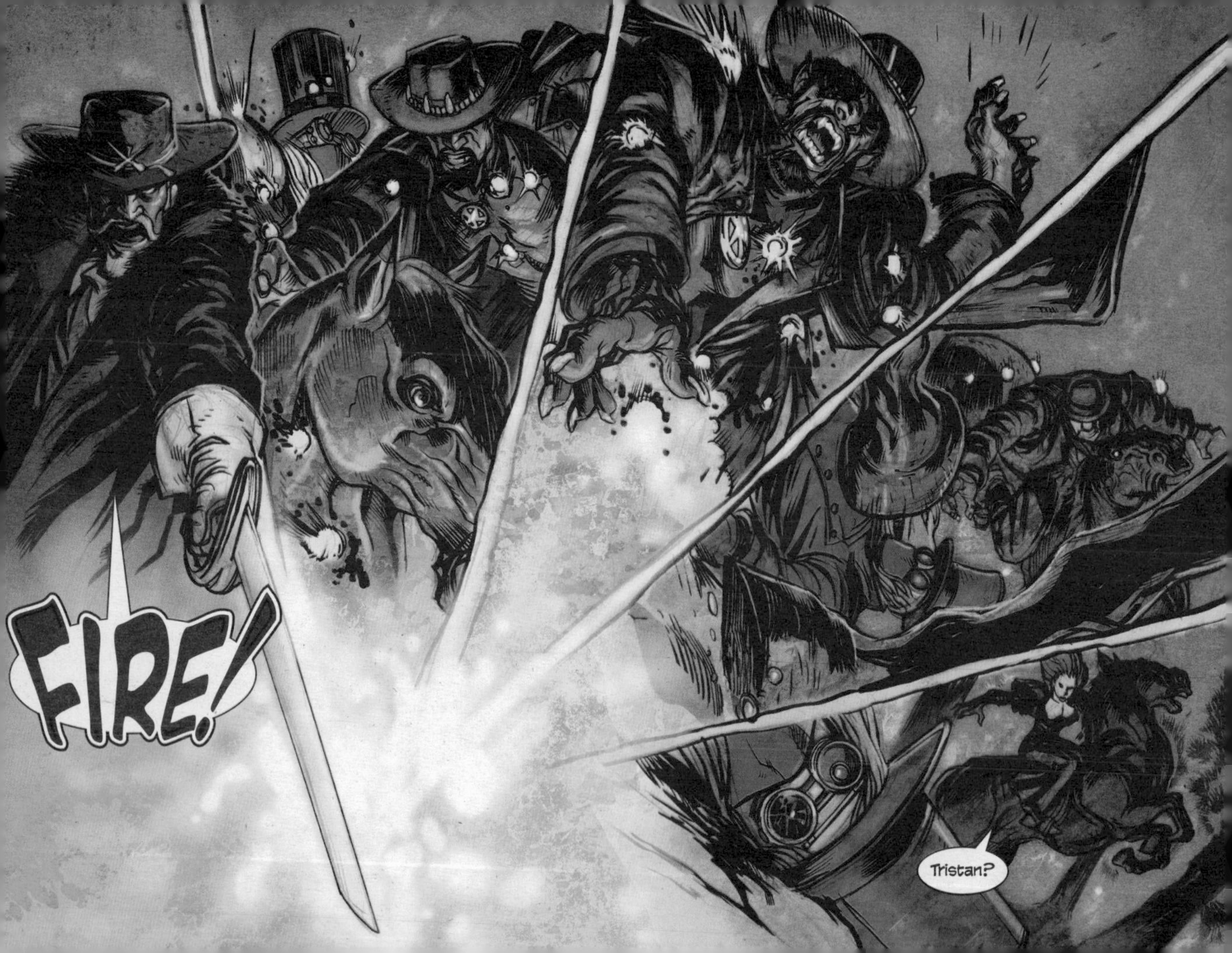
FIRE!
Tristan?

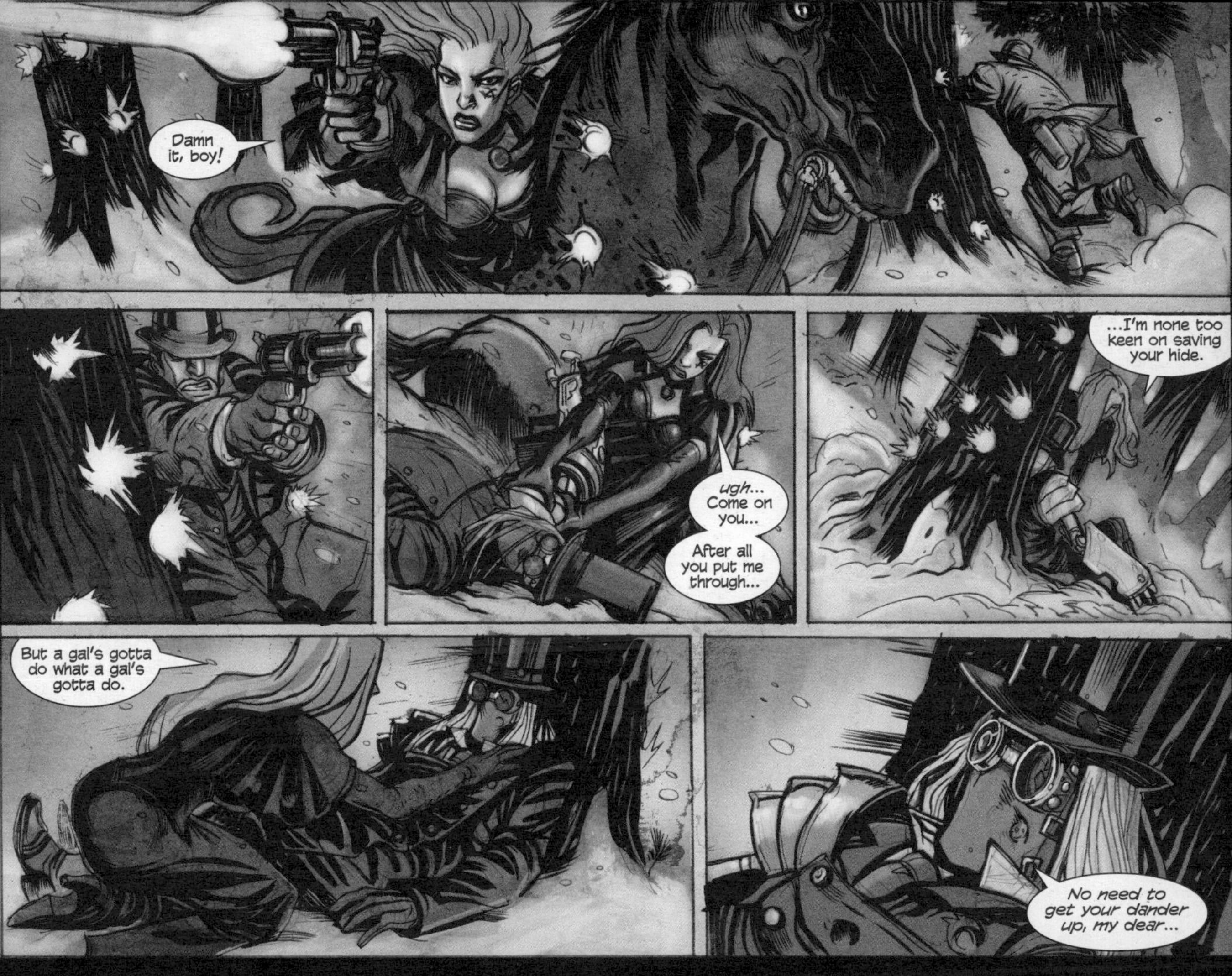

Damn it, boy!
ugh... Come on you...
After all you put me through...
...I'm none too keen on saving your hide.
But a gal's gotta do what a gal's gotta do.
No need to get your dander up, my dear...

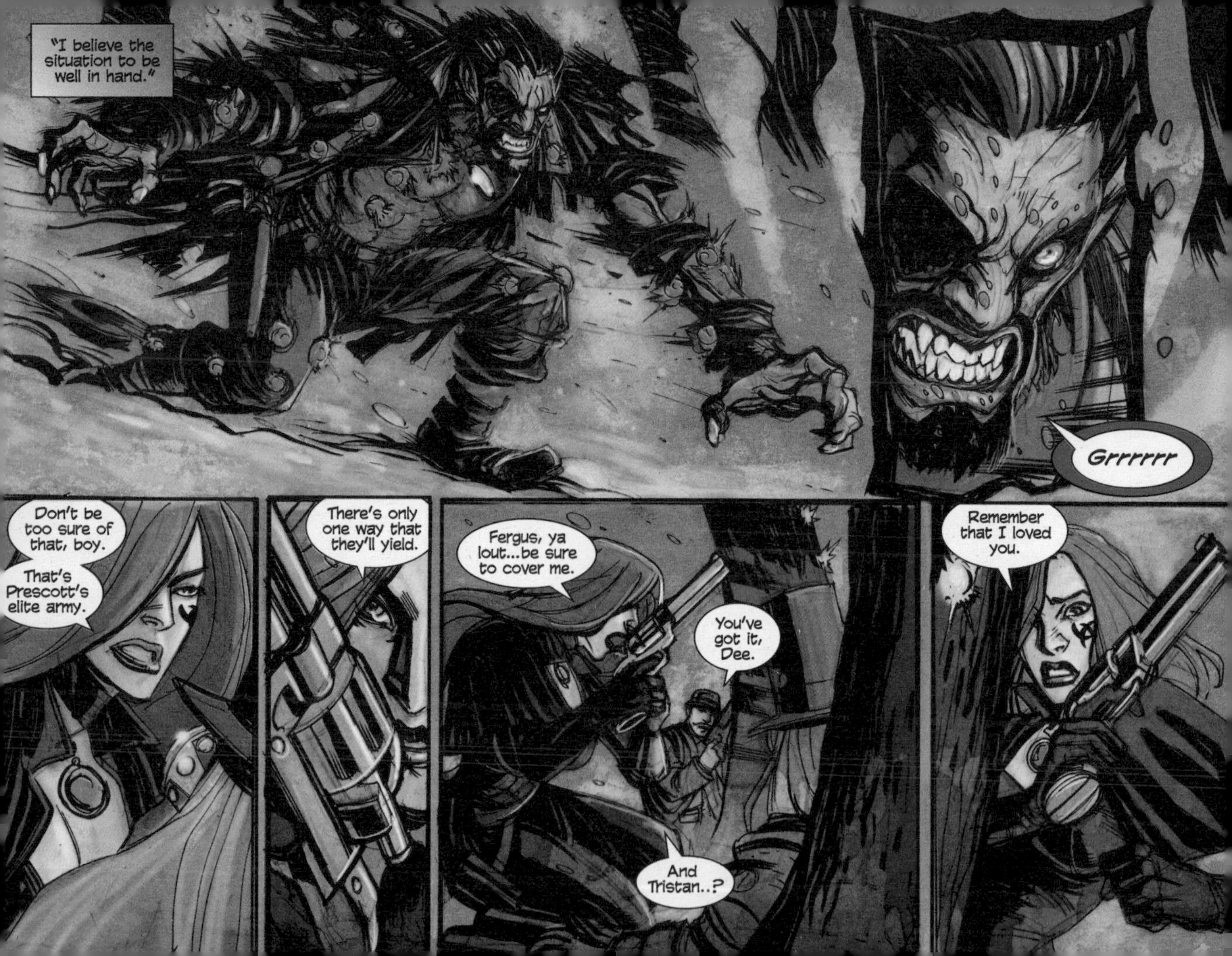
"I believe the situation to be well in hand."
Grrrrrr
Don't be too sure of that, boy.
That's Prescott's elite army.
There's only one way that they'll yield.
Fergus, ya lout...be sure to cover me.
You've got it, Dee.
And Tristan..?
Remember that I loved you.

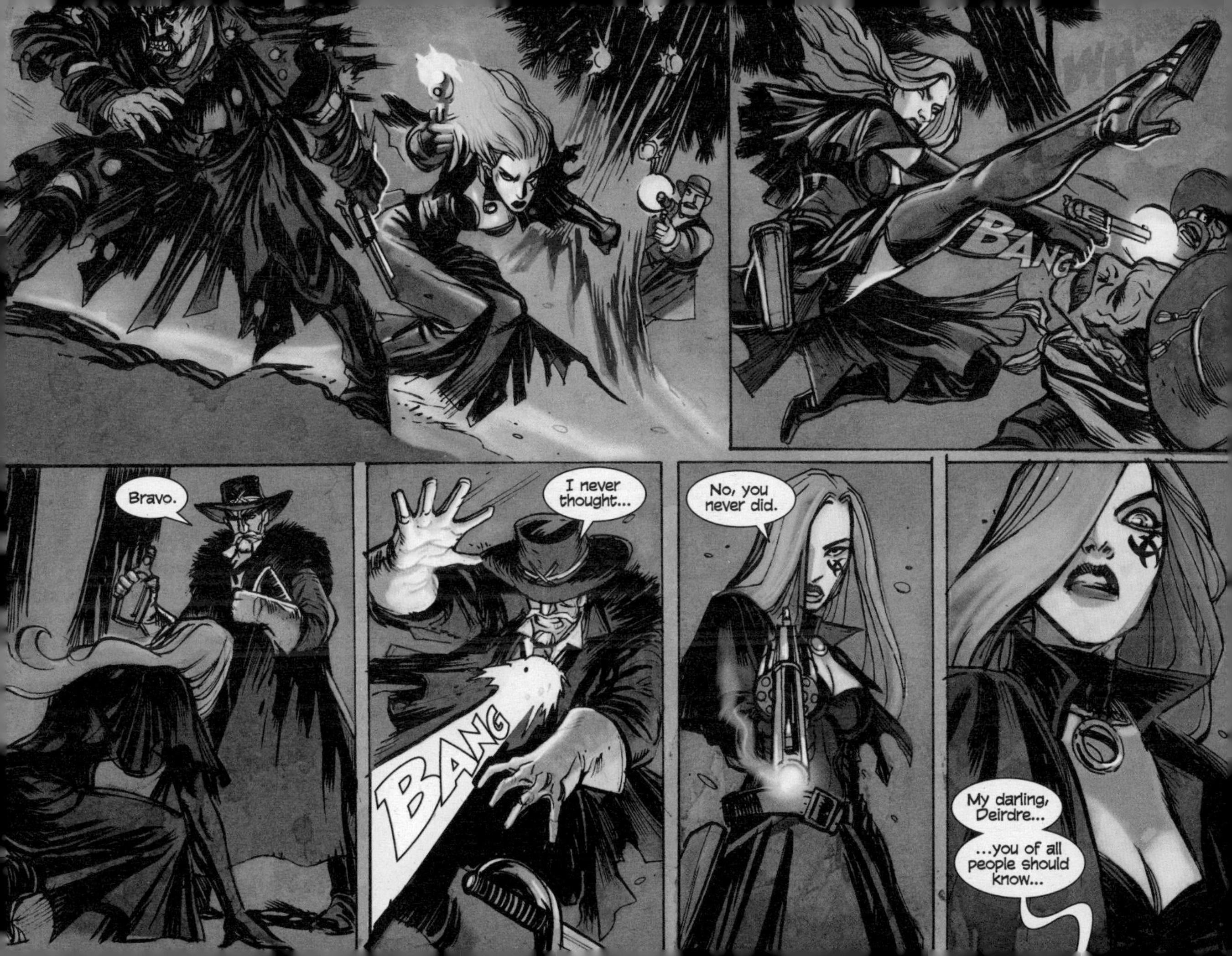
BANG
Bravo.
I never thought...
BANG
No, you never did.
My darling, Deirdre...
...you of all people should know...

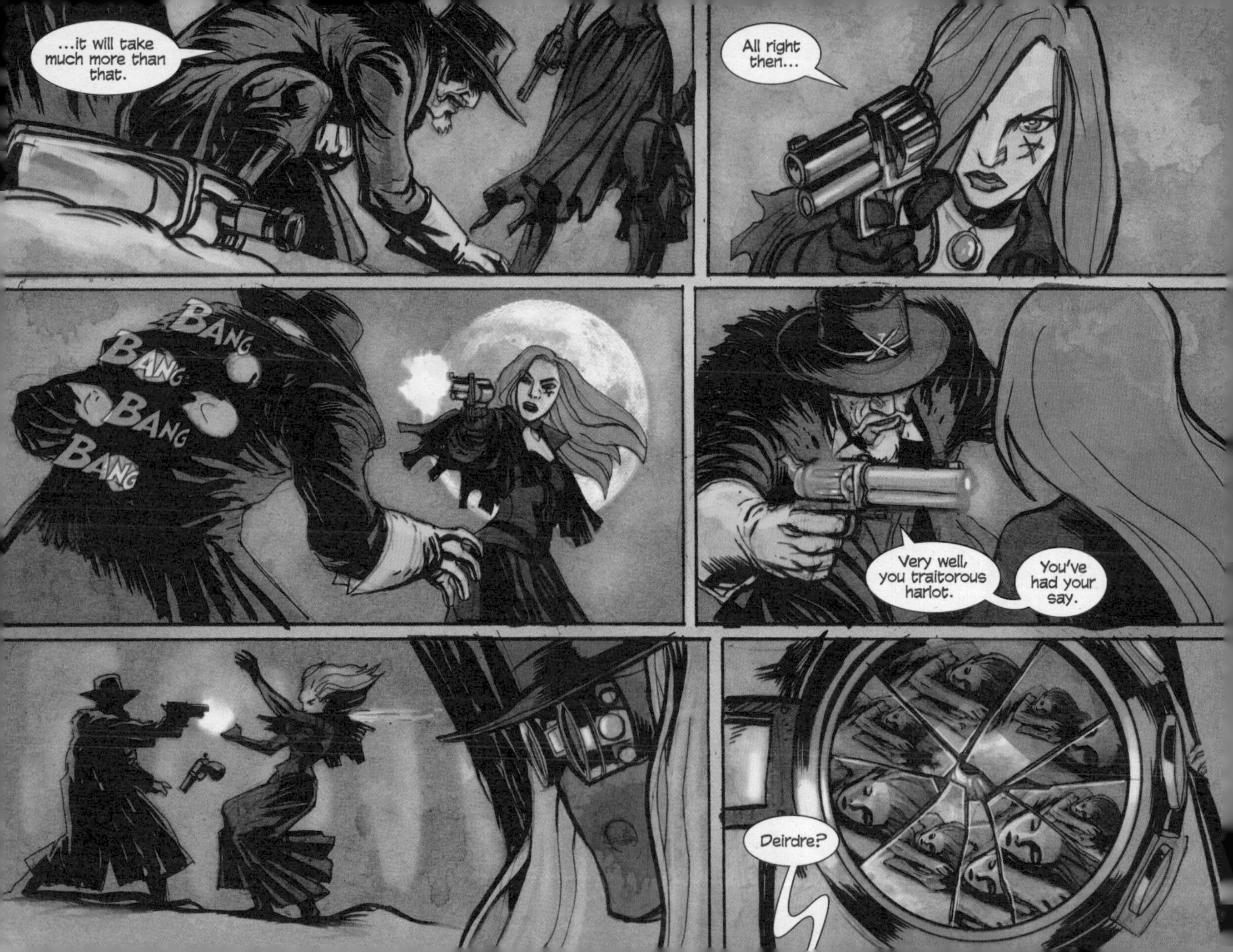
...it will take much more than that.
All right then...
BANG
BANG
BANG
BANG
BANG
BANG
Very well, you traitorous harlot.
You've had your say.
Deirdre?

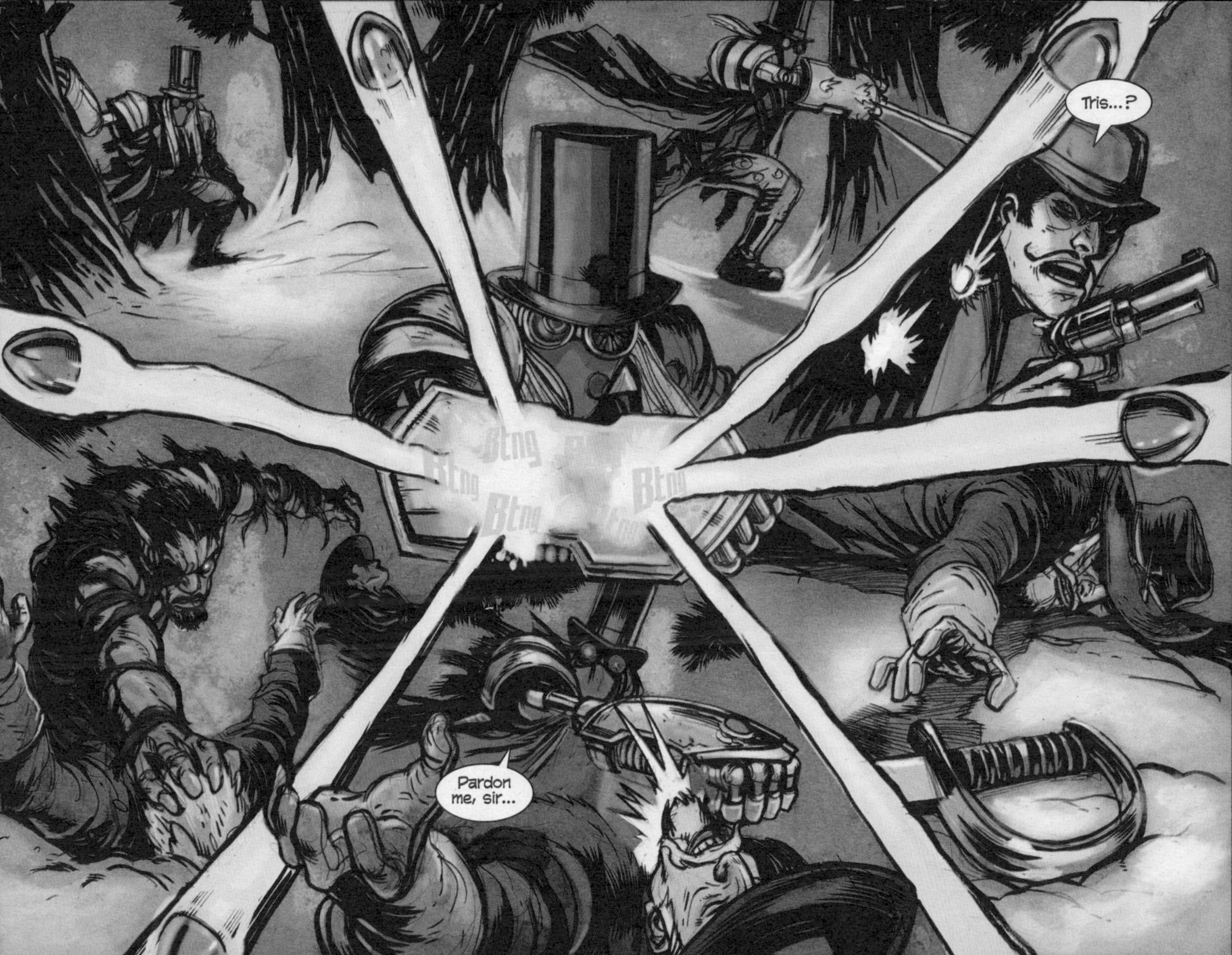
Tris...?
Btng
Btng
Btng
Btng
Pardon me, sir...

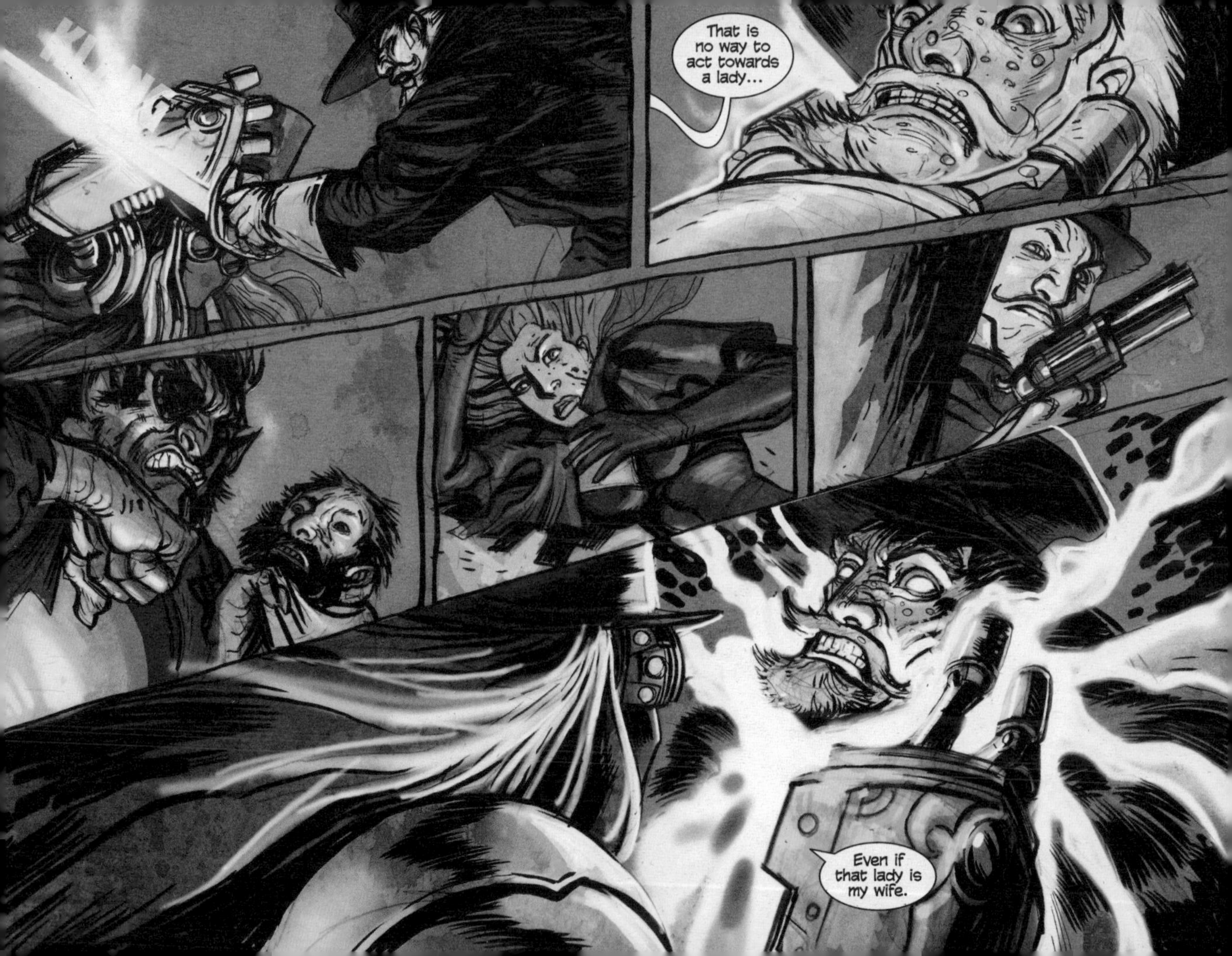
That is no way to act towards a lady...
Even if that lady is my wife.

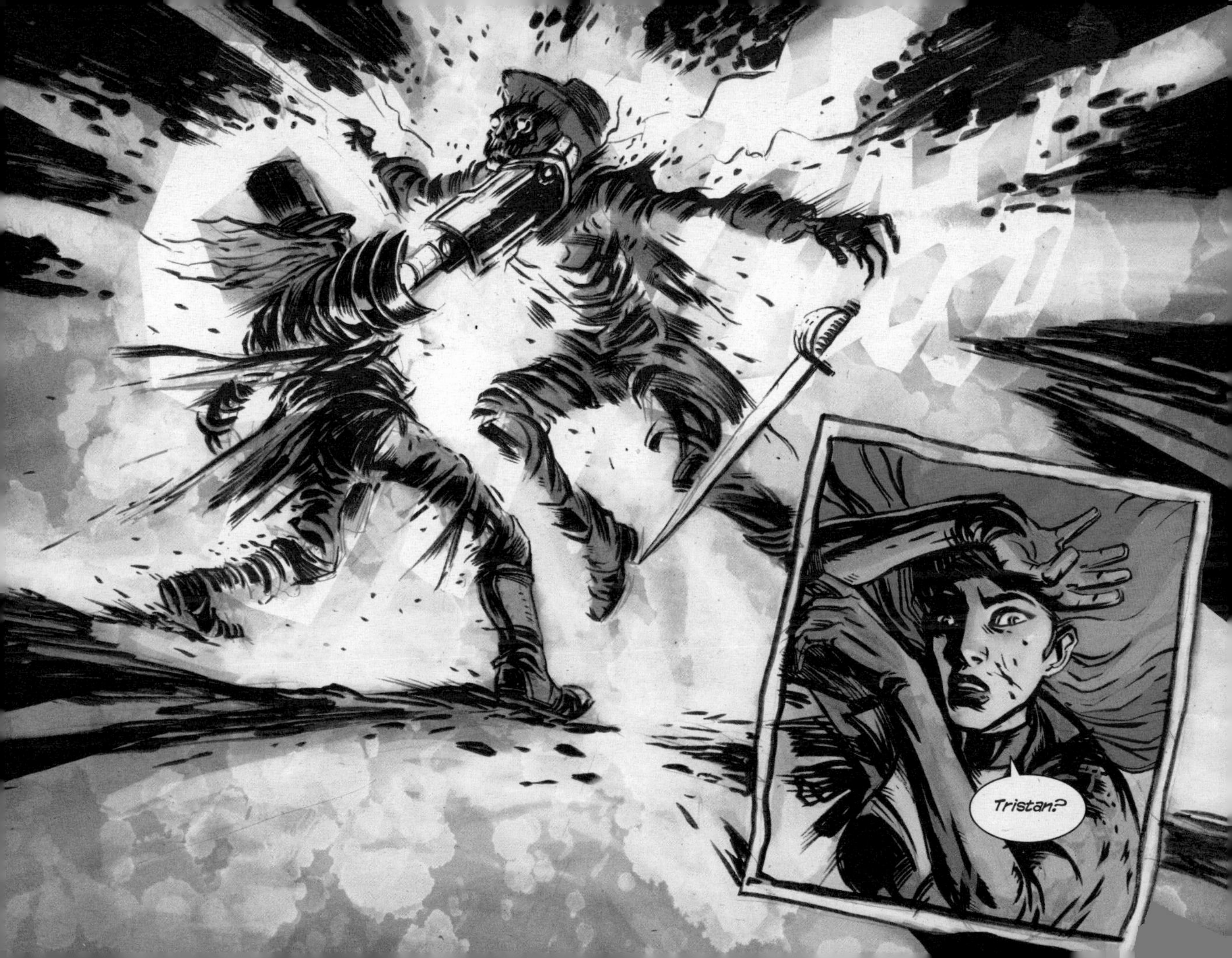
Tristan?

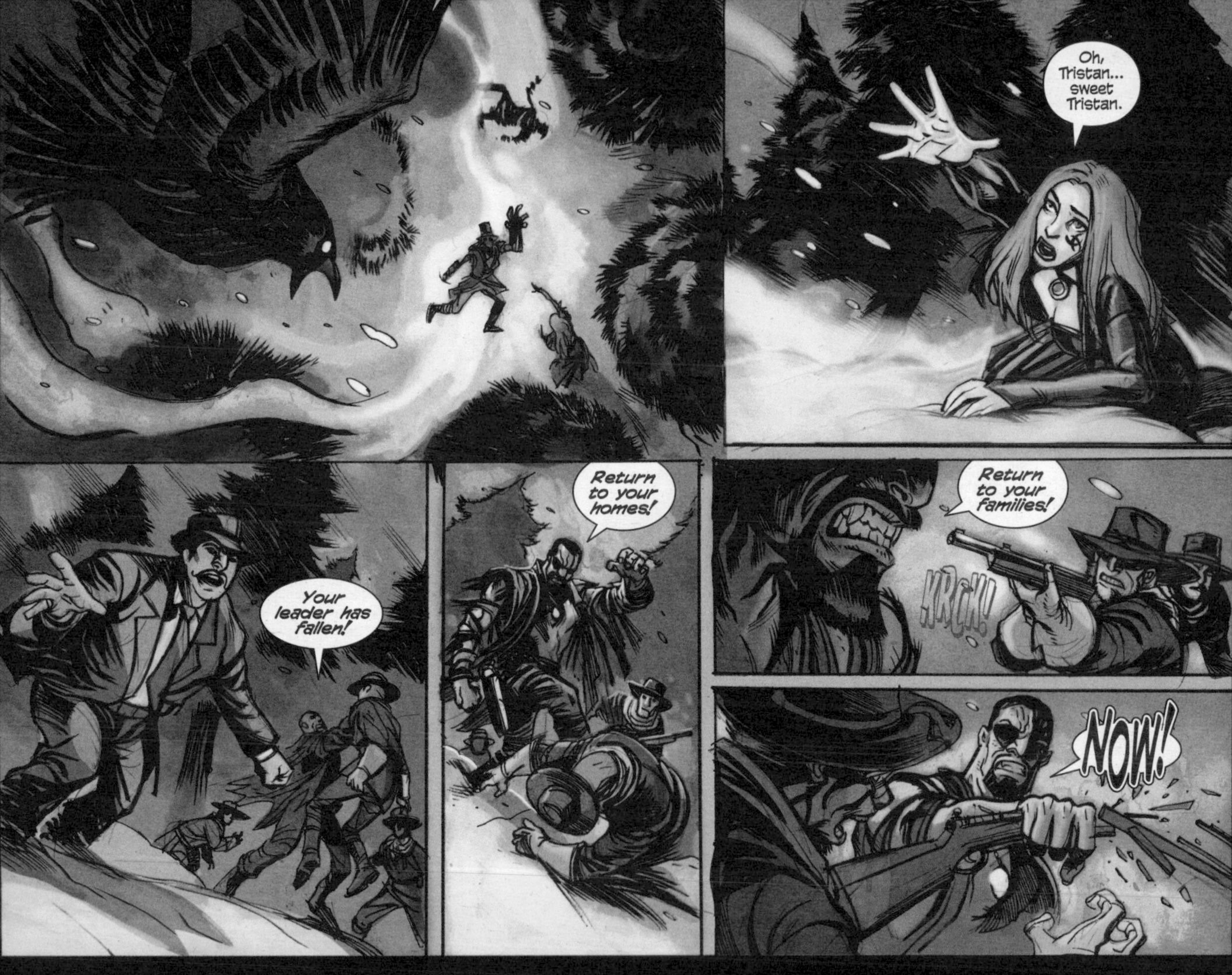
Oh, Tristan... sweet Tristan.
Your leader has fallen!
Return to your homes!
Return to your families!
KRCK!
NOW!

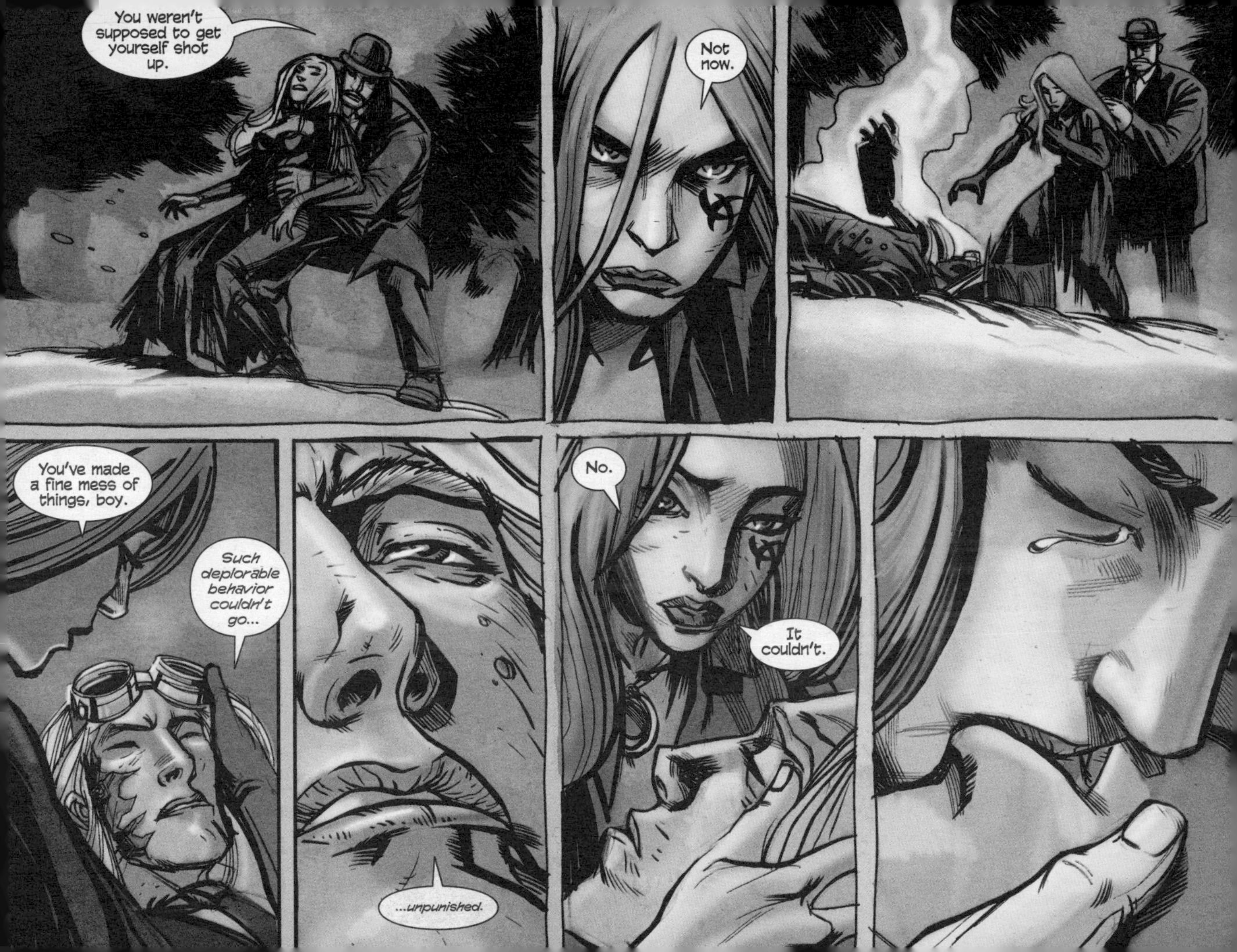
You weren't supposed to get yourself shot up.
Not now.
You've made a fine mess of things, boy.
Such deplorable behavior couldn't go...
...unpunished.
No.
It couldn't.

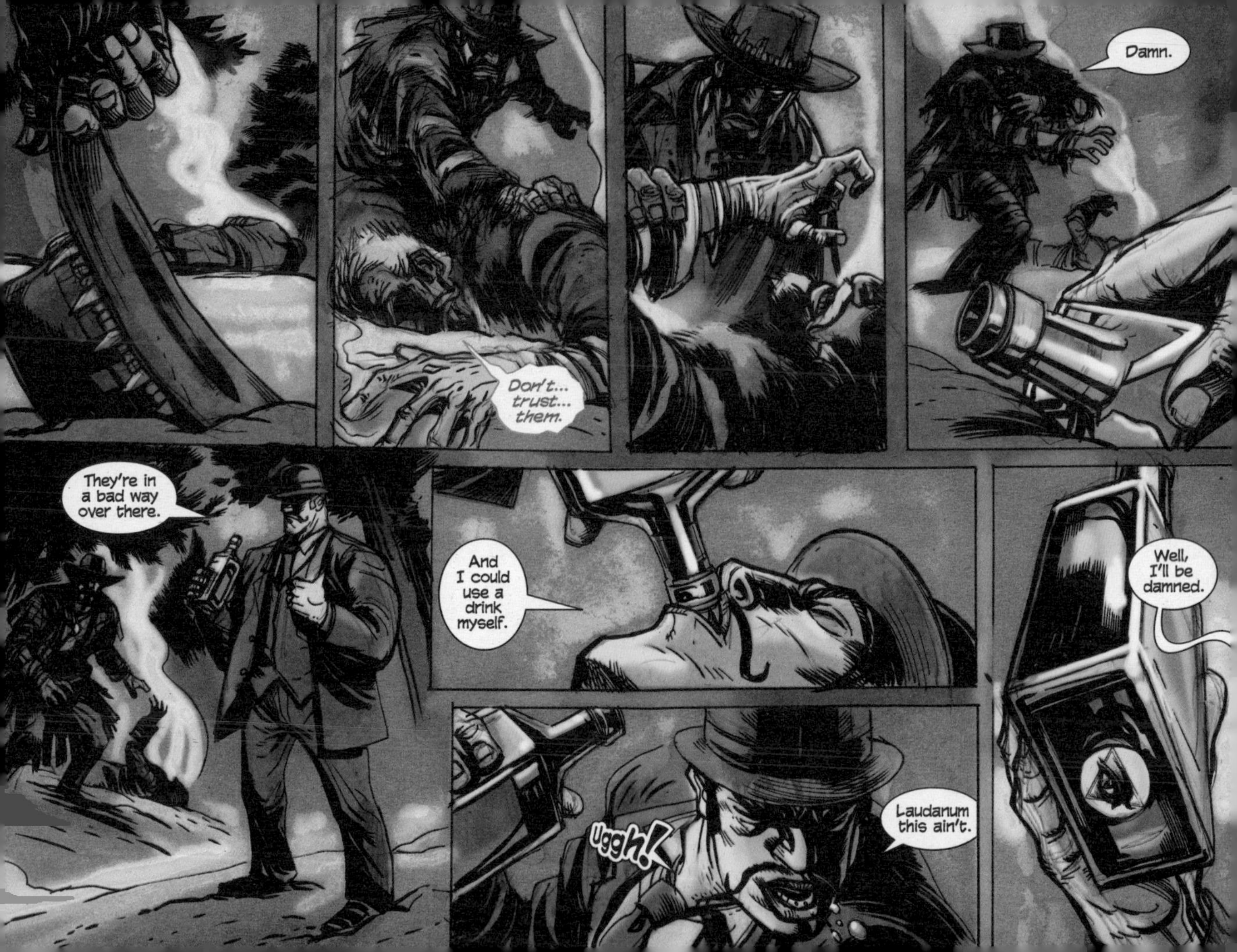

Don't... trust... them.
Damn.
They're in a bad way over there.
And I could use a drink myself.
Uggh!
Laudanum this ain't.
Well, I'll be damned.

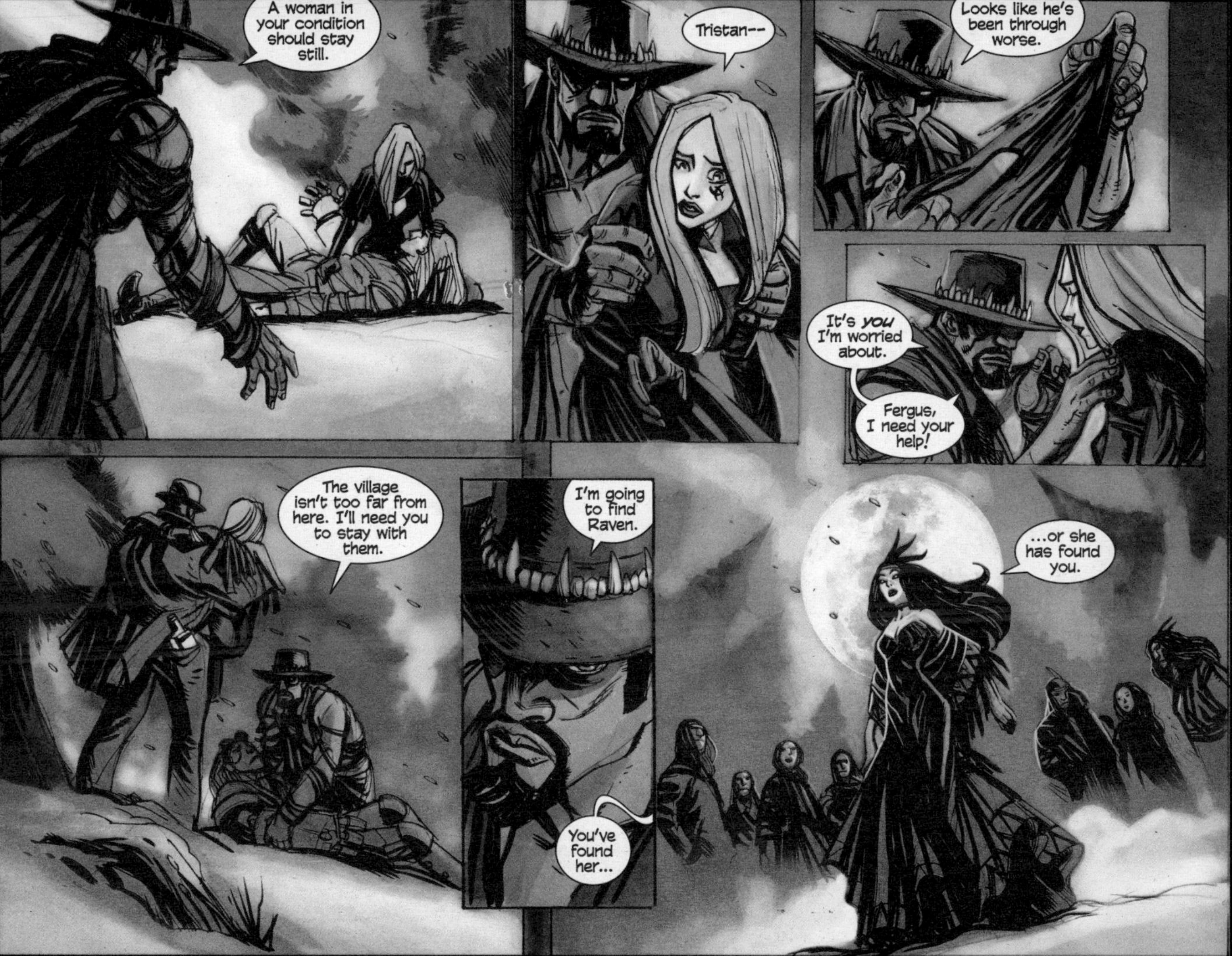
A woman in your condition should stay still.
Tristan--
Looks like he's been through worse.
It's *you* I'm worried about.
Fergus, I need your help!
The village isn't too far from here. I'll need you to stay with them.
I'm going to find Raven.
You've found her...
...or she has found you.

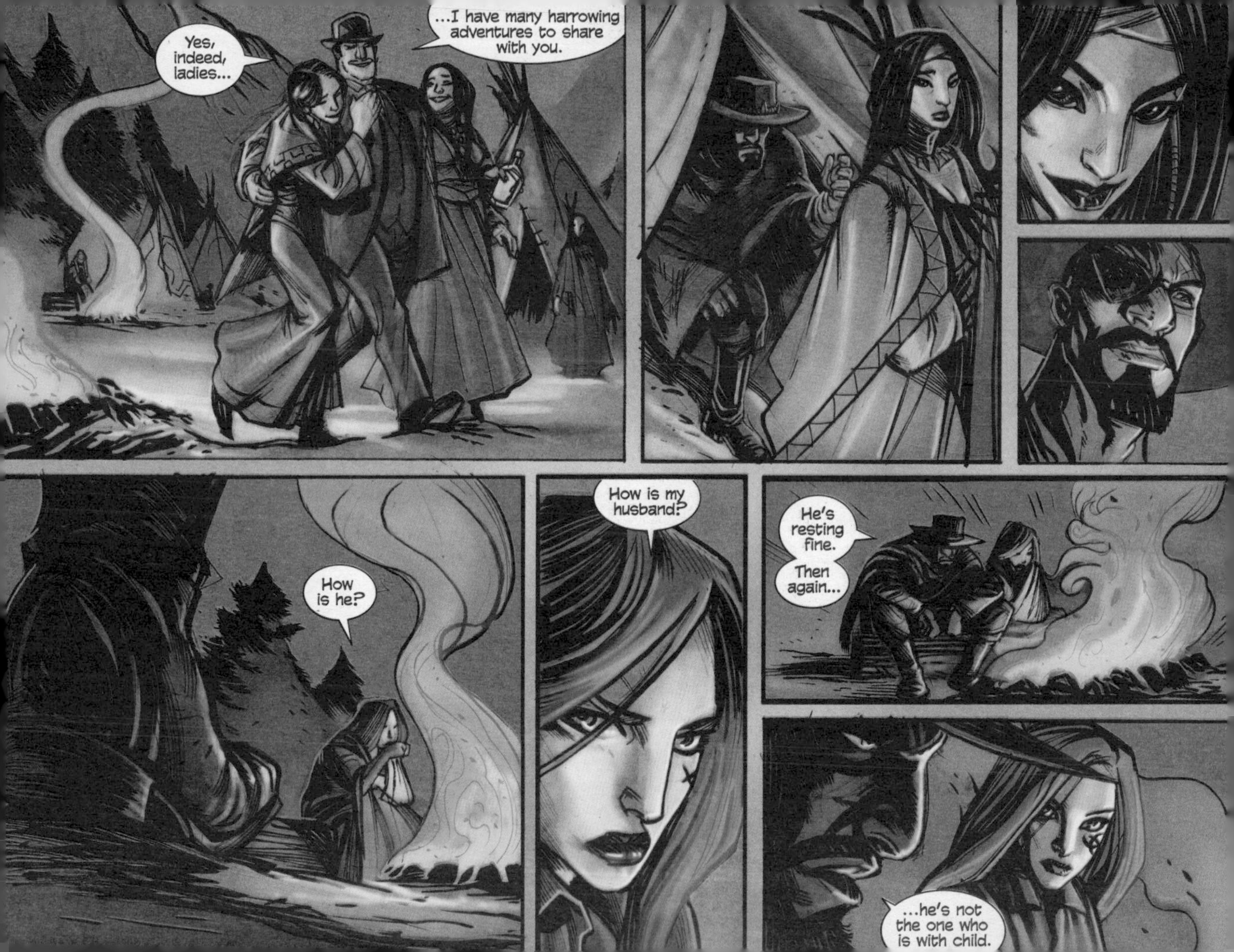
Yes, indeed, ladies...
...I have many harrowing adventures to share with you.
How is he?
How is my husband?
He's resting fine.
Then again...
...he's not the one who is with child.

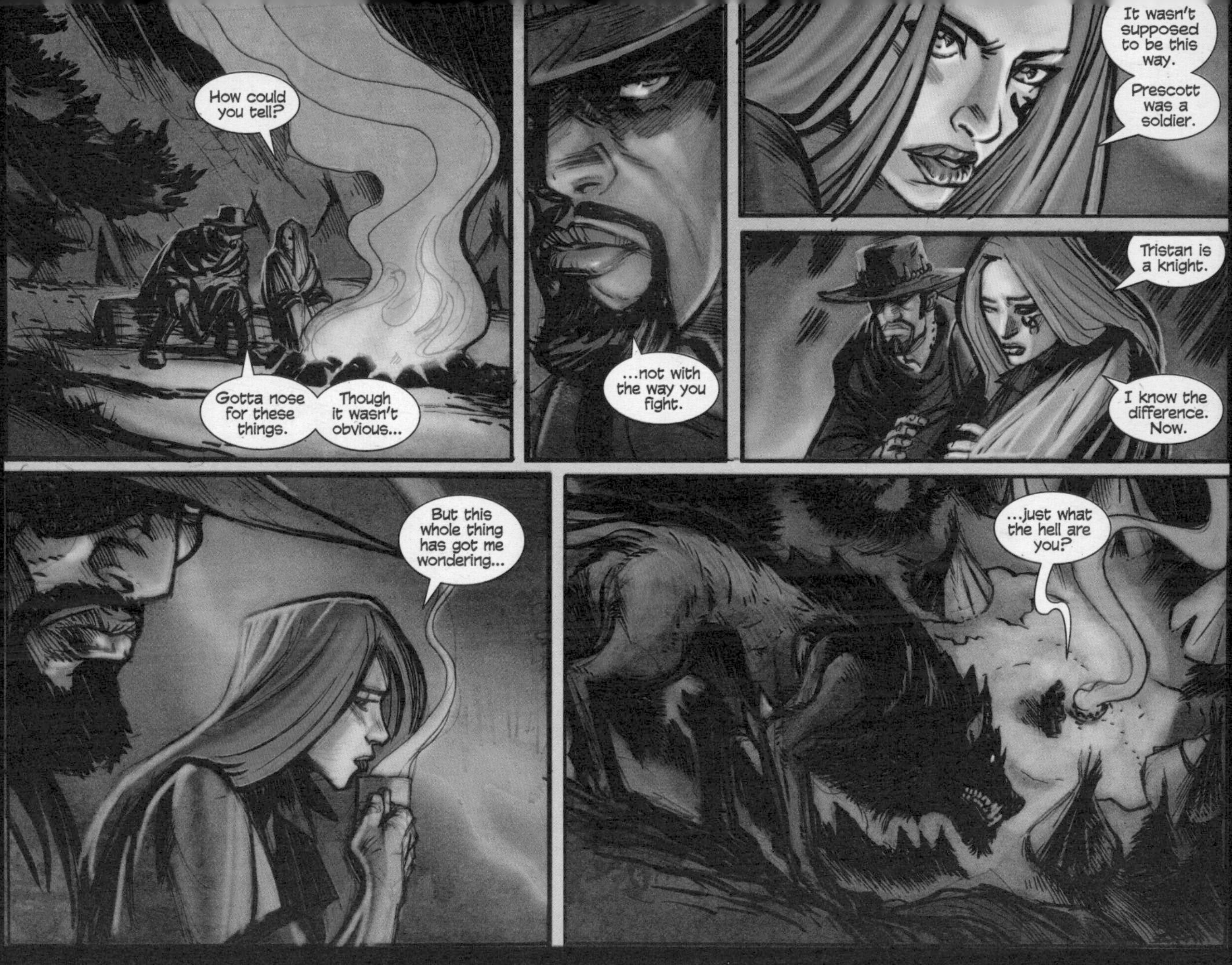
How could you tell?
Gotta nose for these things.
Though it wasn't obvious...
...not with the way you fight.
It wasn't supposed to be this way.
Prescott was a soldier.
Tristan is a knight.
I know the difference. Now.
But this whole thing has got me wondering...
...just what the hell are you?

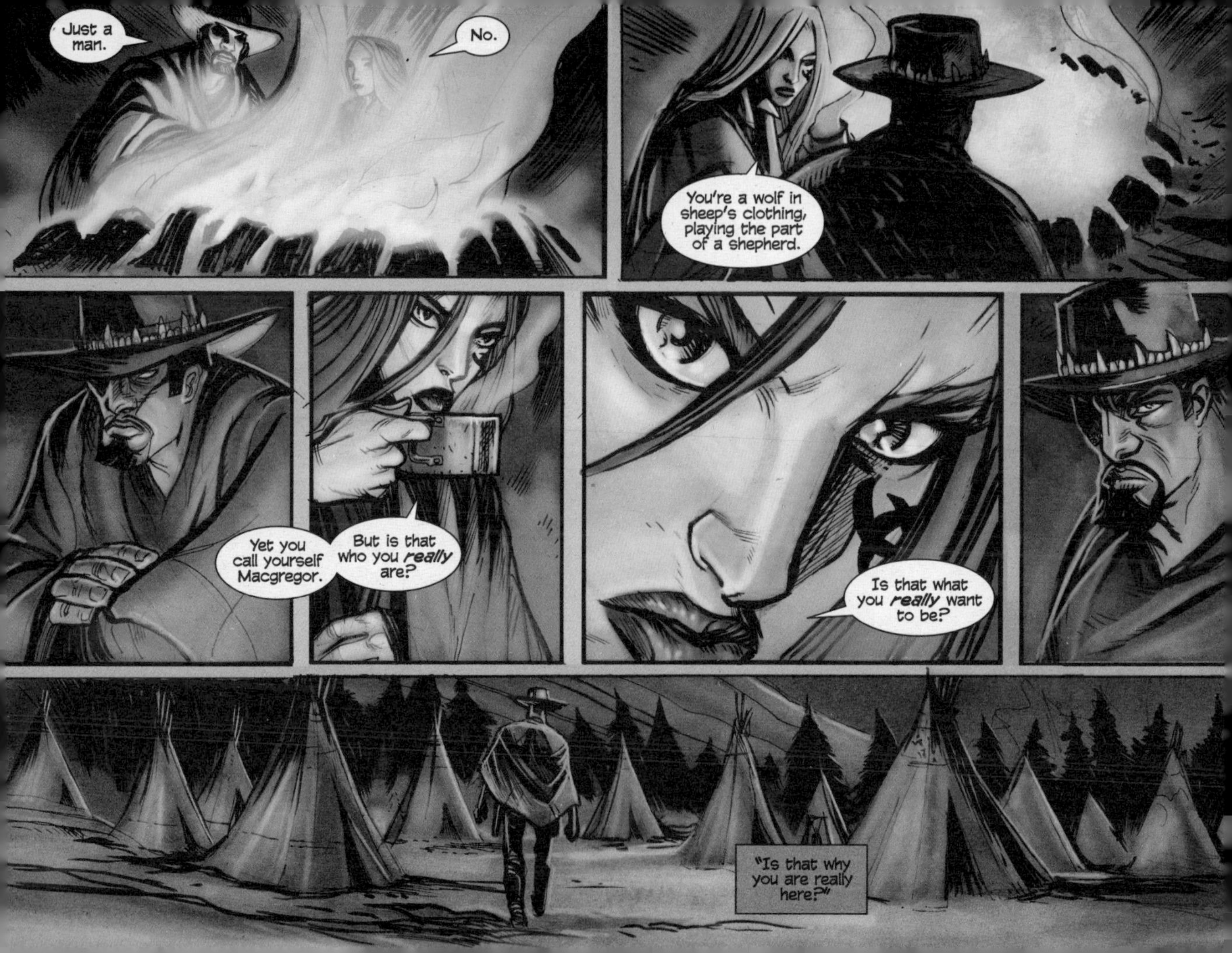
Just a man.
No.
You're a wolf in sheep's clothing, playing the part of a shepherd.
Yet you call yourself Macgregor.
But is that who you *really* are?
Is that what you *really* want to be?
"Is that why you are really here?"

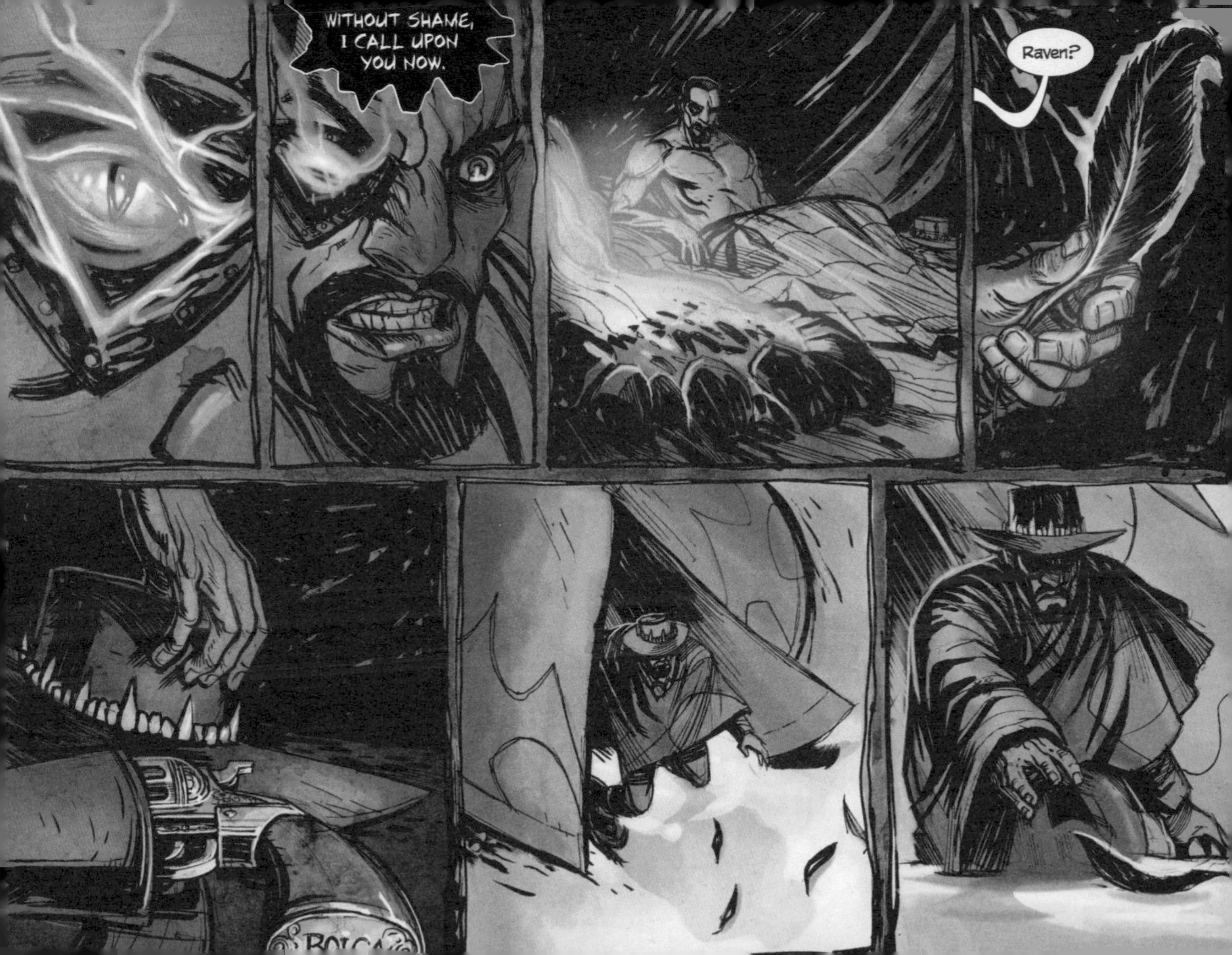
WITHOUT SHAME, I CALL UPON YOU NOW.
Raven?

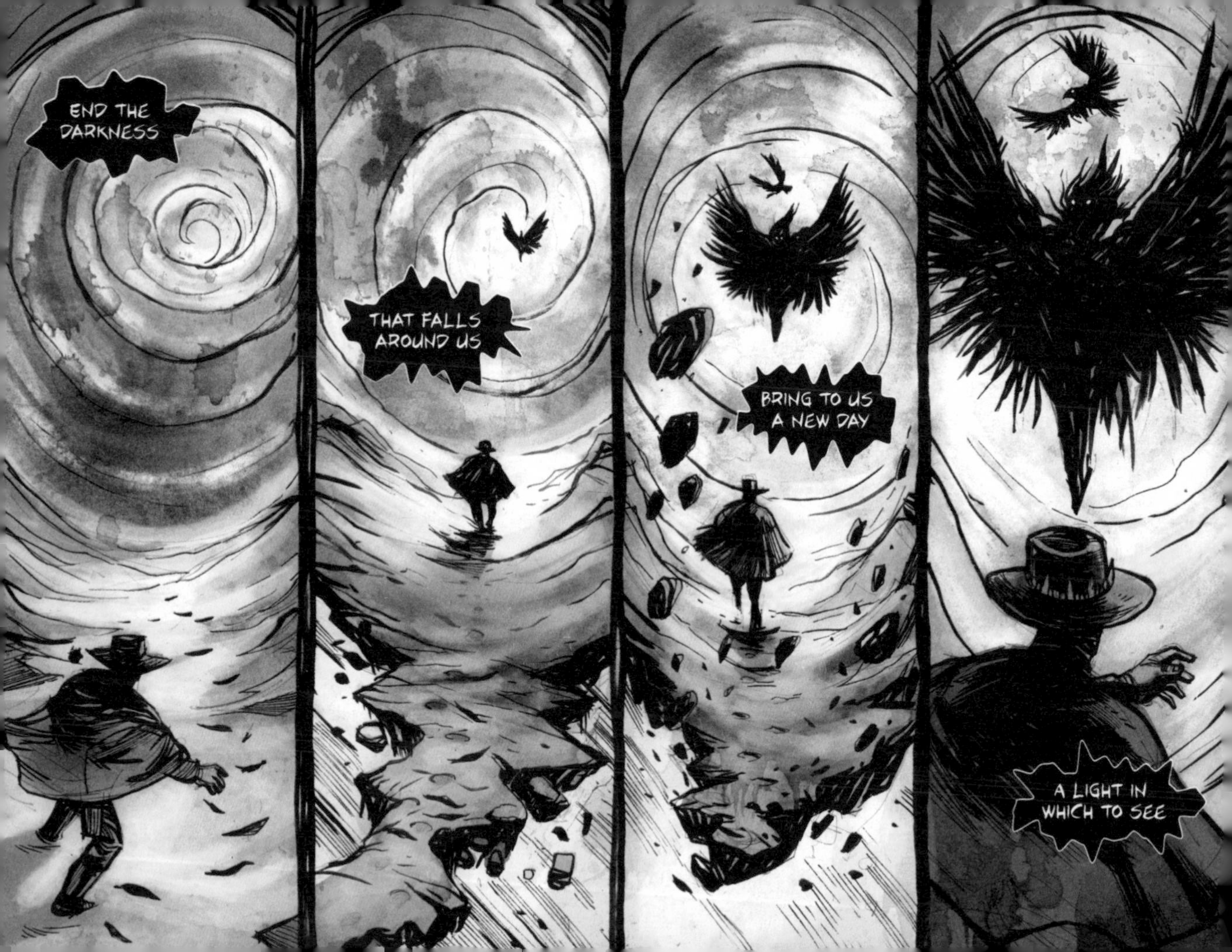
END THE DARKNESS
THAT FALLS AROUND US
BRING TO US A NEW DAY
A LIGHT IN WHICH TO SEE

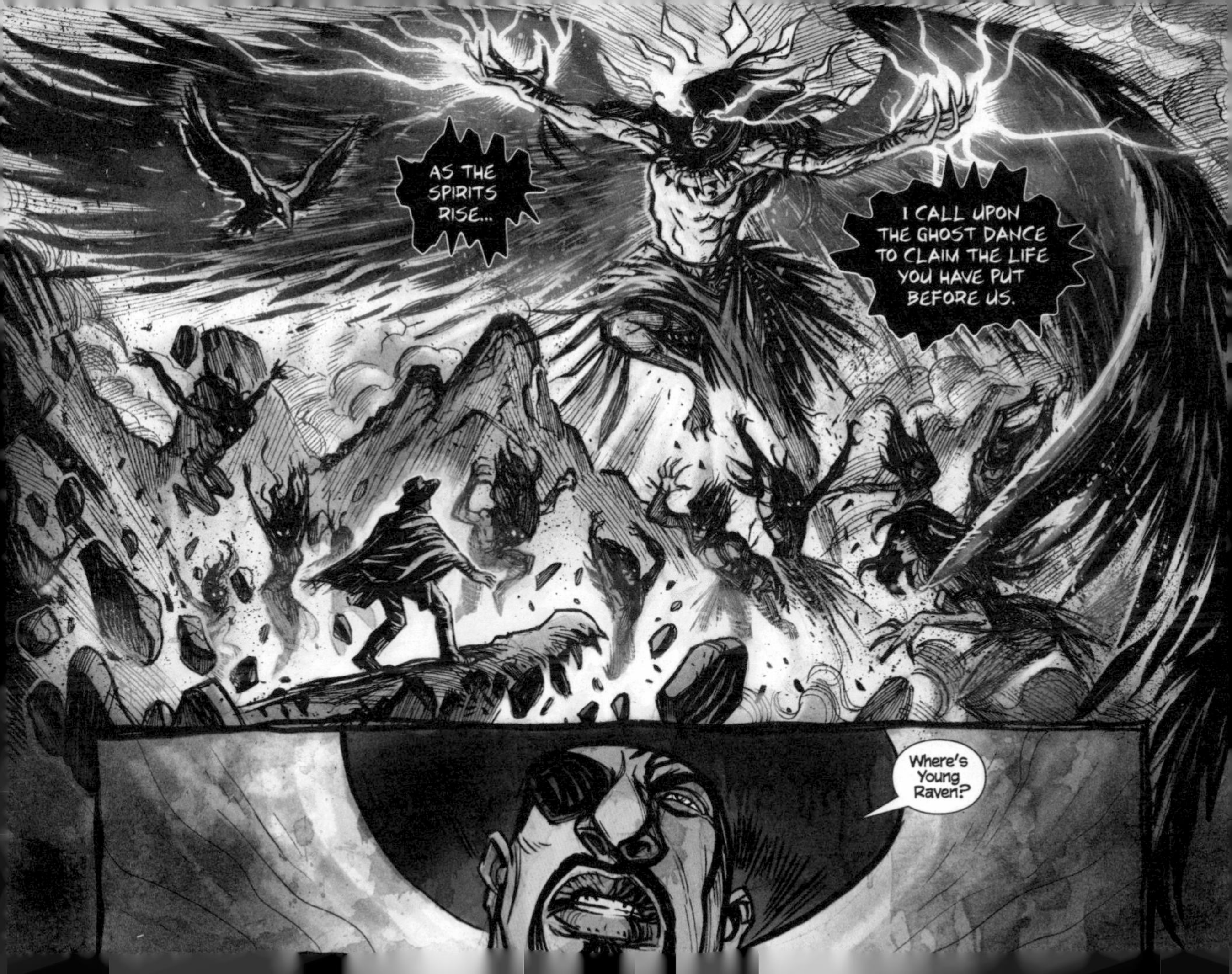
AS THE SPIRITS RISE...
I CALL UPON THE GHOST DANCE TO CLAIM THE LIFE YOU HAVE PUT BEFORE US.
Where's Young Raven?

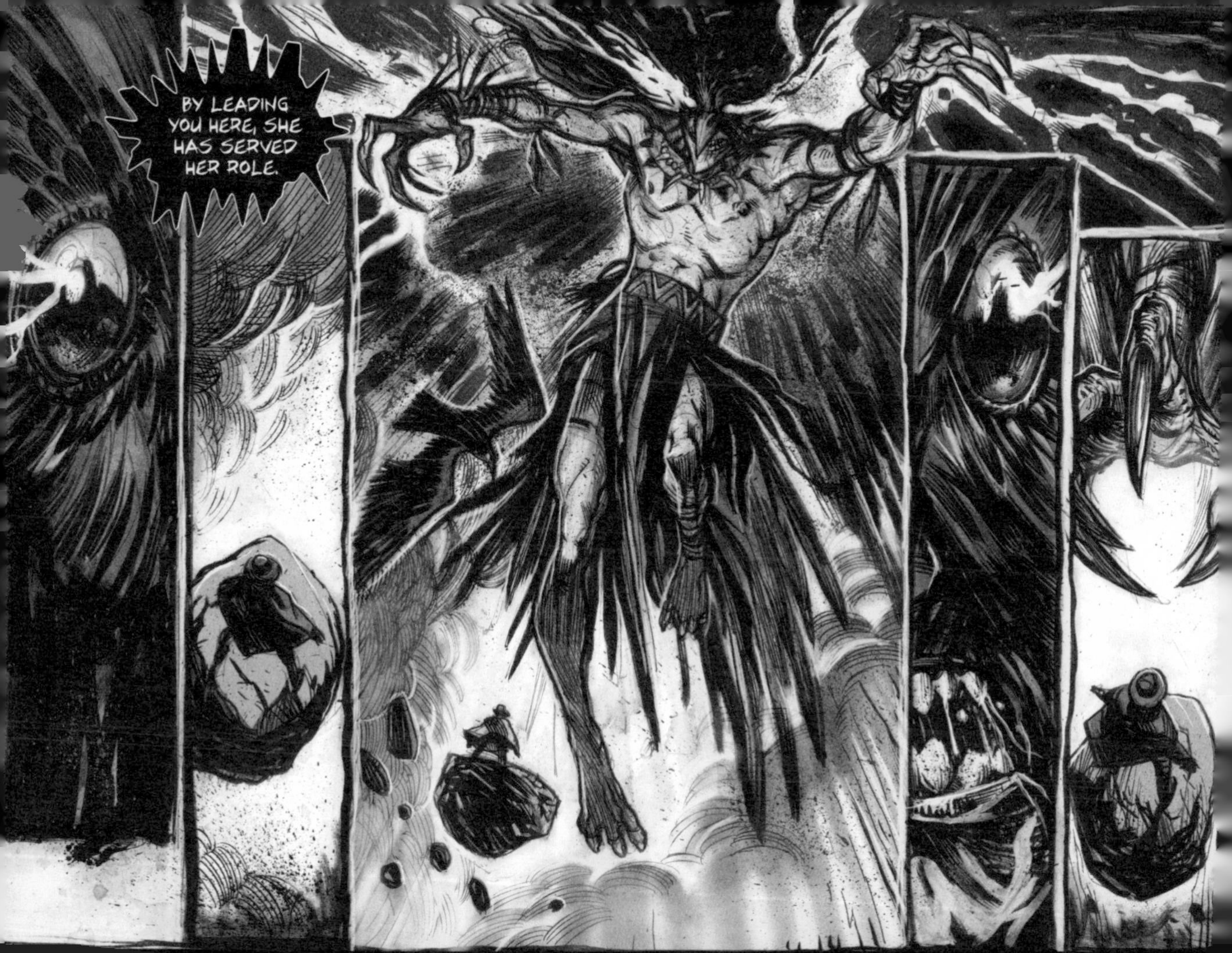
BY LEADING YOU HERE, SHE HAS SERVED HER ROLE.

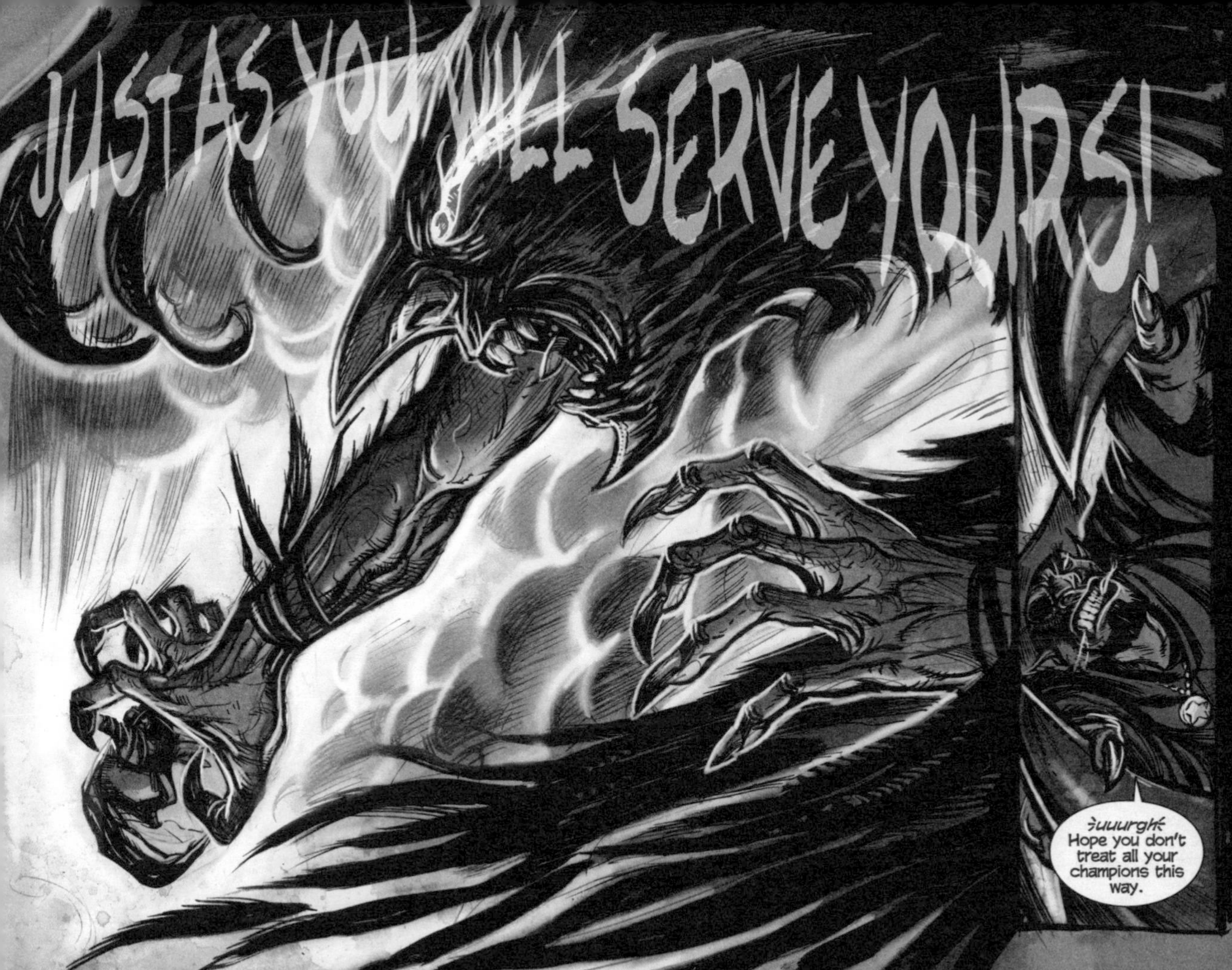
JUST AS YOU WILL SERVE YOURS!
uuurgh
Hope you don't treat all your champions this way.

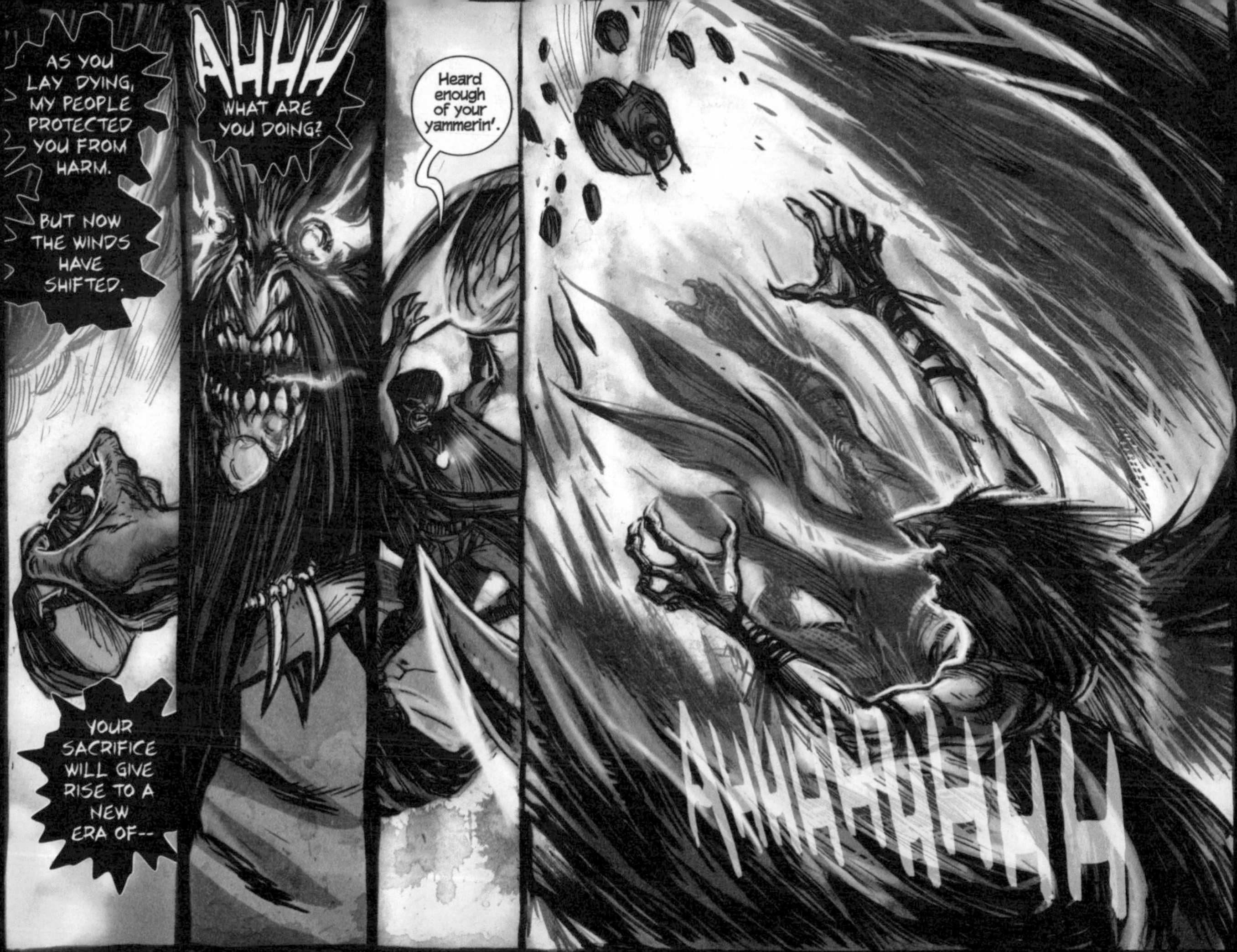
AS YOU LAY DYING, MY PEOPLE PROTECTED YOU FROM HARM.
BUT NOW THE WINDS HAVE SHIFTED.
YOUR SACRIFICE WILL GIVE RISE TO A NEW ERA OF--
AHHH
WHAT ARE YOU DOING?
Heard enough of your yammerin'.
AHHHHHHHHH

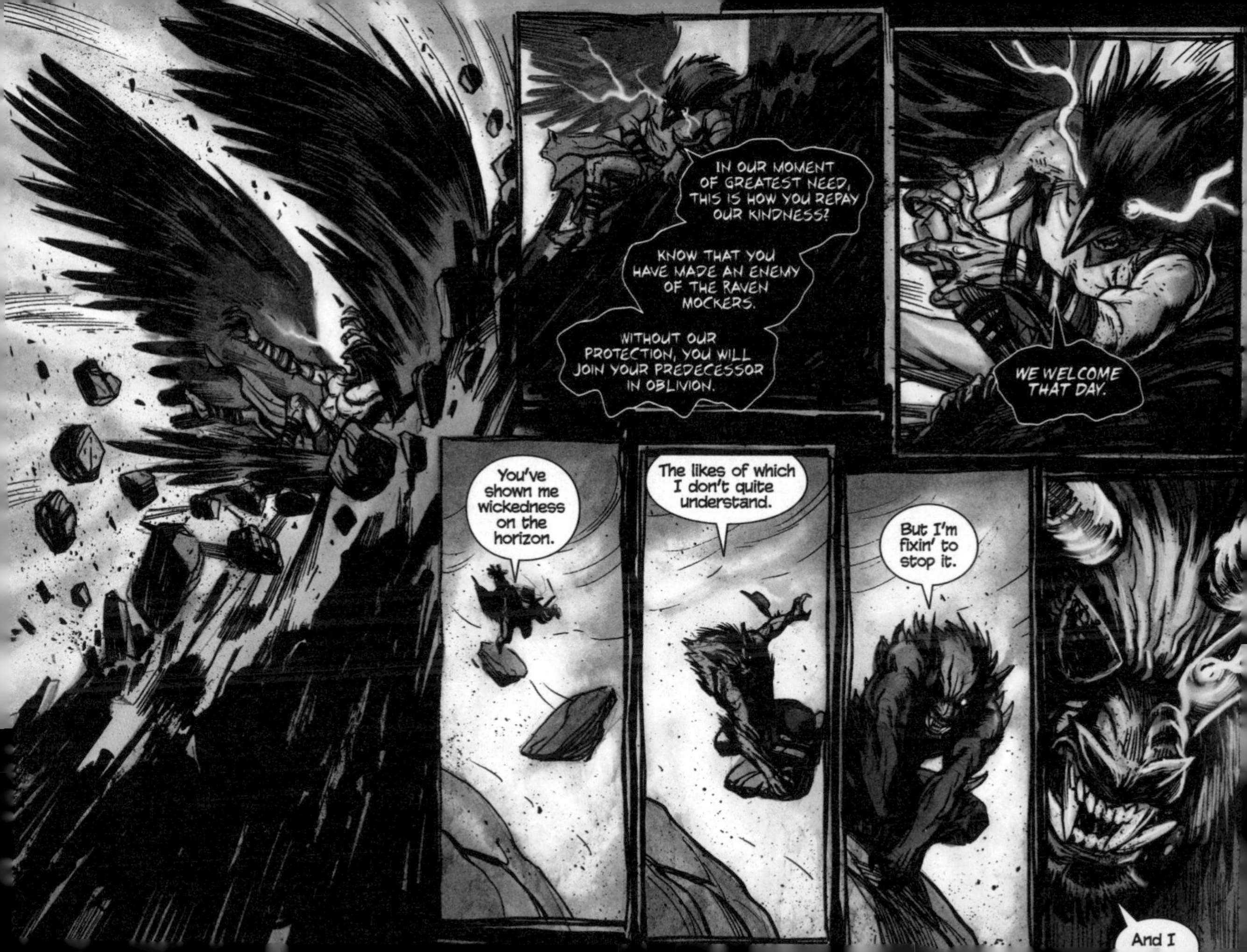
IN OUR MOMENT OF GREATEST NEED, THIS IS HOW YOU REPAY OUR KINDNESS?
KNOW THAT YOU HAVE MADE AN ENEMY OF THE RAVEN MOCKERS.
WITHOUT OUR PROTECTION, YOU WILL JOIN YOUR PREDECESSOR IN OBLIVION.
WE WELCOME THAT DAY.
You've shown me wickedness on the horizon.
The likes of which I don't quite understand.
But I'm fixin' to stop it.
And I

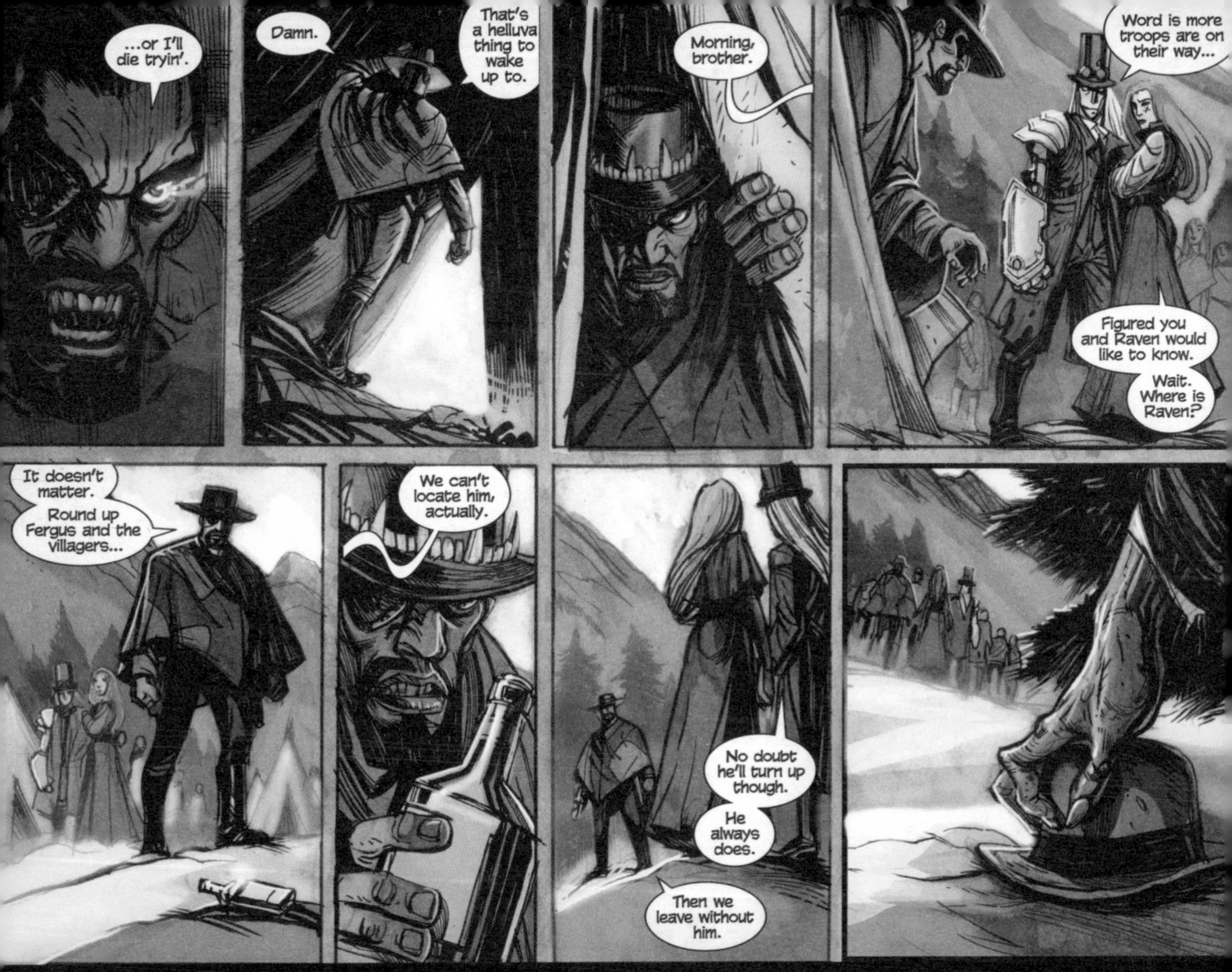
...or I'll die tryin'.
Damn.
That's a helluva thing to wake up to.
Morning, brother.
Word is more troops are on their way...
Figured you and Raven would like to know.
Wait. Where is Raven?
It doesn't matter.
Round up Fergus and the villagers...
We can't locate him, actually.
No doubt he'll turn up though.
He always does.
Then we leave without him.

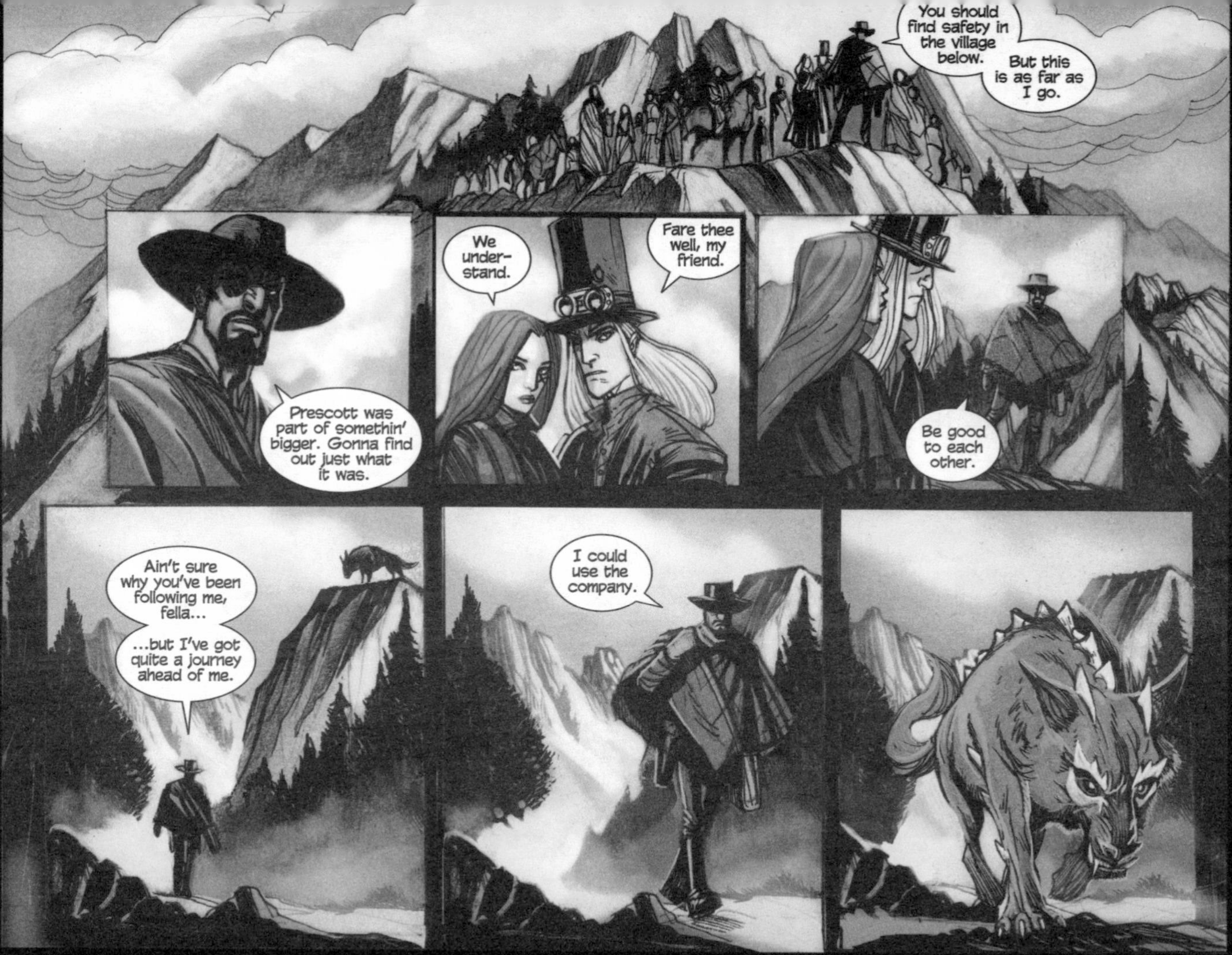
You should find safety in the village below.
But this is as far as I go.
Prescott was part of somethin' bigger. Gonna find out just what it was.
We under-stand.
Fare thee well, my friend.
Be good to each other.
Ain't sure why you've been following me, fella...
...but I've got quite a journey ahead of me.
I could use the company.

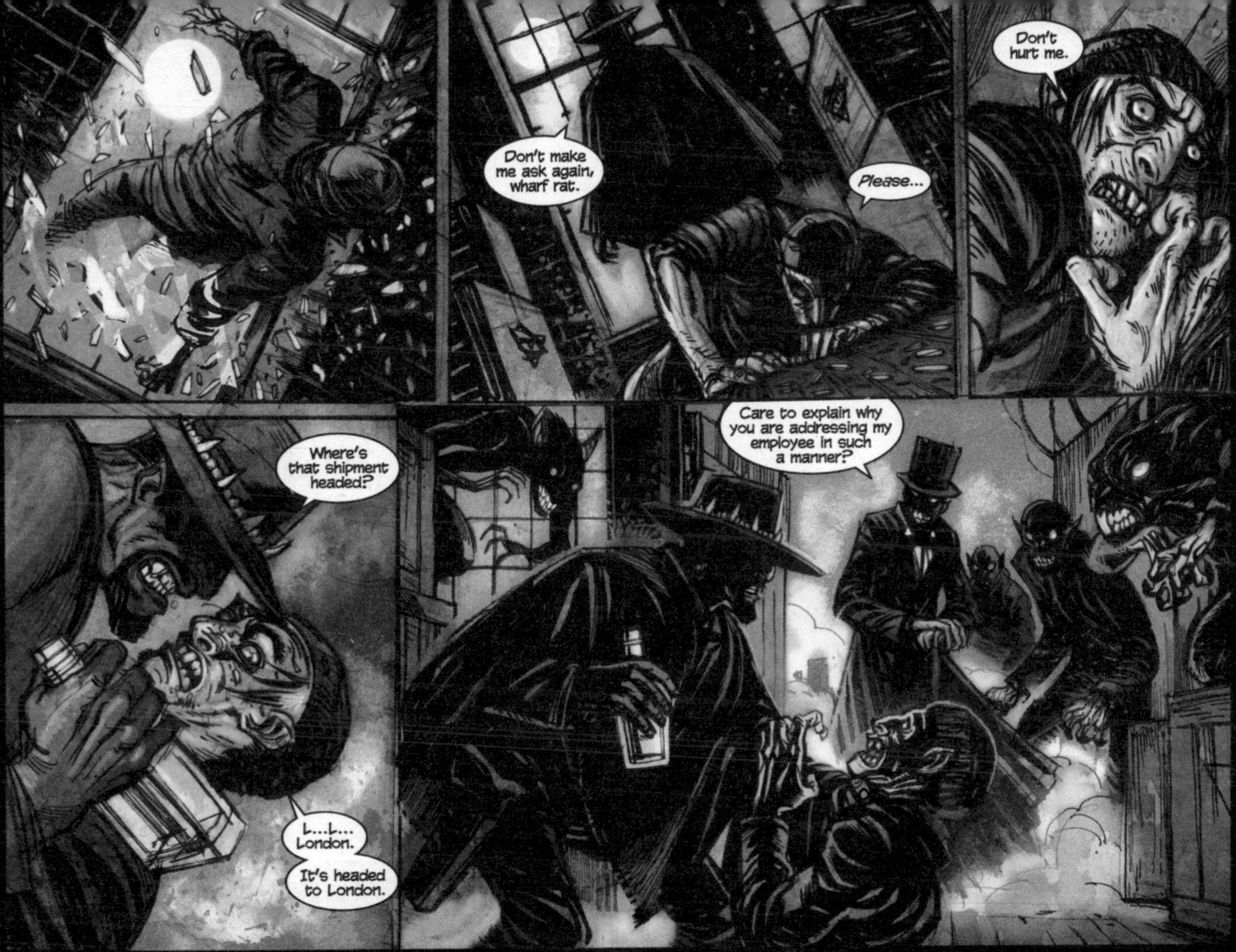
Don't make me ask again, wharf rat.
Please...
Don't hurt me.
Where's that shipment headed?
L...L... London.
It's headed to London.
Care to explain why you are addressing my employee in such a manner?

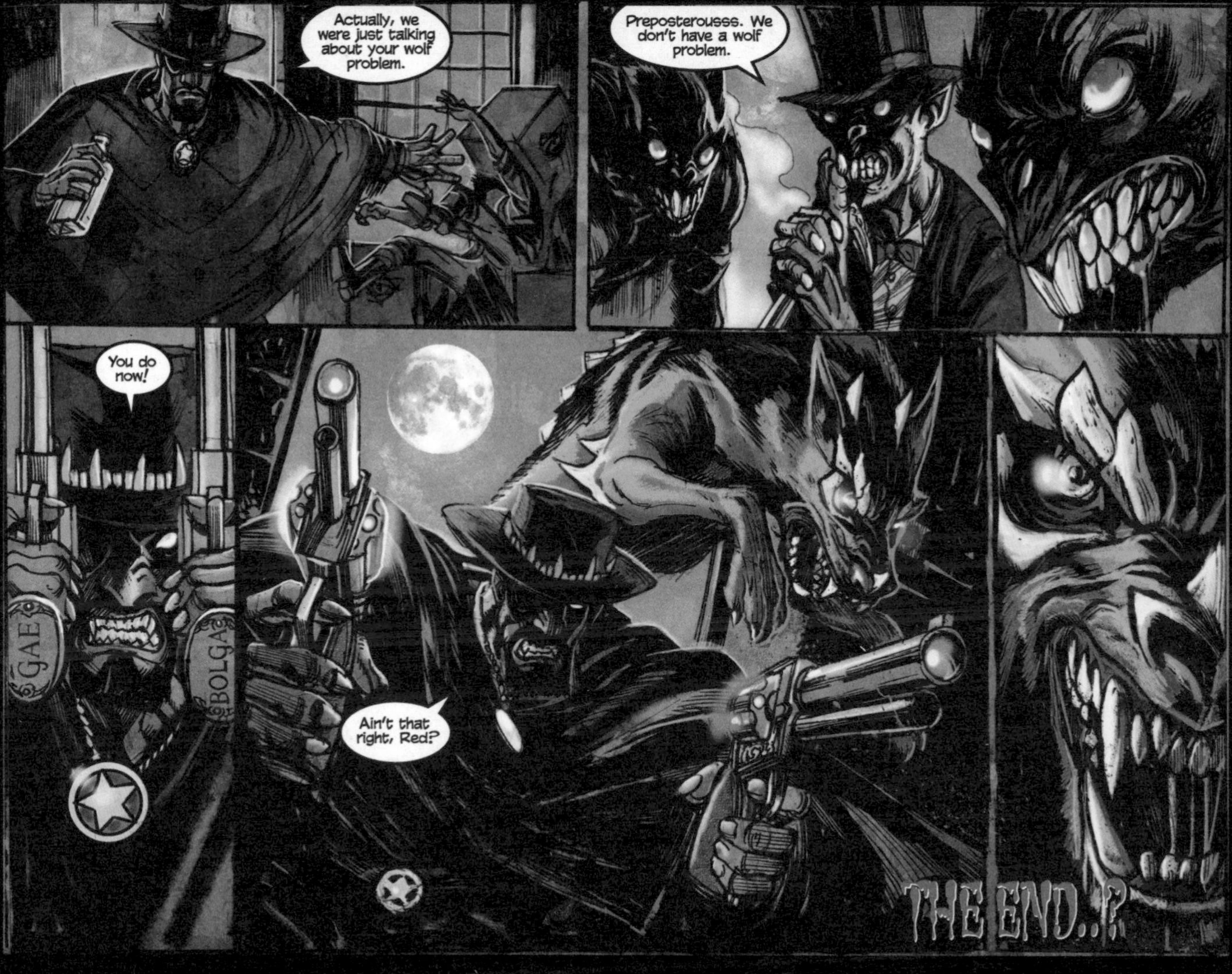
Actually, we were just talking about your wolf problem.
Preposterousss. We don't have a wolf problem.
You do now!
GAE
BOLGA
Ain't that right, Red?
THE END..?

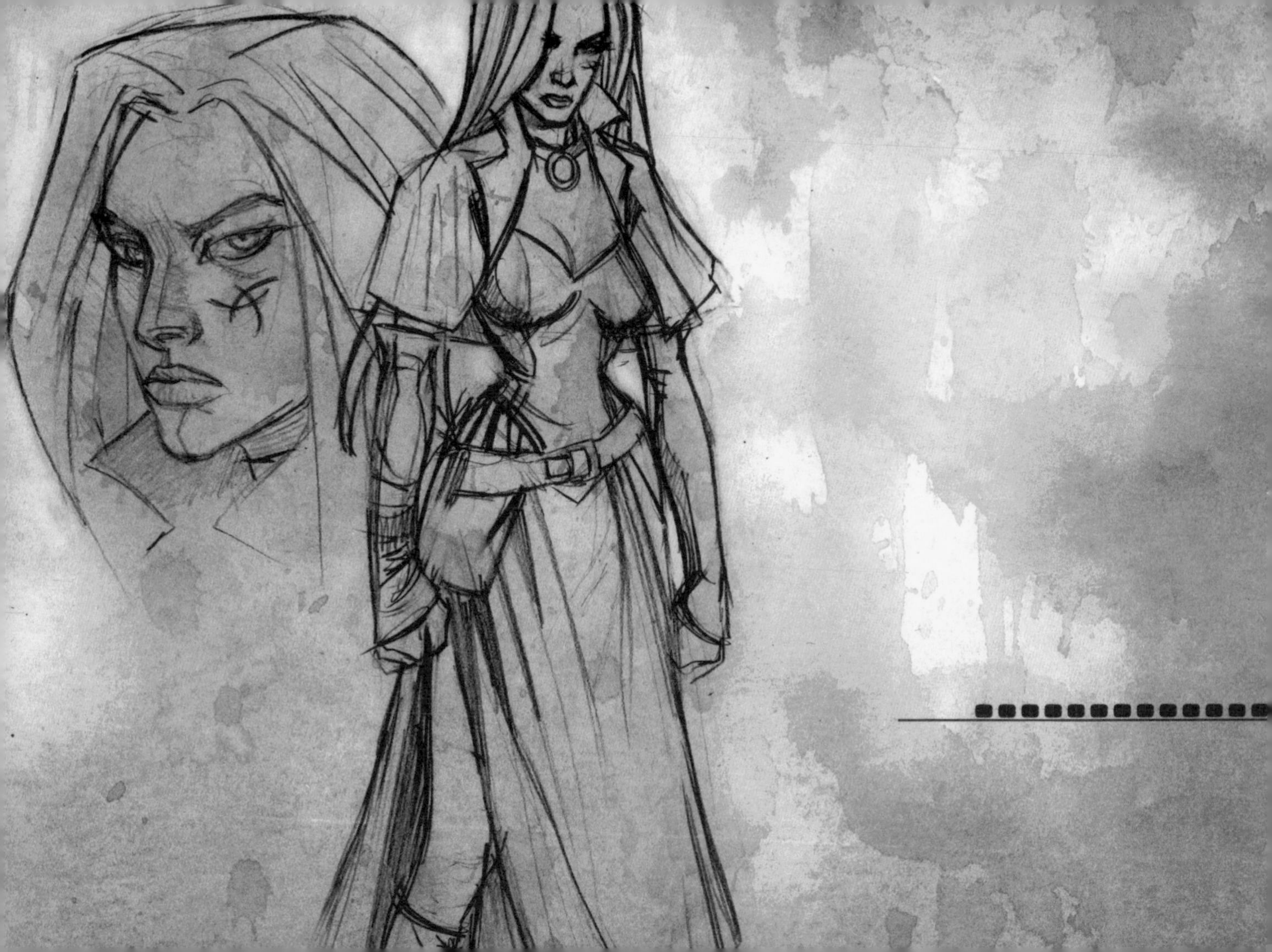

● DAVID GALLAHER Writer

Named "Breakout Creator of 2008" by Comic Foundry Magazine, David Gallaher was the winner of the very first Zuda Comics competition with his high-energy, deeply researched, fusion horror/western webcomic HIGH MOON. In addition to his work for Zuda, David has written *Johnny Dollar* and *Vampire: The Masquerade* for Moonstone Books and *More Fund Comics* for Sky-Dog Press.

● STEVE ELLIS Artist

Steve Ellis's lush and detailed work has been featured across a wide spectrum of science fiction and fantasy books, video games, trading cards, magazines and, of course, comic books. At various points in his professional career, Steve provided artwork for LOBO, HAWKMAN, GREEN LANTERN, *Iron Man*, *Spider-Woman* and other series before dedicating himself fully to HIGH MOON for Zuda Comics.

● SCOTT O. BROWN Letterer

As a "Man of Comics," Scott O. Brown has been a writer, editor, and production artist for a wide range of comic properties. He has written *Nightfall* and *Atlantis Rising* for Platinum Studios and *They Do Not Die* for Ambrosia Publishing.

CREATORS

What are Zuda Comics?

Zuda Comics are webcomics!
Created by you. Chosen by you.

zudacomics.com

NIGHT OWLS By Peter Timony + Bobby Timony
A pair of detectives (and a gargoyle)
solve supernatural crimes in the 1920s
with their minds, mitts and moxie.
zudacomics.com/the_night_owls

I RULE THE NIGHT By Kevin Colden
Years after Night Devil died, his surviving
sidekick starts receiving messages from
beyond that reveal the disturbing truth
about his mentor.
zudacomics.com/i_rule_the_night

CELADORE By Caanan Grall
Two children are thrust into the
monster-slaying world of Celadore,
and it seems they would have it
no other way.
zudacomics.com/celadore

BAYOU By Jeremy Love
To save her father from a lynching,
Lee Wagstaff must enter a world
that is an eerie reflection of her own.
zudacomics.com/bayou